Marquee Series

MICROSOFT®

WINDOWS 8

Nita Rutkosky
Pierce College at Puyallup,
Puyallup, Washington

Denise Seguin
Fanshawe College,
London, Ontario

Audrey Roggenkamp
Pierce College at Puyallup,
Puyallup, Washington

Ian Rutkosky
Pierce College at Puyallup,
Puyallup, Washington

St. Paul

Contents

Managing Editor Christine Hurney
Director of Production Timothy W. Larson
Production Editor Sarah Kearin
Cover and Text Designer Leslie Anderson
Copy Editor Sid Korpi, Proof Positive Editing
Design and Production Specialists Jack Ross and Sara Schmidt Boldon
Testers Desiree Carvel; Ann E. Mills, Ivy Tech Community College of Indiana, Indianapolis, IN; Brienna McWade
Indexer Terry Casey
VP & Director of Digital Projects Chuck Bratton
Digital Project Manager Tom Modl

875 Montreal Way
St. Paul, MN 55102
Email: educate@emcp.com
Website: www.emcp.com

Windows® SECTION 1

Exploring Windows 8

Skills

- Navigate the Windows 8 Start screen
- Navigate the Windows 8 desktop
- Perform actions using the mouse, such as point, click, double-click, and drag
- Start and close a program
- Open and close a window
- Shut down Windows 8
- Move a window
- Minimize, maximize, and restore a window
- Stack and cascade windows
- Use the snap feature to position windows on the desktop
- Change the date and time
- Use components of a dialog box
- Adjust the volume using the Speaker slider bar
- Customize the Taskbar
- Use the Help and Support feature
- Turn on the display of file extensions

Projects Overview

Your department at Worldwide Enterprises has received new computers with the Windows 8 operating system. You will explore the Windows 8 Start screen and desktop; open, close, and manipulate windows; open a program; customize the Taskbar; explore the online help for Windows 8; and turn on the display of file extensions.

Activity 1.1

Exploring the Windows 8 Start Screen

When you turn on your computer, the Windows 8 operating system loads and the Windows 8 Start screen displays on your monitor. The Windows 8 Start screen contains tiles you can use to open programs or access features within Windows 8. By default, the Windows 8 Start screen displays tiles for the most commonly used applications and features. Display all of the applications installed on your computer by right-clicking a blank area of the Start screen and then clicking the All apps icon that displays in the lower right corner of the screen. Windows 8 includes a Charm bar containing five buttons you can use to perform tasks such as searching apps, sharing apps, and shutting down the computer. Display the Charm bar by hovering the mouse over the upper or lower right corner of the screen.

Project

Tutorial 1.1
Exploring the Windows 8 Start Screen

Your department has received new computers with Windows 8 installed. You decide to take some time to explore the Windows 8 Start screen to familiarize yourself with this new operating system.

1. Complete the step(s) needed to display the Windows 8 Start screen.

   Check with your instructor to determine the specific step(s) required to display the Windows 8 Start screen on your computer. If you are at school, you may need a user name and password to log on to the computer system. When Windows 8 starts, you will see a Start screen similar to the one shown in Figure 1.1. Your Start screen may contain additional tiles or have a different background than the one shown in Figure 1.1.

2. Move your mouse and notice how the corresponding pointer moves in the Windows 8 Start screen.

   The ***mouse*** is a device that controls the pointer that identifies your location on the screen. Move the mouse on your desk (preferably on a mouse pad) and the pointer moves on the screen. For information on mouse terms, refer to Table 1.1 and for information on mouse icons, refer to Table 1.2.

FIGURE 1.1 Windows 8 Start Screen

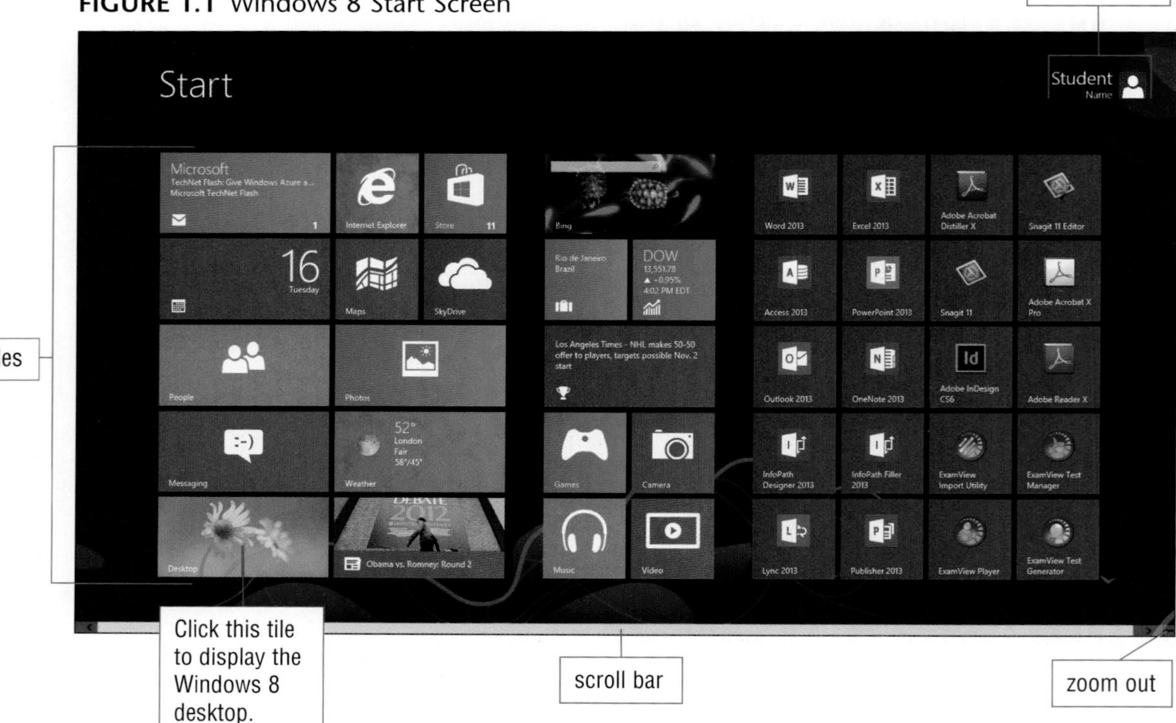

TABLE 1.1 Mouse Terms and Actions

Term	Action
point	Position the mouse pointer on the desired item.
click	Quickly tap the left button on the mouse once.
right-click	Quickly tap the right button on the mouse once.
double-click	Tap the left mouse button twice in quick succession.
drag	Press and hold down the left mouse button, move the mouse pointer to a specific location, and then release the mouse button.

TABLE 1.2 Mouse Icons

Icon	Description
I	The mouse appears as an I-beam pointer in a program screen in which you enter text (such as Microsoft Word) and also in text boxes. You can use the I-beam pointer to move the insertion point or select text.
	The mouse pointer appears as an arrow pointing up and to the left (called the *arrow pointer*) on the Windows desktop and also in other program title bars, menu bars, and toolbars.
	The mouse pointer becomes a double-headed arrow (either pointing left and right, up and down, or diagonally) when performing certain functions, such as changing the size of a window.
	Select an object in a program, such as a picture or image, and the mouse pointer displays with a four-headed arrow attached. Use this four-headed arrow pointer to move the object left, right, up, or down.
	When you position the mouse pointer inside selected text in a document (such as a Microsoft Word document) and then drag the selected text to a new location in the document, the pointer displays with a gray box attached, indicating that you are moving the text.
	When a request is being processed or a program is being loaded, the mouse pointer may display with a moving circle icon beside it. The moving circle means "please wait." When the process is completed, the moving circle disappears.
	When you position the mouse pointer on certain icons or hyperlinks, it turns into a hand with a pointing index finger. This image indicates that clicking the icon or hyperlink will display additional information.

3 Click the Desktop tile in the Start screen.

The desktop is the main screen in Windows 8. Different tools and applications can be opened on the desktop, similar to how different tools, documents, and items can be placed on a desk.

continues

4 Position the mouse in the upper right corner of the desktop screen until the Charm bar displays.

The Charm bar contains five buttons you can use to access different features and tools in Windows 8.

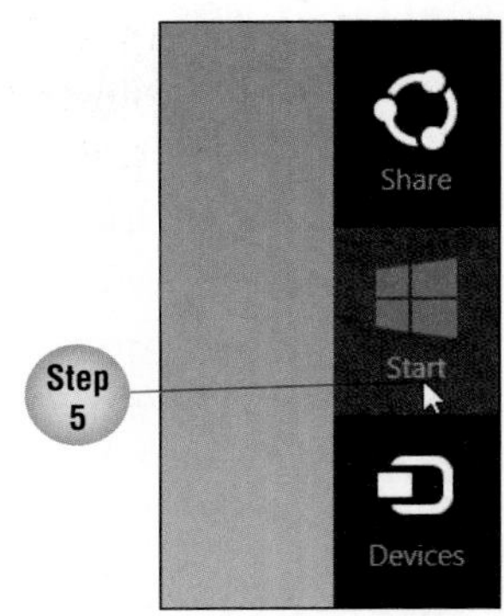

5 With the Charm bar displayed, click the Start button to return to the Start screen.

Alternatively, you can return to the Start screen by positioning the mouse pointer in the lower left corner of the desktop until a Start screen thumbnail displays and then clicking the left mouse button.

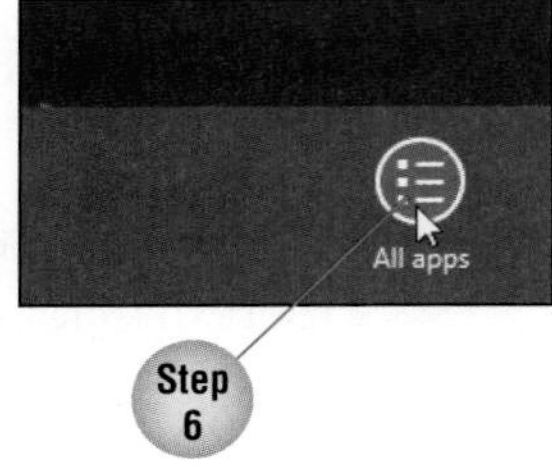

6 Right-click in a blank area of the Start screen and then click the All apps icon that appears in the lower right corner of the screen.

The Windows 8 Start screen displays the most commonly used applications and features. Display all applications (grouped in categories) in the Start screen if you cannot find a desired application.

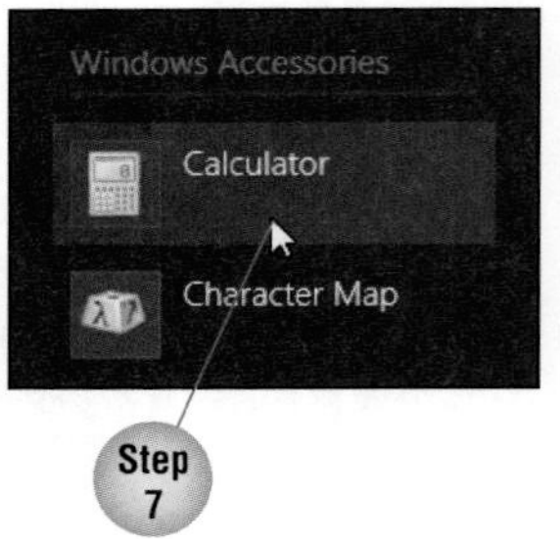

7 Click the Calculator tile that displays in the *Windows Accessories* section.

Clicking the Calculator tile causes the Calculator tool to open and display on the desktop.

8 Close the Calculator by clicking the Close button ✕ that displays in the upper right corner of the program.

9 Complete Steps 4 and 5 to return to the Start screen.

10 Click the Internet Explorer tile.

Certain applications, such as Internet Explorer, can be opened in the Start screen as well as on the desktop. Applications opened in the Start screen have been optimized to be used on touch devices.

11 Close Internet Explorer by positioning the mouse pointer at the top of the screen until the pointer turns into a hand, holding down the left mouse button, dragging the mouse pointer to the bottom of the screen, and then releasing the left mouse button.

Closing applications in the Windows 8 Start screen is different than closing applications on the desktop. Dragging an application down to the bottom of the screen closes it, while dragging an application to the left or right portion of the screen resizes the application and positions it on the side to which it was dragged.

12 Display the Charm bar by positioning the mouse in the upper right corner of the screen and then click the Settings button on the Charm bar.

The Settings button contains options for changing Windows 8 settings. It also contains the controls to shut down the computer.

13 Click the Power tile located toward the bottom of the Settings panel.

14 Click the *Shut down* option at the pop-up list that displays.

The Power tile contains three options. The *Sleep* option turns off the monitor and hard drives to conserve power. The *Shut down* option turns off the computer, and the *Restart* option turns off the computer and then restarts it.

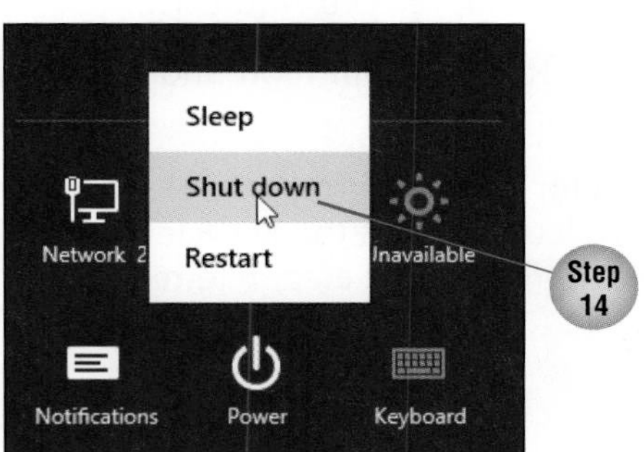

In Brief

Start Program
1. Display Windows 8 Start screen.
2. Click desired program tile.

Shut Down Windows
1. Display Charm bar.
2. Click Settings button.
3. Click Power tile.
4. Click *Shut down*.

Need Help?

Check with your instructor before shutting down Windows 8. If you are working in a computer lab at your school, a shared computer lab policy may prevent you from shutting down the computer. In this case, proceed to the next activity.

In Addition

Putting the Computer to Sleep

In Windows 8, Sleep mode saves all of your work and places the computer in a low power state by turning off the monitor and hard drive. A light on the outside of the computer case blinks or turns a different color to indicate Sleep mode is active. Wake up the computer by pressing the Power button on the front of the computer case, or by moving the mouse. After you log on, the screen will display exactly as you left it when you activated Sleep mode. Sleep mode causes Windows to automatically save your work, whereas shutting down does not.

Activity 1.2

Exploring the Windows 8 Desktop

The Windows 8 desktop can be compared to the top of a desk in an office. A person places necessary tools—such as pencils, pens, paper, files, or a calculator—on his or her desktop to perform functions. Similarly, the Windows 8 desktop contains tools for operating the computer. These tools are logically grouped and placed in dialog boxes or windows that can be accessed using the icons located on the desktop. The desktop is the most common screen in Windows 8 and is the screen in which most applications and tools will open and run.

Project

You decide to take some time to explore the Windows 8 desktop to familiarize yourself with this important screen of the operating system.

Tutorial 1.2
Exploring the Windows 8 Desktop

1. If necessary, turn on the power to your computer to start Windows. At the Windows 8 Start screen, click the Desktop tile.

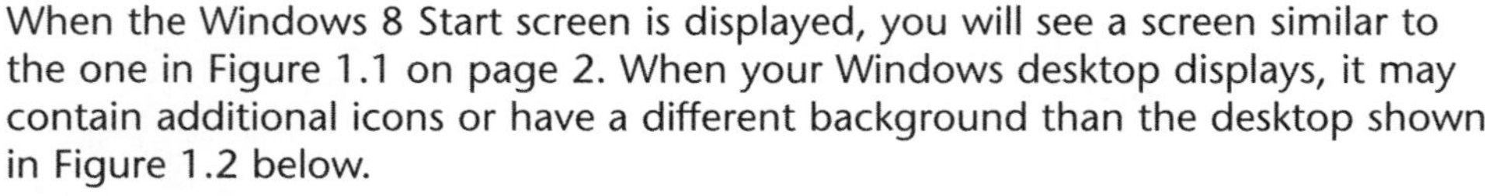

When the Windows 8 Start screen is displayed, you will see a screen similar to the one in Figure 1.1 on page 2. When your Windows desktop displays, it may contain additional icons or have a different background than the desktop shown in Figure 1.2 below.

2. Move the mouse pointer to the bottom right corner of the desktop where the current day and time display at the right side of the Taskbar. After approximately one second, a pop-up box appears with the current day of the week as well as the current date.

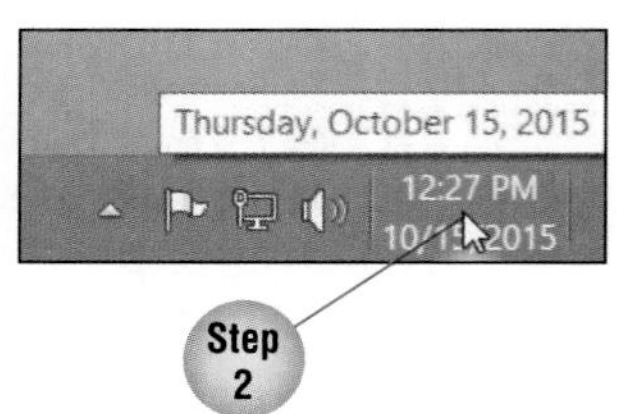

To identify the location of the Taskbar, refer to Figure 1.2.

3. Position the mouse pointer on the Recycle Bin icon and then double-click the left mouse button.

Icons provide an easy method for opening programs or documents. Double-clicking the *Recycle Bin* icon displays the Recycle Bin window. When you open a program, a defined work area, referred to as a ***window***, appears on the screen.

FIGURE 1.2 Windows 8 Desktop

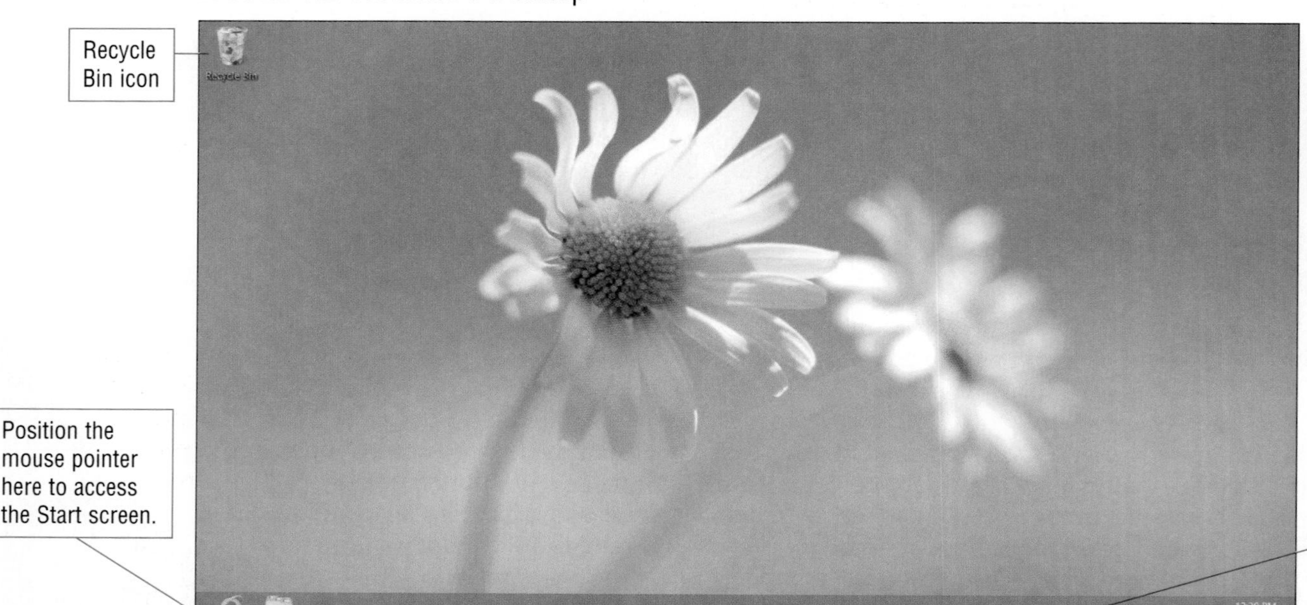

4 Close the Recycle Bin window by clicking the Close button that displays in the upper right corner of the window.

5 Position the mouse pointer in the lower left corner of the screen until the Start screen thumbnail displays and then click the right mouse button.

When you right-click the Start screen thumbnail, a pop-up list displays with various options. You can use these options to access computer and operating system management features such as the Control Panel, Task Manager, and Device Manager.

In Brief

Display Windows 8 Desktop
Click Desktop tile.

6 Click the *System* option in the pop-up list to display information about your computer in a new window.

Your computer's information will appear in the System window. This information can be useful when determining if your computer is capable of running advanced software, or when you want to upgrade hardware such as RAM or a processor.

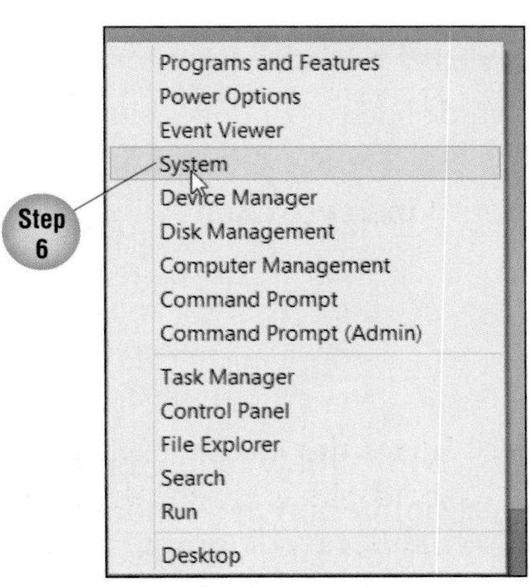

7 Close the System window by clicking the Close button that displays in the upper right corner of the window.

8 Right-click in a blank area of the desktop (not on an icon or the Taskbar).

A shortcut menu will display with various options you can use to manage files and/or change the way the desktop appears on your monitor.

9 Click the *Personalize* option at the shortcut menu.

The Personalization window contains options such as the Desktop Background, Color, Sounds, and Screen Saver, which you can customize.

10 Close the Personalization window by clicking the Close button in the upper right corner of the window.

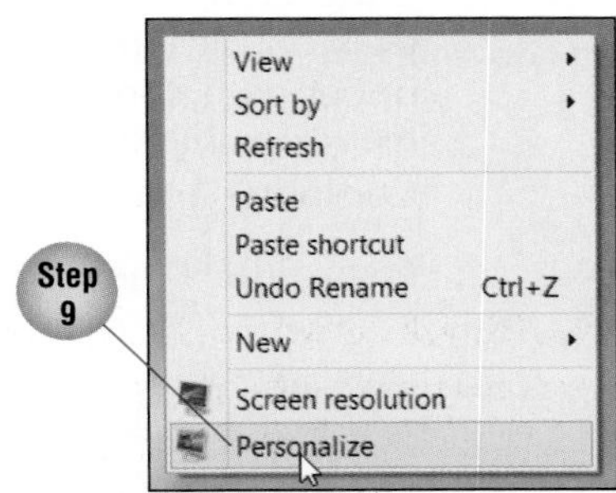

In Addition

Changing the Appearance of Windows 8

You can change the appearance of Windows 8 with options that display when you right-click a blank area of the desktop. Click the *Personalize* option at the shortcut menu if you want to change the Windows theme, desktop background, color, sounds, or screen saver. You can also change how the desktop icons and mouse pointers display. Click the *Screen resolution* option at the shortcut menu if you want to change the screen resolution, the monitor orientation, or the size of text or other items. The Screen Resolution window also contains controls for setting up multiple displays. Customizing how Windows 8 appears on your monitor by increasing the size of certain elements or changing certain colors can make Windows easier to use.

Activity 1.3

Opening and Manipulating Windows

When you open a program, a defined work area, referred to as a ***window***, appears on the screen. You can move a window on the desktop and change the size of a window. The top of a window is called the Title bar and generally contains buttons at the right side for closing, minimizing, maximizing, and/or restoring the size of the window. More than one window can be open at a time, and open windows can be cascaded or stacked. When a window is moved to the left or right side of the screen, the Snap feature in Windows 8 causes it to "stick" to the edge of the screen. When the window is moved to the top of the screen, the window is automatically maximized, and when a maximized window is dragged down, the window is automatically restored down.

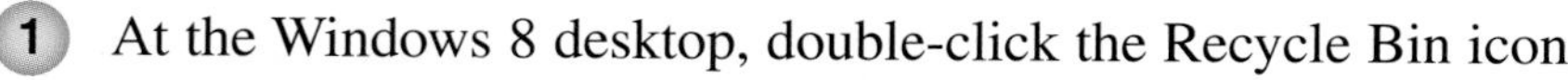

Project

You decide to continue your exploration of the Windows 8 desktop by opening and manipulating windows.

SNAP

Tutorial 1.3
Opening and Using Windows

1. At the Windows 8 desktop, double-click the Recycle Bin icon.

   This opens the Recycle Bin window on the desktop. If the Recycle Bin window fills the entire desktop, click the Restore Down button, which is the second button from the right (immediately left of the Close button) in the upper right corner of the window.

Step 1

2. Move the window on the desktop. To do this, position the mouse pointer on the window's Title bar (the bar along the top of the window), hold down the left mouse button, drag the window to a different location on the desktop, and then release the mouse button.

3. Position the mouse pointer in the lower left corner of the desktop to display the Start screen thumbnail, click the right mouse button, and then click the *File Explorer* option in the pop-up list.

   If the Computer window fills the entire desktop, click the Restore Down button in the upper right corner of the window. You now have two windows open on the desktop—Computer and Recycle Bin.

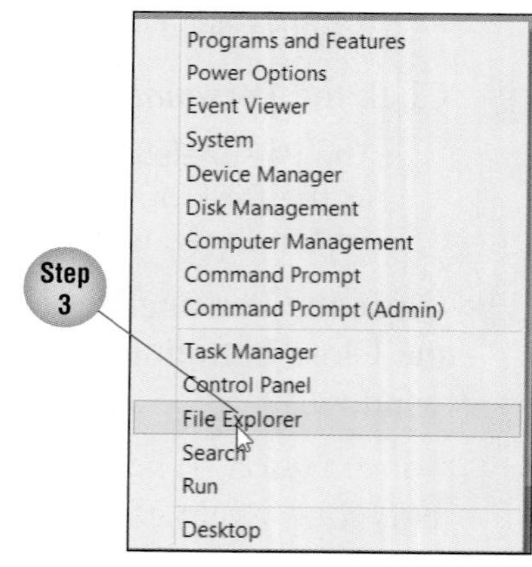

Step 3

4. Make sure the Title bar of the Recycle Bin window is visible (if not, move the Computer window) and then click the Recycle Bin Title bar.

   Clicking the Recycle Bin Title bar makes the Recycle Bin window active and moves it in front of the Computer window.

5. Minimize the Recycle Bin window to the Taskbar by clicking the Minimize button (located toward the right side of the Recycle Bin Title bar).

   The minimized Recycle Bin window is positioned behind the File Explorer button (displays as a group of file folders) on the Taskbar. Notice the File Explorer button now appears with another button stacked behind it.

Step 5

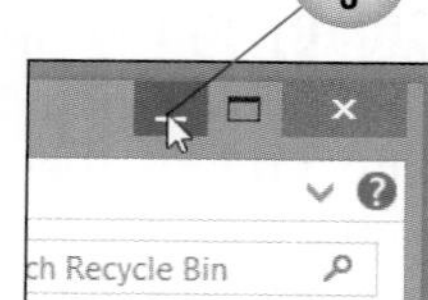

6. Minimize the Computer window to the Taskbar (behind the File Explorer button) by clicking the Minimize button located at the right side of the Title bar.

7. Move the pointer over the File Explorer button at the left side of the Taskbar.

   The two minimized windows are stacked behind the File Explorer button. Resting the pointer on the File Explorer button causes a thumbnail preview of each window to display.

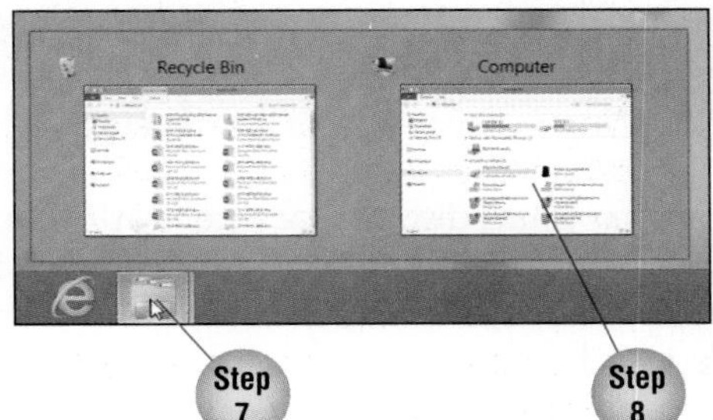

8. Click the thumbnail preview for the Computer window to redisplay the window on the desktop.
9. Rest the pointer over the File Explorer button on the Taskbar and then click the thumbnail preview for the Recycle Bin window.
10. Drag the Title bar for the Recycle Bin window to the top of the desktop and then release the mouse button.

    Dragging a window to the top of the desktop causes the window to automatically maximize when you release the mouse button. The Snap feature allows you to resize a window by dragging the window to the edge of a screen. You can also maximize the window by clicking the Maximize button adjacent to the Close button at the right side of the Title bar.

11. Drag the Title bar for the Recycle Bin window down from the top of the desktop to restore the window to its previous size before it was maximized.
12. Right-click a blank, unused section of the Taskbar and then click *Show windows stacked* at the shortcut menu.

    The Taskbar shortcut menu provides three options to display windows: *Cascade windows,* which places the windows in a fanned, single stack with the title bar of each open window visible; *stacked,* which places windows in a horizontal stack with a portion of each window visible; or *side by side,* which places open windows next to each other.

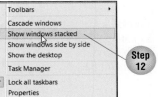

    Toolbars
    Cascade windows
    Show windows stacked
    Show windows side by side
    Show the desktop
    Task Manager
    ✓ Lock all taskbars
    Properties

    Step 12

13. Drag the Recycle Bin window off the right edge of the screen and then release the mouse button. When you release the mouse button, the window resizes to fill one-half the width of the screen.
14. Drag the Computer window off the left edge of the screen and then release the mouse button. When you release the mouse button, the window resizes to fill the remaining width of the screen.
15. Close each of the two windows by clicking the Close button located at the right side of the Title bar.

In Brief

Move Window
1. Position mouse pointer on window Title bar.
2. Hold down left mouse button.
3. Drag window to desired position.
4. Release mouse button.

Stack Windows
1. Right-click an unused section of Taskbar.
2. Click *Show windows stacked* at shortcut menu.

Cascade Windows
1. Right-click an unused section of Taskbar.
2. Click *Cascade windows* at shortcut menu.

In Addition

Sizing a Window

Using the mouse, you can increase or decrease the size of a window. To change the width, position the mouse pointer on the border at the right or left side of the window until the mouse turns into a left-and-right-pointing arrow. Hold down the left mouse button, drag the border to the right or left, and then release the mouse button. Complete similar steps to increase or decrease the height of the window using the top or bottom borders. To change the width and height of the window at the same time, position the mouse pointer at the left or right corner of the window until the pointer turns into a diagonally pointing, double-headed arrow and then drag in the desired direction to change the size.

Activity 1.4

Exploring the Taskbar, Charm Bar, and Dialog Box Components

The bar that displays at the bottom of the desktop is called the ***Taskbar*** and it is divided into three sections: the Start screen area, the task button area, and the notification area. Position the mouse in the Start screen area to display the Start screen thumbnail. Open programs display as task buttons in the task button area of the Taskbar. The notification area displays at the right side of the Taskbar and contains a clock and the program icons for programs that run in the background on your computer. You can right-click a blank, unused portion of the Taskbar to display a shortcut menu with options for customizing the Taskbar. The bar that displays at the right side of the desktop when the mouse pointer is positioned in the upper or lower right corner of the desktop is called the *Charm bar*. Click buttons in the Charm bar to access common operating system features. Some settings are changed in a window called a *dialog box*. Dialog boxes contain similar features such as tabs, text boxes, and option buttons that you can use to change settings.

Project

As you continue exploring Windows 8, you want to learn more about the features available on the Taskbar.

Tutorial 1.4
Exploring the Taskbar and the Charm Bar

1. At the Windows 8 desktop, click the current time that displays at the far right side of the Taskbar and then click the Change date and time settings hyperlink in the pop-up box.

   Figure 1.3 identifies the components of the Taskbar. Clicking the current time and then clicking the Change date and time settings hyperlink causes the Date and Time dialog box to display. Refer to Table 1.3 on the next page for information on dialog box components. Each listed component will not be present in every dialog box.

2. Check to make sure the correct date and time display in the Date and Time dialog box.

   If the date is incorrect, click the Change date and time button. At the Date and Time Settings dialog box, click the correct date in the calendar box. If necessary, use the left- or right-pointing arrows to change the calendar display to a different month. To change the time, double-click the hour, minutes, or seconds and then type the correct entry or use the up- or down-pointing arrows to adjust the time. Click OK when finished.

3. Click the Additional Clocks tab located toward the top of the Date and Time dialog box.

   At this tab, you can add the ability to show a second clock when you hover over or click the current time in the Taskbar. For example, you could show the current time for Cairo, Egypt, in addition to the current time for your time zone.

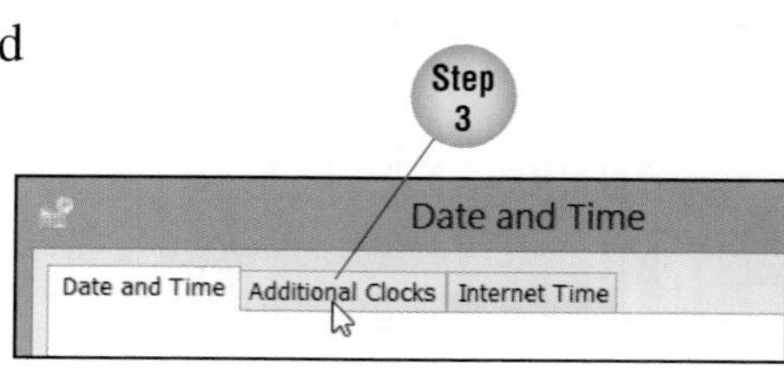

FIGURE 1.3 Taskbar

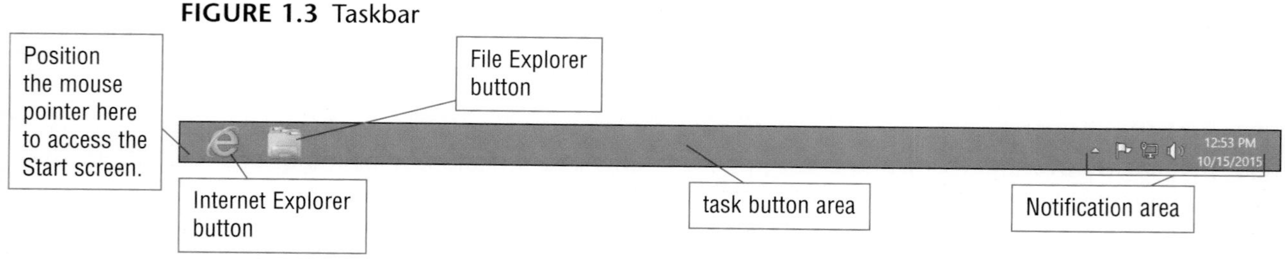

TABLE 1.3 Possible Dialog Box Components

Name	Image	Function
tabs	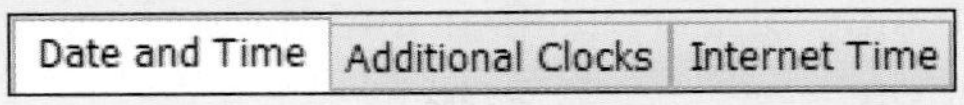 Date and Time / Additional Clocks / Internet Time	Click a dialog box tab and the dialog box options change.
text box	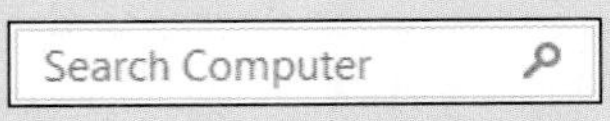 Search Computer	Type or edit text in a text box. A text box may contain up- or down-pointing arrows to allow you to choose a number or an option instead of typing it.
drop-down list box	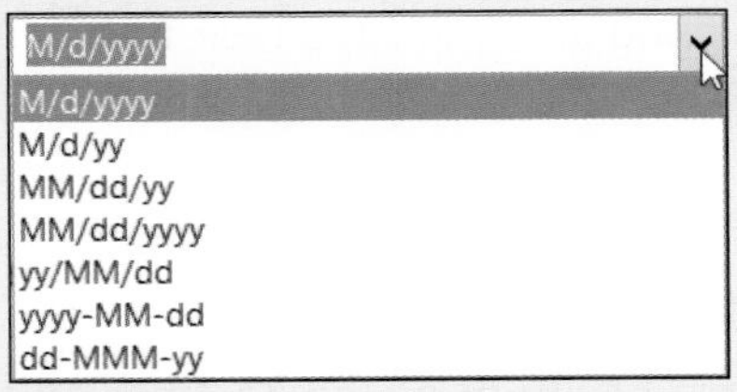 M/d/yyyy; M/d/yyyy, M/d/yy, MM/dd/yy, MM/dd/yyyy, yy/MM/dd, yyyy-MM-dd, dd-MMM-yy	Click the down-pointing arrow at the right side of an option box and a drop-down list displays.
list box	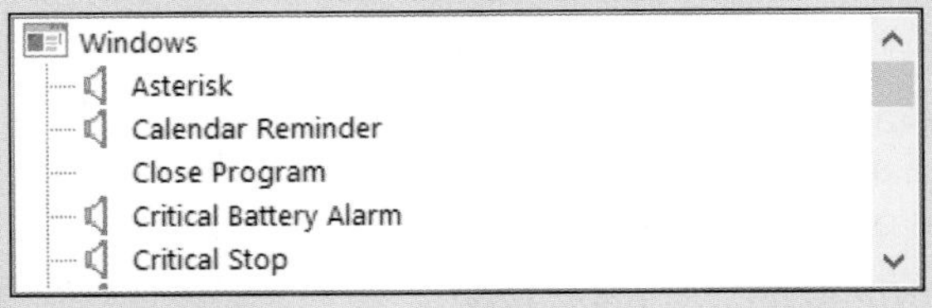 Windows; Asterisk, Calendar Reminder, Close Program, Critical Battery Alarm, Critical Stop	A list box displays a list of options.
check boxes	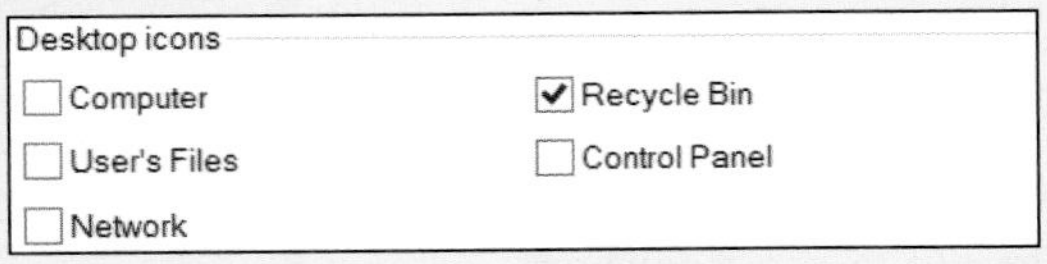 Desktop icons: Computer, Recycle Bin, User's Files, Control Panel, Network	If a check box contains a check mark, the option is active; if the check box is empty, the option is inactive. In some cases, any number of check boxes may be active.
option buttons	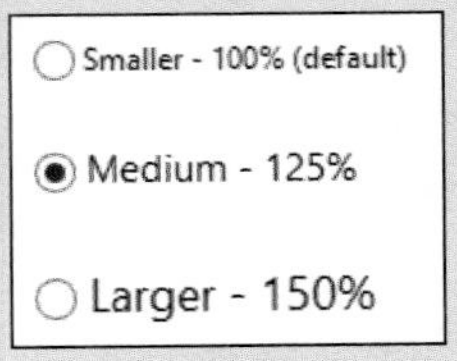 Smaller - 100% (default); Medium - 125%; Larger - 150%	Only one option button in a dialog box section can be selected at once. An active option button contains a dark or colored circle.
command buttons	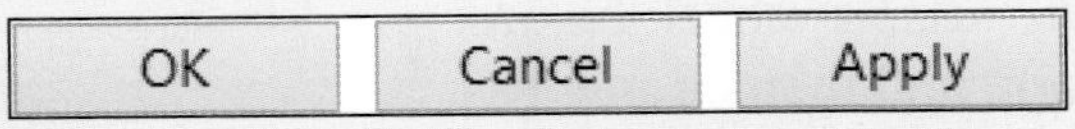 OK / Cancel / Apply	Click a command button to execute or cancel a command. If a command button name is followed by an ellipsis (...),clicking the button will open another dialog box.
slider bar	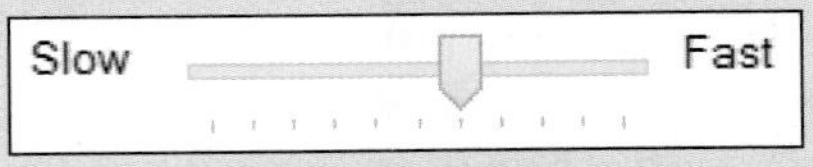 Slow — Fast	Using the mouse, drag a slider button on a slider bar to increase or decrease the number, speed, or percentage of the option.
scroll bar	 (UTC-12:00) International Date Line West; (UTC-11:00) Coordinated Universal Time-11; (UTC-10:00) Hawaii; (UTC-09:00) Alaska; (UTC-08:00) Baja California; (UTC-08:00) Pacific Time (US & Canada); (UTC-07:00) Arizona; (UTC-07:00) Chihuahua, La Paz, Mazatlan; (UTC-07:00) Mountain Time (US & Canada); (UTC-06:00) Central America; (UTC-06:00) Central Time (US & Canada)	A scroll bar displays when the amount of information in a list is larger than can fit in a single window.

continues

4. Click the OK button to close the Date and Time dialog box.

5. Position the mouse pointer on the Speakers button located toward the right side of the Taskbar and then click the left mouse button.

    Clicking the Speakers button causes a slider bar to display. Use this slider bar to increase or decrease the volume. Click the Mute Speakers button located at the bottom of the slider bar if you want to turn off the sound. If the Speakers button is not visible on the Taskbar, click the up-pointing arrow located near the left side of the notification area. This expands the area to show hidden icons.

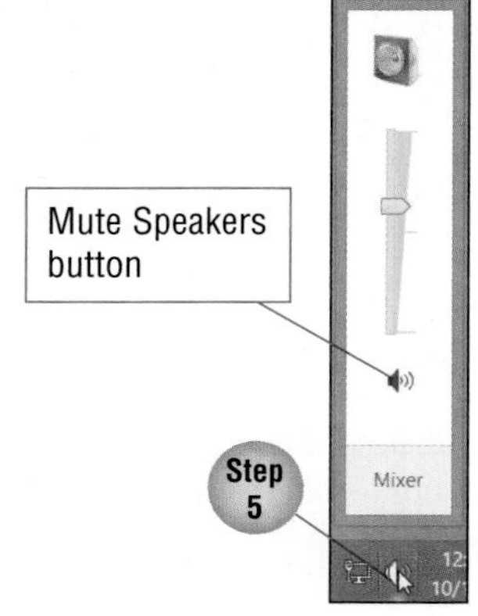

6. After viewing the Speakers slider bar, click in a blank, unused area on the desktop to hide the slider bar.

7. Right-click in a blank, unused section of the Taskbar and then click *Properties* at the shortcut menu.

    This displays the Taskbar Properties dialog box with the Taskbar tab selected. Notice that the dialog box contains check boxes. A check mark in a check box indicates that the option is active.

8. Click the *Auto-hide the taskbar* check box to insert a check mark.

9. Click the Apply button located toward the bottom of the dialog box.

10. Click the OK button to close the Taskbar Properties dialog box.

    Notice that the Taskbar is no longer visible.

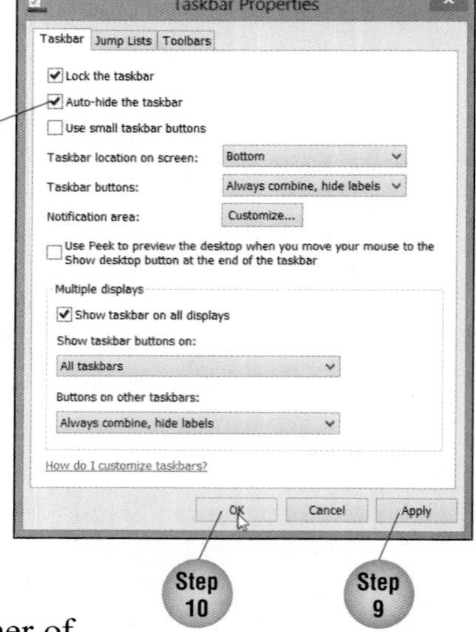

11. Display the Taskbar by moving the mouse pointer to the bottom of the desktop.

12. Right-click in a blank, unused section of the Taskbar, click *Properties* at the shortcut menu, click the *Auto-hide the taskbar* check box to remove the check mark, and then click OK.

13. Position the mouse pointer in the upper right corner of the desktop to display the Charm bar.

    The Charm bar displays transparently until the mouse pointer is moved onto any area of the bar, which activates the bar. When the Charm bar is active, it changes from transparent to black, and a box with the current time and date displays in the lower left corner of the screen.

14. Make the Charm bar active by moving the mouse onto the bar and then click the Search button.

    Clicking the Search button opens the Windows 8 Start screen and makes the search text box active. You can search for applications, settings, or files by clicking the desired option below the search text box.

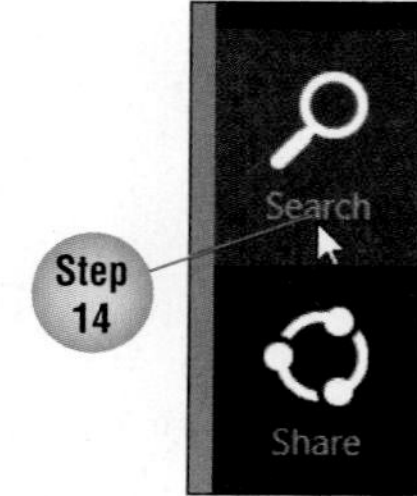

15 Type **snipping tool** in the search text box.

Notice that Windows 8 actively narrows the search results in the *Apps* section of the screen as you type.

16 Press the Enter key on the keyboard.

Pressing the Enter key opens the Snipping Tool in a new window on the desktop. If the search does not return a match for what you typed in the text box, a list of possible results will display.

17 Close the Snipping Tool window by clicking the Close button in the upper right corner of the window.

18 Make the Charm bar active and then click the Settings button.

19 At the Settings panel, click the *Change PC settings* option located at the bottom of the panel.

When you click the *Change PC settings* option in the Settings panel, the PC settings screen displays. This screen contains a variety of options for changing the settings of your computer. These options are grouped into categories that display at the left side of the PC settings screen.

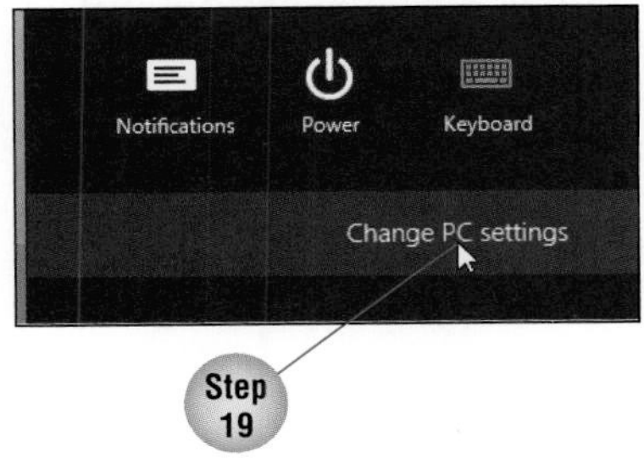

20 Close the PC settings screen by positioning the mouse pointer at the top of the screen until it turns into a hand, holding down the left mouse button, dragging the PC settings screen to the bottom of the screen until it dims, and then releasing the left mouse button.

In Windows 8, certain applications and tools open in the Start screen instead of in a window on the desktop. To close applications or tools that open in the Start screen, drag the top of the screen to the bottom of the screen until it becomes dim and then release the mouse button.

In Brief

Display Date and Time Dialog Box
1. Click current time at right side of Taskbar.
2. Click Change date and time settings.

Display Speakers Slider Bar
Click Speakers button on Taskbar.

Display Taskbar Properties Dialog Box
1. Right-click an unused section on Taskbar.
2. Click *Properties* at shortcut menu.

In Addition

Managing Devices Using the Charm Bar

The Charm bar contains the Devices button, which you can use to manage devices plugged into your computer. Click the Devices button on the Charm bar and the Devices panel displays at the right side of the screen. Devices plugged into your computer display as a list in the Devices panel. Click a device in the Devices list to display options for a particular device. Devices that are commonly listed in the Devices panel are monitors, projectors, and other peripheral devices that may be plugged into your computer.

Activity 1.5

Getting Help in Windows; Displaying File Extensions

Windows 8 includes an on-screen reference guide, called Windows Help and Support, that provides information, explanations, and interactive help on learning Windows features. The Windows Help and Support feature contains complex files with hypertext that can be clicked to display additional information. Display the Windows Help and Support window by right-clicking a blank area of the Start screen, clicking the All apps icon and then clicking the Help and Support tile in the Windows System section. You can also press F1 at the desktop and the Windows Help and Support window will display with information on your current task. At the Windows Help and Support window, you can perform such actions as choosing a specific help topic, searching for a keyword, and displaying a list of help topics.

Project

You decide to use the Windows Help and Support feature to learn how to pin an application to the Taskbar. You also want to find out how to turn on the display of file extensions.

Tutorial 1.5
Getting Help in Windows 8

1. Display the Windows 8 Start screen, right-click a blank area of the screen, and then click the All apps icon.
2. Use the horizontal scroll bar at the bottom of the screen to display the *Windows System* section and then click the Help and Support tile.
3. At the Windows Help and Support window with the insertion point positioned in the search text box, type **taskbar** and press Enter.

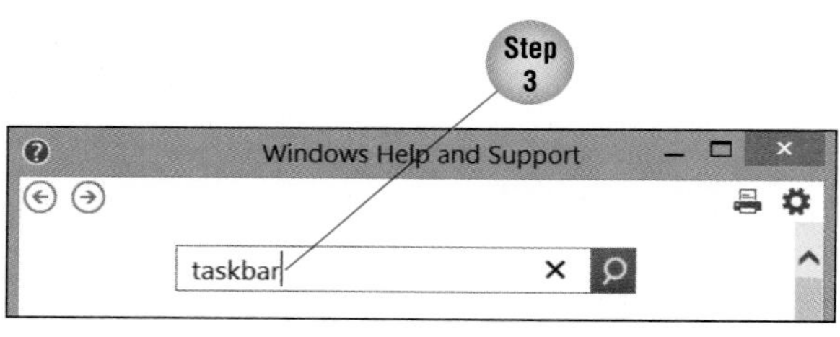

4. Click the How to use the taskbar hyperlink in the search results list.
5. Scroll down the Windows Help and Support window and then read the information under the heading *Pin an app to the taskbar*.

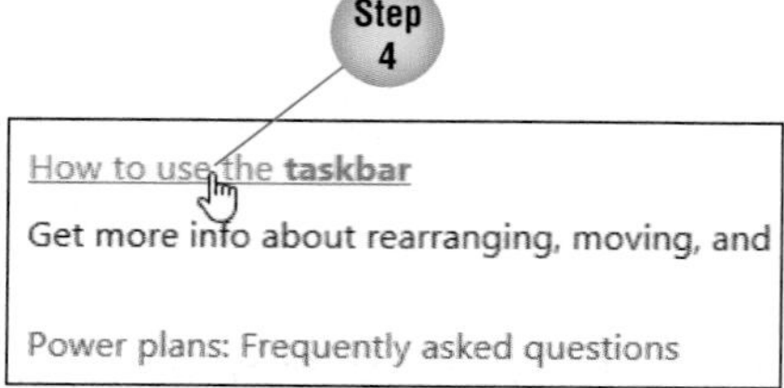

   You will open and then pin the Snipping Tool application to the Taskbar in the following steps.

6. Open the Snipping Tool from the Windows 8 Start screen or by using the Charm bar to conduct a search for the Snipping Tool application.
7. Return to the Windows Help and Support window by clicking the Windows Help and Support button on the Taskbar.

8 Follow the instructions in the *Pin an app to the taskbar* section of the Windows Help and Support window to pin the Snipping Tool to the Taskbar.

When you pin an application to the Taskbar, the button for the application will be added to and remain on the Taskbar until it is unpinned (even if you restart the computer). Pinning applications you use often to the Taskbar reduces the steps required to open them.

9 Read information in the *Pin an app to the taskbar* section of the Windows Help and Support Window on how to remove a pinned application from the Taskbar and then unpin the Snipping Tool.

Note that unpinning the Snipping Tool application while the application is still open will unpin the button, but the button will display on the taskbar until the Snipping Tool application is closed.

10 Close the Windows Help and Support window and the Snipping Tool application by clicking the Close button located in the upper right corner of each window.

Worldwide Enterprises requires that employees work with the display of file extensions turned on. This practice helps employees identify source applications associated with files and can prevent employees from accidentally opening email attachments that contain harmful data. In the next steps, you will turn on the display of file extensions.

11 Click the File Explorer button on the Taskbar.

12 Click the View tab on the ribbon.

Windows 8 File Explorer contains a ribbon with four tabs: File, Home, Share, and View. These tabs contain options and buttons to change File Explorer settings and manage folders and files.

13 Click the *File name extensions* check box in the Show/hide group to insert a check mark. ***Note: If the check box appears with a check mark in it, then file extensions are already turned on—skip this step.***

Inserting a check mark in a check box makes the option active.

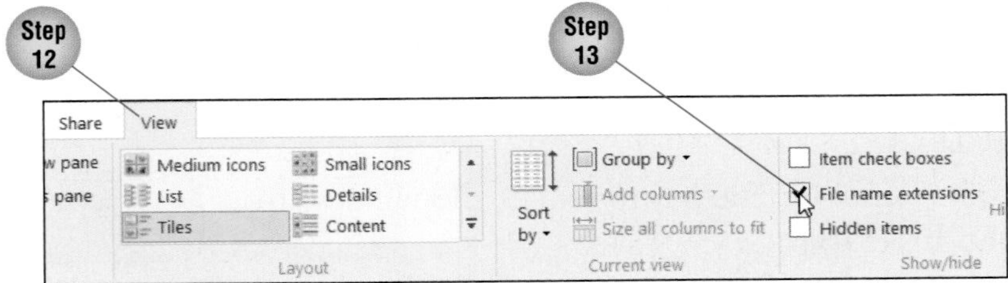

14 Close the File Explorer window by clicking the Close button located at the right side of the Title bar.

In Brief

Display Help and Support Window

1. Open Start screen.
2. Right-click blank area of Start screen.
3. Click All apps icon.
4. Click Help and Support tile.

In Addition

Browsing the Windows Help and Support Window by Topic Lists

You can locate Help information by browsing the Contents list of topics instead of typing key words in the search text box. Click the Browse help button (located below the search text box) in the Windows Help and Support window. This displays the Windows Help topics list. Click the hyperlink to a topic category in the Windows Help topics list and then continue clicking hyperlinks until you find the information you need.

Features Summary

Feature	Button	Action
close window	×	Click Close button on Title bar.
Computer window		Right-click Start screen thumbnail, click *File Explorer*.
Date and Time dialog box		Click time on Taskbar, click Change date and time settings.
maximize window		Drag window to top of screen or click Maximize button on Title bar.
minimize window		Click Minimize button on Title bar.
move window on desktop		Drag window Title bar.
restore window		Drag maximized window down or click Restore Down button on Title bar.
shut down computer		Click Settings button on Charm bar, click Power, click *Shut down*.
Start screen		Click Start screen area on Taskbar.
Taskbar and Start Menu Properties dialog box		Right-click unused section of Taskbar, click *Properties* at shortcut menu.
Taskbar shortcut menu		Right-click unused section of Taskbar.
Speakers slider bar		Click Speakers button on Taskbar.
Windows Help and Support window		Open Start screen, right-click blank area, click All apps icon, click *Help and Support*.

Knowledge Check SNAP

Completion: In the space provided at the right, indicate the correct term, command, or option.

1. This mouse term refers to tapping the left mouse button twice in quick succession. ________________
2. Click this button on a window Title bar to reduce the window to a task button on the Taskbar. ________________
3. Click this button on a window Title bar to expand the window so it fills the entire screen. ________________
4. Click the time located at the right side of the Taskbar and then click this option to open the Date and Time dialog box. ________________
5. This is the name of a bar you can display on the desktop for quick access to a variety of Windows 8 features. ________________
6. Windows Help and Support is accessed from this screen. ________________

Skills Review

Review 1 Opening and Manipulating Windows

1. At the Windows 8 desktop, click the File Explorer button on the Taskbar. (If the Libraries window fills the desktop, drag the window down from the top of the screen or click the Restore Down button located in the upper right corner of the window.)
2. Double-click the Recycle Bin icon on the desktop. (If the Recycle Bin window fills the desktop, drag the window down from the top of the screen or click the Restore Down button.)
3. Position the mouse pointer on the Recycle Bin Title bar, hold down the left mouse button, and then drag the Recycle Bin window so the Libraries Title bar is visible.
4. Click the Libraries Title bar to make the window active.
5. Right-click in a blank, unused section of the Taskbar and then click *Cascade windows* at the shortcut menu.
6. Click the Minimize button (located toward the right side of the Title bar) on the Libraries Title bar to reduce the window to a task button behind the File Explorer button on the Taskbar.
7. Click the Minimize button on the Recycle Bin window to reduce the window to a task button behind the File Explorer button on the Taskbar.
8. Point to the File Explorer button on the Taskbar and then click the thumbnail preview for the Recycle Bin window to restore the Recycle Bin window on the desktop.
9. Point to the File Explorer button on the Taskbar and then click the thumbnail preview for the Libraries window to restore the Libraries window on the desktop.
10. Drag the Libraries window to the top of the screen and then release the mouse button. (The window expands to fill the entire screen.)
11. Drag the Libraries window down from the top of the screen to restore the window to its previous size and then release the mouse button.
12. Drag the Libraries window off the right edge of the screen until a transparent box displays on the right half of the screen and then release the mouse button.
13. Drag the Recycle Bin window off the left edge of the screen until a transparent box displays on the left half of the screen and then release the mouse button.
14. Close the Libraries window.
15. Close the Recycle Bin window.

Review 2 Exploring the Taskbar

1. At the Windows 8 desktop, click the time that displays in the notification area at the right side of the Taskbar and then click Change date and time settings hyperlink in the pop-up box.
2. At the Date and Time dialog box, click the Change date and time button.
3. At the Date and Time Settings dialog box, click the right arrow in the calendar to display the next month (from the current month).
4. Click the OK button twice.
5. Click the Start screen thumbnail, right-click in a blank area of the Start screen, click the All apps icon, and then click the Notepad tile in the *Windows Accessories* section. (Notepad is a program used for creating and editing text files.)
6. Close Notepad by clicking the Close button at the right side of the Notepad Title bar.

Skills Assessment

Assessment 1 **Manipulating Windows**

1. Click the File Explorer button on the Taskbar and then double-click the Pictures icon. (If the Pictures window fills the entire desktop, drag the window down from the top of the screen or click the Restore Down button.)
2. Right-click the File Explorer button on the Taskbar, click *File Explorer* in the pop-up list, and then double-click the Music icon. (If the Music window fills the entire desktop, drag the window down from the top of the screen or click the Restore Down button.)
3. Stack the two windows.
4. Make the Pictures window active and then reduce it to a task button on the Taskbar.
5. Reduce the Music window to a task button on the Taskbar.
6. Restore the Pictures window.
7. Restore the Music window.
8. Arrange the two windows side-by-side on the desktop with each window filling one-half the width of the screen.
9. Close the Music window and then close the Pictures window.

Assessment 2 **Customizing the Taskbar**

1. At the Windows 8 desktop, display the Date and Time dialog box.
2. Change the current hour to one hour ahead and then close the dialog box.
3. Display the Speakers slider bar, drag the slider to increase the volume, and then click the desktop outside the slider to hide the slider bar.
4. Display the Taskbar Properties dialog box, use the *Taskbar location on screen* option box to change the Taskbar location on the screen to *Top*, and then close the dialog box. (Notice that the Taskbar is now positioned along the top edge of the screen.)
5. Display the Charm bar and then click the Search button.
6. At the Search panel, type **calculator** in the text box and then press Enter.
7. Close the Calculator application.

Assessment 3 **Restoring the Taskbar**

1. At the Windows 8 desktop, display the Date and Time dialog box and then change the date and time to today's date and the current time.
2. Display the Speakers slider bar and then drag the slider button back to the original position.
3. Display the Taskbar Properties dialog box and change the Taskbar location so that the Taskbar displays back at the bottom of the screen.

Windows SECTION 2

Maintaining Files and Customizing Windows

Skills

- Browse the contents of storage devices
- Change folder and view options
- Create a folder
- Rename a folder or file
- Select, move, copy, and paste folders or files
- Delete files/folders to and restore files/folders from the Recycle Bin
- Explore the Control Panel
- Use search tools to find applications, folders, and/or files
- Customize the desktop
- Change screen resolution

Student Resources

Before beginning the activities in Windows Section 2, copy to your storage medium the Windows folder on the Student Resources CD. This folder contains the data files you need to complete the projects in Windows Section 2.

Projects Overview

Explore options for browsing and viewing folders and files and then organize folders and files for your department at Worldwide Enterprises. This organization includes creating and renaming folders, as well as moving, copying, renaming, deleting, and restoring files. You will also search for specific files and customize your desktop to the corporate computer standard.

Organize files for Performance Threads including creating folders and copying, moving, renaming, and deleting files.

Organize files for First Choice Travel including creating folders and copying, moving, renaming, and deleting files. Assist your supervisor by searching for information on how to set up a computer for multiple users and how to work with libraries.

Activity 2.1

Browsing Storage Devices and Files in a Computer Window

Open a Computer window to view the various storage devices connected to your computer. The Content pane of the Computer window displays an icon for each hard disk drive and each removable storage medium such as a CD, DVD, or USB device. Next to each storage device icon, you can see the amount of storage space available as well as a bar with the amount of used space shaded with color. This visual cue allows you to see at a glance the proportion of space available relative to the capacity of the device. Double-click a device icon in the Content pane to show the contents stored on the device. You can display contents from another device or folder using the Navigation pane or the Computer window Address bar.

Project

You decide to explore the contents of the various storage devices on the computer you are using as you become familiar with the Windows 8 environment.

Note: To complete the projects in this section, you will need to use a USB flash drive or computer hard drive rather than your SkyDrive. Before beginning the projects in this section, make sure you have copied the WindowsS2 folder from the Student Resources CD to your storage medium. If necessary, refer to the inside back cover of this textbook for instructions on how to copy a folder from the Student Resources CD to your storage medium.

Tutorial 2.1
Browsing Devices and Files

1 If necessary, insert into an empty USB port the storage medium that you are using for the files in this course.

FIGURE 2.1 Computer Window

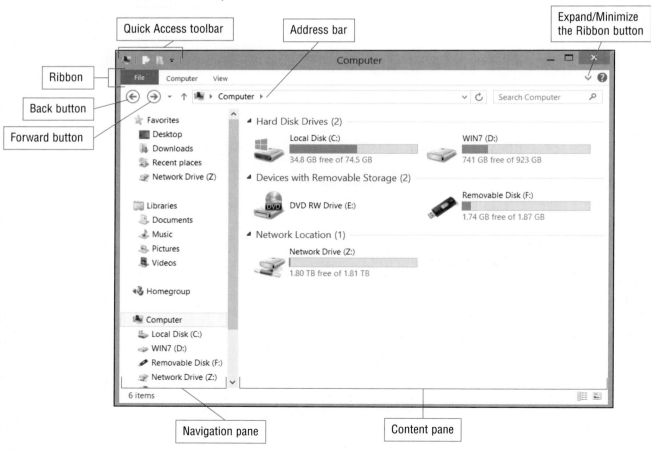

Quick Access toolbar
Address bar
Expand/Minimize the Ribbon button
Ribbon
Back button
Forward button
Navigation pane
Content pane

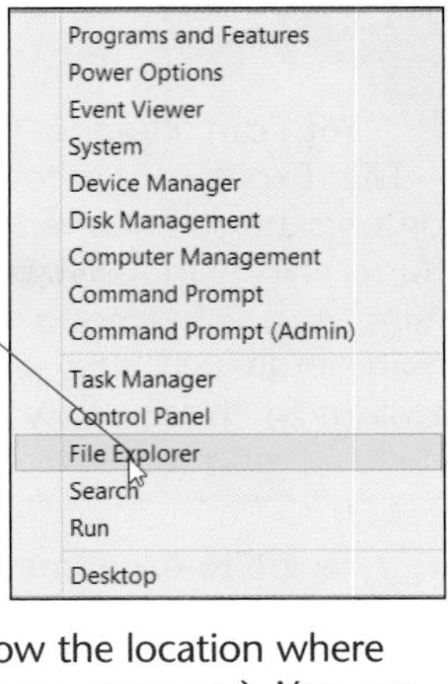

In Brief
Display Computer Window
1. Right-click Start screen thumbnail.
2. Click File Explorer at pop-up list.

2 At the Windows desktop, position the mouse in the lower left corner of the screen to display the Start screen thumbnail, right-click the thumbnail to display a pop-up list, and then click *File Explorer*.

The Computer window displays. It should appear similar to the one shown in Figure 2.1.

3 Double-click the icon for the hard disk drive named *Local Disk (C:)*.

The Computer window changes so that the Content pane displays the files and folders that are stored on the local hard disk drive assigned drive letter C:. Notice also that the Address bar in the Computer window updates to show the location where you are viewing *Local Disk (C:)* within *Computer* (your drive name may vary). You can navigate back using either the Back button or by clicking *Computer* in the Address bar.

4 Click the Back button to return to the Computer window.

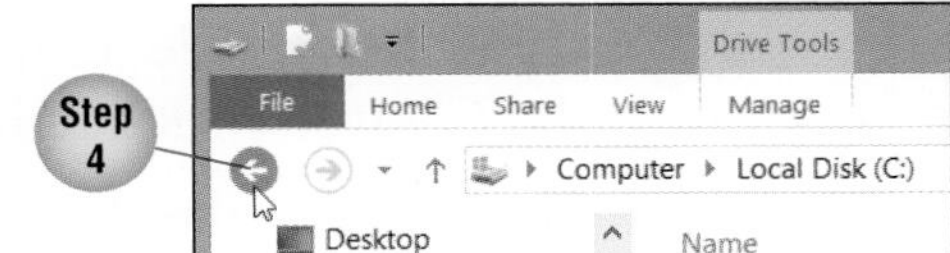

5 Double-click the icon for the storage medium onto which you copied the WindowsS2 folder. ***Note: The screens shown in this section show* Removable Disk (F:) *as the storage medium in the Computer window. Your icon label and drive letter may vary.***

Devices with Removable Storage (2)
DVD RW Drive (E:)
MarqueeStudentCD
0 bytes free of 152 MB
Removable Disk (F:)
1.72 GB free of 1.87 GB
Step 5

USB flash drives are shown in the section of the Content pane labeled *Devices with Removable Storage*. Each device is assigned a drive letter by Windows, usually starting at E or F and continuing through the alphabet depending on the number of removable devices that are currently in use. The label that displays next to the drive letter depends on the manufacturer of the USB flash drive. If no manufacturer label is present, Windows displays *Removable Disk*.

6 Double-click the *WindowsS2* folder to view the contents of the folder in the Content pane.

7 Look at the Address bar and notice how it displays the path to the current content list: Computer ▶ Removable Disk (F:) ▶ WindowsS2.

You can use the Address bar to navigate to any other device or folder by clicking a drive or folder name or by clicking the right-pointing black arrow to view a drop-down list of folders or other devices.

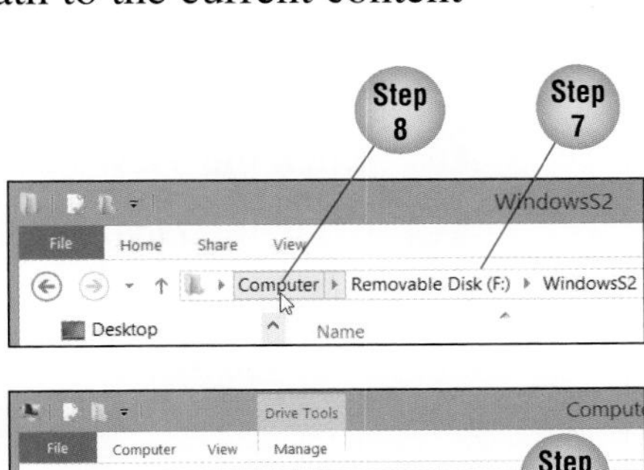

8 Click *Computer* in the Address bar.

9 Click the right-pointing arrow ▶ next to *Computer* in the Address bar (the arrow becomes a down-pointing arrow when clicked) and then click the drive letter representing the removable storage device that contains the WindowsS2 folder.

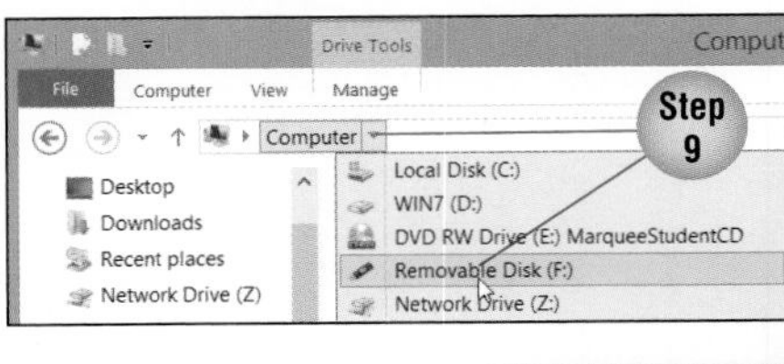

10 Click *Desktop* in the *Favorites* section of the Navigation pane.

You can also change what displays in the Content pane by clicking the device or folder name in the Navigation pane. Click the white right-pointing arrow next to a device or folder name in the Navigation pane to expand the list and view what is stored within the item.

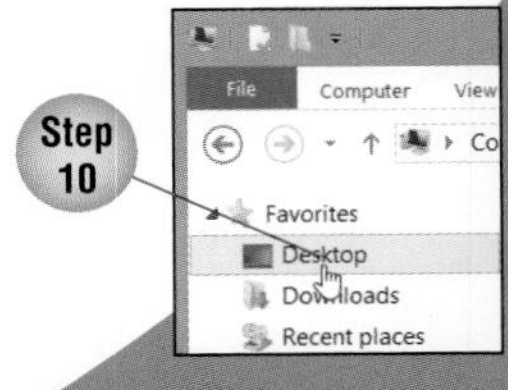

11 Close the Computer window.

Activity 2.2

Changing Folder and View Options

You can change the view of the File Explorer window to show the contents of your current location (drive or folder) in various formats, including icons, tiles, or a list, among others. With the Content pane in Details view, you can click the column headings to change how the contents are sorted and whether they are sorted in ascending or descending order. You can customize a window's environment by using buttons and options on the File Explorer View tab. You can change how panes are displayed, how content is arranged in the Content pane, how content is sorted, and which features are hidden.

Project

You decide to experiment with various folder and view options as you continue to become acquainted with the Windows 8 environment.

Tutorial 2.2
Changing Folder and View Options

1. Click the File Explorer button on the Taskbar.

   A Libraries window opens. For a description of libraries, refer to the In Addition section at the end of this activity.

2. Click the drive letter representing your storage medium in the *Computer* section in the Navigation pane.

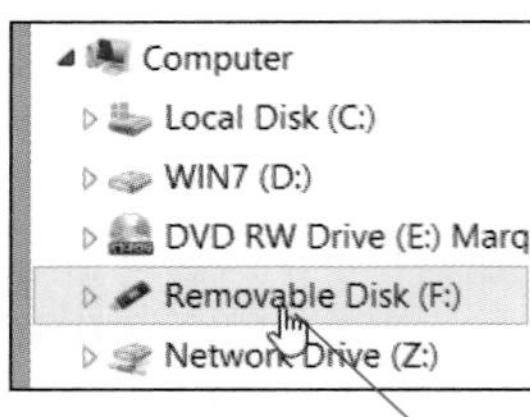

3. Double-click the *WindowsS2* folder in the Content pane.
4. Click the View tab located below the WindowsS2 Title bar.
5. Click the *Large icons* option in the Layout group.

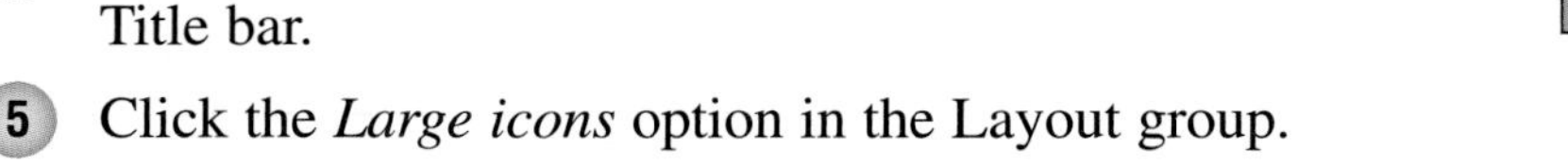

   After you click an option on the View tab, the View tab collapses to provide more space in the File Explorer window.

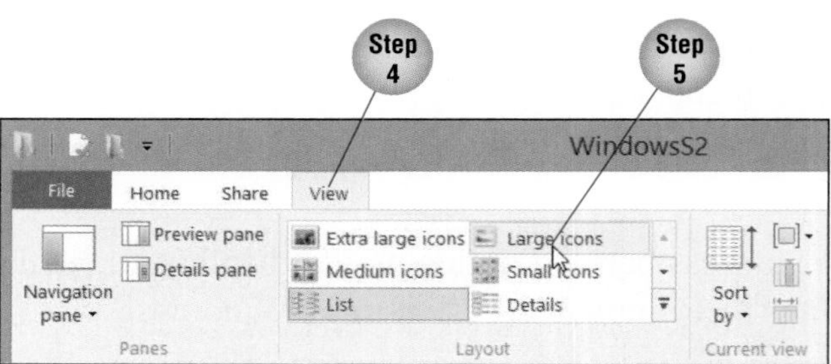

6. Click the View tab.
7. Click the *Details* option in the Layout group.

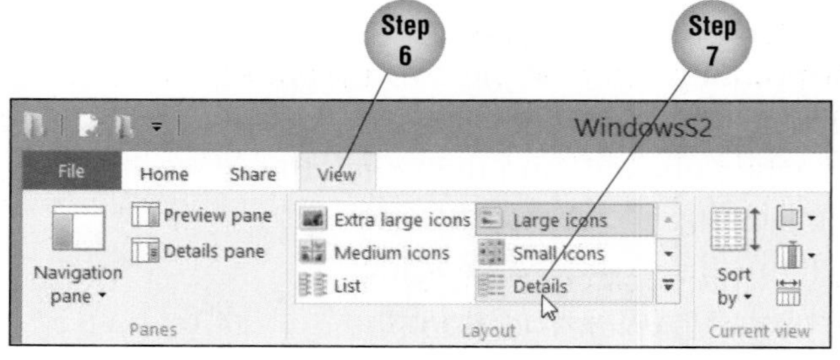

8. With folders now displayed in Details view, click the *Name* column heading to sort the list in descending order by name.

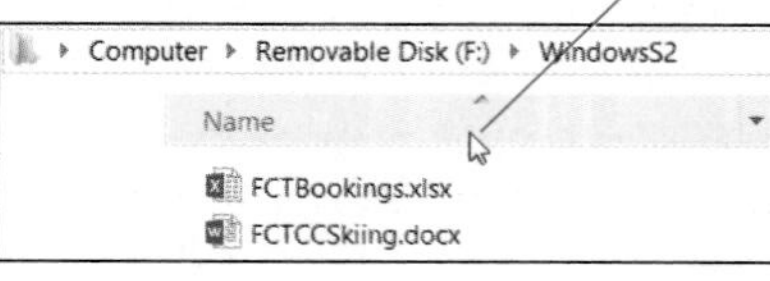

9. Click the *Name* column heading again to restore the list to ascending order by name.
10. Click the View tab and then click the Options button to open the Folder Options dialog box.
11. Click the *Open each folder in its own window* option in the *Browse folders* section on the General tab and then click OK.
12. Close the WindowsS2 window.
13. Click the File Explorer button on the Taskbar and then click the drive representing your storage medium in the *Computer* section in the Navigation pane.
14. Double-click the *WindowsS2* folder.

    Notice that this time a new window opens with the WindowsS2 content list layered on top of the original window.
15. Close the WindowsS2 folder window.
16. Click the View tab, click the Options button, click the Restore Defaults button located near the bottom of the General tab, and then click OK.
17. Close the Removable Disk (F:) window.

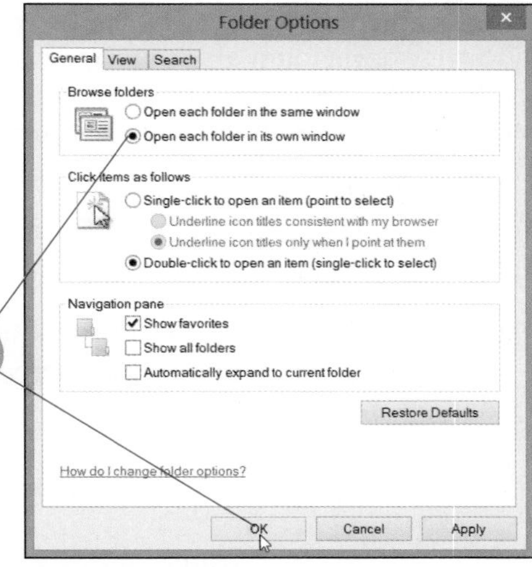

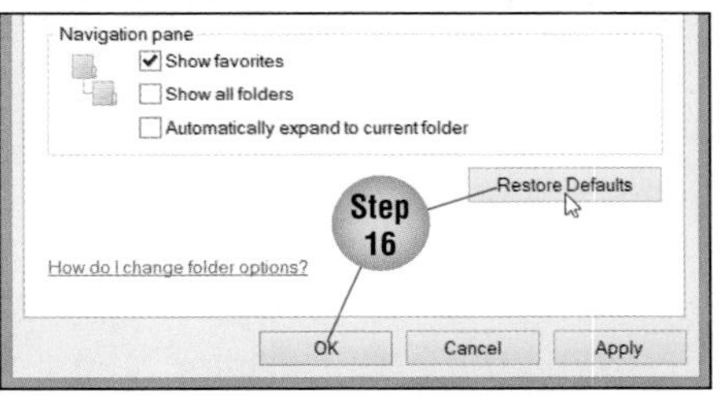

In Brief

Change Current View
Click desired view in Layout group on View tab.

Change Folder and View Options
1. Click View tab.
2. Click Options button.
3. Click desired option(s).
4. Click OK.

In Addition

Windows Libraries

While browsing the Computer window you may have noticed a section in the Navigation pane with the title *Libraries*. Libraries are tools you can use to keep track of and/or organize files that have something in common, regardless of where they are stored. A library does not store the actual files but instead keeps track of locations where the source files are stored. When you click the library name in the Navigation pane, the library displays all of the files in the locations that it is keeping track of associated with that library. For example, in the Pictures library, you could have Windows show you the contents of a Pictures folder on the local disk, from another folder on an external hard disk, and from a folder on a networked computer. Four default libraries are created when Windows 8 is installed: Documents, Music, Pictures, and Videos. You can create your own library and customize the locations associated with the default libraries. You will explore Libraries further in an assessment at the end of this section.

Changing the Default View for All Folders

You can set a view to display by default for all folders of a similar type (such as all disk drive folders or all documents folders). To do this, change the current view to the desired view for the type of folder that you want to set, such as a disk drive folder or a documents folder. Next, click the Options button on the View tab and then click the View tab at the Folder Options dialog box. Click the Apply to Folders button in the *Folder views* section and then click OK. Click Yes at the Folder Views message asking if you want all folders of this type to match this folder's view settings.

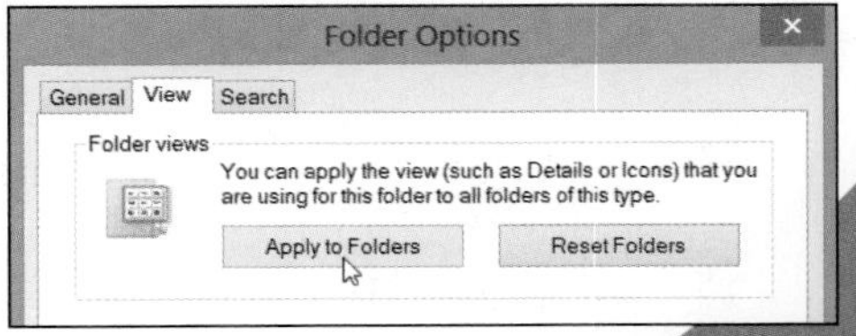

Activity 2.3

Creating a Folder; Renaming a Folder or File

As you begin working with programs, you will create files in which data (information) is saved. A file might be a Word document, an Excel workbook, or a PowerPoint presentation. Files can also be pictures or videos that you transfer from your digital camera to your computer. As you begin creating files, developing a system by which to organize those files becomes important so that you can easily retrieve a document or photograph when you need it. The first step in organizing your files is to create folders. Creating a folder is like creating a separate container in which you can place similar types of files. File management tasks such as creating a folder, renaming a folder or file, and copying and moving files and folders can be completed at a variety of locations, including the Computer and Documents windows.

Project

You need to organize files for your department at Worldwide Enterprises, so you decide to start by creating a folder.

SNAP

Tutorial 2.3
Creating a Folder and Renaming a Folder or File

1. At the Windows desktop, position the mouse in the lower left corner of the screen to display the Start screen thumbnail, right-click the thumbnail, and then click *File Explorer* in the pop-up list.

2. Double-click the icon representing the storage medium onto which you copied the WindowsS2 folder.

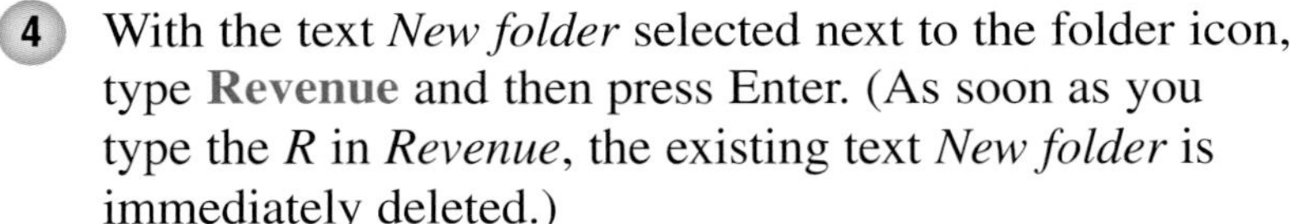

3. Click the New folder button on the Quick Access toolbar.

   A new folder icon is added to the Content pane with the text *New folder* already selected.

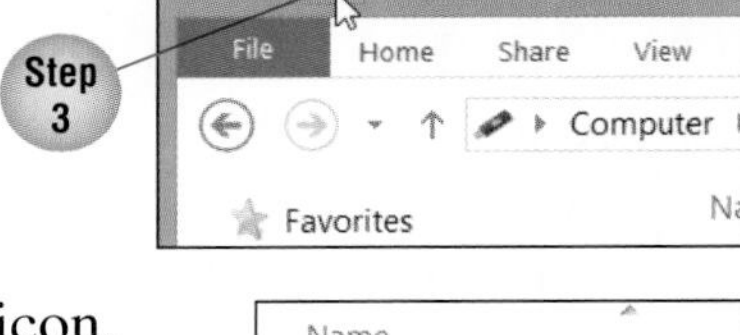

4. With the text *New folder* selected next to the folder icon, type **Revenue** and then press Enter. (As soon as you type the *R* in *Revenue*, the existing text *New folder* is immediately deleted.)

   This changes the folder name from *New folder* to *Revenue*.

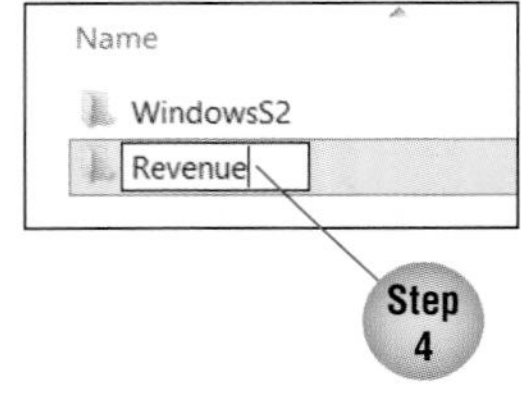

5. You can also create a new folder using a shortcut menu. To begin, right-click in a blank, unused area of the Content pane, point to *New*, and then click *Folder*.

6. With the text *New folder* already selected next to the folder icon, type **Contracts** and then press Enter.

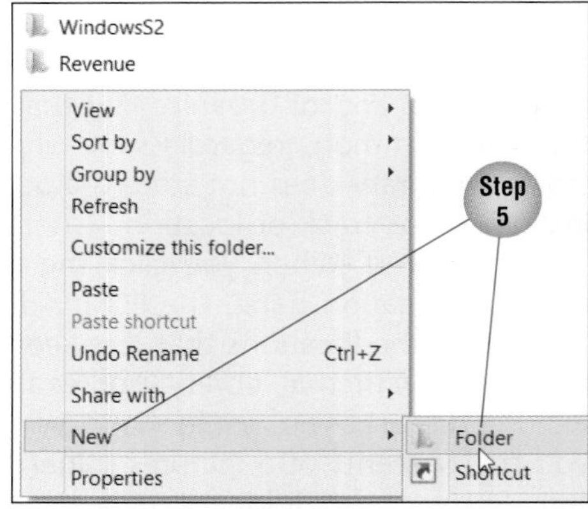

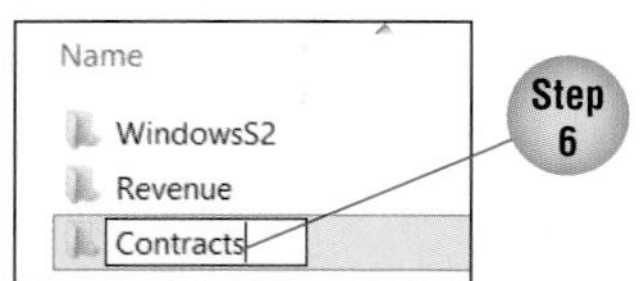

7. Click once on the *Revenue* folder to select the folder.

8. Click the Home tab and then click the Rename button in the Organize group.

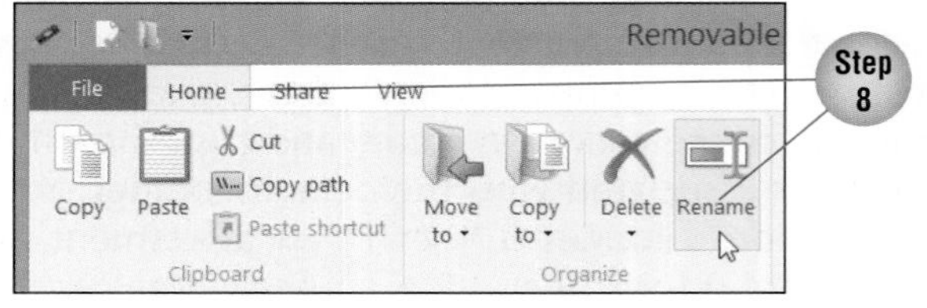

9 With the text *Revenue* selected, type **Income** and then press Enter.

You can also use the shortcut menu to rename a file or folder.

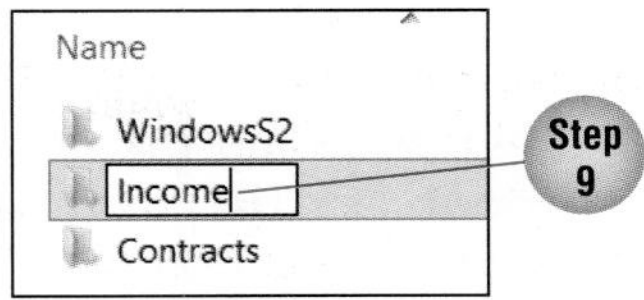

10 Right-click the *Contracts* folder and then click *Rename* at the shortcut menu.

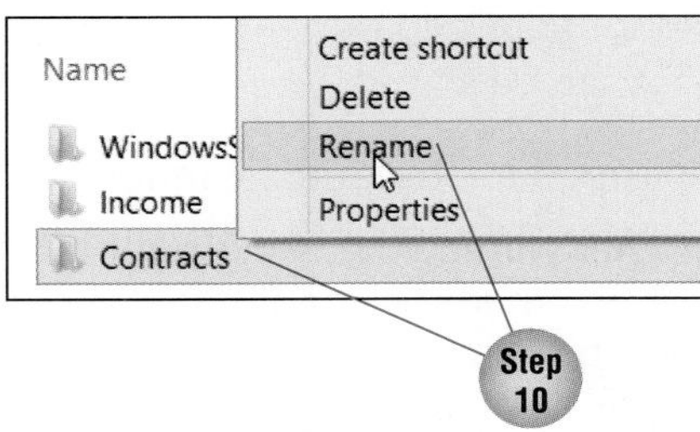

11 With the text *Contracts* selected, type **Administration** and then press Enter.

12 Double-click the *WindowsS2* folder.

13 Right-click the file ***FCTExcelSalesCom.xlsx*** and then click *Rename* at the shortcut menu.

14 Type **FCTSalesCommissions** and then press Enter.

Notice when you rename a file that Windows does not select the file extension. Programs such as Microsoft Word and Microsoft Excel automatically assign a file extension to each file (in this case, Word documents or Excel workbooks). These file extensions should remain intact. If you rename or remove a file extension by accident, Windows prompts you with a message that the file may no longer be usable and asks you if you are sure.

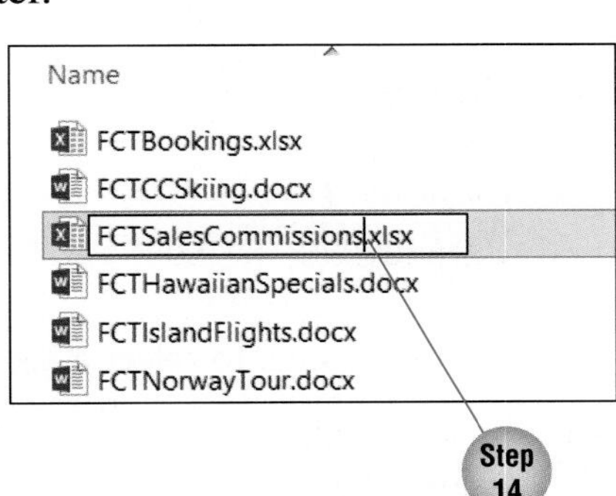

15 Close the Computer window.

In Brief

Create New Folder

1. Display Computer window.
2. Double-click device in which to create folder.
3. Click New folder button on Quick Access toolbar.
4. Type folder name and press Enter.

Rename Folder or File

1. Display Computer window.
2. Navigate to desired drive and/or folder.
3. Right-click folder or file to be renamed.
4. At shortcut menu, click *Rename*.
5. Type new folder or file name and press Enter.

In Addition

More about Organizing Files into Folders

Think of a ***folder*** on the computer the same way you think of a file folder in which you would store paper documents in your filing cabinet. Generally, you put similar types of documents into the same folder. For example, all of your rent receipts might be placed inside a file folder on which you have written the label *Rent* on the folder tab. Similarly, on the computer, you could create a folder named *Rent* and store all of the electronic copies of all of your rental documents within that folder. On the computer, a folder can have another folder stored inside it. The folder within the folder is referred to as a ***subfolder***. For example, you may have thousands of pictures stored on your computer. Saving all of the pictures in one folder named *Pictures* would be too cumbersome when the content list contains thousands of images. You would be scrolling a long time to locate a particular picture. Instead, consider creating subfolders in the Pictures folder so that related pictures are grouped together in one place.

Activity 2.4

Selecting and Copying Folders and Files

In addition to creating and renaming files and folders, file management activities include selecting, moving, copying, and deleting files or folders. Open a Computer or Documents window to perform file management tasks. Use options on the Home tab or at a shortcut menu. More than one file or folder can be moved, copied, or deleted at one time. Select adjacent files and folders using the Shift key, and select nonadjacent files and folders using the Ctrl key. When selecting multiple files or folders, you may want to change the view to *List* in the Computer window.

Project

As you continue to organize files for your department, you will copy files to the Income folder you created in Activity 2.3.

Tutorial 2.4
Selecting, Copying, and Moving Folders and Files

1. At the Windows desktop, open a Computer window.

   You can open a Computer window by either right-clicking the Start screen thumbnail and then clicking *File Explorer* or by clicking the File Explorer button on the Taskbar and then clicking *Computer* in the Navigation pane.

2. Double-click the icon representing the storage medium onto which you copied the WindowsS2 folder.

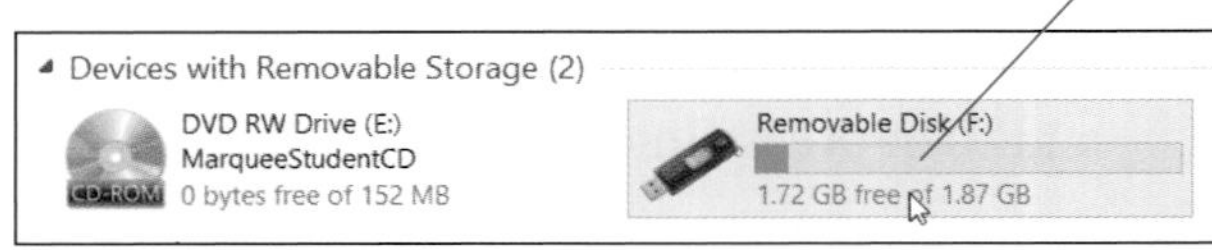

3. Double-click the *WindowsS2* folder in the Content pane.
4. Click the View tab and then click the *List* option in the Layout group.
5. Click the file named ***WEExcelRevenues.xlsx*** in the Content pane.

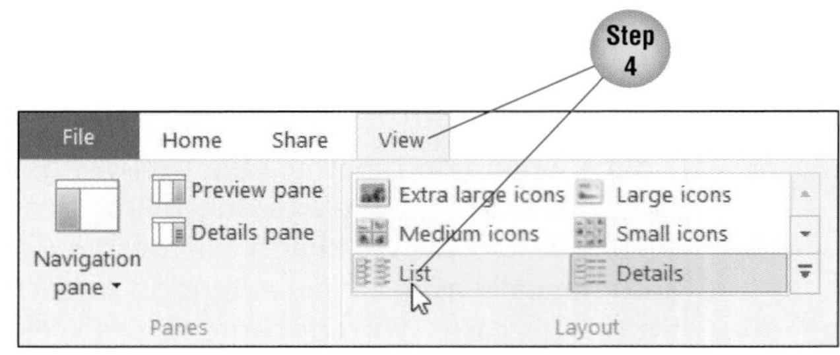

   Click once to select a file. Windows displays file properties for the selected file in the bottom left corner of the WindowsS2 window.

6. Hold down the Shift key, click the file named ***WETable02.docx***, and then release the Shift key.

   Clicking ***WETable02.docx*** while holding down the Shift key causes all files from ***WEExcelRevenues.xlsx*** through ***WETable02.docx*** to be selected.

7. Position the mouse pointer within the selected group of files, right-click, and then click *Copy* at the shortcut menu.

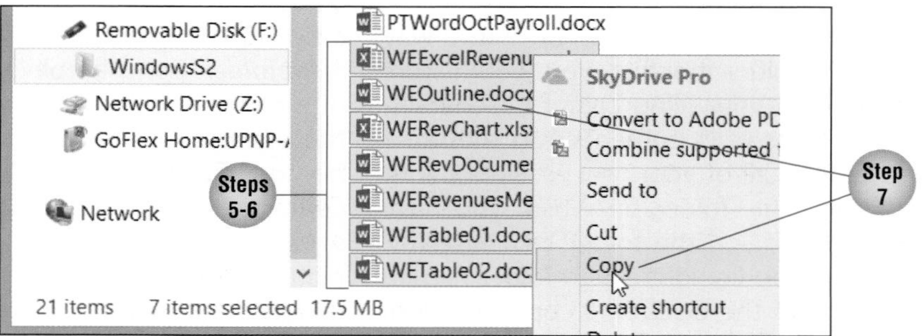

8 Click the Back button located left of the Address bar.

9 Double-click the *Income* folder.

10 Right-click in the Content pane and then click *Paste* at the shortcut menu.

When a large file or large group of files is copied, Windows displays a message box with a progress bar to indicate the approximate time required to copy the files, as shown in Figure 2.2. The message box closes when the copying process is complete.

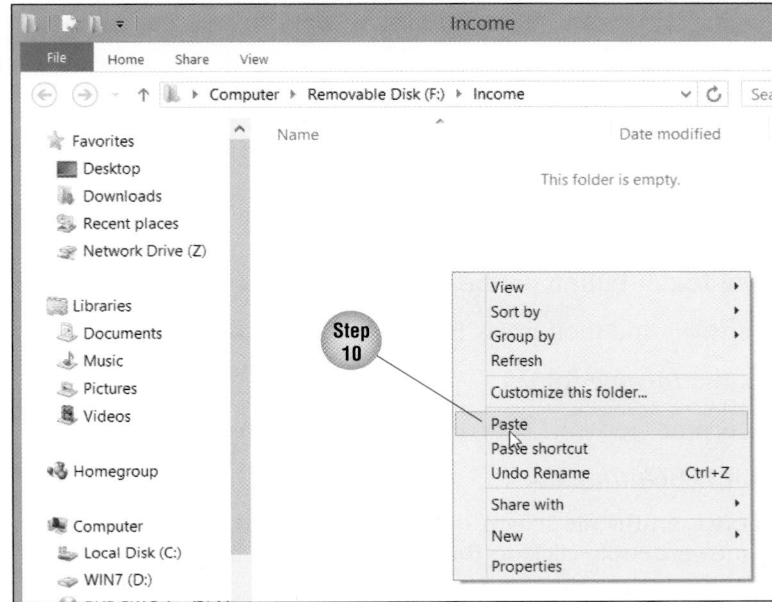

11 Click in a blank area of the Content pane to deselect the file names.

12 Close the Computer window.

FIGURE 2.2 Time to Complete Message Box

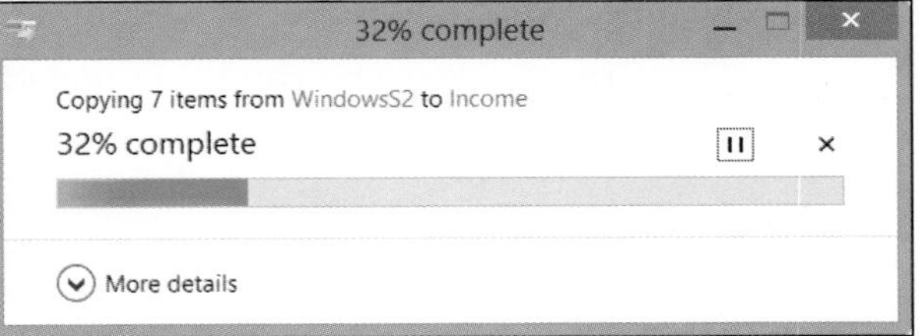

In Brief

Copy Adjacent Files to New Folder

1. Display Computer window.
2. Navigate to desired drive and/or folder.
3. If necessary, change current view to *List*.
4. Click first file name.
5. Hold down Shift key and then click last file name.
6. Right-click in selected group of files and click *Copy*.
7. Navigate to desired destination drive and/or folder.
8. Right-click in blank area of Content pane and click *Paste*.

In Addition

Copying by Dragging

You can also copy a file or folder to another location using a drag-and-drop technique. To do this, open a Computer or Documents window and display the desired file or folder in the Content pane. Position the mouse pointer on the file or folder to be copied, hold down the left mouse button, drag to the destination drive or folder name in the *Favorites, Libraries,* or *Computer* list in the Navigation pane, and then release the mouse button. By default, if you drag a file from one disk drive to another, Windows copies the file. However, to copy a file from one folder to another on the same disk drive, you must hold down the Ctrl key as you drag. To make dragging and dropping easier, you can open two windows and arrange them side-by-side on the desktop. In one window, display the files you want to copy. In the other window, display the destination folder. Select the files to be copied and then hold down the Ctrl key while dragging them to the destination window.

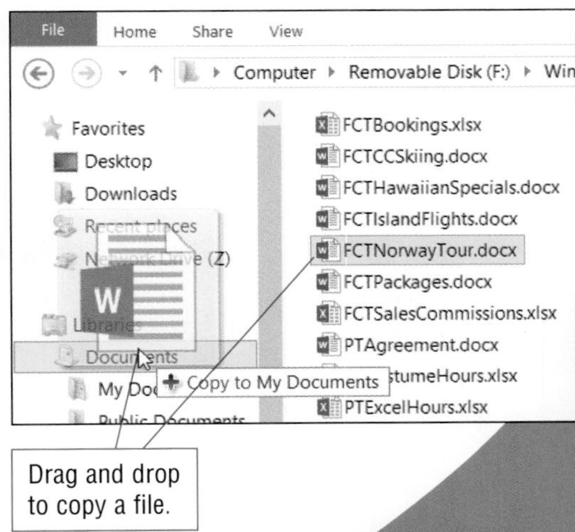

Drag and drop to copy a file.

Activity 2.5

Moving Folders and Files

Move files in a Computer or Documents window in a manner similar to copying files. Select the file(s) or folder(s) you want to move, position the mouse pointer over the selected file(s) or folder(s), right-click, and then click *Cut* at the shortcut menu. Navigate to the desired destination location, right-click a blank area in the Content pane, and then click *Paste* at the shortcut menu. You can also use the Copy, Cut, and Paste buttons in the Clipboard group on the Home tab.

Project

After further review of the files you copied into the Income folder, you decide to create another folder and move some of the files from the Income folder into the new folder.

Review Tutorial 2.4
Selecting, Copying, and Moving Folders and Files

1. At the Windows desktop, display a Computer window.
2. Double-click the icon representing the storage medium onto which you copied the WindowsS2 folder.

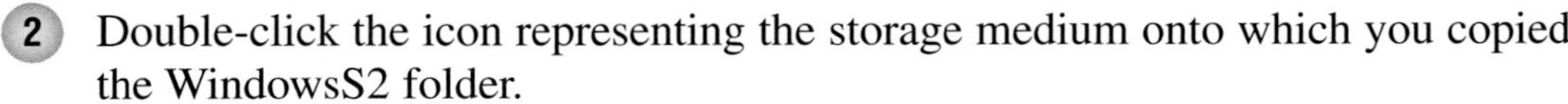

3. Click the New folder button on the Quick Access toolbar.
4. Type **Distribution** and then press Enter.
5. Double-click the *Income* folder.
6. Change the current view to *List.*
7. Click once on ***WEOutline.docx***.

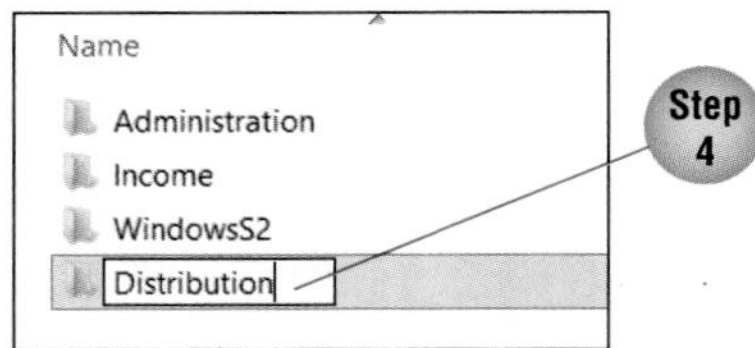

Clicking once on the file selects the file name, thereby identifying the item you want to move; double-clicking the file would instruct Windows to open Word and then open the document.

8. Hold down the Ctrl key, click once on ***WETable01.docx***, click once on ***WETable02.docx***, and then release the Ctrl key.

Using the Ctrl key, you can select nonadjacent files.

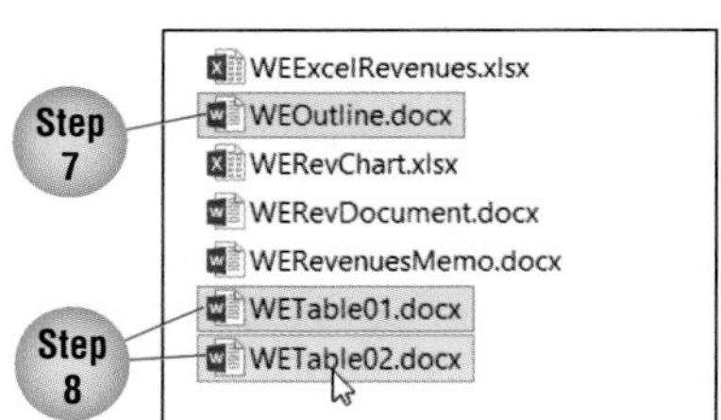

9. Click the Home tab and then click the Cut button in the Clipboard group.

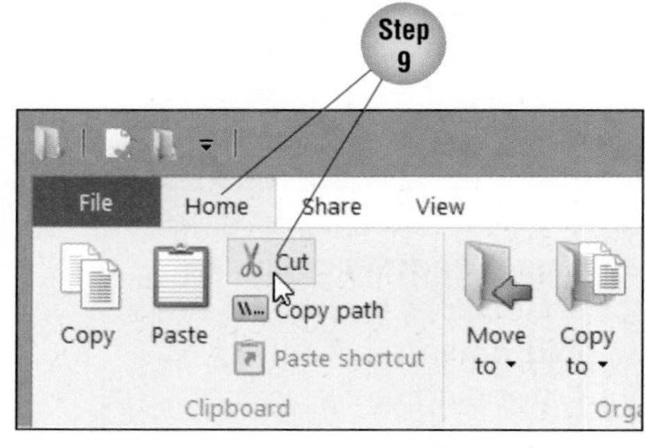

10 Click the Back button at the left of the Address bar.

11 Double-click the *Distribution* folder.

12 Click the Home tab and then click the Paste button in the Clipboard group.

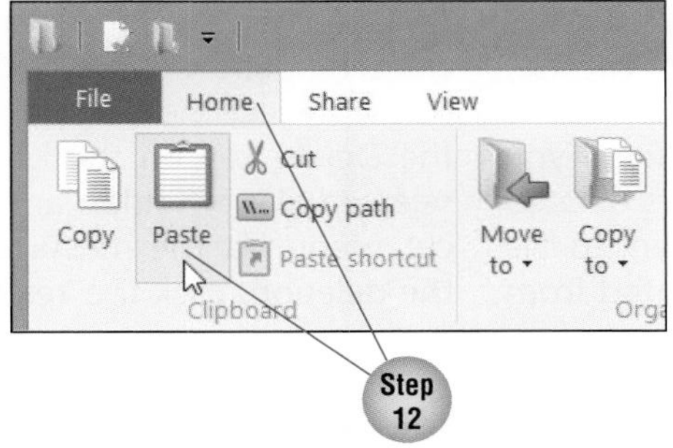

13 Click in a blank area of the Content pane to deselect the file names.

14 Click the Back button at the left of the Address bar.

15 Double-click the *Income* folder.

16 Notice the three files ***WEOutline.docx***, ***WETable01.docx***, and ***WETable02.docx*** no longer reside in the Income folder.

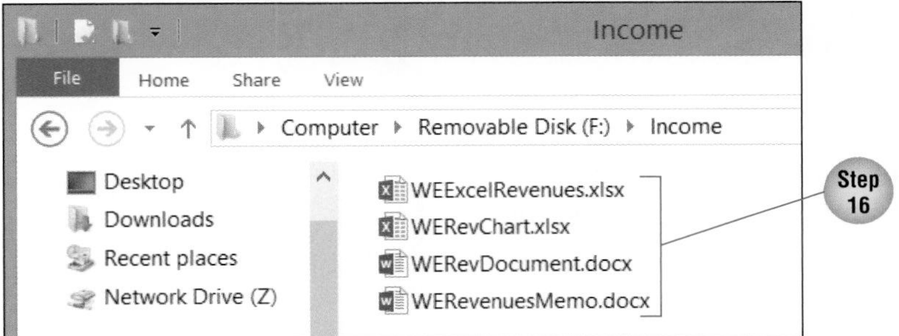

17 Close the Computer window.

In Brief

Move Nonadjacent Files to New Folder

1. Display Computer window.
2. Navigate to desired drive and/or folder.
3. If necessary, change current view to *List*.
4. Click first file name.
5. Hold down Ctrl key, click each additional file name, and then release Ctrl key.
6. Click Cut button in Clipboard group on Home tab.
7. Navigate to desired destination drive and/or folder.
8. Click Paste button in Clipboard group on Home tab.

In Addition

Displaying Disk or Drive Properties

Information such as the amount of used space and free space on a disk or drive and the disk or drive hardware is available at the Properties dialog box. To display the Local Disk (C:) Properties dialog box, similar to the one shown at the right, open a Computer window. At the Computer window, right-click *Local Disk (C:)* and then click *Properties* at the shortcut menu. With the General tab selected, information displays about used and free space on the drive. Click the Tools tab to display error-checking, backup, and defragmentation options. The Hardware tab displays the name and type of all disk drives as well as the device properties. The Sharing tab displays options for sharing folders, and change user permissions at the Security tab. To enable quota management wherein you can assign space limits for each user, click the Quota tab.

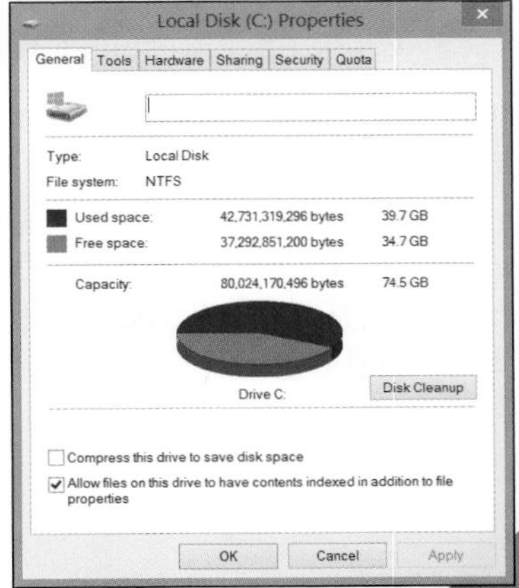

Activity 2.6

Deleting Folders and Files to the Recycle Bin

Deleting the wrong file can be a disaster, but Windows helps protect your work with the Recycle Bin. The Recycle Bin acts just like an office waste-paper basket: you can "throw away" (delete) unwanted files, but you also can "reach in" to the Recycle Bin and take out (restore) a file if you threw it away by accident. Files or folders deleted from a hard disk drive are automatically sent to the Recycle Bin. However, files or folders deleted from a removable disk such as your USB flash drive are deleted permanently.

To delete a file or folder, display a Computer or Documents window and then display in the Content pane the file(s) or folder(s) you want to delete. Select the file(s) or folder(s) and then press the Delete key on the keyboard or right-click the selected files or folders and click *Delete* at the shortcut menu. At the message asking you to confirm the deletion, click the Yes button.

Project

As you continue to organize your files, you will copy a file and a folder from your storage medium to the My Documents folder on the hard drive and then delete a file and folder, moving them to the Recycle Bin.

Tutorial 2.6
Using the Recycle Bin

1. At the Windows desktop, display a Computer window.
2. Double-click the icon representing the storage medium onto which you copied the WindowsS2 folder.
3. Click once to select the *Distribution* folder.
4. Position the mouse pointer over the selected folder name, hold down the left mouse button, drag to *Documents* in the *Libraries* section of the Navigation pane, and then release the mouse button.

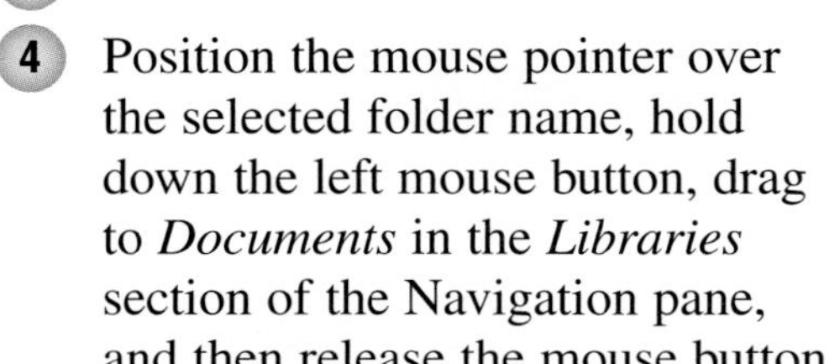

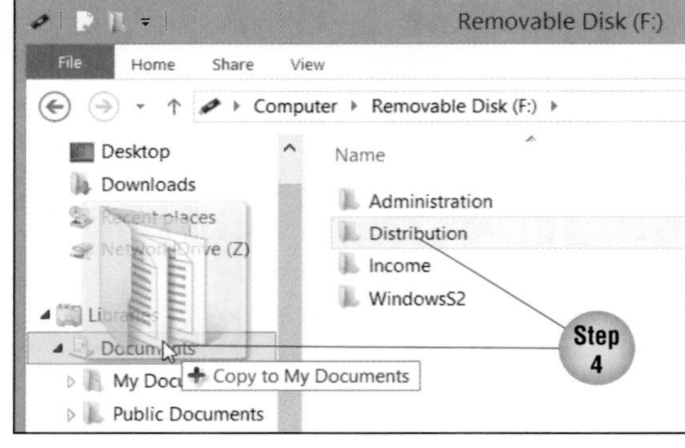

As you point to the Documents library in the Navigation pane, Windows displays the ScreenTip *Copy to My Documents*. If you drag a file or folder from a removable storage device to a location on the computer's hard drive, the file or folder is copied. However, if you drag a file or folder from a location on the hard drive to another location on the hard drive, the file or folder is moved rather than copied.

5. Double-click the *Income* folder.
6. Click once to select ***WERevDocument.docx***.
7. Position the mouse pointer over the selected file name, hold down the left mouse button, drag to *Documents* in the *Libraries* section of the Navigation pane, and then release the mouse button.

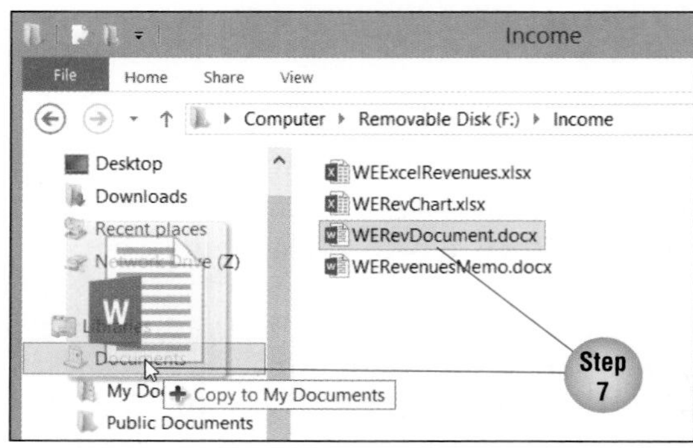

8 Click *Documents* in the *Libraries* section of the Navigation pane to display the files and folders associated with the Documents library in the Content pane.

The Documents library displays the contents of two folders by default: *My Documents* and *Public Documents*. My Documents is the default folder in which files and folders associated with the Documents library are stored. You can add and remove folders associated with a library. You will learn more about libraries in an assessment at the end of this section.

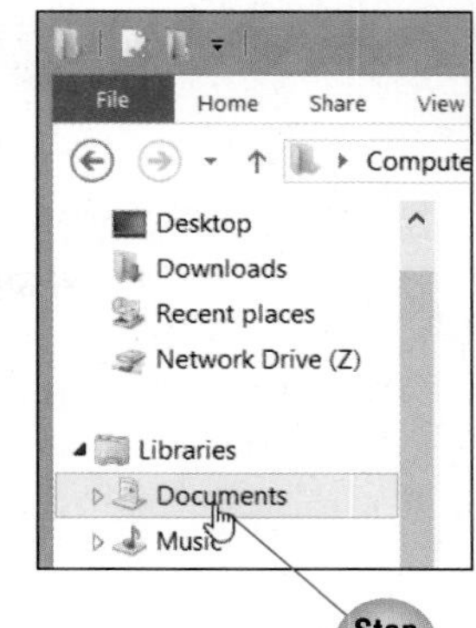

In Brief

Delete File/Folder

1. Display Computer window and navigate to desired drive and/or folder.
2. Click file/folder to select it.
3. Press Delete key.

9 Click once to select the *Distribution* folder.

Step 9

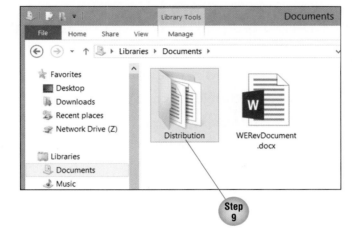

10 Press the Delete key on the keyboard.

11 Right-click ***WERevDocument.docx*** in the Content pane and then click *Delete* at the shortcut menu.

12 Close the Documents library window.

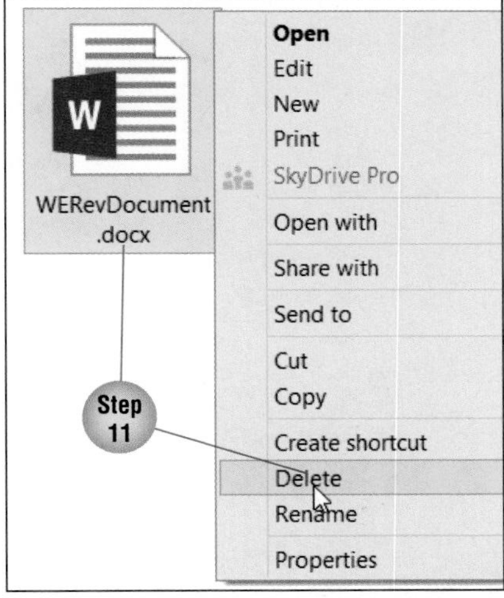

In Addition

Dragging and Dropping Files and Folders

Another method for deleting a file or folder is to drag the file or folder to the Recycle Bin icon on the desktop. This moves the file into the Recycle Bin. You can also select multiple files or folders and then drag and drop the selected items into the Recycle Bin.

Activity 2.7

Restoring Folders and Files; Emptying Files from the Recycle Bin

A file or folder deleted to the Recycle Bin can be restored. Restore a file or folder with options at the Recycle Bin window. Display this window by double-clicking the Recycle Bin icon on the Windows desktop. Once you restore a file or folder, it is removed from the Recycle Bin and returned to its original location. Just like a wastepaper basket can overflow, the Recycle Bin can contain too many files and folders. Emptying the Recycle Bin permanently deletes all files and folders. You can also delete a single file or folder from the Recycle Bin (rather than all files and folders).

Project

You decide to experiment with the Recycle Bin by learning how to restore a file and how to empty the Recycle Bin.

Review Tutorial 2.4 Selecting, Copying, and Moving Folders and Files

1. At the Windows desktop, display the contents of the Recycle Bin by double-clicking the Recycle Bin icon.

   The Recycle Bin window displays, similar to the one shown in Figure 2.3.

2. At the Recycle Bin window, change the current view to *List.*
3. Click once to select ***WERevDocument.docx***.

   Depending on the contents of the Recycle Bin, you may need to scroll down the list to display this document.

FIGURE 2.3 Recycle Bin Window

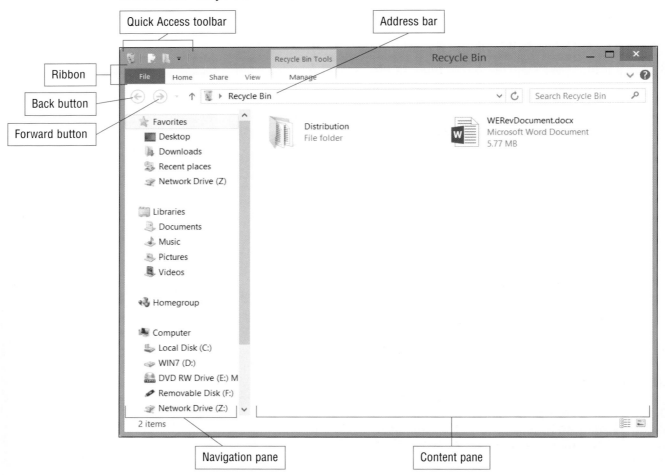

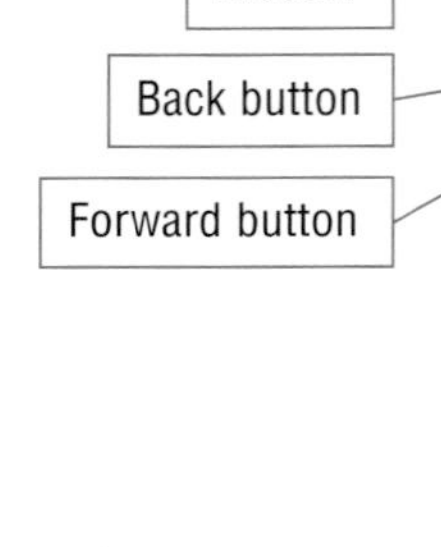

4. Click the Recycle Bin Tools Manage tab and then click the Restore the selected items button in the Restore group.

   The file is removed from the Recycle Bin and returned to the location from which it was deleted. Once a file or folder is moved into the Recycle Bin, you are limited to the following options: Restore, Cut, or Delete.

5. Click once to select the *Distribution* folder.
6. Click the Restore the selected items button in the Restore group.
7. Close the Recycle Bin window.
8. At the Windows desktop, open a Computer window.
9. Click *Documents* in the *Libraries* section of the Navigation pane.

   Notice that the file and folder have been restored from the Recycle Bin.

10. Delete the file and folder you restored. To do this, click once on the *Distribution* folder, hold down the Ctrl key, click once on the ***WERevDocument.docx*** file name, and then release the Ctrl key.
11. Press the Delete key.
12. Close the Documents window.
13. At the Windows desktop, double-click the Recycle Bin icon.
14. Click once on the *Distribution* folder, hold down the Ctrl key, click once on the ***WERevDocument.docx*** file name, and then release the Ctrl key.
15. Click the Home tab and then click the Delete button in the Organize group.

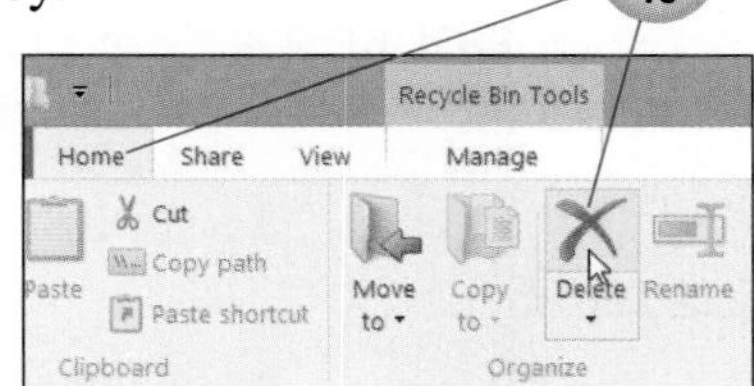

16. At the Delete Multiple Items message box asking if you are sure you want to permanently delete the two items, click Yes.

    To empty the entire contents of the Recycle Bin, click the Empty Recycle Bin button in the Manage group on the Recycle Bin Tools Manage tab.

17. Close the Recycle Bin window.

In Brief

Restore File/Folder from Recycle Bin

1. At Windows desktop, double-click Recycle Bin icon.
2. At Recycle Bin window, click file/folder to select it (or select multiple files/folders).
3. Click Restore the selected items button on Recycle Bin Tools Manage tab.

Delete File/Folder from Recycle Bin

1. At Windows desktop, double-click Recycle Bin icon.
2. At Recycle Bin window, click file/folder to select it (or select multiple files/folders).
3. Press Delete key.
4. At confirmation message, click Yes.

In Addition

Showing or Hiding the Recycle Bin on the Desktop

The Recycle Bin icon is displayed on the desktop by default. To remove it, right-click a blank area of the desktop and then click *Personalize* at the shortcut menu. At the Personalization window, click Change desktop icons in the left pane. At the Desktop Icon Settings dialog box, shown at the right, click the *Recycle Bin* check box to remove the check mark and then click OK. Note the other desktop icons you can choose to show or hide at this dialog box.

Activity 2.8

Exploring the Control Panel

The Control Panel offers a variety of categories, each containing icons you can use to customize the functionality of your computer. Display the Control Panel window by right-clicking the Start screen thumbnail and then clicking *Control Panel* at the pop-up list. At the Control Panel window, available categories display in the Content pane. (By default, the Control Panel window opens in Category view. If your window opens in Large icons view or Small icons view, click the down-pointing arrow next to *View by*, located near the top right of the Control Panel window, and then click *Category* at the drop-down list.) Click a category or hyperlinked option below a category and a list of tasks, a list of icons, or a separate window displays.

Project

You want to know how to customize your computer, so you decide to explore the Control Panel window.

Tutorial 2.8
Exploring the Control Panel

1. At the Windows desktop, right-click the Start screen thumbnail and then click *Control Panel* at the pop-up list.

   The Control Panel window displays, similar to the one shown in Figure 2.4.

2. At the Control Panel window, click the Appearance and Personalization hyperlink.

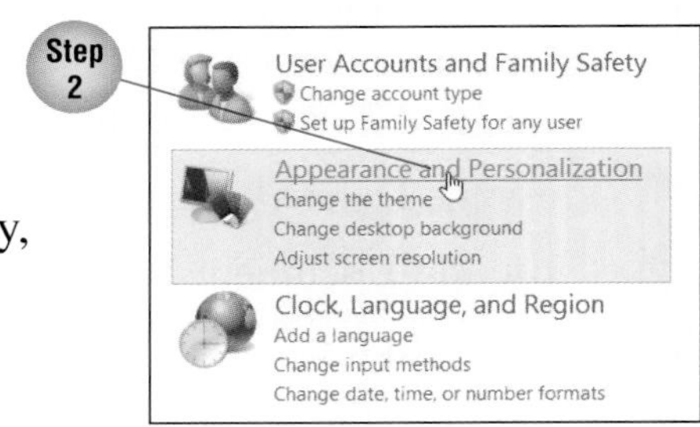

3. After viewing the tasks and icons available in the Appearance and Personalization category, click the Back button.
4. Click the Hardware and Sound hyperlink.

FIGURE 2.4 Control Panel Window

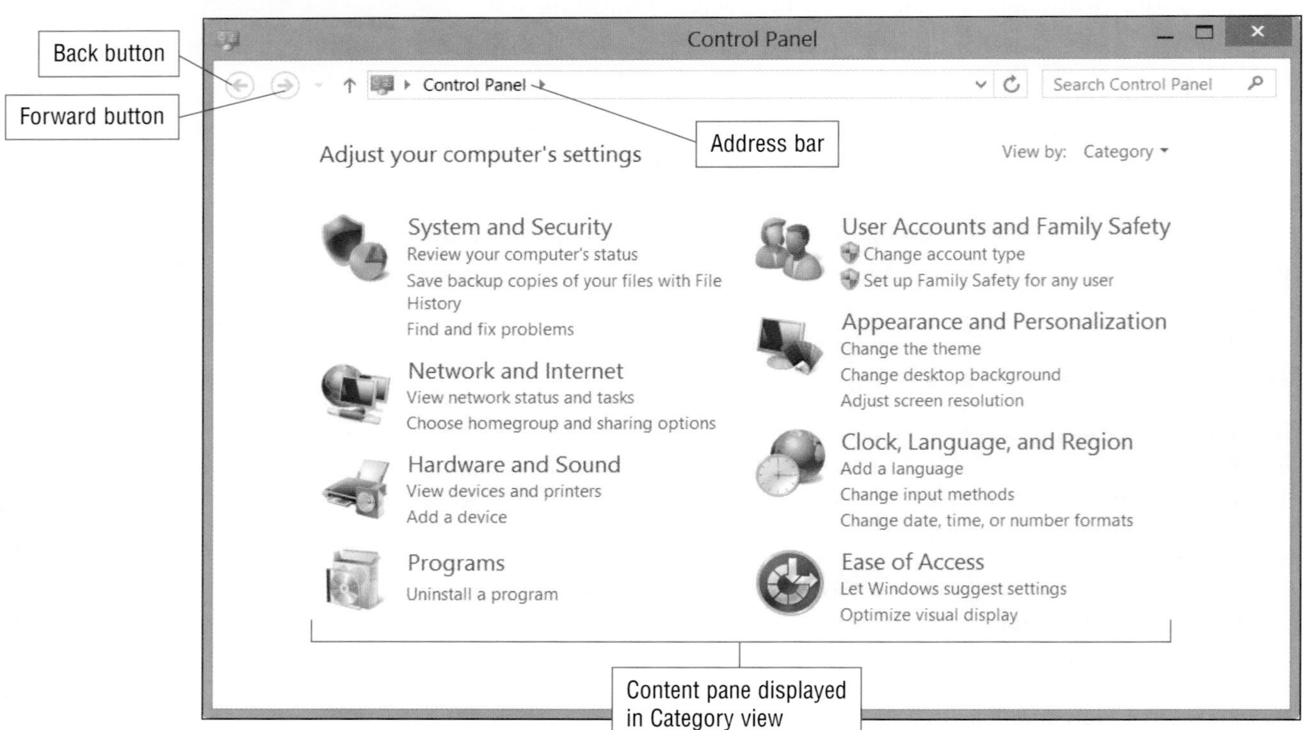

5 Click the Mouse hyperlink in the Devices and Printers category.

This displays the Mouse Properties dialog box.

In Brief

Display Control Panel Window

1. Right-click Start screen thumbnail.
2. Click *Control Panel*.

6 At the Mouse Properties dialog box, click each tab and review the available options.

7 Click the Cancel button to close the Mouse Properties dialog box.

8 Click the Back button.

9 Click the Programs hyperlink in the Content pane.

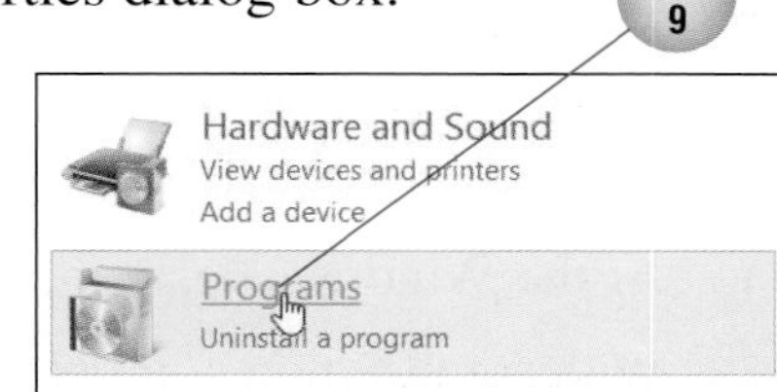

10 At the Programs window, click the Programs and Features hyperlink.

This is where you would uninstall a program on your computer.

11 Click the Back button twice.

12 Click the System and Security hyperlink.

13 Click the System hyperlink.

14 Maximize the window.

15 Close the System window.

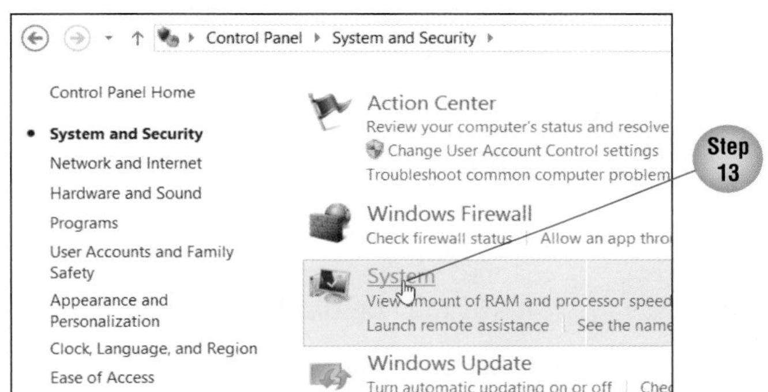

In Addition

Changing the Control Panel View

By default, the Control Panel window displays categories of tasks in what is called Category view. This view can be changed to *Large icons* or *Small icons*. In the Large icons view, shown at the right, options in the Control Panel window are shown alphabetically by icon name. To change from Category view to Large icons or Small icons, click the down-pointing arrow next to *View by* located near the top right of the Control Panel window and then click the desired option at the drop-down list.

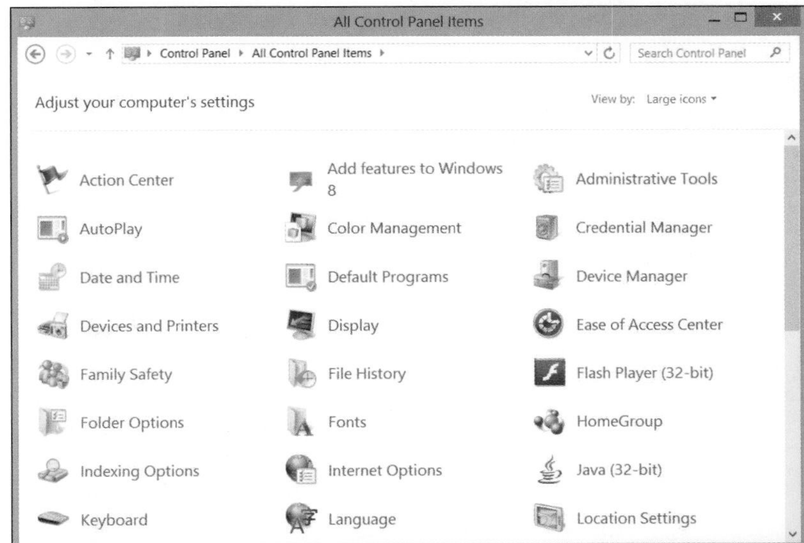

Activity 2.9

Using Windows Search Tools

Windows includes a Search feature you can access through the Charm bar. You can quickly find an application, setting, or file by typing the first few letters of the application, setting, or file name. You can choose whether to search for an application, setting or file by selecting one of the three tiles located below the search text box—Apps, Settings, or Files. If your computer has many applications and files stored on the hard disk, using the search tool allows you to locate what you need in a few seconds and with minimal mouse clicks. At the right of the Address bar in a Computer or Documents window is a search text box. Type in this text box the first few letters of a file you need to locate. The Content pane is filtered instantly to display items that match your criterion.

Windows performs fast searching because the operating system maintains an index in the background in which all of the key words associated with the applications, settings, and files on your computer are referenced. This index is constantly updated as you work. When you type an entry in a search text box, Windows consults the index rather than conducting a search of the entire hard drive.

Project

You want to experiment with the search capabilities of Windows to see how you can quickly locate applications and files.

Worldwide Enterprises

SNAP

Tutorial 2.9
Using Windows Search Tools

1. At the Windows desktop, display the Charm bar and then click the Search button.
2. With the insertion point positioned in the search text box located at the top of the Search panel, make sure the Apps tile is selected below the search text box, and then type **calc** in the search text box.

   As soon as you begin typing an entry in the search text box, Windows begins to display relevant results. Notice that the Calculator program is shown below the heading *Apps* at the top of the list. Depending on the contents stored in the computer you are using, additional items may be displayed below *Calculator*.

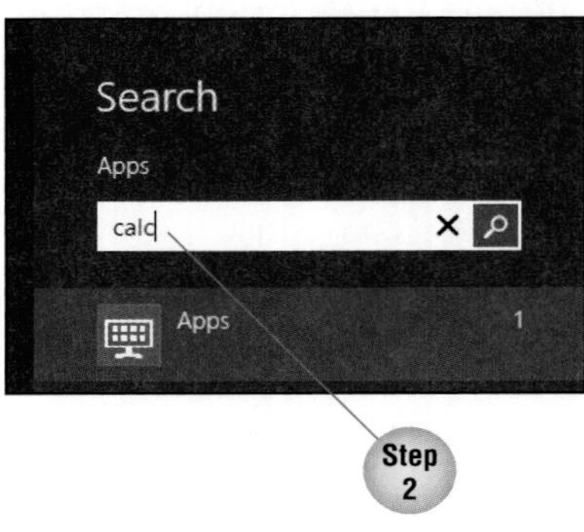

3. Click the Calculator tile in the *Apps* list at the upper left side of the Start screen.

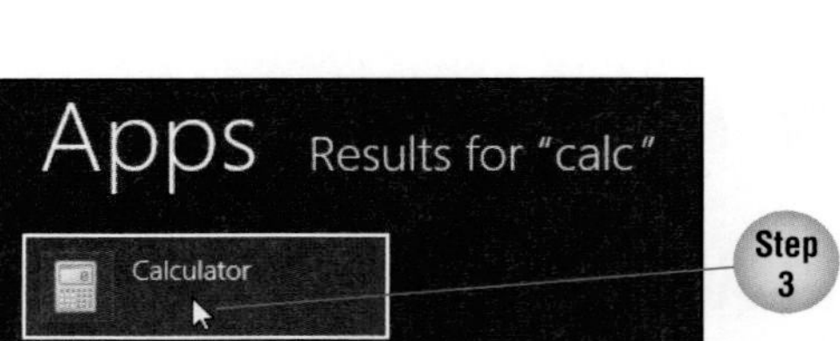

4. Close the Calculator window.
5. Display the Charm bar and then click the Search button.
6. Make sure the Apps tile is selected below the search text box and then type **note** in the search text box.

   Windows lists all app elements stored on the computer you are using that are associated with the text *note*, including the Notepad application, which you can use to create, edit, and save simple, text-based documents.

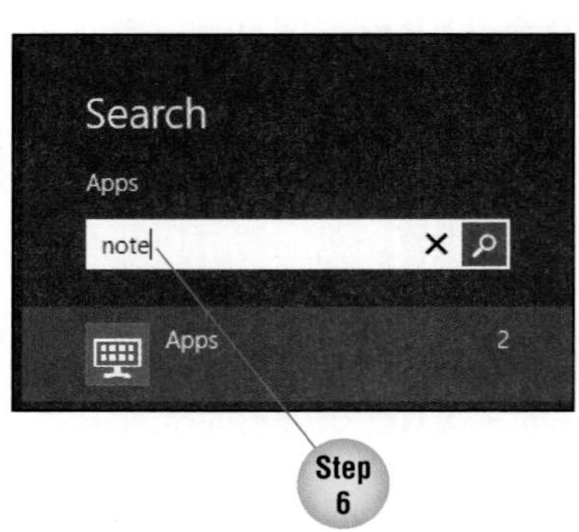

7. Press the Esc key.

   Pressing the Esc key clears the search results list and the search text box.

8. Display the desktop and then open a Computer window.
9. Double-click the icon representing the storage medium onto which you copied the WindowsS2 folder.

10 Double-click the *WindowsS2* folder and then change the view to Large Icons.

11 Click in the Search WindowsS2 text box located at the right of the Address bar.

12 Type **werev**.

As soon as you begin typing in the search WindowsS2 text box, Windows filters the list of files in the Content pane to those that begin with the letters you type. Notice that the Address bar displays *Search Results in WindowsS2* to indicate that the files displayed that match your criteria were limited to the current folder. If you want to search other locations or by other file properties, click one of the option buttons located on the Search Tools Search tab.

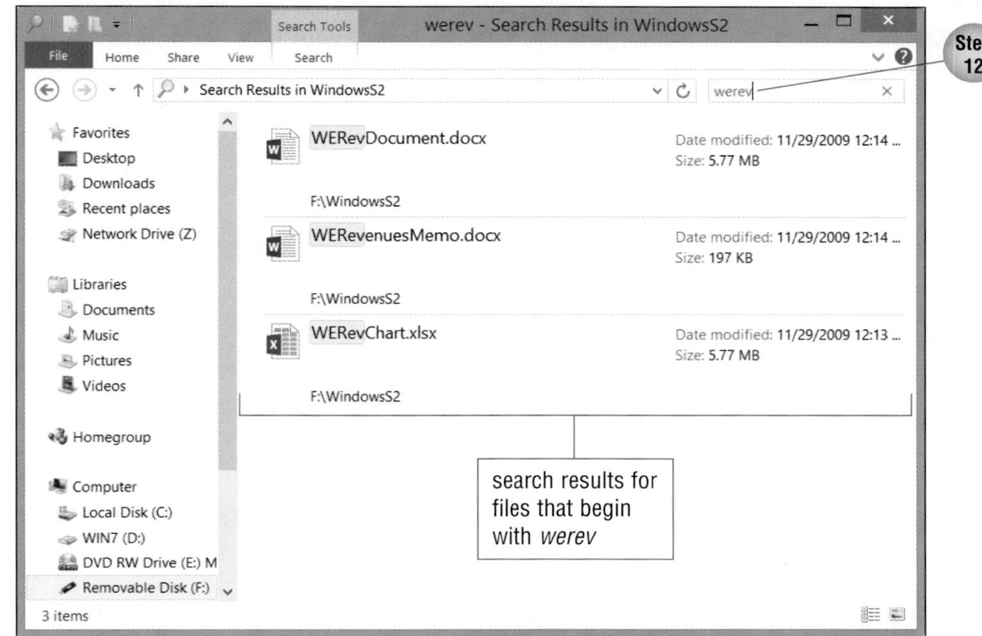

13 With the insertion point still positioned in the search text box, press the Backspace key to remove *werev* and then type **pte**.

The list of files in the Content pane is updated to display those files that begin with *pte*.

14 Double-click the file named ***PTExcelOctPayroll.xlsx***.

The file opens in Microsoft Excel.

15 Close Microsoft Excel by clicking the Close button at the right side of the Title bar.

16 Close the Computer window.

In Brief

Search for Applications or Files from Charm bar

1. Click Search button on Charm bar.
2. Click Apps, Settings, or Files tile.
3. Type search criteria in search text box.

Search for Document

1. Open Computer or Documents library window.
2. Type search criteria in search text box.

In Addition

Using a Wildcard Character in a Search

When conducting a search, you can type an asterisk (*) in place of any number of letters, numbers, or symbols within a file name to find files based on a pattern of characters. For example, typing ***hours*** would locate the files listed at the right in your WindowsS2 folder. Notice the pattern is that all files have *hours* in the middle of the file name but any number of other characters before and after *hours*.

PTWordHours.docx
PTExcelHours.xlsx
PTCostumeHours.xlsx

Activity 2.10

Customizing the Desktop

The Windows operating environment is customizable. You can change background patterns and colors; specify a screen saver that will display when the screen sits idle for a specific period of time; change the scheme for windows, title bars, and system fonts; and change screen resolution and text size. Make these types of changes at the Control Panel Personalization window. Many companies adopt a corporate standard for display properties on their computers.

Project

You decide to look at the customization options available for the desktop and set the screen resolution to the corporate standard for computers at Worldwide Enterprises.

Note: Before completing this activity, check with your instructor to determine if you can customize the desktop. If necessary, practice these steps on your home computer.

Tutorial 2.10
Customizing the Desktop

1. At the Windows desktop, position the arrow pointer in a blank area of the desktop, right-click the mouse, and then click *Personalize* at the shortcut menu.
2. At the Personalization window, click the Desktop Background hyperlink located along the bottom of the window.

   Make a note of the current background.

3. Make sure *Windows Desktop Backgrounds* displays in the Picture location option box. If necessary, scroll up or down the available images, click an image that you like, and click the Save changes button.

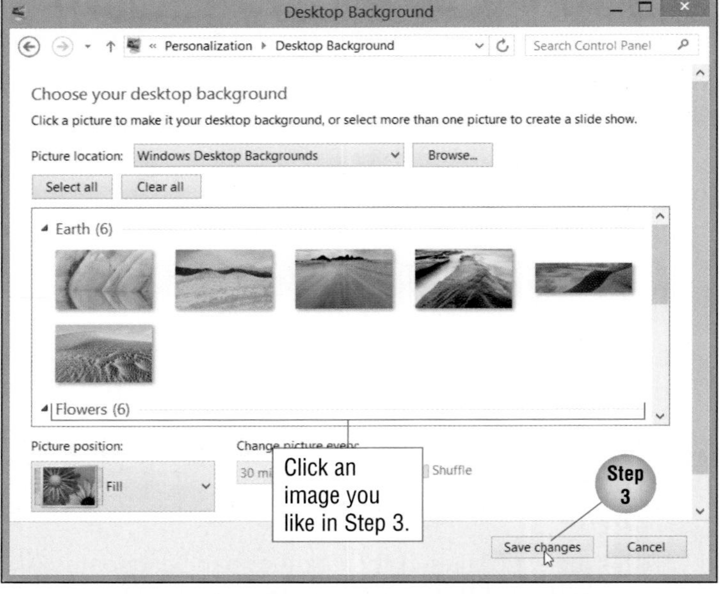

4. Click the Screen Saver hyperlink.

   Make a note of the current screen saver name.

5. At the Screen Saver Settings dialog box, click the option box arrow below *Screen saver* and then click *Ribbons* at the drop-down list.

   A preview of the screen saver displays in the screen located toward the top of the dialog box.

6. Click the up- or down-pointing arrow next to the *Wait* measurement box until *1* displays.
7. Click the OK button.

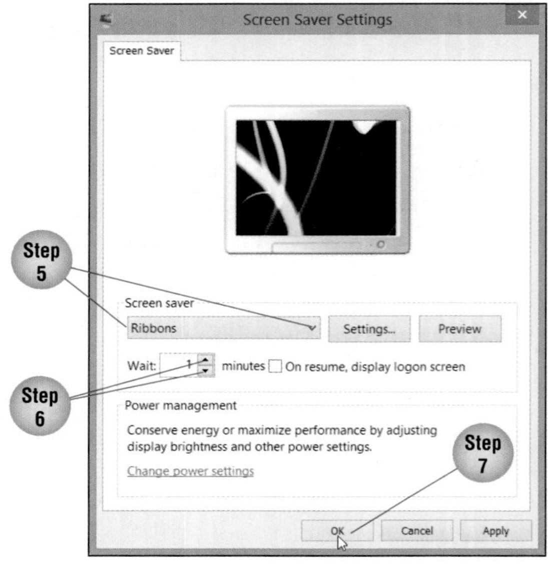

8. Click the Color hyperlink.

   Make a note of the color box that is currently selected.

9. Click the *Color 9* color box (second column in the bottom row) and then click the Save changes button. ***Note: Skip this step if your window does not display as shown below.***

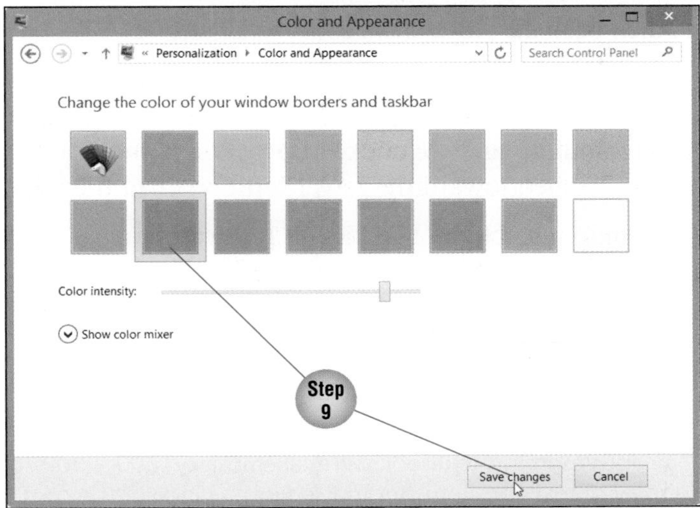

10. Close the Personalization window. Let the screen remain idle for one minute so that the screen saver displays.

11. Move the mouse to deactivate the screen saver and then double-click the Recycle Bin icon.

    Notice the Color 9 color scheme applied to the Taskbar and the window borders.

12. Close the Recycle Bin window.

13. Reinstate the original desktop settings by right-clicking a blank area of the desktop, clicking *Personalize* at the shortcut menu, and then returning the desktop background, screen saver, and window color to the original settings.

    In the next steps, you will set the screen resolution to *1600 × 900 pixels,* which is the corporate standard for all desktop computers at Worldwide Enterprises. Standardizing display properties is considered a best practice in large companies that support many computer users.

14. Right-click a blank area of the desktop and then click *Screen resolution* at the shortcut menu.

15. At the Screen Resolution window, look at the current setting displayed in the *Resolution* option box. For example, your screen may be currently set at *1920 × 1080.* If your screen is already set to *1600 × 900*, click OK to close the window and complete this activity.

    Screen resolution is set in pixels. ***Pixel*** is the abbreviation of *picture element* and refers to a single dot or point on the display monitor. Changing the screen resolution to a higher number of pixels means that more information can be seen on the screen as items are scaled to a smaller size.

continues

16 Click the *Resolution* option box and then drag the slider bar up or down as necessary until the screen resolution is set to *1600 × 900*. If necessary, check with your instructor for alternate instructions.

17 Click in the window outside the slider box, click OK, and then click the Keep changes button at the Display Settings message box asking if you want to keep the display settings.

18 At the Screen resolution window, click the Make text and other items larger or smaller hyperlink located toward the lower left corner of the window.

19 At the display window, click the Medium – 125% option.

20 Click the Apply button.

21 At the message indicating that you must sign out of your computer, click the Sign out now button.

22 Log back into your account.

The screen captures in this textbook were taken using 1600 × 900 screen resolution and the display of text and items set to Medium - 125%. If the computer you are using has a different screen resolution, what you will see on your screen may not match the textbook illustrations. For additional information, refer to the In Addition section below.

In Addition

Windows Screen Resolution and the Microsoft Office Ribbon

Before you begin learning the applications in the Microsoft Office 2013 suite, take a moment to check the display settings on the computer you are using. The ribbon in the Microsoft Office suite adjusts to the screen resolution setting of your computer monitor. A computer monitor set at a high resolution will have the ability to show more buttons in the ribbon than will a monitor set to a low resolution. The screen captures in this textbook were taken at a resolution of 1600 x 900 pixels. Below, the Word ribbon is shown three ways: at a lower screen resolution (1366 x 768 pixels), at the screen resolution featured throughout this textbook, and at a higher screen resolution (1920 x 1080 pixels). Note the variances in the ribbon in all three examples. If possible, set your display to 1600 x 900 pixels to match the illustrations you will see in this textbook.

Appearance of Microsoft Word ribbon with computer monitor set at:

1366 x 768 screen resolution

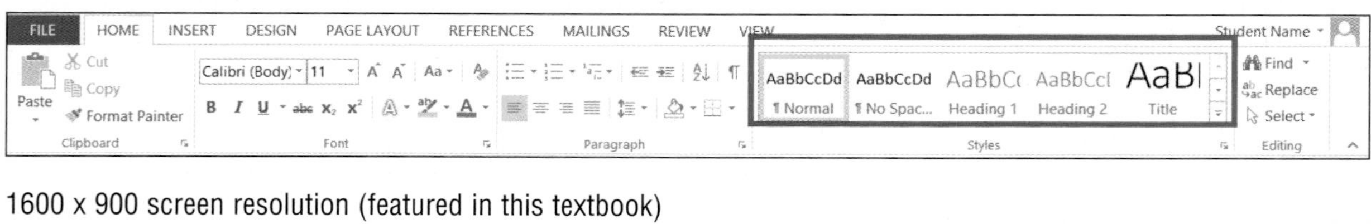

1600 x 900 screen resolution (featured in this textbook)

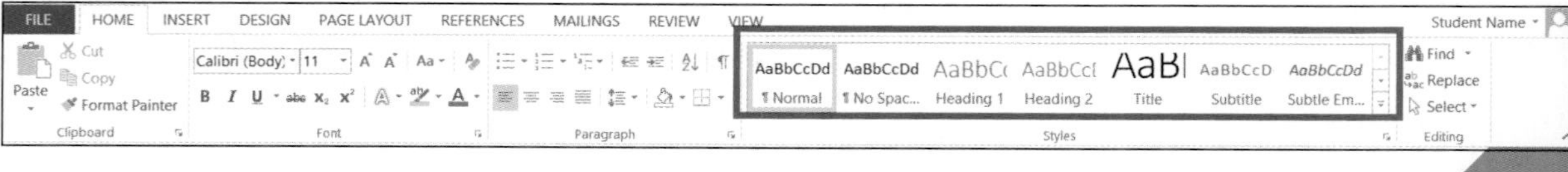

1920 x 1080 screen resolution

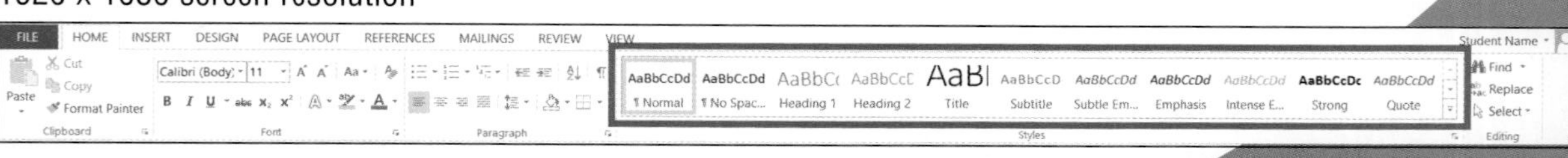

Features Summary

Feature	Button/Icon	Action
Computer window		Right-click Start screen thumbnail, click *File Explorer*.
Control Panel window		Right-click Start screen thumbnail, click *Control Panel*.
copy selected files/folders		At Computer or Documents library window, select files/folders to be copied, right-click in selected group, click *Copy*, navigate to destination folder, right-click in Content pane, click *Paste*.
create new folder		At Computer or Documents library window, click New Folder button on Quick Access toolbar.
delete selected files/folders		At Computer or Documents library window, select files to be deleted, press Delete key, click Yes.
folder options		Click View tab, click Options button.
move selected files/folders		At Computer or Documents library window, select files/folders to be moved, right-click in selected group, click *Cut*, navigate to destination folder, right-click in Content pane, click *Paste*.
Recycle Bin		Double-click *Recycle Bin* icon.
rename file/folder		At Computer or Documents library window, right-click file or folder, click *Rename,* type new name, press Enter.
restore files/folders from Recycle Bin		At Recycle Bin, select desired files/folders, click Recycle Bin Tools Manage tab, click Restore the selected items button on tab.
search for programs or documents		Display Charm bar, click Search button, type search criterion in search text box; or open Computer or Documents library window, type search criterion in search text box.
select adjacent files/folders		Click first file/folder, hold down Shift key, click last file/folder.
select nonadjacent files/folders		Click first file/folder, hold down Ctrl key, click any other files/folders.

Completion: In the space provided at the right, indicate the correct term, command, or option.

1. Navigate to any other device or folder from the current device and folder using the Navigation pane or this bar in the Computer window. ________________
2. Specify the option to open each folder in its own window at this dialog box. ________________
3. Click this button on the Quick Access toolbar to create a new folder in the Computer window. ________________
4. Change the display of files and folders in the Computer window to *List* or *Details* using this group on the View tab. ________________
5. To select adjacent files, click the first file, hold down this key, and then click the last file. ________________
6. To select nonadjacent files, click the first file, hold down this key, and then click any other desired files. ________________
7. Click this button to display in the Content pane the files in the previous folder viewed. ________________
8. Click this button in the Clipboard group on the Home tab to move selected files. ________________
9. Files deleted from the hard drive are sent here. ________________
10. Open this window to display a list of categories or icons in which you can customize the appearance and functionality of your computer. ________________
11. Access search tools using this bar at the desktop. ________________
12. Customize the desktop by changing the background, screen saver, and/or color option at this window. ________________

Skills Review

Review 1 Browsing Devices and Changing the View

1. Open the Computer window.
2. Change to Large Icons view.
3. Change the folder option to open each folder in its own window.
4. Display the contents of your storage medium.
5. Display the contents of the WindowsS2 folder.
6. Change to Details view.
7. Close the WindowsS2 window.
8. Close the window for your storage medium.
9. Change the folder option to open each folder in the same window.
10. Change to Tiles view and then close the Computer window.

Review 2 Creating a Folder

1. Open the Computer window.
2. Display the contents of your storage medium.
3. Right-click a blank area in the Content pane, point to *New*, and then click *Folder*.
4. Type **Worksheets** and then press Enter.
5. Close the window.

Review 3 Selecting, Copying, Moving, and Deleting Files

1. Open the Computer window.
2. Display the contents of your storage medium.
3. Display the contents of the WindowsS2 folder.
4. Change the current view to List if the display is not already set to List.
5. Click once on ***FCTBookings.xlsx*** to select it, hold down the Shift key, and then click ***FCTPackages.docx***.
6. Right-click within the selected group of files and then click *Copy* at the shortcut menu.
7. Click the Back button.
8. Double-click the *Worksheets* folder.
9. Right-click in the Content pane, click *Paste*, and then click in a blank area to deselect the files.
10. Click the Back button and then double-click *WindowsS2*.
11. Click ***WEExcelRevenues.xlsx*** in the Content pane, hold down the Ctrl key, and then click ***WERevChart.xlsx***.
12. Click the Cut button in the Clipboard group on the Home tab.
13. Click the Back button and then double-click *Worksheets*.
14. Click the Paste button in the Clipboard group on the Home tab.
15. Click the right-pointing arrow next to your storage medium in the Address bar and then click *WindowsS2* at the drop-down list.
16. Click ***FCTCCSkiing.docx*** in the Content pane, hold down the Ctrl key, and then click ***FCTNorwayTour.docx***.
17. Press the Delete key and then click Yes at the Delete Multiple Items confirmation message.
18. Close the Computer window.

Review 4 Renaming a File

1. Open the Computer window.
2. Display the contents of your storage medium.
3. Display the contents of the WindowsS2 folder.
4. Right-click ***WETable01.docx*** and then click *Rename*.
5. Type **WEPreviewDistribution** and then press Enter.
6. Right-click ***WETable02.docx*** and then click *Rename*.
7. Type **WEGeneralDistribution** and then press Enter.
8. Close the Computer window.

Review 5 Searching for Files

1. Open the Computer window.
2. Display the contents of the WindowsS2 folder on your storage medium.
3. Type *rev* in the search WindowsS2 text box.
4. Press the Esc key until the filter is cleared and all files are redisplayed.
5. Type *excel* in the search WindowsS2 text box.
6. Close the Computer window.
7. Click the Search button on the Charm bar.
8. Type *word* in the search text box. Notice the applications displayed in the Start screen.
9. Press the Esc key and then click in the Start screen area outside the Search panel to close the Search panel.

Skills Assessment

Assessment 1 Managing Folders and Files

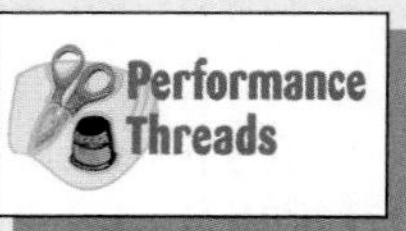

1. Create a new folder on your storage medium named PerformanceThreads.
2. Display the contents of the WindowsS2 folder.
3. If necessary, change to List view.
4. Copy all files beginning with *PT* to the PerformanceThreads folder.
5. If necessary, display the contents of the PerformanceThreads folder and change to List view.
6. Create a new folder within PerformanceThreads named Payroll. (A folder created within a folder is referred to as a subfolder.)
7. Move **PTExcelOctPayroll.xlsx** and **PTWordOctPayroll.docx** from the PerformanceThreads folder into the Payroll subfolder.
8. Delete **PTMarqueeLetter.docx** from the PerformanceThreads folder.
9. Rename the file named **PTAgreement.docx** located in the PerformanceThreads folder to **CostumeAgreement.docx**.

Assessment 2 Managing Folders and Files

First Choice TRAVEL

1. Display the contents of your storage medium.
2. Create a new folder named FirstChoiceTravel.
3. Display the contents of the WindowsS2 folder.
4. Copy all files beginning with *FCT* to the FirstChoiceTravel folder.
5. If necessary, display the contents of the FirstChoiceTravel folder and change to List view.
6. Create a new folder within FirstChoiceTravel and name it *Accounting*.
7. Create a new folder within the Accounting folder and name it *Commissions*.
8. Move **FCTBookings.xlsx** from the FirstChoiceTravel folder into the Accounting subfolder.
9. Move **FCTSalesCommissions.xlsx** from the FirstChoiceTravel folder into the Commissions subfolder.
10. Delete **FCTIslandFlights.docx** from the FirstChoiceTravel folder.
11. Rename the file named **FCTPackages.docx** located in the FirstChoiceTravel folder to **FCTOregonNevadaPkgs.docx**.

Assessment 3 Managing Folders and Files

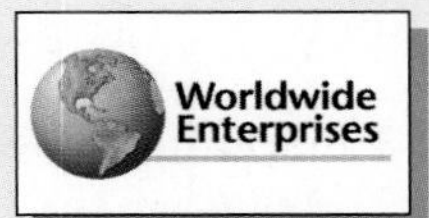

1. Display the contents of your storage medium.
2. Create a new folder named WorldwideEnt.
3. Display the contents of the WindowsS2 folder.
4. Copy all files beginning with *WE* to the WorldwideEnt folder.
5. If necessary, display the contents of the WorldwideEnt folder and change to List view.
6. Delete **WEOutline.docx** from the WorldwideEnt folder.
7. Change the name of the WorldwideEnt folder to *WorldwideEnterprises*.

Assessment 4 Deleting Folders and Files

Note: Check with your Instructor before completing this assessment in case you need to show him or her that you completed the activities within this section before deleting the folders.

1. Display the contents of your storage medium.
2. Delete the folder named Administration.
3. Delete the folder named Distribution.
4. Delete the folder named Income.

Assessment 5 Copying Folders from the Student CD to Storage Medium

1. Display the contents of the Marquee student CD that accompanies this textbook in the Computer window.
2. Display the contents of the Word folder in the Content pane.
3. Select all of the subfolders in the Word folder and then copy them to your storage medium.
4. Display the contents of the Excel folder in the Content pane and then copy all of the subfolders in the Excel folder to your storage medium.
5. Display the contents of the Access folder in the Content pane and then copy all of the subfolders in the Access folder to your storage medium.
6. Display the contents of the PowerPoint folder in the Content pane and then copy all of the subfolders in the PowerPoint folder to your storage medium.
7. Copy the AudioandVideo folder to your storage medium.
8. Display the contents of the Integrating folder and then copy all of the subfolders to your storage medium.

Assessment 6 Searching for Information on User Accounts

1. You have been asked by your supervisor at First Choice Travel to learn about sharing your computer with other users. Your supervisor is considering adding an evening shift and wants to find out how existing computer equipment can be set up for other users. Using the Windows Help and Support feature, search for information on user accounts. ***Hint: Type** user accounts **in the search text box and press Enter. Consider reading the topic*** **Which user account is right for me** ***as your first step***.
2. Locate topics with information about the three types of user accounts: *Standard*, *Administrator*, and *Guest*. Specifically, your supervisor is interested in which type of account would be best suited for day-to-day work and why this type of account is your recommendation.
3. Create a new folder on your storage medium named WindowsEOS.
4. Using WordPad or Word, compose a memo to your instructor that describes the differences among the three types of user accounts and then provide your recommendation for which type of account should be used for individuals on each shift.
5. Save the memo in the WindowsEOS folder and name it **WS2-UserAccounts**.
6. Print the memo and then close the application you used to compose the memo.

Assessment 7 Searching for Information on Windows Libraries

1. You have been asked by your supervisor at First Choice Travel to learn about a feature in Windows 8 called Libraries. Your supervisor is not sure about the difference between a library and a normal folder for managing folders and files. She wants you to find out how a library can be useful to her and how to create her own library and add folders to it. She also wonders if the default libraries Windows created can have other folders added to them. Using the Windows Help and Support feature, search for information on libraries. ***Hint: Type** libraries **in the search text box and then press Enter. Consider reading the topic*** **Library basics** ***as your first step***.
2. Locate topics with information about libraries.
3. Using WordPad or Word, compose a memo to your instructor that provides her or him with answers to the following questions:
   a. What is the difference between a library and a folder?
   b. How can I create my own library?
   c. How can I add or remove folders in a library?
   d. What is the limit on the number of folders that can be added to a library?
4. Save the memo and name it **WS2-Libraries** in the WindowsEOS folder.
5. Print the memo and then close the application you used to compose the memo.

Marquee Series

MICROSOFT®

INTERNET EXPLORER 10

Nita Rutkosky
Pierce College at Puyallup,
Puyallup, Washington

Denise Seguin
Fanshawe College,
London, Ontario

Audrey Roggenkamp
Pierce College at Puyallup,
Puyallup, Washington

Ian Rutkosky
Pierce College at Puyallup,
Puyallup, Washington

St. Paul

Contents

Managing Editor Christine Hurney
Director of Production Timothy W. Larson
Production Editor Sarah Kearin
Cover and Text Designer Leslie Anderson
Copy Editor Sid Korpi, Proof Positive Editing
Design and Production Specialists Jack Ross and Sara Schmidt Boldon
Testers Desiree Carvel; Ann E. Mills, Ivy Tech Community College of Indiana, Indianapolis, IN; Brienna McWade
Indexer Terry Casey
VP & Director of Digital Projects Chuck Bratton
Digital Project Manager Tom Modl

875 Montreal Way
St. Paul, MN 55102
Email: educate@emcp.com
Website: www.emcp.com

Internet Explorer

Browsing the Internet Using Internet Explorer 10

Skills

- Visit sites by typing a web address
- Use hyperlinks to navigate to web pages
- Search for information using search tools
- Narrow a search using advanced search options
- Download content from a web page
- Evaluate content found on a web page

Projects Overview

Visit websites for two national parks. Search for websites pertaining to historical costume design. Use advanced search options to locate information on skydiving companies in the state of Oregon. Locate and save images of Banff National Park. Find information on Apollo lunar missions and evaluate the source and date of publication of the information.

Visit the home pages for the *New York Times* and *USA Today* and read a current article.

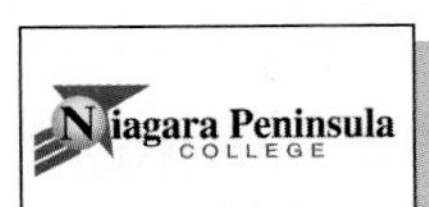

Search for and locate the web page for the Theatre Department at York University and the web page for the Department of Drama at New York University.

Locate a website for a snow skiing resort in Utah and then download an image from the web page.

Activity 1.1

Navigating the Internet Using Web Addresses

In today's world, the Internet is used for a variety of tasks, including locating information about any topic one can imagine, communicating with others through email or social networking sites, and buying and selling goods and services. In this section, you will use Microsoft's Internet Explorer web browser to locate information on the Internet. A ***web browser*** is software that allows you to view the text, images, and other content that has been stored on a web page on the Internet. ***Uniform Resource Locators***, referred to as URLs, identify web servers that have content on the Internet. A URL is often referred to as a ***web address***. Just as you need a specific mailing address to identify your location to the post office, a web server needs a unique web address to identify its location to the Internet.

Project

Dennis Chun, the location director for Marquee Productions, is gathering information for a new movie project. He has asked you to browse the websites for Yosemite National Park and Glacier National Park.

Note: Printing instructions are not included in the project steps in this section. Check with your instructor to find out if you need to print the web pages you visit.

Tutorial 1.1
Navigating the Internet Using Web Addresses

1. Make sure you are connected to the Internet and that the Windows desktop displays.

   Check with your instructor to determine if you need to complete steps to access the Internet.

2. Open Microsoft Internet Explorer by clicking the Internet Explorer icon on the Windows Taskbar.

   Figure 1.1 identifies the elements of the Internet Explorer window. The web page that displays in your Internet Explorer window may vary from what you see in Figure 1.1. Refer to Figure 1.2 on the next page for descriptions of the tools available in Internet Explorer.

3. At the Internet Explorer window, click in the Address bar (refer to Figure 1.1), type **www.nps.gov/yose**, and then press Enter.

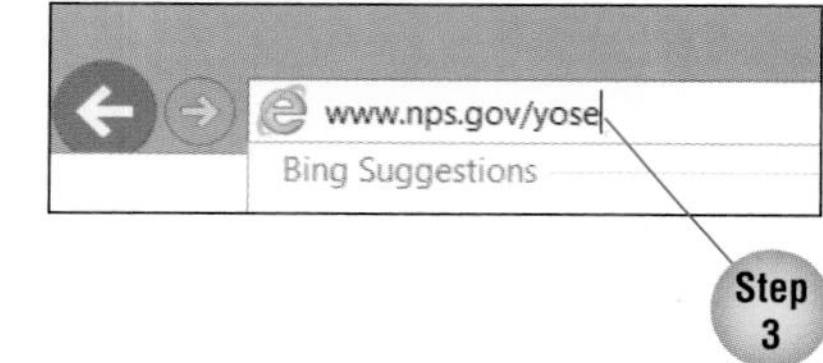

FIGURE 1.1 Internet Explorer Window

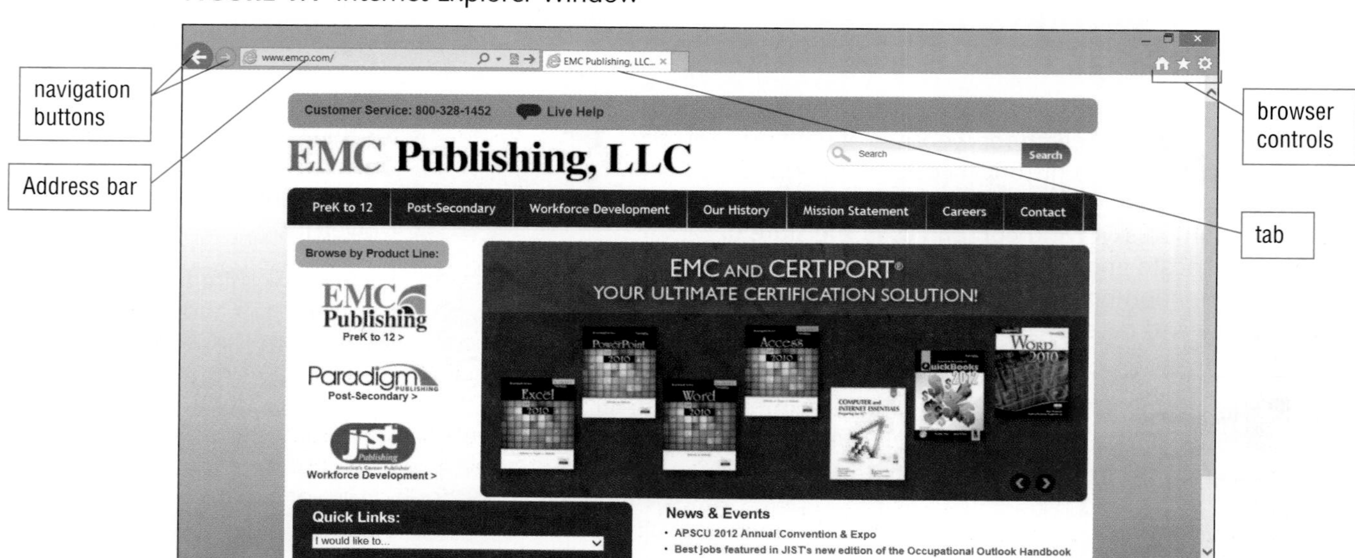

4 Scroll down the home page for Yosemite National Park by pressing the Down Arrow key on the keyboard, or by clicking the down-pointing arrow on the vertical scroll bar located at the right side of the Internet Explorer window.

The first web page that appears for a website is called the site's *home page.*

In Brief

Display Specific Website

1. At Windows desktop, click *Internet Explorer* icon on Taskbar.
2. Click in Address bar, type web address, and then press Enter.

5 Display the home page for Glacier National Park by clicking in the Address bar, typing **www.nps.gov/glac**, and then pressing Enter.

As you begin to type the first few characters in the Address bar, a drop-down list appears with the names of websites you have already visited that are spelled the same. Matched characters are displayed in blue for quick reference. If the web address you want displays in the drop-down list, you do not need to type the entire address—simply click the desired web address in the drop-down list.

6 Click the History & Culture hyperlink in the navigation area at the left side of the page.

Most web pages contain hyperlinks that you click to connect to another page within the website or to another site on the Internet. Hyperlinks display in a web page in a variety of ways such as underlined text, text in a navigation bar, buttons, images, or icons. To use a hyperlink, position the mouse pointer on the hyperlink until the mouse pointer turns into a hand and then click the left mouse button.

7 Scroll down and view the content on the History & Culture web page.

8 Click the Back button located in the upper left corner of the screen (see Figure 1.2) to return to the Glacier National Park home page.

9 Click the Forward button located to the right of the Back button to return to the History & Culture page.

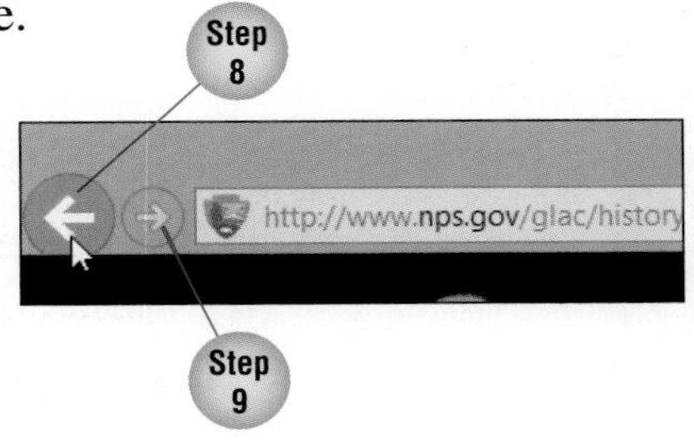

FIGURE 1.2 Browsing, Navigating, and Other Internet Explorer Tools

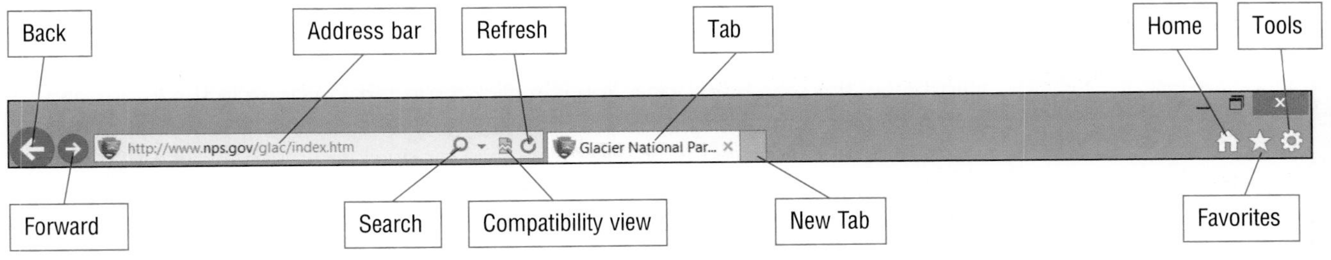

In Addition

Using Internet Explorer in the Modern UI

Windows 8 contains a new user interface, which has been optimized for touch devices. If you access Internet Explorer through the Windows 8 start screen, the Modern UI version of Internet Explorer displays. This version displays differently than the desktop version of Internet Explorer and is designed for use on touch devices. To open the Modern UI version of Internet Explorer, display the Windows 8 start screen and then click the Internet Explorer tile. The address bar and buttons appear at the bottom of the screen and are increased in size. All of the activities in this section use the desktop version of Internet Explorer. If the Internet Explorer button does not appear on the Taskbar, ask your instructor for help on how to access the desktop version of Internet Explorer.

Activity 1.2

Finding Information Using Search Tools

If you do not know the web address for a specific site or you want to find information on the Internet but do not know what site to visit, you can search the Internet using a search engine. A variety of search engines are available, and each offers the opportunity to search for specific information. One method for searching for information is to click in the Address bar, type a keyword or phrase related to your search, and then press Enter. Another method for completing a search is to go to the home page for a search engine and use options at the search engine's site.

Project

Allan Herron, research coordinator for Marquee Productions, has asked you to locate sites with historical costumes for a new movie project. Specifically, she has asked you to locate information on Elizabethan and Renaissance costumes.

Tutorial 1.2
Finding Information Using Search Tools

1. With the Internet Explorer window active, click in the Address bar.
2. Type **Renaissance costumes** and then press Enter.

   When you press the Enter key, a Bing page with the search results displays. Bing is Microsoft's online search portal and is the default search engine used by Internet Explorer. Bing organizes search results by topic category and provides related search suggestions.

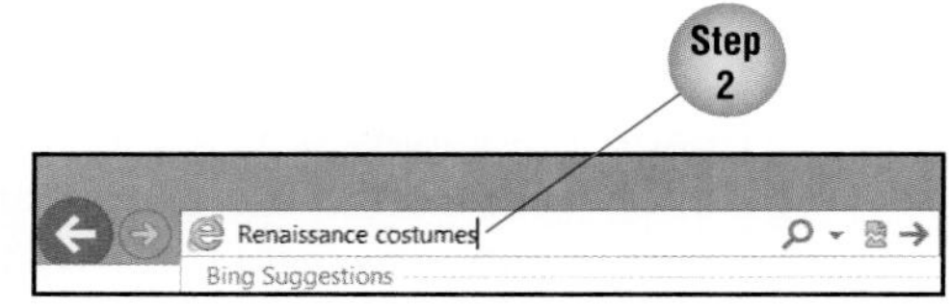

3. Scroll down the search results list and click a hyperlink that interests you by positioning the mouse pointer on the hyperlink text until the pointer turns into a hand and then clicking the left mouse button.
4. Browse the content at the page you selected.
5. Use the Yahoo! search engine to find sites on Renaissance costumes by clicking in the Address bar, typing **www.yahoo.com**, and then pressing Enter.
6. At the Yahoo! website, type **Renaissance costumes** in the search text box and then press Enter.

   As you begin to type, the Yahoo! search assist feature displays search suggestions in a list below the search text box. You can click a suggested phrase in the list instead of completing your typing. Characters in each suggested search phrase that match your typing are displayed in another font style for quick reference. Notice that Bing and Yahoo!'s suggested search phrases are different. Each search engine has its own way of cataloging and indexing search terms.

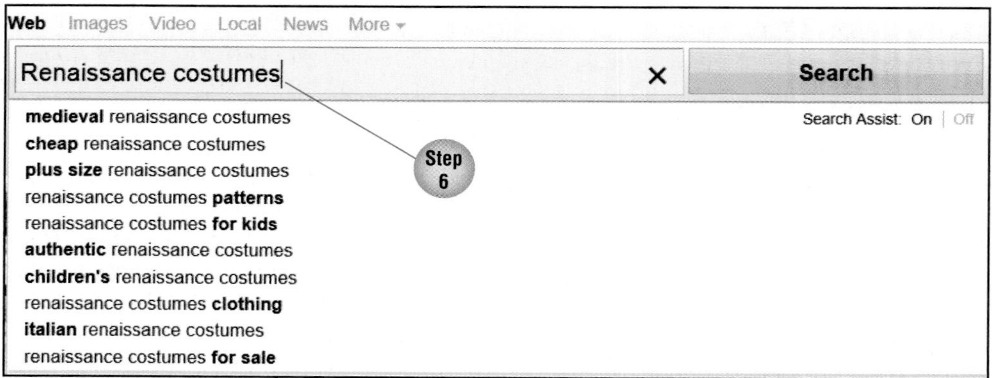

7 Click a hyperlink to a site that interests you.

8 Use the Google search engine to find sites on Elizabethan costumes by clicking in the Address bar, typing **www.google.com**, and then pressing Enter.

9 At the Google website, type **Elizabethan costumes** in the search text box and then press Enter.

Notice that Google also provides a drop-down list of suggested search phrases based on the characters you type.

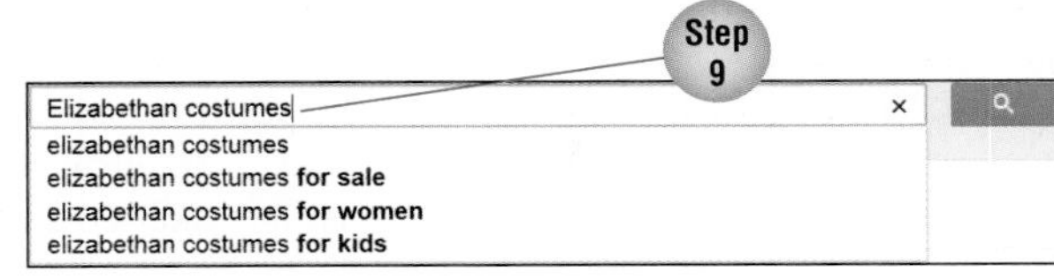

10 Click a hyperlink to a site that interests you.

11 Use the Dogpile search engine to find sites on Elizabethan costumes by clicking in the Address bar, typing **www.dogpile.com**, and then pressing Enter.

Dogpile is a metasearch search engine. A ***metasearch search engine*** sends your search phrase to other search engines and then compiles the results into one list, allowing you to type the search phrase once and access results from a variety of search engines that index web pages. Dogpile provides search results from Google, Yahoo!, and Yandex.

12 At the Dogpile website, type **Elizabethan costumes** in the search text box and then press Enter.

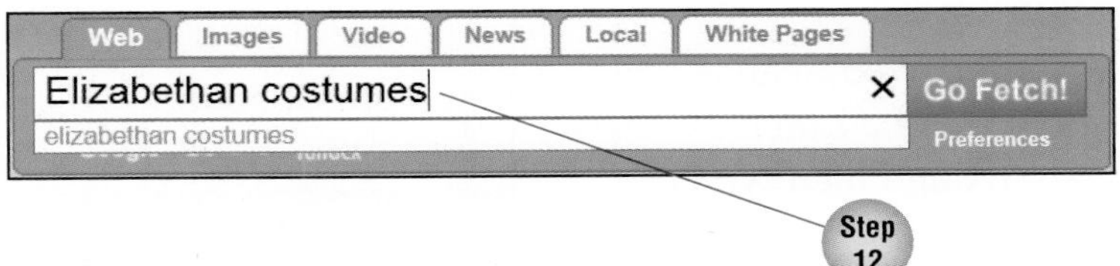

13 Click a hyperlink to a site that interests you.

In Brief

Search for Website
At Internet Explorer window, type search terms text in the Address bar and then press Enter.

In Addition

Customizing Internet Explorer

Internet Explorer 10 has been streamlined to provide users with more browsing space and reduced clutter. By default, Microsoft has turned off many features in Internet Explorer 10 such as the Menu bar, Command bar, and Status bar. You can turn these features on by right-clicking the empty space above the Address bar (see Figure 1.1 on page 2) and then clicking the desired option at the drop-down list that displays. For example, if you want to turn on the Menu bar (the bar that contains File, Edit, and so on), right-click the empty space above the Address bar and then click *Menu bar* at the drop-down list. (This inserts a check mark next to *Menu bar.*)

Adding Frequently Used Web Pages to Favorites

If you visit a web page on a regular basis, add the page to the Favorites Center or add a button to the web page on the Favorites bar. To display the Favorites bar, right-click the empty space above the Address bar and then click *Favorites bar* at the drop-down list. To add the web page to the Favorites bar, display the web page and then click the Favorites button (which displays as a white star located in the upper right corner of the window). When the Favorites Center displays, click the down-pointing arrow on the Add to favorites button and then click *Add to Favorites bar* at the drop-down list. If you prefer, you can add the website to the Favorites Center list. To do this, click the Favorites button and then click the Add to favorites button at the Favorites Center. At the Add a Favorite dialog box that displays, make sure the information in the *Name* text box is the title by which you want to refer to the website (if not, type your own title for the page) and then click the Add button. The new website is added to the Favorites Center drop-down list. Jump quickly to the site by clicking the Favorites button and then clicking the site name at the drop-down list.

Activity 1.3

Refining Your Search Using Advanced Search Tools

The Internet contains an extraordinary amount of information. Depending on what you are searching for on the Internet and the search engine you use, some searches can result in several thousand "hits" (sites). Wading through a large number of sites can be very time-consuming. You can achieve a more targeted search results list if you hone your search technique using the advanced search options offered by a search engine. Look for an advanced search options link at your favorite search engine site the next time you need to locate information, and experiment with various methods to limit the search results. Effective searching is a skill you obtain through practice.

Project

James Vecchio, stunt coordinator at Marquee Productions, has asked you to locate information on skydiving companies in the state of Oregon.

Tutorial 1.3
Researching Information Using Advanced Search Tools

1. With the Internet Explorer window active, click in the Address bar, type **www.yahoo.com**, and then press Enter.
2. At the Yahoo! home page, click the Search button **Search** next to the search text box.

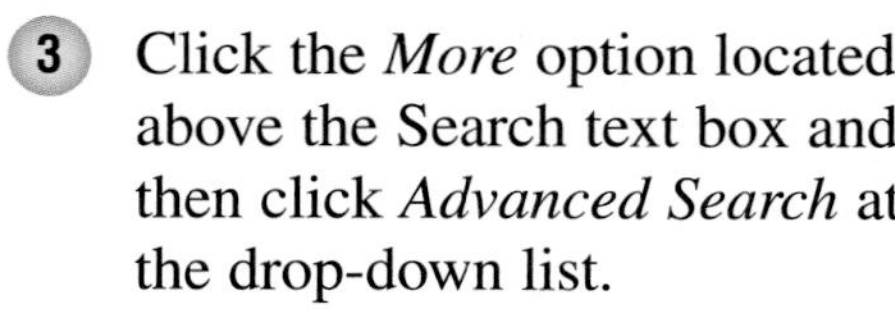

3. Click the *More* option located above the Search text box and then click *Advanced Search* at the drop-down list.

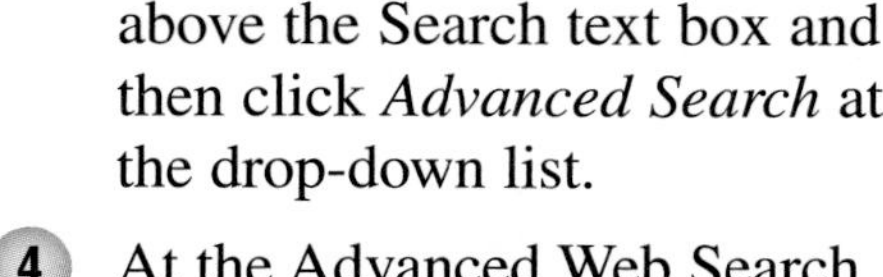

4. At the Advanced Web Search page, click in the *the exact phrase* text box and then type **skydiving in Oregon**.

   This limits the search to websites with the exact phrase "skydiving in Oregon."

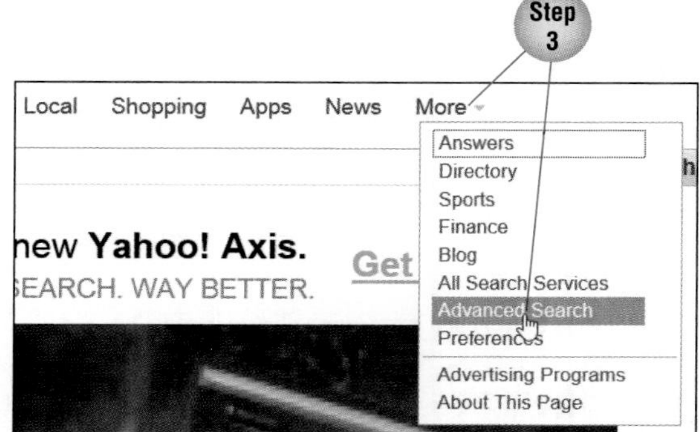

5. Click the *Only .com domains* option.

   Clicking this option tells Yahoo! to only display websites with a *.com* extension and to ignore any other extension.

6. Click the Yahoo! Search button.

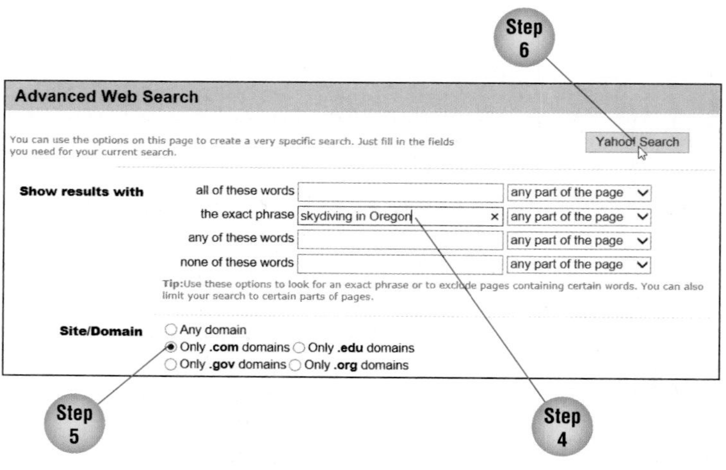

7 When the list of websites displays, click a hyperlink that interests you.

8 Click the Back button until the Yahoo! Advanced Web Search page displays.

9 Select and then delete the text *skydiving in Oregon* located in the *the exact phrase* text box.

10 Click in the *all of these words* text box and then type **skydiving Oregon tandem static line**.

You want to focus on websites that offer tandem and static line skydiving in Oregon. Enter specific text in the *all of these words* text box to limit the search only to those websites containing all of the words.

11 Click the *Any domain* option.

12 Click the Yahoo! Search button.

In Brief

Complete Advanced Search Using Yahoo!

1. At Internet Explorer window, click in Address bar, type *www.yahoo.com*, then press Enter.
2. Click Search button, click *More* option, click *Advanced Search*.
3. Click in desired search text box, type search criteria text.
4. Select search method and search options.
5. Click Yahoo! Search button.

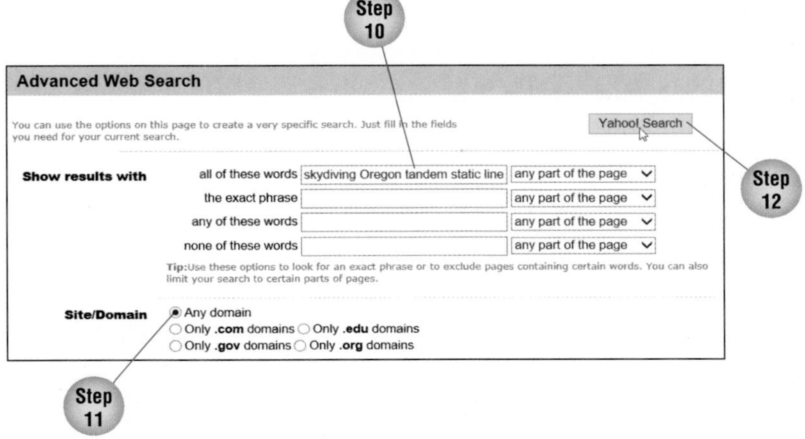

13 When the list of websites displays, click a hyperlink that interests you.

In Addition

Displaying a List of Sites Visited

As you view various web pages, Internet Explorer keeps track of the websites you visit. Display the History pane by clicking the Favorites button and then clicking the History tab in the Favorites Center. Click a timeframe to expand the list and display the sites visited during that period. For example, click *Last Week* to expand the list and view the pages you visited within the past week. Click a hyperlink to revisit the page. At the top of the History pane, click the View option box (currently displays *View By Date*) to change the order in which the history list is displayed. You can display websites in the History pane to *View By Date, View By Site, View By Most Visited,* or *View By Order Visited Today*. Click *Search History* at the View button drop-down list to search the websites in the History pane by keyword or phrase.

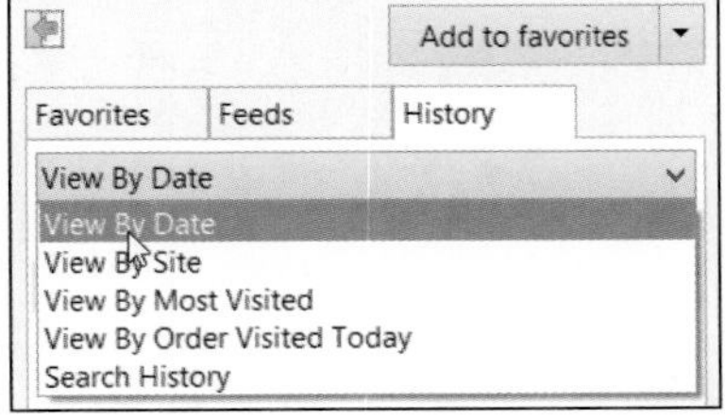

Activity 1.4

Downloading Content from a Web Page

Downloading content from a web page can involve saving to your hard disk or other storage medium images, text, video, audio, or an entire web page. Copyright laws protect much of the information on the Internet. Before using information or media files you have downloaded from the Internet, check the source site for restrictions. When in doubt, contact the website administrator or another contact person identified on the site and request permission to use the content. Finally, make sure to credit the source of any content you use that was obtained from a web page. Generally, you can use content from a website that is considered public domain, such as a government website, without obtaining permission.

Project

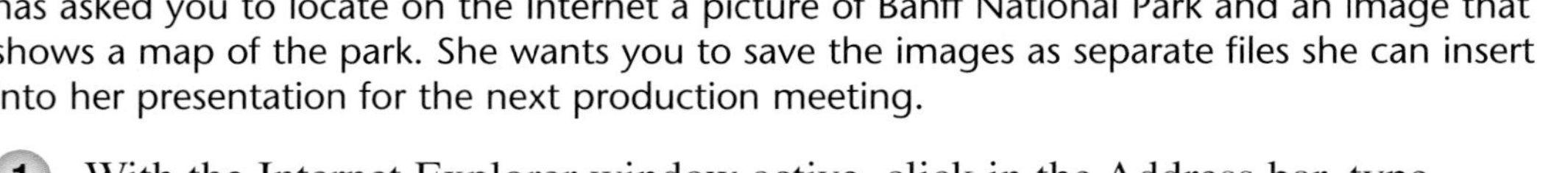

Chris Greenbaum, the production manager of the new movie project at Marquee Productions, has asked you to locate on the Internet a picture of Banff National Park and an image that shows a map of the park. She wants you to save the images as separate files she can insert into her presentation for the next production meeting.

Tutorial 1.4
Downloading Content from a Web Page

1. With the Internet Explorer window active, click in the Address bar, type **www.google.com**, and then press Enter.
2. At the Google home page, click the Images hyperlink at the top left of the home page.

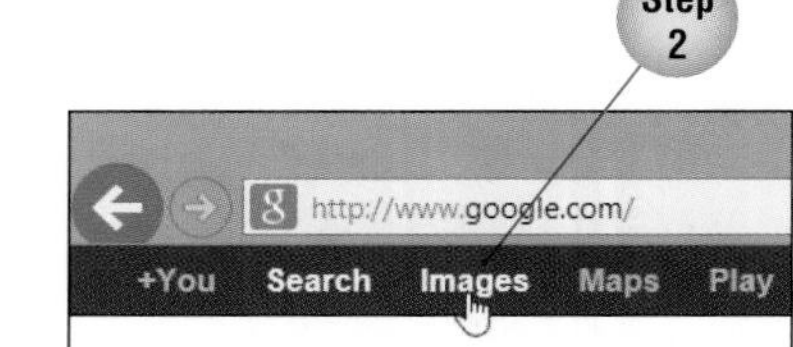

3. At the Google images page, type **Banff National Park** in the search text box and then press Enter or click the Search button.
4. Browse the images that display in the search results.

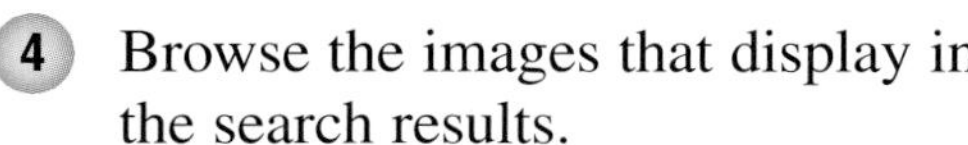

Your image may vary.

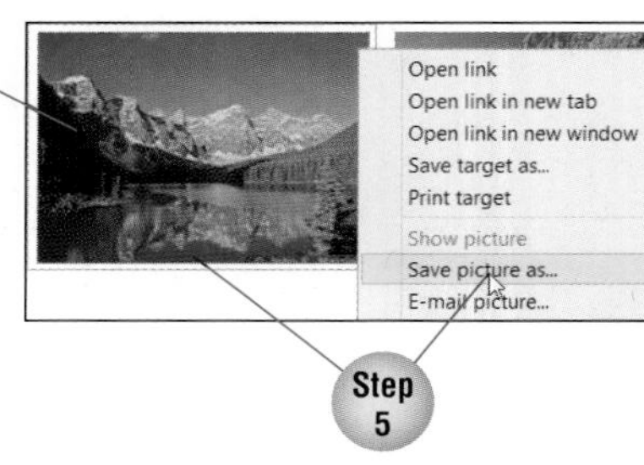

5. Position the mouse pointer over an image you want to download, right-click the mouse, and then click *Save picture as* at the shortcut menu.

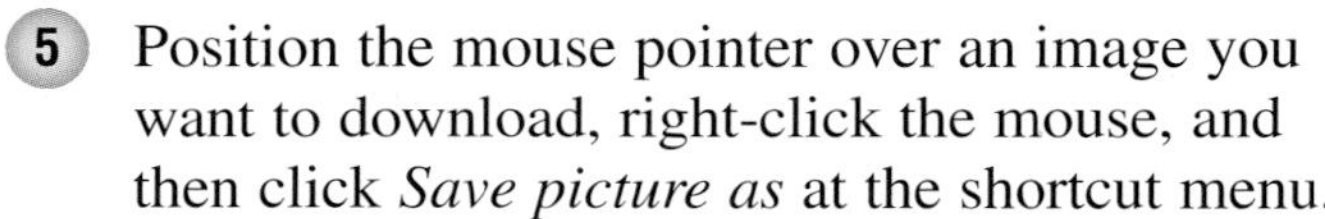

   The image you choose may vary from the one shown here.

6. At the Save Picture dialog box, click *Desktop* in the *Favorites* section of the Navigation pane, select the current text in the *File name* text box, type **BanffPicture1**, and then click Save or press Enter.

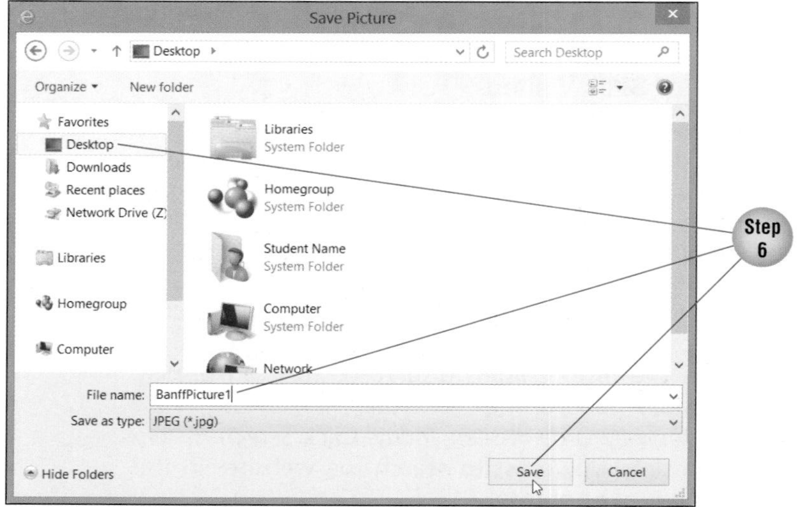

7 Click in the Address bar, type **www.dogpile.com**, and then press Enter.

8 Click the Images tab at the Dogpile home page.

9 Click in the search text box, type **Banff National Park map**, and then press Enter or click the Go Fetch! button.

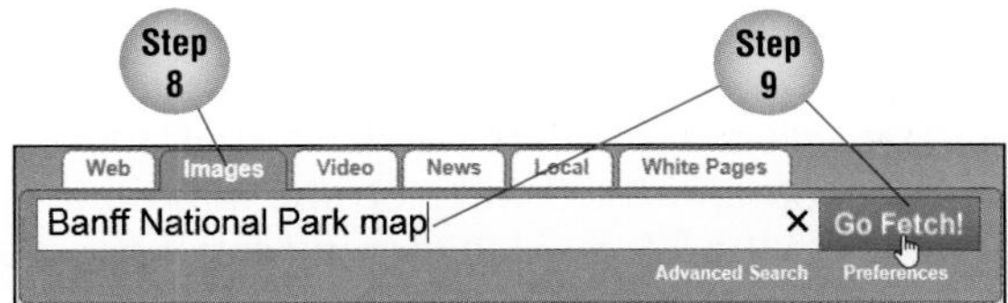

10 Browse the map images that display in the search results, right-click the mouse over one of the maps you want to download, and then click *Save picture as* at the shortcut menu.

11 At the Save Picture dialog box, with *Desktop* already selected in the Address bar and with the current file name already selected in the *File name* text box, type **BanffMap1** and then click Save or press Enter.

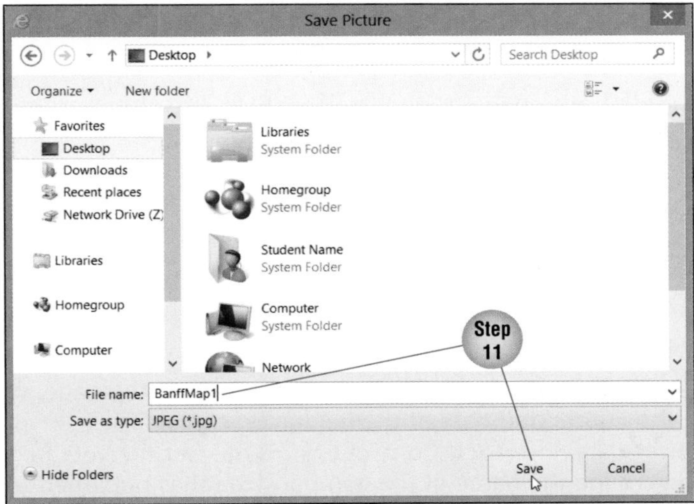

In Brief

Download Images from Web Page

1. Display desired web page in Internet Explorer window.
2. Right-click desired image.
3. Click *Save picture as*.
4. Navigate to desired drive and/or folder.
5. Type file name in *File name* text box.
6. Click Save.

In Addition

Downloading an Application

Using Internet Explorer, you can download applications and programs to install onto your computer. When an application is downloaded, Internet Explorer displays the download bar toward the bottom of the screen (as shown below) asking if you want to run or save the application. If you want to install the application, click the Run button. Click the Save button if you want Internet Explorer to save the application in a temporary folder. If you want to save the application in a specific location on your computer, click the down-pointing arrow on the Save button and then click *Save As* at the drop-down list that displays. This displays the Save As dialog box where you can specify the drive or file in which you want to save the file. Applications downloaded from the Internet can potentially contain viruses, so make sure the website and file are from a trusted source.

Activity 1.5

Evaluating Content on the Web

The Web is a vast repository of information that is easily accessible and constantly changing. Although a wealth of accurate and timely information is available at your fingertips, some information on the Internet may be outdated, inaccurate, or of poor quality, and therefore should not be relied upon. Since anyone with an Internet connection and the right software can publish information on the Web, knowing the clues to recognizing accurate and current content is a worthwhile skill. The following are some tips to help you develop this skill.

First, look for an author, publisher, or website owner name and consider if the source is credible. For example, is the author associated with a recognizable company, government, or news organization? Second, look for the date the information was published. Is the content outdated? If yes, consider the impact that more current information might have on the information you are evaluating. Third, look for indications that a bias may exist in the content. For example, is there a sponsor on the site that might indicate the information is one-sided? Can the information be validated by another source?

Project

Allan Herron, research coordinator at Marquee Productions, is working on research for a new documentary about the Apollo space missions. She has asked you to locate information on the Web that she can add to her research. You want to be careful that the information you provide for the project is credible.

1. With the Internet Explorer window active, click in the Address bar, type **www.google.com**, and then press Enter.
2. At the Google home page, type **Apollo lunar missions** in the search text box and then click the Search button or press Enter.
3. Click a hyperlink to a page that interests you.
4. At the web page, try to locate the author or publisher name, the date the article was published, and/or the date the page was last updated. If the web page contains any ads or sponsors, consider if this advertising has an impact on the content you are reading.

   Some pages put this information at the bottom of the page, while other pages place the author and date at the beginning of the article. If you cannot find an author or date, look for a Contact link on the website you are viewing to see if you can determine the name of the company that has published the information. Also, look over the web address to see if the address provides a clue to the authorship. For example, a web address with a *.edu* domain indicates the source is from a page connected with an educational institution.

5. Click the New Tab tab to open a new browsing window.

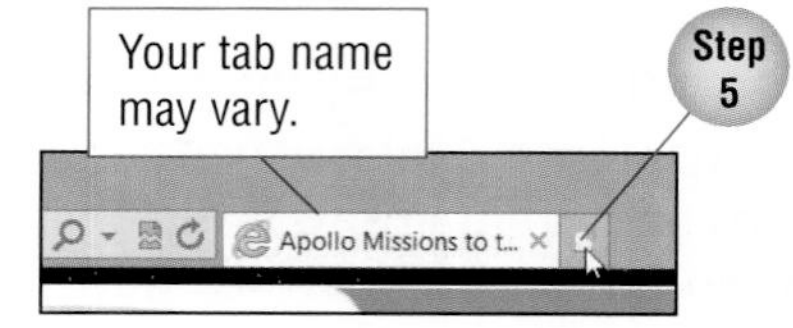

6. Click in the Address bar, type **www.nasa.gov/mission_pages/apollo**, and then press Enter.
7. Scroll to the bottom of the page and read the information in the banner next to the NASA logo that provides information about the date the page was last updated, the page editor, and the NASA official.

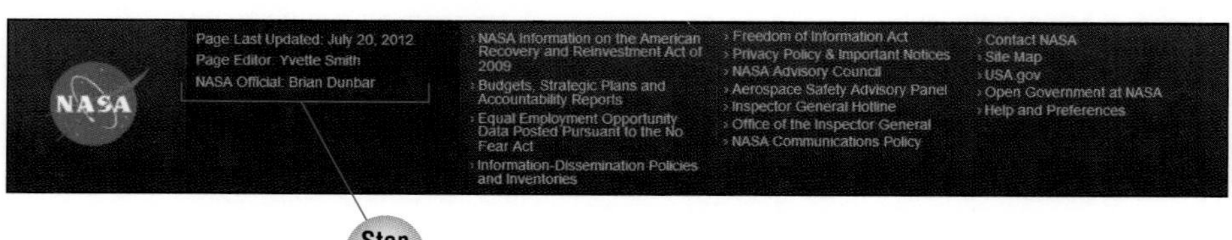

8 Click the tab for the first web page you visited about Apollo lunar missions and click the Back button to return to the search results list.

9 Click another link that interests you and try to locate information about the date, author, and publisher similar to that which you viewed at NASA's website.

10 Compare the two pages shown side by side in Figure 1.3 below. Note that one page provides details about dates and authors while the other page does not have the same references.

The page without the references may not necessarily have inaccurate data or be an otherwise poor-quality source of information about the Apollo missions; however, the absence of an author or date of revision means that you would have difficulty citing this source for a research paper or other academic assignment.

11 Close Internet Explorer. Click the Close all tabs button at the Internet Explorer dialog box.

FIGURE 1.3 Step 10

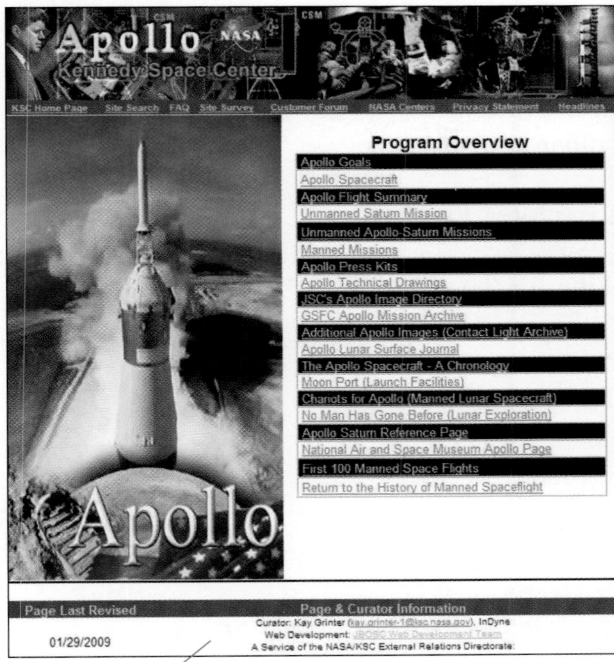

This page has source and date references.

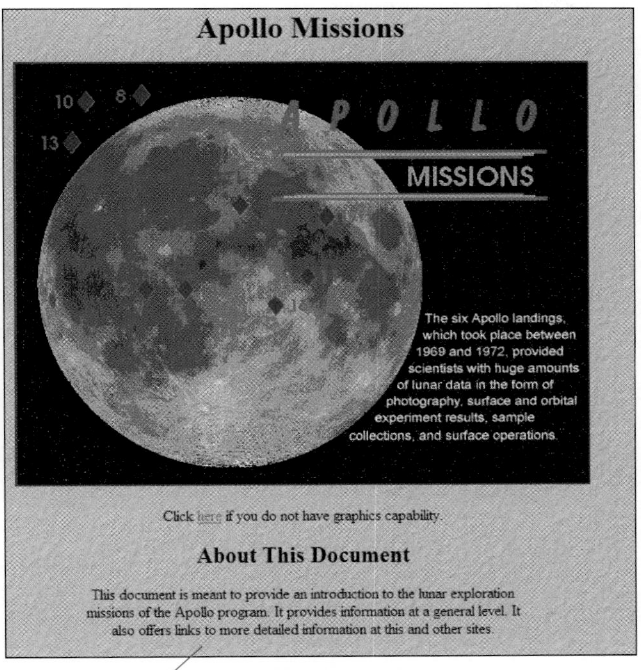

This page has no author, publisher, or date reference.

Features Summary

Feature	Button	Keyboard Shortcut
go back to previous web page		Alt + Left Arrow OR Backspace
go forward to next web page		Alt + Right Arrow
go to home page		Alt + Home
display Favorites Center		Alt + C
display Tools drop-down list		Alt + X

Knowledge Check

Completion: In the space provided at the right, indicate the correct term, command, or option.

1. The letters *URL* stand for this. ________________
2. Type a URL in this bar at the Internet Explorer window. ________________
3. Click this button on the Internet Explorer toolbar to display the previous web page. ________________
4. Bing is the default search engine in Internet Explorer. List two other search engines. ________________
5. Reduce the number of search results by looking for these options at the search engine's website. ________________
6. Download an image from a website to a file on your computer by right-clicking the image and then selecting this option at the shortcut menu. ________________

Skills Review

Note: Check with your instructor before completing the Skills Review activities to find out if you have to print the pages you visit.

Review 1 Browsing the Internet and Navigating with Hyperlinks

1. Open Internet Explorer.
2. Click in the Address bar, type **www.si.edu**, and then press Enter. (This is the home page for the Smithsonian Institution.)
3. Click a hyperlink to a topic that interests you and then read the page.
4. Click another hyperlink and then read the page.
5. Click the Back button until the Smithsonian Institution home page displays.

Review 2 Searching for Specific Sites

1. At the Internet Explorer window, search for websites on mountain climbing.
2. In the search results, click a hyperlink to a site that interests you.
3. Display the Yahoo! website and then use advanced options to search for websites with the *.com* domain on mountain climbing in British Columbia, Canada.
4. Visit at least two sites in the search results that interest you.

Review 3 Downloading Content from a Web Page

1. Using your favorite search engine, search for websites on parasailing in Hawaii. Find a site that contains a parasailing image that you like.
2. Download the parasailing image to the desktop, saving it as **ParasailImage1**.
3. Search for maps of Hawaii.
4. Browse the map images and then select one to download to the desktop, saving it as **HawaiiMap1**.
5. Close Internet Explorer.

Skills Assessment

Note: Check with your instructor before completing the Skills Assessment activities to find out if you have to print the pages you visit.

Assessment 1 Visiting Web Pages for Current News Articles

Worldwide Enterprises

1. Sam Vestering, a manager at Worldwide Enterprises, likes to keep up to date with current events by reading the daily headlines for various newspapers. He has asked you to scan the home pages for two online newspapers—the *New York Times* and *USA Today*—for articles of interest. To begin, open Internet Explorer.
2. Go to the website of the *New York Times* at www.nytimes.com. Scan the headlines for today's publication, click the hyperlink to an article that interests you, and then read the article.
3. Visit the website of *USA Today* at www.usatoday.com, click the hyperlink to an article that interests you, and then read the article.

Assessment 2 Navigating Websites for Theatre Programs

1. Cal Rubine, the chair of the Theatre Arts Division at Niagara Peninsula College, has asked you to visit the web pages for the theatre and/or drama departments at two universities to compare programs. Visit the home page for York University, Toronto, Canada, at www.yorku.ca.
2. Locate the web page for the Theatre Department and then read about the program.
3. Visit the home page for New York University at www.nyu.edu.
4. Using NYU's home-page search feature, locate the web page for the Department of Drama (undergraduate) and then read about the program. If necessary, click hyperlinks to more pages to find program details.

Assessment 3 Downloading Content on Ski Resorts

1. You work for First Choice Travel and are preparing a brochure on snow skiing vacations. You need some information and images for the brochure. Search for information on snow-skiing resorts in Utah.
2. Visit a website that interests you and that contains an image of a resort or mountains.
3. Download an image from the web page to the desktop, saving it as **UtahResortImage1**.
4. Close Internet Explorer.

Assessment 4 Deleting Downloaded Content on the Desktop

1. At the Windows 8 desktop, right-click the ***UtahResortImage1*** file and then click *Delete* at the shortcut menu. Click *Yes* at the Delete File dialog box to move the file to the Recycle Bin.
2. Delete all of the other downloaded files you saved to the desktop during this section.

Marquee Series

MICROSOFT®

WORD 2013

Nita Rutkosky
Pierce College at Puyallup,
Puyallup, Washington

Denise Seguin
Fanshawe College,
London, Ontario

Audrey Roggenkamp
Pierce College at Puyallup,
Puyallup, Washington

Ian Rutkosky
Pierce College at Puyallup,
Puyallup, Washington

St. Paul

Managing Editor Christine Hurney
Director of Production Timothy W. Larson
Production Editor Sarah Kearin
Cover and Text Designer Leslie Anderson
Copy Editor Sid Korpi, Proof Positive Editing
Design and Production Specialists Jack Ross and Sara Schmidt Boldon
Testers Desiree Carvel; Ann E. Mills, Ivy Tech Community College of Indiana, Indianapolis, IN; Brienna McWade
Indexer Terry Casey
VP & Director of Digital Projects Chuck Bratton
Digital Projects Manager Tom Modl

The authors, editors, and publisher thank the following instructors for their helpful suggestions during the planning and development of the Marquee Office 2013 series: Olugbemiga Adekunle, Blue Ridge Community College, Harrisonburg, VA; Letty Barnes, Lake WA Institute of Technology, Kirkland, WA; Erika Nadas, Wilbur Wright College, Chicago, IL; Carolyn Walker, Greenville Technical College, Greenville, SC; Carla Anderson, National College, Lynchburg, VA; Judy A. McLaney, Lurleen B. Wallace Community College, Opp, AL; Sue Canter, Guilford Technical Community College, Jamestown, NC; Reuel Sample, National College, Knoxville, TN; Regina Young, Wiregrass Georgia Technical College, Valdosta, GA; William Roxbury, National College, Stow, OH; Charles Adams, II, Danville Community College, Danville, VA; Karen Spray, Northeast Community College, Norfolk, NE; Deborah Miller, Augusta Technical College, Augusta, GA; Wanda Stuparits, Lanier Technical College, Cumming, GA; Gale Wilson, Brookhaven College, Farmers Branch, TX; Jocelyn S. Pinkard, Arlington Career Institute, Grand Prairie, TX; Ann Blackman, Parkland College, Champaign, IL; Fathia Williams, Fletcher Technical Community College, Houma, LA; Leslie Martin, Gaston College, Dallas, NC; Tom Rose, Kellogg Community College, Battle Creek, MI; Casey Thompson, Wiregrass Georgia Technical College, Douglas, GA; Larry Bush, University of Cincinnati, Clermont College, Amelia, OH; Tim Ellis, Schoolcraft College, Liconia, MI; Miles Cannon, Lanier Technical College, Oakwood, GA; Irvin LaFleur, Lanier Technical College, Cumming, GA; Patricia Partyka, Schoolcraft College, Prudenville, MI.

Text: ISBN 978-0-76385-246-7
Text & CD: ISBN 978-0-76385-267-2

875 Montreal Way
St. Paul, MN 55102
Email: educate@emcp.com
Website: www.emcp.com

Printed in the United States of America

22 21 20 19 18 17 16 15 14 13 2 3 4 5 6 7 8 9 10

Contents

Introducing

WORD 2013

Microsoft Word 2013 is a word processing program used to create documents such as letters, reports, research papers, brochures, announcements, newsletters, envelopes, labels, and much more. Word is a full-featured program that provides a wide variety of editing and formatting features as well as sophisticated visual elements. While working in Word, you will produce business documents for the following six companies.

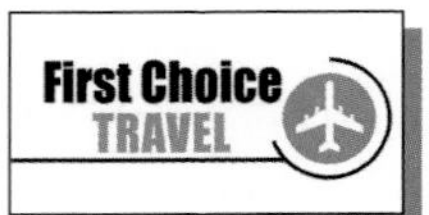

First Choice Travel is a travel center offering a full range of traveling services from booking flights, hotel reservations, and rental cars to offering travel seminars.

The Waterfront Bistro offers fine dining for lunch and dinner and also offers banquet facilities, a wine cellar, and catering services.

Worldwide Enterprises is a national and international distributor of products for a variety of companies and is the exclusive movie distribution agent for Marquee Productions.

Marquee Productions is involved in all aspects of creating movies from script writing and development to filming. The company produces documentaries, biographies, as well as historical and action movies.

Performance Threads maintains an inventory of rental costumes and also researches, designs, and sews special-order and custom-made costumes.

The mission of the Niagara Peninsula College Theatre Arts Division is to offer a curriculum designed to provide students with a thorough exposure to all aspects of the theater arts.

In Section 1 you will learn how to

Create and Edit Documents

Using Microsoft Word, you can create, edit, and format a variety of business documents and use Word's powerful editing and formatting features to produce well-written and visually appealing documents. Some powerful editing features include checking the spelling and grammar in a document and using Thesaurus to find appropriate synonyms for words; using AutoCorrect to improve the efficiency of entering information in a document; and creating a document using a predesigned template.

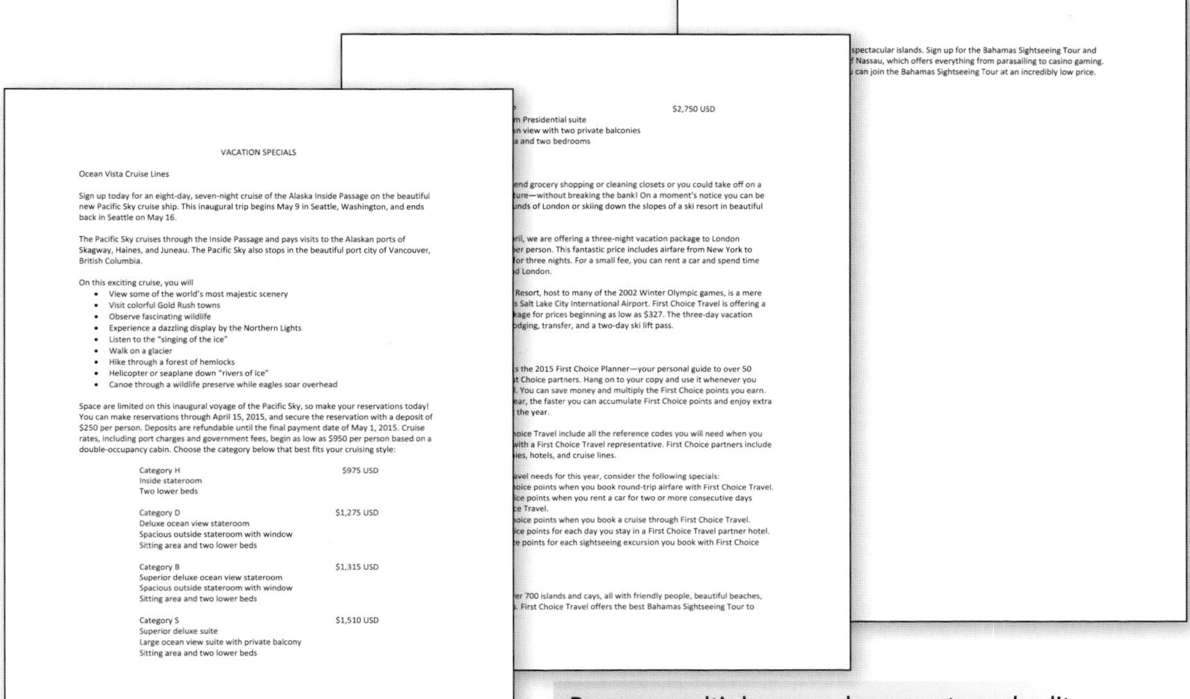

VACATION SPECIALS

Ocean Vista Cruise Lines

Sign up today for an eight-day, seven-night cruise of the Alaska Inside Passage on the beautiful new Pacific Sky cruise ship. This inaugural trip begins May 9 in Seattle, Washington, and ends back in Seattle on May 16.

The Pacific Sky cruises through the Inside Passage and pays visits to the Alaskan ports of Skagway, Haines, and Juneau. The Pacific Sky also stops in the beautiful port city of Vancouver, British Columbia.

On this exciting cruise, you will

- View some of the world's most majestic scenery
- Visit colorful Gold Rush towns
- Observe fascinating wildlife
- Experience a dazzling display by the Northern Lights
- Listen to the "singing of the ice"
- Walk on a glacier
- Hike through a forest of hemlocks
- Helicopter or seaplane down "rivers of ice"
- Canoe through a wildlife preserve while eagles soar overhead

Space are limited on this inaugural voyage of the Pacific Sky, so make your reservations today! You can make reservations through April 15, 2015, and secure the reservation with a deposit of $250 per person. Deposits are refundable until the final payment date of May 1, 2015. Cruise rates, including port charges and government fees, begin as low as $950 per person based on a double-occupancy cabin. Choose the category below that best fits your cruising style:

Category H — $975 USD
Inside stateroom
Two lower beds

Category D — $1,275 USD
Deluxe ocean view stateroom
Spacious outside stateroom with window
Sitting area and two lower beds

Category B — $1,315 USD
Superior deluxe ocean view stateroom
Spacious outside stateroom with window
Sitting area and two lower beds

Category S — $1,510 USD
Superior deluxe suite
Large ocean view suite with private balcony
Sitting area and two lower beds

Prepare multiple-page documents and edit documents by completing a spelling and grammar check and using Thesaurus to find appropriate synonyms for words.

7/20/2015

Student Name
Marquee Productions
955 South Alameda Street
Los Angeles, CA 90037

Ms. Melissa Gehring
First Choice Travel
3588 Ventura Boulevard
Los Angeles, CA 90102

Dear Ms. Gehring:

Marquee Productions will be filming a movie in and around the Toronto area from July 5 through August 27, 2015. I would like scheduling and pricing information for flights from Los Angeles to Toronto, as well as information on lodging.

Approximately 45 people from our company will need flight reservations and hotel rooms. Please locate the best group rates and let me know the approximate costs. I would like to finalize preparations by the end of the month.

Sincerely,

Student Name
Projects Coordinator
Marquee Productions

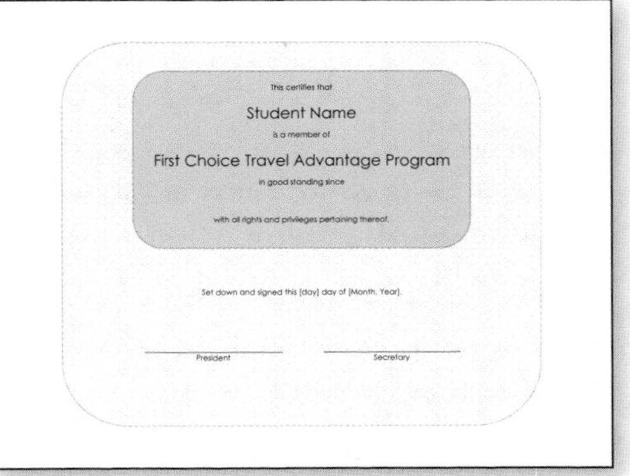

Download templates from Microsoft Office Online and create a variety of documents including letters, faxes, certificates, or awards.

In Section 2 you will learn how to

Format Characters and Paragraphs in Documents

Word contains a number of commands and procedures that affect how the document appears when printed. The appearance of a document in the document screen and how it looks when printed is called the ***format***. Formatting can include such tasks as changing the font; aligning and indenting text; changing line and paragraph spacing; setting tabs; and inserting elements such as bullets, numbers, symbols, and special characters. You can also improve the readability of the document by setting text in tabbed columns and by formatting using styles.

OSLO, NORWAY

History

The founding of Oslo took place in the turbulent period between the *Viking Age* and Norway's *Catholic Middle Ages*. Many remnants and ruins from ancient Oslo can be found in Memorial Park. The city has a fascinating, interesting, and dramatic history.

Oslo's population was substantially reduced during the time of the Black Death in 1348, which claimed over fifty percent of the inhabitants. This epidemic also had political consequences for Norway, which was reduced to a province of Denmark. During this period, Copenhagen was the actual capital of Norway. Oslo was also greatly affected by the Lutheran Protestant Reformation of 1537, with religious conflicts, political separation from the Catholic Church, and the foundation of a Protestant National Church. Many ruins of churches and monasteries bear witness to this process.

Oslo was completely destroyed by fire in 1624. Following intense renewal and advanced city planning in the spirit of the Renaissance, a completely new city was created and named Christiania. In 1814 Norway was united with Sweden, and Christiania experienced strong economic and political growth. In 1905 the union with Sweden was dissolved and Norway gained its independence. The original name of Oslo was reinstated in 1924.

Population

Oslo is the capital of Norway and has more than 500,000 inhabitants. Approximately 900,000 people live in the Greater Oslo area, representing twenty percent of the total population of Norway.

Commerce and Industry

The working population of Oslo distributed according to occupation includes: industry, 16%; building and construction, 6%; transport, 9%; trade, services, and tourism, 69%.

Apply font formatting such as changing the font, font size, and font color. Apply paragraph formatting such as changing alignment, indentations, and line spacing.

Traveling in Europe by Train

Now that you have planned your trip, bought your rail tickets, flown to Europe, and adjusted your body to jet lag, you are ready to start your rail experience. As you do so, remember the following things:

- Have your pass validated.
- Protect your pass.
- Arrive 20 minutes before train departure time.
- Be at the right train station.

Rail Ticket Bonuses

Your rail ticket offers you a variety of bonuses when traveling in Europe, including:

- Free or discount transportation on ferries, steamers, and buses
- Hotel discounts of up to 50% from participating hotels
- Special fare on the high-speed trains linking Paris to London
- Reduced rental rates with most major car rental companies

Some companies offer outstanding reductions on transportation. For example, you can travel on the ferry in Denmark between Århus and Kalundborg and between Nyborg and Korsør at a 75% discount! ScanTravel, a travel company located in Stockholm, offers the StarPass® ticket that provides you with incredible discounts on travel by train, ferry, and bus in Sweden, Norway, and Denmark.

International Airports with Train Connections

Country	City	Airport
Austria	Vienna (Wein)	Schwechat
Belgium	Brussels	Nationaal
France	Paris	Orly
Germany	Berlin	Schoenefeld
Great Britain	London	Heathrow
Italy	Rome	Fiumicino

Airport	Service
Schwechat	Train every 30 minutes
Nationaal	Train every 20 minutes
Orly	RER train every 20 minutes
Schoenefeld	S-Bahn train every 30 minutes
Heathrow	LT train every 10 minutes
Fiumicino	Train every 10 to 20 minutes

Apply formatting such as inserting bullets and special characters, setting text in tabbed columns, applying paragraph shading and lines, and inserting a page border. Use style sets to apply predesigned formatting such as bolding and centering text, changing fonts, and applying border lines to headings.

In Section 3 you will learn how to

Enhance Documents

Improve the formatting of a document using features to rearrange text in a document, add special elements, or change the appearance of text. Use buttons on the HOME tab to move, copy, and paste text in a document. Improve the appearance of documents by inserting page numbering, headers, and footers; changing margins and page orientation; and changing vertical alignment. Add visual appeal to documents by inserting and customizing clip art images and pictures.

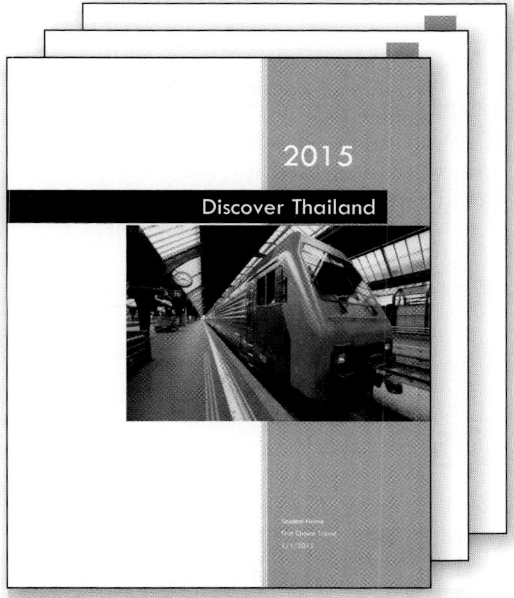

Enhance the appearance of a document by applying a theme, which is a set of formatting choices that includes a color, a font, and effects; inserting a cover page; inserting a watermark, which is a lightened image that displays behind text; and inserting a header and footer.

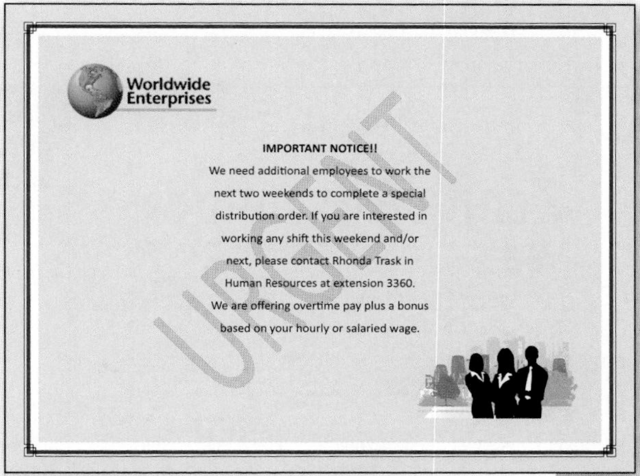

Worldwide Enterprises

IMPORTANT NOTICE!!

We need additional employees to work the next two weekends to complete a special distribution order. If you are interested in working any shift this weekend and/or next, please contact Rhonda Trask in Human Resources at extension 3360. We are offering overtime pay plus a bonus based on your hourly or salaried wage.

URGENT

Enhance the visual appeal of a document by inserting a picture such as a company logo, a clip art image related to text in the document, and a page border and background color.

First Choice Travel
4277 Yonge Street
Toronto, ON M4P 2E6

First Choice Travel
Student Name
3588 Ventura Boulevard
Los Angeles, CA 90102

Camille Matsui
Marquee Productions
955 South Alameda Street
Los Angeles, CA 90037

Create envelopes and mailing labels quickly and automatically.

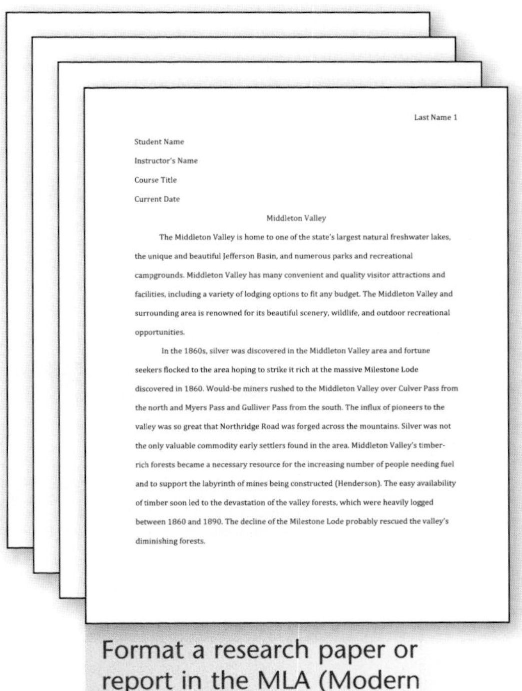

Last Name 1

Student Name

Instructor's Name

Course Title

Current Date

Middleton Valley

The Middleton Valley is home to one of the state's largest natural freshwater lakes, the unique and beautiful Jefferson Basin, and numerous parks and recreational campgrounds. Middleton Valley has many convenient and quality visitor attractions and facilities, including a variety of lodging options to fit any budget. The Middleton Valley and surrounding area is renowned for its beautiful scenery, wildlife, and outdoor recreational opportunities.

In the 1860s, silver was discovered in the Middleton Valley area and fortune seekers flocked to the area hoping to strike it rich at the massive Milestone Lode discovered in 1860. Would-be miners rushed to the Middleton Valley over Culver Pass from the north and Myers Pass and Gulliver Pass from the south. The influx of pioneers to the valley was so great that Northridge Road was forged across the mountains. Silver was not the only valuable commodity early settlers found in the area. Middleton Valley's timber-rich forests became a necessary resource for the increasing number of people needing fuel and to support the labyrinth of mines being constructed (Henderson). The easy availability of timber soon led to the devastation of the valley forests, which were heavily logged between 1860 and 1890. The decline of the Milestone Lode probably rescued the valley's diminishing forests.

Format a research paper or report in the MLA (Modern Language Association) style.

In Section 4 you will learn how to

Apply Special Features

Word contains special formatting features you can apply to a document to enhance the visual display of text. For example, add visual appeal to a document with the WordArt and drop cap features and by inserting shapes. Use the SmartArt feature to create visual representations of data such as organizational charts and graphics, and use the Tables feature to create, modify, and format data in columns and rows. Improve the ease with which others can read and understand text by setting it in columns. You can save a Word document as a web page and insert hyperlinks that will link to another document or a location on the Internet.

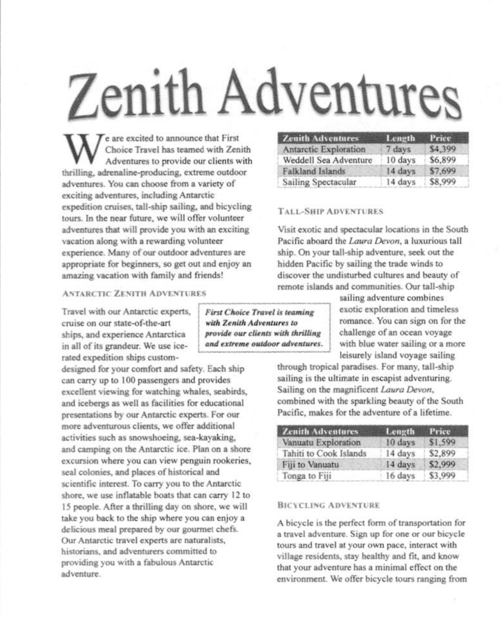

Zenith Adventures

We are excited to announce that First Choice Travel has teamed with Zenith Adventures to provide our clients with thrilling, adrenaline-producing, extreme outdoor adventures. You can choose from a variety of exciting adventures, including Antarctic expedition cruises, tall-ship sailing, and bicycling tours. In the near future, we will offer volunteer adventures that will provide you with an exciting vacation along with a rewarding volunteer experience. Many of our outdoor adventures are appropriate for beginners, so get out and enjoy an amazing vacation with family and friends!

ANTARCTIC ZENITH ADVENTURES

Travel with our Antarctic experts, cruise on our state-of-the-art ships, and experience Antarctica in all of its grandeur. We use ice-rated expedition ships custom-designed for your comfort and safety. Each ship can carry up to 100 passengers and provides excellent viewing for watching whales, seabirds, and icebergs as well as facilities for educational presentations by our Antarctic experts. For our more adventurous clients, we offer additional activities such as snowshoeing, sea-kayaking, and camping on the Antarctic ice. Plan on a shore excursion where you can view penguin rookeries, seal colonies, and places of historical and scientific interest. To carry you to the Antarctic shore, we use inflatable boats that can carry 12 to 15 people. After a thrilling day on shore, we will take you back to the ship where you can enjoy a delicious meal prepared by our gourmet chefs. Our Antarctic travel experts are naturalists, historians, and adventurers committed to providing you with a fabulous Antarctic adventure.

Zenith Adventures	Length	Price
Antarctic Exploration	7 days	$4,399
Weddell Sea Adventure	10 days	$6,899
Falkland Islands	14 days	$7,699
Sailing Spectacular	14 days	$8,999

TALL-SHIP ADVENTURES

Visit exotic and spectacular locations in the South Pacific aboard the *Laura Devon*, a luxurious tall ship. On your tall-ship adventure, seek out the hidden Pacific by sailing the trade winds to discover the undisturbed cultures and beauty of remote islands and communities. Our tall-ship sailing adventure combines exotic exploration and timeless romance. You can sign on for the challenge of an ocean voyage with blue water sailing or a more leisurely island voyage sailing through tropical paradises. For many, tall-ship sailing is the ultimate in escapist adventuring. Sailing on the magnificent *Laura Devon*, combined with the sparkling beauty of the South Pacific, makes for the adventure of a lifetime.

First Choice Travel is teaming with Zenith Adventures to provide our clients with thrilling and extreme outdoor adventures.

Zenith Adventures	Length	Price
Vanuatu Exploration	10 days	$1,599
Tahiti to Cook Islands	14 days	$2,899
Fiji to Vanuatu	14 days	$2,999
Tonga to Fiji	16 days	$3,999

BICYCLING ADVENTURE

A bicycle is the perfect form of transportation for a travel adventure. Sign up for one or our bicycle tours and travel at your own pace, interact with village residents, stay healthy and fit, and know that your adventure has a minimal effect on the environment. We offer bicycle tours ranging from

Use Word's special features to enhance a document with WordArt text, a drop cap, and a built-in text box. Improve the readability of a document by setting text in columns.

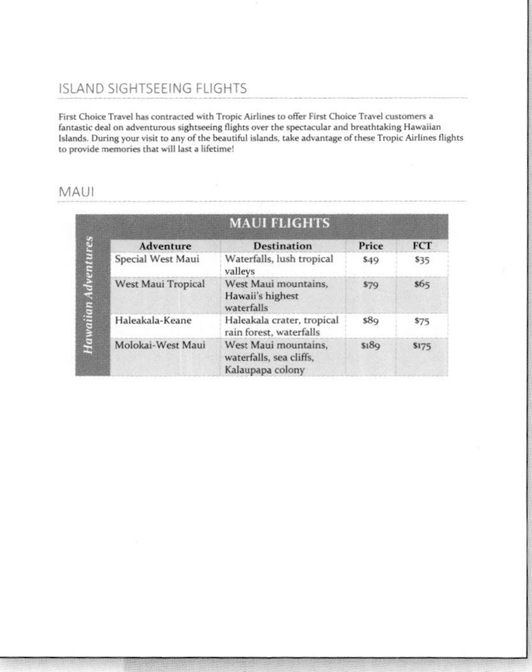

ISLAND SIGHTSEEING FLIGHTS

First Choice Travel has contracted with Tropic Airlines to offer First Choice Travel customers a fantastic deal on adventurous sightseeing flights over the spectacular and breathtaking Hawaiian Islands. During your visit to any of the beautiful islands, take advantage of these Tropic Airlines flights to provide memories that will last a lifetime!

MAUI

Hawaiian Adventures	MAUI FLIGHTS			
	Adventure	Destination	Price	FCT
	Special West Maui	Waterfalls, lush tropical valleys	$49	$35
	West Maui Tropical	West Maui mountains, Hawaii's highest waterfalls	$79	$65
	Haleakala-Keane	Haleakala crater, tropical rain forest, waterfalls	$89	$75
	Molokai-West Maui	West Maui mountains, waterfalls, sea cliffs, Kalaupapa colony	$189	$175

Insert columnar data in a table.

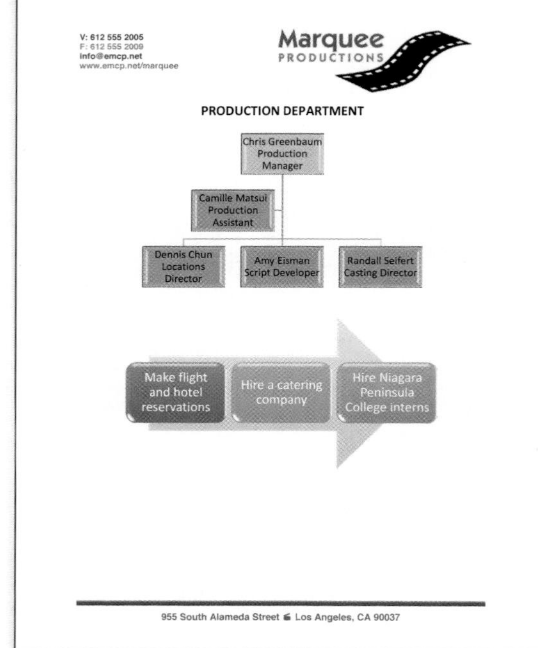

V: 612 555 2005
F: 612 555 2009
info@emcp.net
www.emcp.net/marquee

PRODUCTION DEPARTMENT

955 South Alameda Street ◆ Los Angeles, CA 90037

Use Word's SmartArt feature to illustrate hierarchical data in an organizational chart or create a graphic to show data processes, cycles, or relationships or present data in a matrix or pyramid.

Word SECTION 1

Creating and Editing a Document

Skills

- Complete the word processing cycle
- Move the insertion point
- Insert and delete text
- Scroll in a document
- Select, replace, and delete text
- Use Undo and Redo
- Check the spelling and grammar in a document
- Use AutoCorrect
- Use Thesaurus
- Change document views
- Find specific text
- Find and replace text
- Use the Help feature
- Print a document
- Close a document
- Create a document using a template
- Create and rename a folder
- Save a document in a different format

Student Resources

Before beginning the activities in Word, copy to your storage medium the Word folder on the Student Resources CD. This folder contains the data files you need to complete the projects in each Word section.

Projects Overview

Prepare a document describing a special vacation package and edit and format two documents describing various vacation specials offered by First Choice Travel.

Prepare a letter to First Choice Travel regarding a movie site using a letter template and another to the manager of The Waterfront Bistro requesting catering information.

Customize a sample employee incentive agreement and prepare a fax cover page for the agreement.

Edit a letter to Marquee Productions regarding costuming for a film.

Write a letter to Josh Hart at Marquee Productions explaining the catering services offered by The Waterfront Bistro and then prepare a fax sheet for the letter.

Model Answers for Projects

These model answers for the projects you complete in Section 1 provide a preview of the finished projects before you begin working and also allow you to compare your own results with these models to ensure you have created the materials accurately.

WS1-FCTTravelPkg.docx is the project in Activity 1.1.

First Choice Travel
Los Angeles Office
Travel Package

Are you spontaneous and enjoy doing something on a moment's notice? If this describes you, then you will be interested in the First Choice Travel Moment's Notice Travel Package. For the low price of $599 you can fly from New York to London for a four-day stay. The catch to this incredible deal is that you must make your reservation within the week and complete your London stay within thirty days.

WS1-FCTVacSpecials.docx (a three-page document) is the project in Activities 1.2 to 1.8.

VACATION SPECIALS

Ocean Vista Cruise Lines

Sign up today for an eight-day, seven-night cruise of the Alaska Inside Passage on the beautiful new Pacific Sky cruise ship. This inaugural trip begins May 9 in Seattle, Washington, and ends back in Seattle on May 16.

The Pacific Sky cruises through the Inside Passage and pays visits to the Alaskan ports of Skagway, Haines, and Juneau. The Pacific Sky also stops in the beautiful port city of Vancouver, British Columbia.

On this exciting cruise, you will

- View some of the world's most majestic scenery
- Visit colorful Gold Rush towns
- Observe fascinating wildlife
- Experience a dazzling display by the Northern Lights
- Listen to the "singing of the ice"
- Walk on a glacier
- Hike through a forest of hemlocks
- Helicopter or seaplane down "rivers of ice"
- Canoe through a wildlife preserve while eagles soar overhead

Space are limited on this inaugural voyage of the Pacific Sky, so make your reservations today! You can make reservations through April 15, 2015, and secure the reservation with a deposit of $250 per person. Deposits are refundable until the final payment date of May 1, 2015. Cruise rates, including port charges and government fees, begin as low as $950 per person based on a double-occupancy cabin. Choose the category below that best fits your cruising style:

Category H — $975 USD
Inside stateroom
Two lower beds

Category D — $1,275 USD
Deluxe ocean view stateroom
Spacious outside stateroom with window
Sitting area and two lower beds

Category B — $1,315 USD
Superior deluxe ocean view stateroom
Spacious outside stateroom with window
Sitting area and two lower beds

Category S — $1,510 USD
Superior deluxe suite
Large ocean view suite with private balcony
Sitting area and two lower beds

explore these exciting and spectacular islands. Sign up for the Bahamas Sightseeing Tour and experience the lively city of Nassau, which offers everything from parasailing to casino gaming. Call us to discover how you can join the Bahamas Sightseeing Tour at an incredibly low price.

Category P $2,750 USD
Three-room Presidential suite
Large ocean view with two private balconies
Sitting area and two bedrooms

Getaway Weekends

You could spend the weekend grocery shopping or cleaning closets or you could take off on a romantic three-day adventure—without breaking the bank! On a moment's notice you can be taking in the sights and sounds of London or skiing down the slopes of a ski resort in beautiful Utah.

From February through April, we are offering a three-night vacation package to London beginning as low as $449 per person. This fantastic price includes airfare from New York to London and hotel lodging for three nights. For a small fee, you can rent a car and spend time visiting sights in and around London.

Scenic Park City Mountain Resort, host to many of the 2002 Winter Olympic games, is a mere half-hour drive from Utah's Salt Lake City International Airport. First Choice Travel is offering a three-day ski vacation package for prices beginning as low as $327. The three-day vacation package includes airfare, lodging, transfer, and a two-day ski lift pass.

First Choice Planner

First Choice Travel presents the 2015 First Choice Planner—your personal guide to over 50 special offers from our First Choice partners. Hang on to your copy and use it whenever you travel this summer and fall. You can save money and multiply the First Choice points you earn. The more you travel this year, the faster you can accumulate First Choice points and enjoy extra travel benefits throughout the year.

Specials offered by First Choice Travel include all the reference codes you will need when you make your arrangements with a First Choice Travel representative. First Choice partners include airlines, car rental companies, hotels, and cruise lines.

As you think about your travel needs for this year, consider the following specials:

- Earn 1,000 First Choice points when you book round-trip airfare with First Choice Travel.
- Earn 500 First Choice points when you rent a car for two or more consecutive days through First Choice Travel.
- Earn 5,000 First Choice points when you book a cruise through First Choice Travel.
- Earn 100 First Choice points for each day you stay in a First Choice Travel partner hotel.
- Earn 50 First Choice points for each sightseeing excursion you book with First Choice Travel.

Bahamas Sightseeing Tour

The Bahamas consist of over 700 islands and cays, all with friendly people, beautiful beaches, and magnificent dive spots. First Choice Travel offers the best Bahamas Sightseeing Tour to

WS1-MPLtrtoFCT.docx is the project in Activity 1.9.

7/20/2015

Student Name
Marquee Productions
955 South Alameda Street
Los Angeles, CA 90037

Ms. Melissa Gehring
First Choice Travel
3588 Ventura Boulevard
Los Angeles, CA 90102

Dear Ms. Gehring:

Marquee Productions will be filming a movie in and around the Toronto area from July 5 through August 27, 2015. I would like scheduling and pricing information for flights from Los Angeles to Toronto, as well as information on lodging.

Approximately 45 people from our company will need flight reservations and hotel rooms. Please locate the best group rates and let me know the approximate costs. I would like to finalize preparations by the end of the month.

Sincerely,

Student Name
Projects Coordinator
Marquee Productions

Activity 1.1

Completing the Word Processing Cycle

The process of creating a document in Microsoft Word generally follows a word processing cycle. The steps in the cycle vary but typically include: opening Word; creating and editing the document; saving, printing, and closing the document; and then closing Word.

Project

As an employee of First Choice Travel, you have been asked to create a short document containing information on a travel package offered by First Choice Travel.

Tutorial 1.1
Creating, Saving, and Printing a Word Document

1. At the Windows 8 Start screen, click the Word 2013 tile.

   Depending on your system configuration, these steps may vary.

2. At the Word 2013 opening screen, click the *Blank document* template.

3. At the blank Word document, identify the various features by comparing your screen with the one shown in Figure 1.1.

   Refer to Table 1.1 for a description of the screen features.

4. Type **First Choice Travel** as shown in Figure 1.2 and then hold down the Shift key, press the Enter key, and then release the Shift key.

   Shift + Enter is the New Line command. Use this command to keep lines of text within the same paragraph, which creates less space between one line and the next.

5. Type **Los Angeles Office** and then press Shift + Enter.

FIGURE 1.1 Word Document Screen

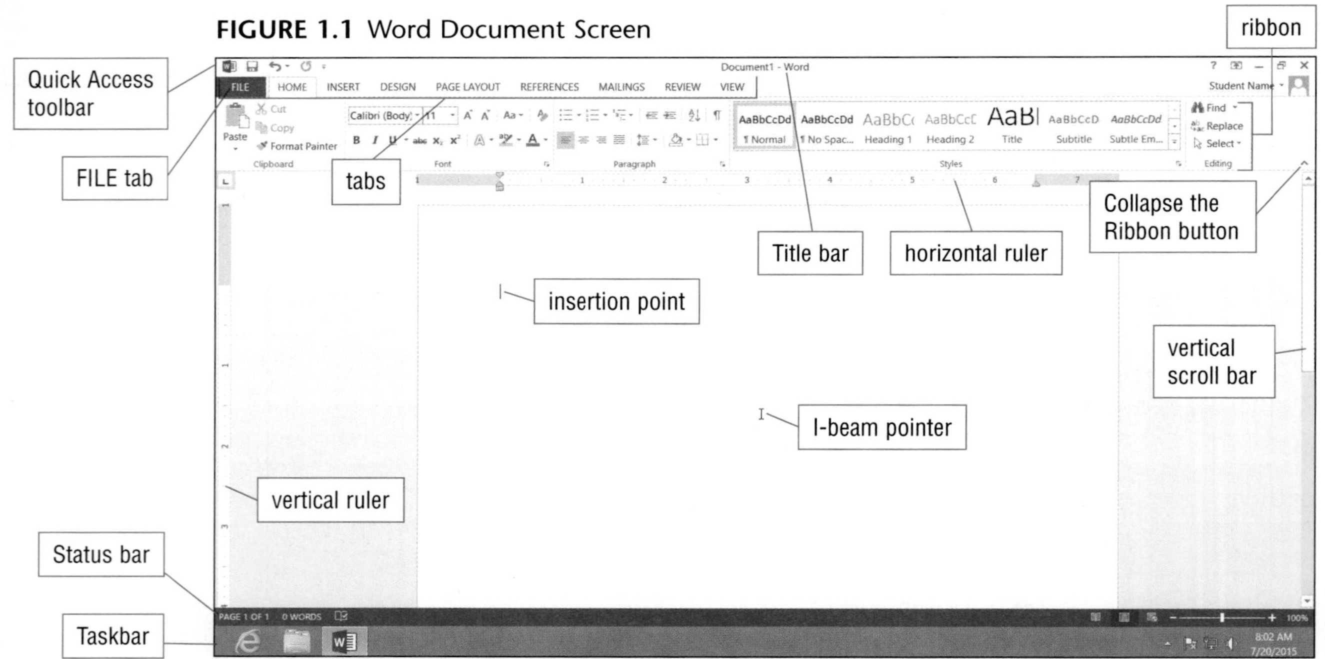

TABLE 1.1 Screen Features and Descriptions

Feature	Description
Collapse the Ribbon button	when clicked, removes the ribbon from the screen
FILE tab	when clicked, displays backstage area that contains options for working with and managing documents
horizontal ruler	used to set margins, indents, and tabs
I-beam pointer	used to move the insertion point or to select text
insertion point	indicates location of next character entered at the keyboard
Quick Access toolbar	contains buttons for commonly used commands
ribbon	area containing the tabs with options and buttons divided into groups
Status bar	displays number of pages and words, view buttons, and Zoom slider bar
tabs	contain commands and buttons organized into groups
Taskbar	divided into three sections—the Start button, the task buttons area, and the notification area
Title bar	displays document name followed by program name
vertical ruler	used to set top and bottom margins
vertical scroll bar	used to view various parts of the document beyond the screen

6 Type **Travel Package** and then press Enter.

Pressing the Enter key begins a new paragraph in the document.

7 Type the remainder of the text shown in Figure 1.2.

Type the text as shown. When you type *adn* and then press the spacebar, the AutoCorrect feature will automatically correct it to *and*. When you type *teh* and then press the spacebar, AutoCorrect corrects it to *the*. Do not press the Enter key to end a line of text within a paragraph. Word will automatically wrap text to the next line.

FIGURE 1.2 Steps 4–7

First Choice Travel
Los Angeles Office
Travel Package

Are you spontaneous adn enjoy doing something on a moment's notice? If this describes you, then you will be interested in the First Choice Travel Moment's Notice Travel Package. For teh low price of $599 you can fly from New York to London for a four-day stay. The catch to this incredible deal is that you must make your reservation within the next week and complete your London stay within thiry days.

continues

8 Save the document by clicking the Save button on the Quick Access toolbar.

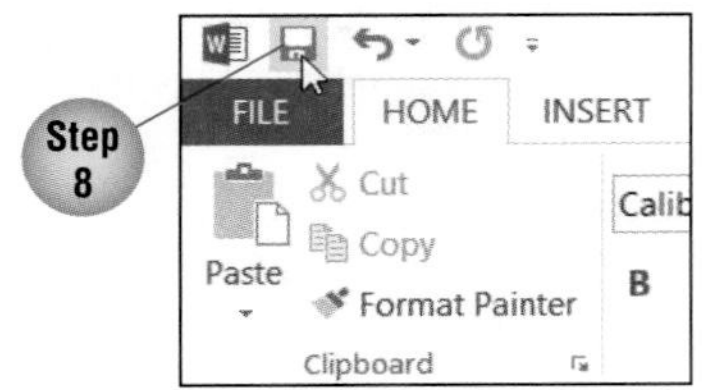

9 At the Save As backstage area, click the desired location in the middle panel of the backstage area (the panel containing the four location options). For example, click the *SkyDrive* option preceded by your name if you are saving to your SkyDrive or click the *Computer* option if you are saving to a USB flash drive.

10 Click the Browse button.

11 At the Save As dialog box, double-click the *WordS1* folder.

Press the F12 function key to display the Save As dialog box without displaying the Save As backstage area.

12 Click in the *File name* text box, type **WS1-FCTTravelPkg**, and then press Enter (or click the Save button).

Word automatically adds the file extension *.docx* to the end of a document name. The Address bar at the Save As dialog box displays the active folder. If you need to make the WordS1 folder active, click the drive in the Navigation pane that contains your storage medium and then double-click the *WordS1* folder in the Content pane.

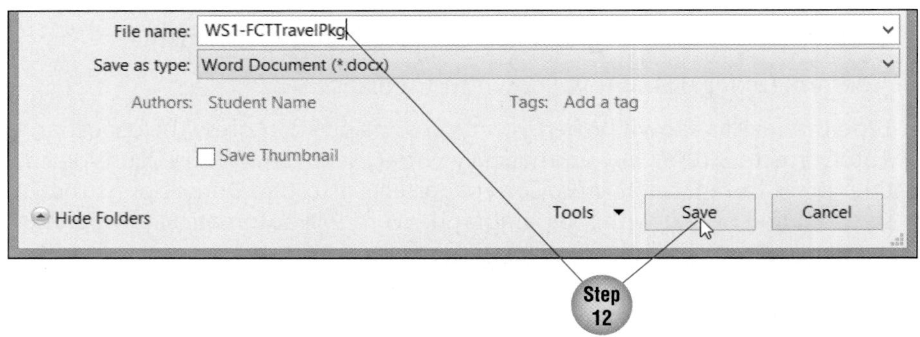

13 Print the document by clicking the FILE tab, clicking the *Print* option, and then clicking the Print button at the backstage area.

The FILE tab is located in the upper left corner of the screen at the left side of the HOME tab. When you click the FILE tab, the backstage area displays with options for working with and managing documents. Refer to Table 1.2 for descriptions of the options and information you will find in each option's backstage area.

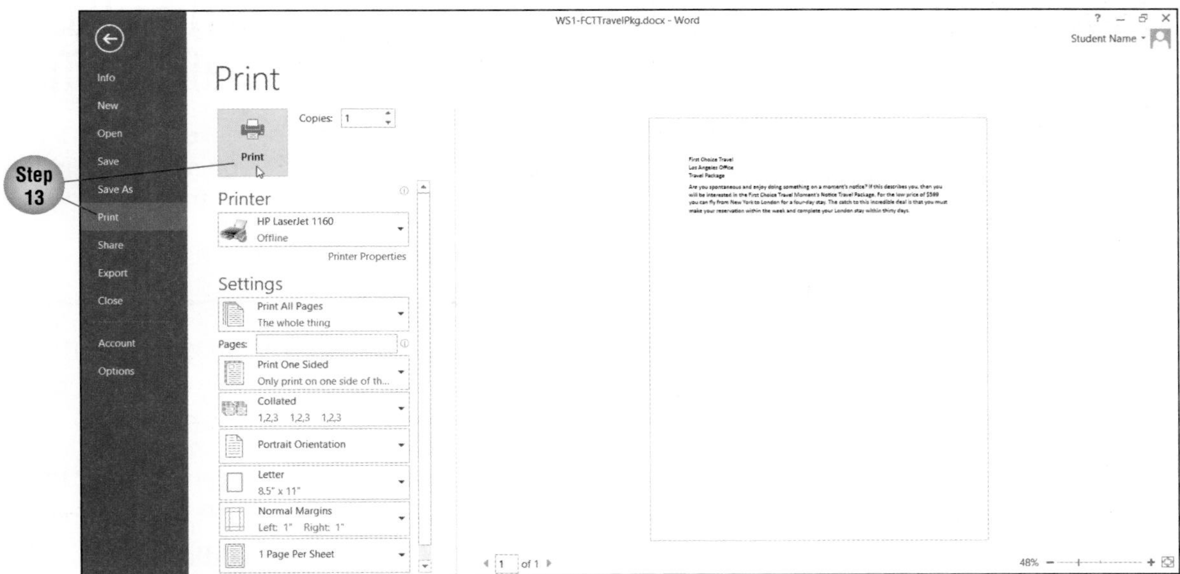

14 Close the document by clicking the FILE tab and then clicking the *Close* option.

TABLE 1.2 Backstage Area Options

Option	Information
Info	permissions, possible issues with sharing the document, document versions, properties (for example, number of pages, number of words), date created, date last modified, date last printed, author
New	available templates such as Blank document as well as templates from Office.com
Open	options for opening documents; list of recently opened documents
Save	saves previously saved document or displays Save As backstage area with options for saving a document, current folder, and recent folders
Save As	options for saving a document, current folder, and recent folders
Print	number of copies, printer, settings (for example, one-sided pages, letter size, normal margins, one page per sheet)
Share	share document with specific people; share document using email, present document online, and share as a blog post
Export	export document as PDF or XPS document; change file type
Close	close currently open document
Account	user information, connected services, product information
Options	Word Options dialog box with options for customizing Word

In Addition

Default Document Formatting

A Word document is based on a template that applies default formatting. Default formatting refers to formatting automatically applied by Word. Some of the default formats include 11-point Calibri as the font, line spacing of 1.08, and 8 points of spacing after each paragraph (added when you press the Enter key). You will learn more about fonts and paragraph spacing in Section 2.

Correcting Errors

Word contains a spelling feature that inserts wavy red lines below words it cannot find in the Spelling dictionary. You can edit these words or leave them as written. The wavy red lines do not print.

Activity 1.2

Moving the Insertion Point; Inserting and Deleting Text

After you create a document, you will often want to make changes to it. These changes may include adding text, called ***inserting***, or removing text, called ***deleting***. To insert text, position the insertion point in the desired location and then type the text. Delete text in a document by positioning the insertion point in the desired location and then pressing the Backspace key or the Delete key.

Project

First Choice Travel marketing staff members have reviewed your document on vacation specials and have recommended a few changes. You need to create a revised version.

Tutorial 1.2A
Opening a Document

Tutorial 1.2B
Pinning Documents and Folders to the Recent Lists

1. At the blank Word screen, click the FILE tab.

   This displays the Open backstage area. If you have a document open and click the FILE tab, you will need to click the *Open* option to display the Open backstage area.

2. At the Open backstage area, click the desired location in the middle panel.

   For example, click the *SkyDrive* option preceded by your name if you are opening a document from your SkyDrive or click the *Computer* option if you are opening a document from your USB flash drive.

3. Click the Browse button.

4. At the Open dialog box, double-click the *WordS1* folder.

   Press Ctrl + F12 to display the Open dialog box without displaying the Open backstage area.

5. Double-click ***FCTVacSpecials.docx*** in the Open dialog box list box.

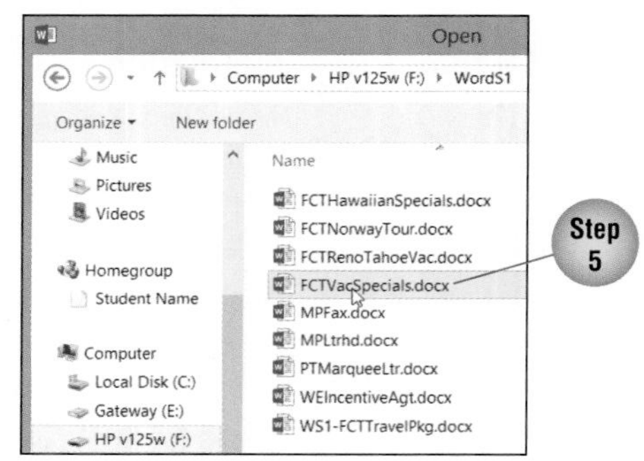

6. At the document, click the FILE tab and then click the *Save As* option.

7. At the Save As backstage area, click the *WordS1* folder name that displays below the Current Folder heading in the *Computer* section.

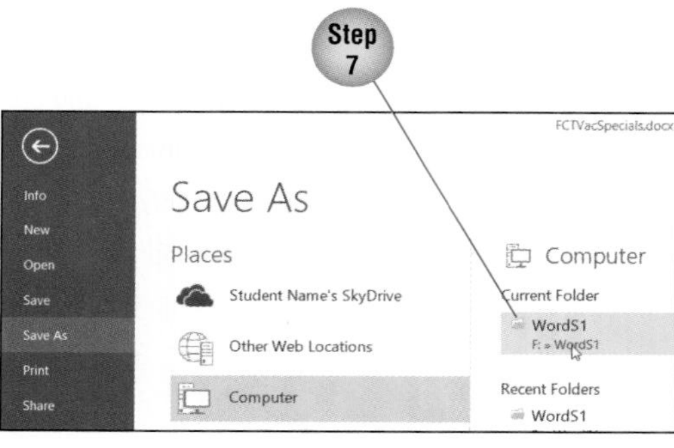

8. At the Save As dialog box, press the Home key to move the insertion point to the beginning of the file name, type **WS1-** in the *File name* text box, and then press the Enter key. (The document name in the *File name* text box should display as **WS1-FCTVacSpecials.docx**.)

   Pressing the Home key saves you from having to type the entire document name. If you open an existing document, make changes to it, and then want to save it with the same name, click the Save button on the Quick Access toolbar. If you want to keep the original document and save the edited document with a new name, click the FILE tab and then click the *Save As* option.

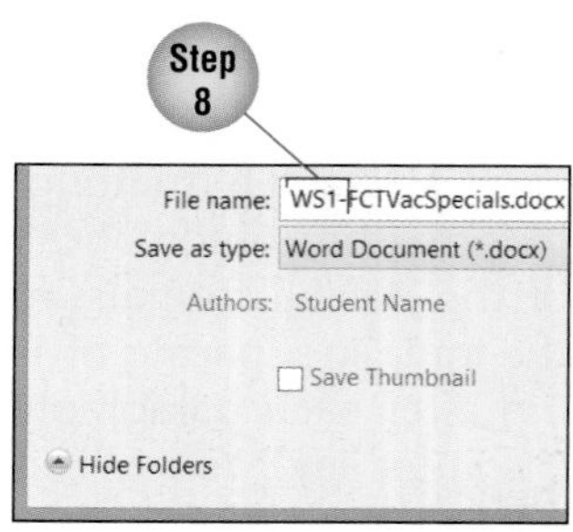

9 Position the mouse pointer at the beginning of the second paragraph and then click the left mouse button.

This moves the insertion point to the location of the mouse pointer.

10 Press the Up, Down, Left, and Right arrow keys located to the right of the regular keys on the keyboard.

Use the information shown in Table 1.3 to practice moving the insertion point in the document.

11 Press Ctrl + Home to move the insertion point to the beginning of the document.

12 Click at the beginning of the paragraph that begins *Sign up today for* and then type **Ocean Vista Cruise Lines announces the inaugural voyage of the Pacific Sky ocean liner.** Press the spacebar once after typing the period.

By default (automatically determined by Word), text you type in a document is inserted in the document and existing text is moved to the right.

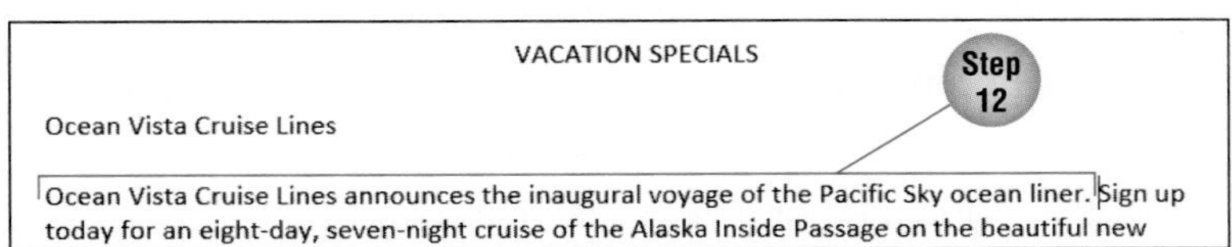

13 Press Ctrl + End to move the insertion point to the end of the document and then click anywhere in the last sentence in the document (the sentence that begins *Let First Choice Travel take*).

14 Press the Backspace key until the insertion point is positioned at the left margin and then press the Delete key until you have deleted the remainder of the sentence.

Pressing the Backspace key deletes any characters to the left of the insertion point. Press the Delete key to delete any characters to the right of the insertion point.

15 Click the Save button on the Quick Access toolbar.

Clicking the Save button saves the document with the same name (**WS1-FCTVacSpecials.docx**).

TABLE 1.3 Insertion Point Keyboard Commands

Press	To move insertion point
End	to end of line
Home	to beginning of line
Page Up	up one screen
Page Down	down one screen
Ctrl + Home	to beginning of document
Ctrl + End	to end of document

In Brief

Open Document

1. Click FILE tab.
2. At Open backstage area, click desired location.
3. Click Browse button.
4. At Open dialog box, navigate to desired folder.
5. Double-click document name.

Save Document

1. Click Save button on Quick Access toolbar.
2. At Save As backstage area, click desired location.
3. Click Browse button.
4. At Save As dialog box, navigate to desired folder.
5. Type document name.
6. Click Save or press Enter.

In Addition

Adding Buttons to the Quick Access Toolbar

You can add to the Quick Access toolbar buttons that represent commonly used features. For example, you might want to add the Open button to save steps when opening a document or the Quick Print button to save steps when printing a document. To add a button to the Quick Access toolbar, click the Customize Quick Access Toolbar button that displays at the right side of the toolbar and then click the desired button name at the drop-down list.

Activity 1.3

Scrolling; Selecting, Replacing, and Deleting Text; Using Undo and Redo

In addition to moving the insertion point to a specific location, you can use the mouse to move the display of text in the document screen. Use the mouse with the vertical scroll bar to scroll through text in a document. The vertical scroll bar displays toward the right side of the screen. Scrolling in a document changes the text displayed but does not move the insertion point. Previously, you learned to delete text by pressing the Backspace key or Delete key. You can also select text and then delete it, replace it with other text, or apply formatting to the selected text. If you make a change to text, such as deleting selected text, and then change your mind, use the Undo and/or Redo buttons on the Quick Access toolbar.

Project

The assistant manager, Jordan Keyes, has reviewed the document and asked you to make a few changes.

SNAP

Tutorial 1.3
Editing a Document

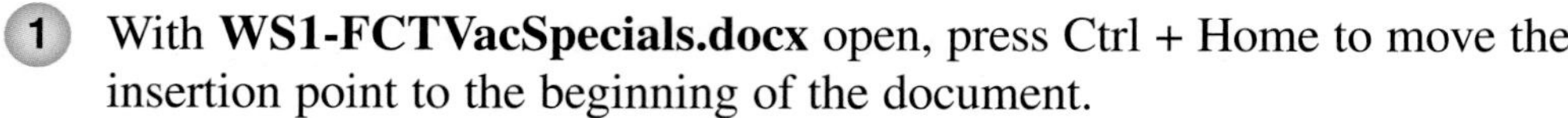

1. With **WS1-FCTVacSpecials.docx** open, press Ctrl + Home to move the insertion point to the beginning of the document.

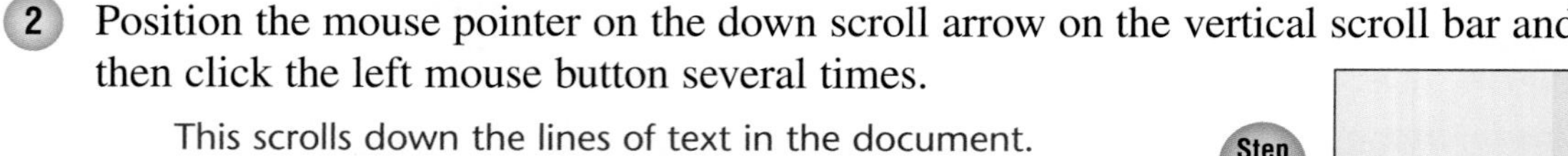

2. Position the mouse pointer on the down scroll arrow on the vertical scroll bar and then click the left mouse button several times.

   This scrolls down the lines of text in the document. Scrolling changes the display of text but does not move the insertion point.

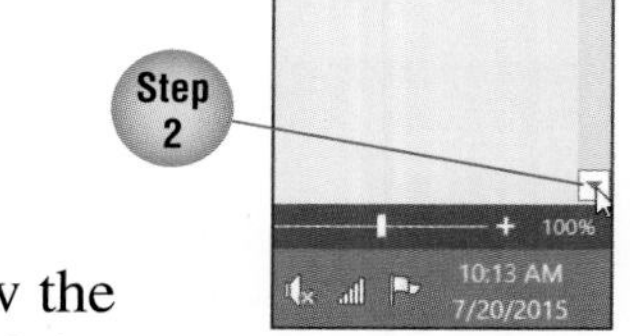

3. Position the mouse pointer on the vertical scroll bar below the scroll box and then click the left mouse button a couple of times.

   The scroll box on the vertical scroll bar indicates the location of the text in the document screen in relation to the remainder of the document. Clicking below the scroll box on the vertical scroll bar scrolls down one screen of text at a time.

4. Position the mouse pointer on the scroll box on the vertical scroll bar, hold down the left mouse button, drag the scroll box to the top of the vertical scroll bar, and then release the mouse button.

5. Position the mouse pointer on the word *Behold* (located immediately after the first bullet) and then double-click the left mouse button.

   Selected text displays with a gray background. You can also drag through text with the mouse to select the text. When you select text, a Mini toolbar displays. You will learn more about the Mini toolbar in Activity 2.1.

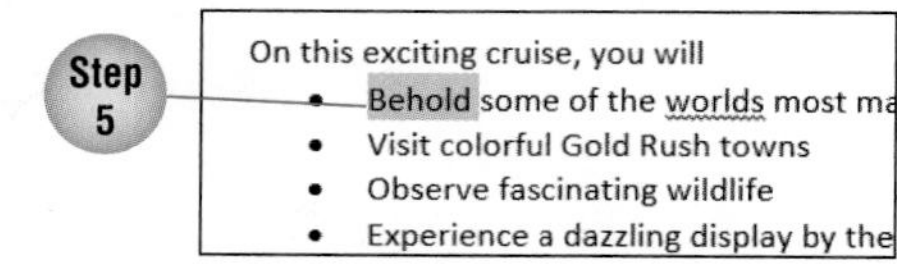

6. Type **View**.

   When you type *View*, it takes the place of *Behold*.

7. Move the insertion point to the beginning of the word *Glacier* (located in the second paragraph) and then press the F8 function key on the keyboard. Press the Right Arrow key until the words *Glacier Bay and* are selected.

   Pressing the F8 function key turns on Extend mode. Use the insertion point movement keys to select text in Extend mode.

Step 7

The Pacific Skye cruises through Glacier Bay and the I
ports of Skagway, Haines, and Juneau. The Pacific Sky
Vancouver, British Columbia.

8. Press the Delete key.

9 Hold down the Ctrl key, click on any character in the first sentence (begins with *Ocean Vista Cruise Lines announces*), and then release the Ctrl key.

Holding down the Ctrl key while clicking the mouse button selects the entire sentence.

10 Press the Delete key to delete the selected sentence.

11 Click the Undo button on the Quick Access toolbar.

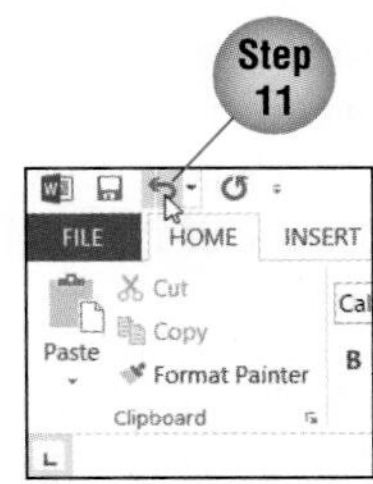

When you click the Undo button, the deleted sentence reappears. Clicking the Undo button reverses the last command or deletes the last entry you typed. Click the down-pointing arrow at the right side of the Undo button and a drop-down list displays the changes made to the document since it was opened. Click an action and the action, along with any actions listed above it in the drop-down list, is undone.

12 Click the Redo button on the Quick Access toolbar.

Clicking the Redo button deletes the selected sentence. If you click the Undo button and then decide you do not want to reverse the original action, click the Redo button.

13 Position the mouse pointer between the left edge of the page and the first line of text in the second paragraph until the pointer turns into an arrow pointing up and to the right (instead of the left) and then click the left mouse button.

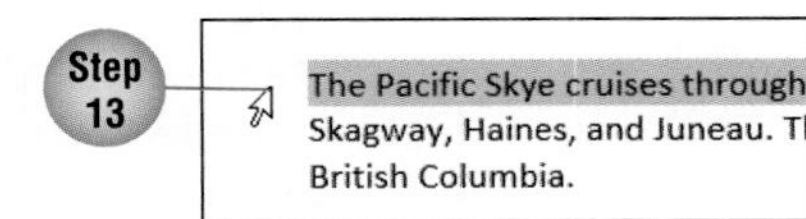

The space between the left edge of the page and the text is referred to as the **selection bar**. Use the selection bar to select specific amounts of text. Refer to Table 1.4 for more information on selecting text.

14 Deselect the text by clicking in the document.

Deselecting cancels the selection of text.

15 Save the document by clicking the Save button on the Quick Access toolbar.

TABLE 1.4 Selecting with the Mouse

To select	Complete these steps using the mouse
a word	Double-click the word.
a line of text	Click in the selection bar to the left of the line.
multiple lines of text	Drag in the selection bar to the left of the lines.
a sentence	Hold down the Ctrl key and then click anywhere in the sentence.
a paragraph	Double-click in the selection bar next to the paragraph or triple-click anywhere in the paragraph.
multiple paragraphs	Drag in the selection bar.
an entire document	Triple-click in the selection bar.

In Addition

Resuming Reading or Editing a Document

When you work in a multiple-page document and then close the document, Word remembers the page where the insertion point was last positioned. When you reopen the document, Word displays a Welcome Back message at the right side of the screen near the vertical scroll bar. The message tells you that you can pick up where you left off and identifies the page where your insertion point was last located. Click the message and the insertion point is positioned at the top of that page.

Activity 1.4

Checking the Spelling and Grammar in a Document

Use Word's spelling checker to find and correct misspelled words and find duplicated words (such as *and and*). The spelling checker compares words in your document with words in its dictionary. If a match is found, the word is passed over. If no match is found for the word, the spelling checker stops, selects the word, and offers replacements. The grammar checker will search a document for errors in grammar, punctuation, and word usage. The spelling checker and the grammar checker can help you create a well-written document but do not replace the need for proofreading.

Project

Continuing with the editing process, you are ready to check the spelling and grammar in the First Choice Travel vacation specials document.

Tutorial 1.4A
Checking the Spelling and Grammar in a Document

Tutorial 1.4B
Customizing Spelling and Grammar Checking

1. With **WS1-FCTVacSpecials.docx** open, press Ctrl + Home to move the insertion point to the beginning of the document.

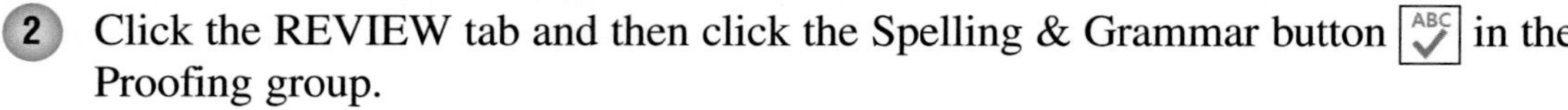

2. Click the REVIEW tab and then click the Spelling & Grammar button in the Proofing group.

   When you click the Spelling & Grammar button, Word selects the first misspelled word or grammar error and displays the Spelling task pane at the right side of the screen with options for correcting the error, ignoring the error, or adding the word to the spelling dictionary. It also contains a brief definition of the selected word in the list box.

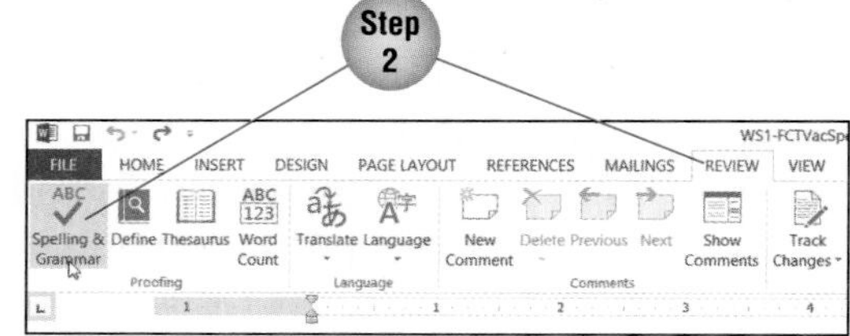

3. When the word *inagural* is selected in the document and *inaugural* is selected in the list box in the Spelling task pane, click the Change button in the pane.

   Refer to Table 1.5 for an explanation of the buttons in the Spelling task pane and Grammar task pane.

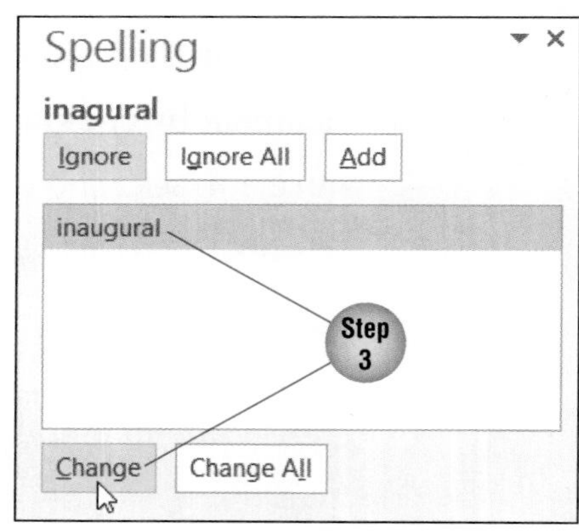

4. When the word *worlds* is selected in the document and *world's* is selected in the list box in the Grammar task pane, click the Change button in the pane.

5. When the word *Your* is selected in the document and *You* is selected in the list box in the Grammar task pane, click the Change button.

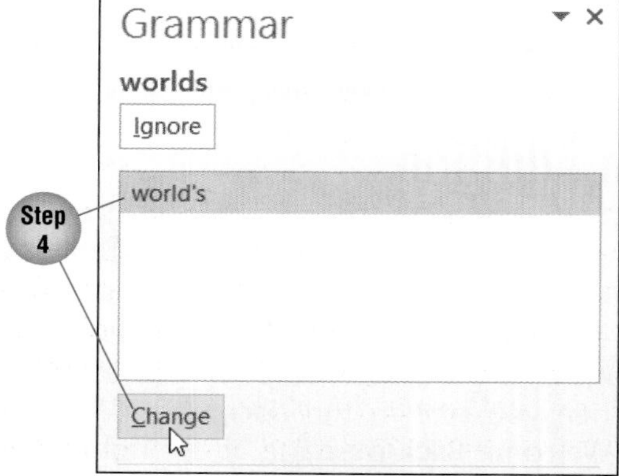

6. When the word *the* is selected (this word occurs twice), click the Delete button in the Spelling task pane.

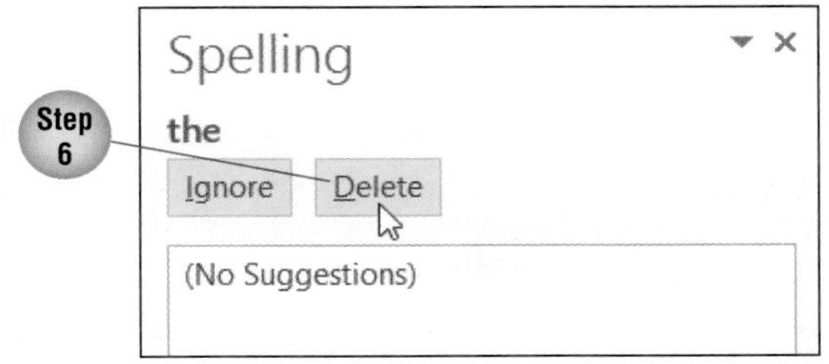

7. When the word *of* is selected in the document and *off* is selected in the list box in the Grammar task pane, click the Change button.

8. When the word *utah* is selected in the document and *Utah* is selected in the list box in the Spelling task pane, click the Change button in the Spelling task pane.

9. Click OK at the message box telling you the spelling and grammar check is complete.

10. Click the Save button on the Quick Access toolbar to save the changes made to the document.

In Brief

Check Spelling and Grammar

1. Click REVIEW tab.
2. Click Spelling & Grammar button in Proofing group.
3. Ignore or change as needed.
4. Click OK.

TABLE 1.5 Spelling and Grammar Task Pane Buttons

Button	Function
Ignore	during spell checking, skips that occurrence of the word; in grammar checking, leaves currently selected text as written
Ignore All	during spell checking, skips that occurrence and all other occurrences of the word in the document
Add	adds selected word to the main spelling check dictionary
Delete	deletes the currently selected word(s)
Change	replaces selected word in sentence with selected word in list box
Change All	replaces selected word in sentence with selected word in list box and all other occurrences of the word

In Addition

Changing Spelling Options

Control spelling and grammar checking options at the Word Options dialog box with the *Proofing* option selected. Display this dialog box by clicking the FILE tab and then clicking *Options*. At the Word Options dialog box, click *Proofing* in the left panel in the dialog box. With options in the dialog box, you can tell the spelling checker to ignore certain types of text, create custom dictionaries, show readability statistics, and hide spelling and/or grammar errors in the document.

Editing While Checking Spelling and Grammar

When checking a document, you can temporarily leave the Spelling task pane or Grammar task pane by clicking in the document. To resume the spelling and grammar check, click the Resume button in the Spelling task pane or Grammar task pane.

Activity 1.5

Using AutoCorrect and Thesaurus

The AutoCorrect feature automatically detects and corrects some typographical errors, misspelled words, and incorrect capitalization. In addition to correcting errors, you can use the AutoCorrect feature to insert frequently used text. Use the Thesaurus to find synonyms, antonyms, and related words for a particular word.

Project

You need to insert additional text in the First Choice Travel vacation specials document. To speed up the process, you will add an entry to AutoCorrect. You will also use the Thesaurus to find synonyms for specific words in the document.

Tutorial 1.5A
Using the AutoCorrect Feature

Tutorial 1.5B
Using the Thesaurus

1. With **WS1-FCTVacSpecials.docx** open, click the FILE tab and then click *Options*.

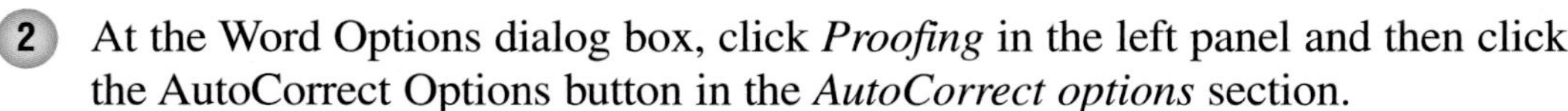

2. At the Word Options dialog box, click *Proofing* in the left panel and then click the AutoCorrect Options button in the *AutoCorrect options* section.
3. At the AutoCorrect dialog box, type **bst** in the *Replace* text box and then press the Tab key.
4. Type **Bahamas Sightseeing Tour** in the *With* text box and then click the Add button.
5. Click OK to close the AutoCorrect dialog box.
6. Click OK to close the Word Options dialog box.
7. Press Ctrl + End to move the insertion point to the end of the document, make sure the insertion point is positioned a double space below the last bulleted item, and then type the text shown in Figure 1.3. (Type the text exactly as shown. AutoCorrect will correct *bst* to *Bahamas Sightseeing Tour* when you press the Enter key or the spacebar.)

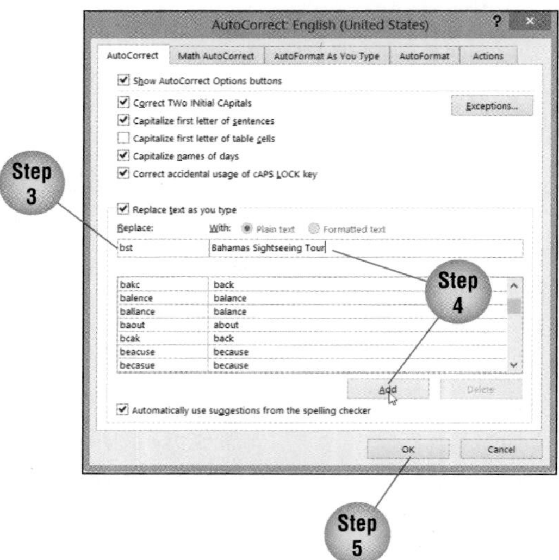

FIGURE 1.3 Step 7

> bst
>
> The Bahamas consist of over 700 islands and cays, all with friendly people, beautiful beaches, and magnificent dive spots. First Choice Travel offers the bst to explore these exciting and breathtaking islands. Sign up for the bst and experience the bustling city of Nassau, which offers everything from parasailing to casino gaming. Call us to discover how you can join the bst at an incredibly low price.

8. Click anywhere in the word *breathtaking* (located in the second sentence in the paragraph you just typed), click the REVIEW tab, and then click the Thesaurus button in the Proofing group.

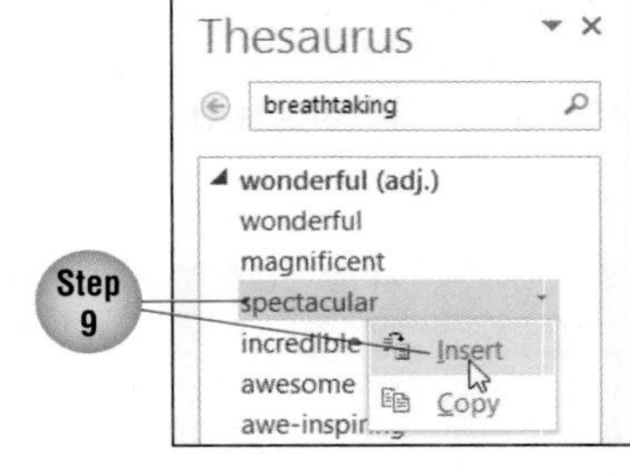

9. At the Thesaurus task pane, right-click the word *spectacular* in the task pane list box and then click *Insert* at the drop-down list.

10. Close the Thesaurus task pane by clicking the Close button located in the upper right corner of the task pane.

11. Position the mouse pointer on the word *bustling* (located in the third sentence in the paragraph you just typed) and then click the right mouse button. At the shortcut menu that displays, point to *Synonyms* and then click *lively* at the side menu.

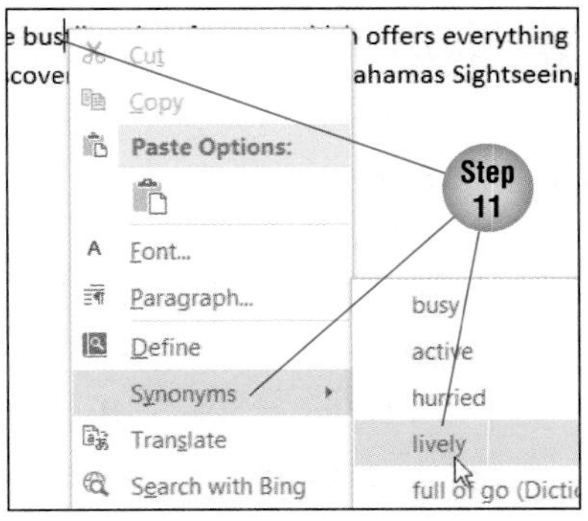

12. Click the Save button to save the document with the same name.

13. Click the FILE tab and then click *Options*. At the Word Options dialog box, click *Proofing* in the left panel and then click the AutoCorrect Options button.

14. At the AutoCorrect dialog box, type **bst** in the *Replace* text box.

    This selects *bst* and *Bahamas Sightseeing Tour* in the list box.

15. Click the Delete button and then click OK to close the dialog box.

16. Click OK to close the Word Options dialog box.

Step 14

Step 15

In Brief

Add AutoCorrect Entry

1. Click FILE tab.
2. Click *Options*.
3. Click *Proofing*.
4. Click AutoCorrect Options button.
5. Type text in *Replace* text box.
6. Type text in *With* text box.
7. Click Add button.
8. Click OK.
9. Click OK.

Use Thesaurus

1. Click in desired word.
2. Click REVIEW tab.
3. Click Thesaurus button.
4. Right-click desired word.
5. Click *Insert*.

In Addition

Using the Thesaurus Task Pane

Depending on the word you are looking up, the words in the Thesaurus task pane list box may display followed by *(n.)* for *noun*, *(v.)* for *verb*, *(adj.)* for *adjective*, or *(adv.)* for *adverb*. Click a word in the list box and a definition of the word displays below the list box. (You may need to install a dictionary before you will see a definition. To install a dictionary, click the Get a dictionary hyperlink. At the Dictionaries pane, click the desired dictionary and then click the Download button.)

Activity 1.6

Changing Document Views

By default, a document generally displays in Print Layout view. You can change this default to Read Mode, Web Layout, Outline, or Draft. You can also change the zoom percentage for viewing a document. In Print Layout view, you can show and/or hide white space at the top and bottom of each page. With the Zoom button on the VIEW tab and the Zoom slider bar on the Status bar, you can change the percentage of display. Use the Navigation pane to browse in a document, search for specific text or items in the document, and re-arrange the content of your document.

Project

Several people will be reviewing the First Choice Travel vacation specials document on the screen so you decide to experiment with various views to determine the best view for reviewing on the screen.

Tutorial 1.6
Changing Document Views

1. With **WS1-FCTVacSpecials.docx** open, press Ctrl + Home to move the insertion point to the beginning of the document and then change to Draft view by clicking the VIEW tab and then clicking the Draft button in the Views group.
2. Click the Print Layout button in the Views group.
3. Change the zoom by clicking the Zoom button in the Zoom group. At the Zoom dialog box, click *75%* in the *Zoom to* section and then click OK.

   You can also display the Zoom dialog box by clicking the percentage that displays at the right side of the Zoom slider bar located toward the bottom of the screen at the right side of the Status bar.

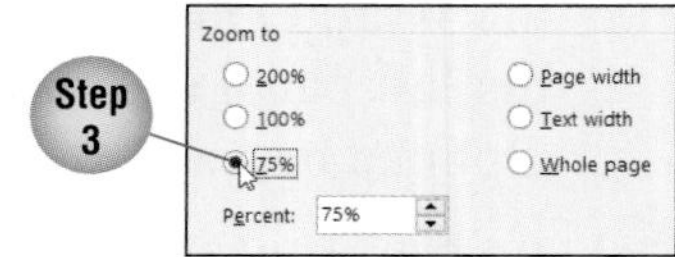

4. Return the view percentage to 100% by positioning the mouse pointer on the button on the Zoom slider bar and then dragging the button to the right until *100%* displays at the right side of the bar.

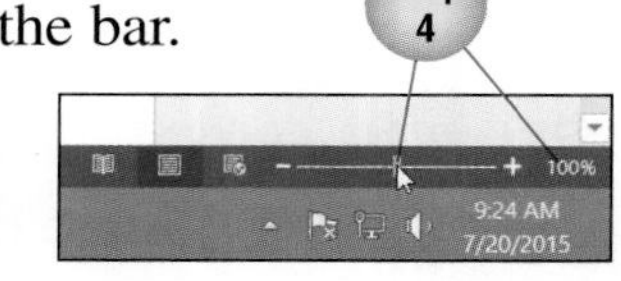

5. To save space on the screen, you decide to remove the white and light gray space that displays at the top and bottom of each page. To do this, position the mouse pointer on the light gray space above the page until the pointer turns into the hide white space icon and then double-click the left mouse button.

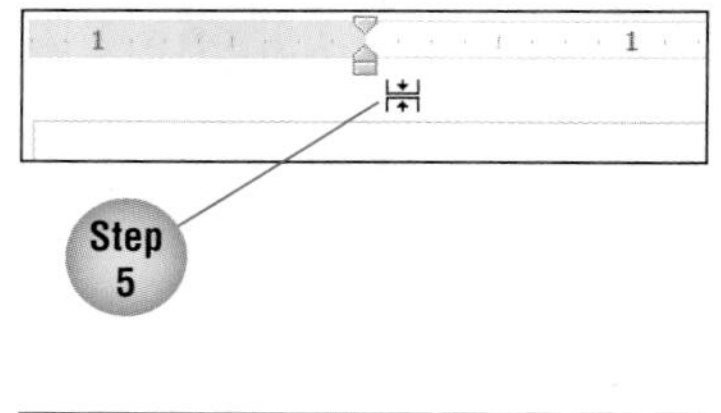

6. Scroll through the document and then redisplay the white and light gray space at the top and bottom of each page. To do this, position the mouse pointer on the gray line at the top of the page until the pointer turns into a show white space icon and then double-click the left mouse button.

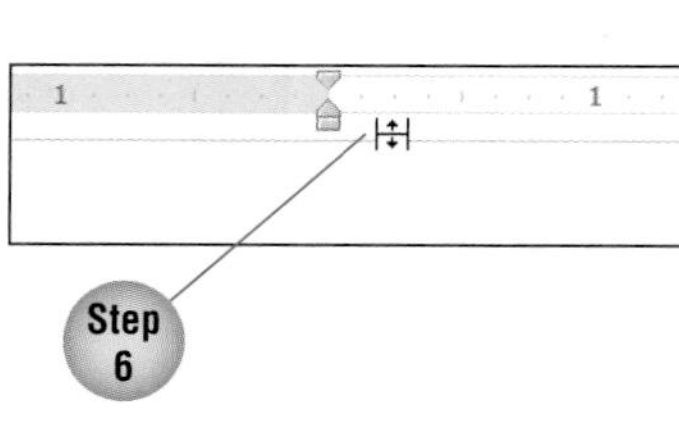

7. Click the Read Mode button in the Views group and then navigate in the document using the commands shown in Table 1.6.

   Read Mode displays a document for easy viewing and reading. You can also display the document in Read Mode by clicking the Read Mode button located in the view area on the Status bar.
8. Return to Print Layout view by pressing the Esc key on your keyboard.

   Pressing the Esc key displays the document in Print Layout view. You can also return to the Print Layout view by clicking the VIEW tab and then clicking *Edit Document* at the drop-down list.

In Brief

Display Draft View
1. Click VIEW tab.
2. Click Draft button in Views group.

Display Read Mode View
1. Click VIEW tab.
2. Click Read Mode button in Views group.

OR
Click Read Mode button in view area on Status bar.

Display Navigation Pane
1. Click VIEW tab.
2. Click *Navigation Pane* check box.

9. Click the *Navigation Pane* check box in the Show group on the VIEW tab.

   The Navigation pane displays at the left side of the screen and includes a search text box and a pane with three tabs. Click the HEADINGS tab to browse headings in a document (heading styles must be applied to text in the document for headings to display in the pane), click the PAGES tab to browse pages in the document, and click the RESULTS tab to browse the current search results in the document.

10. Click the PAGES tab in the Navigation pane.

    Clicking the PAGES tab displays miniatures of each page in the document in the Navigation pane.

11. Click the page 2 thumbnail in the Navigation pane.

    This moves the insertion point to the beginning of page 2.

12. Click in the search text box in the Navigation pane (contains the text *Search document*) and then type **Pacific Skye**.

    When you type *Pacific Skye*, each occurrence of the text is highlighted in the document.

13. Click the Next Search Result button in the Navigation pane (displays as a down-pointing arrow) to select the next occurrence of *Pacific Skye*. Click the button again to select the next occurrence.

    You can click the Previous Search Result button to display the previous occurrence of the search text.

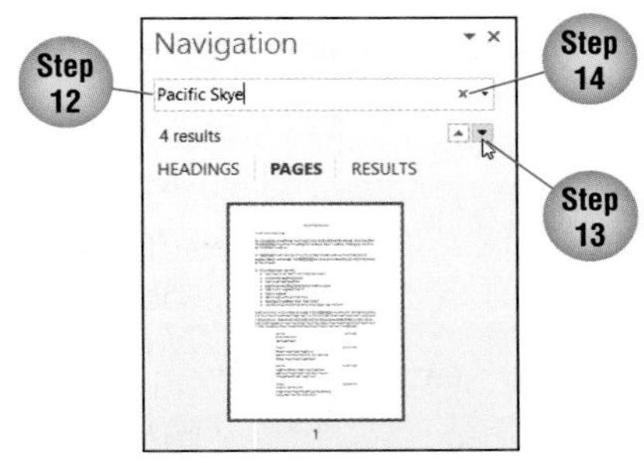

14. Click the button containing an X that displays at the right side of the search text box.

    Clicking this button ends the current search, removes the search text in the Navigation pane, and selects the current search result in the document.

15. Close the Navigation pane by clicking the Close button that displays in the upper right corner of the pane or by clicking the *Navigation Pane* check box in the Show group on the VIEW tab.

16. Click the Multiple Pages button in the Zoom group to display two pages on the screen and then click the One Page button in the Zoom group.

17. Drag the button on the Zoom slider bar or click the Zoom Out button or Zoom In button until *100%* displays at the right side of the bar.

TABLE 1.6 Navigating in Read Mode

Press this key	To complete this action
Page Down or spacebar	Move to next page or section.
Page Up or Backspace key	Move to previous page or section.
Right Arrow	Move to next page.
Left Arrow	Move to previous page.
Home	Move to first page in document.
End	Move to last page in document.
Esc	Return to previous view.

In Addition

Displaying the Ribbon Options

Control how much of the ribbon displays on screen with the Ribbon Display Options button located in the upper right corner of the screen. Click this button and a drop-down list displays with options for hiding the ribbon, showing only the tabs, or showing tabs and commands. You can also turn off the display of the ribbon by clicking the Collapse the Ribbon button located above the vertical scroll bar or with the keyboard shortcut Ctrl + F1. Redisplay the ribbon by double-clicking any tab or by pressing Ctrl + F1.

Activity 1.7

Finding and Replacing Text

In the previous activity you displayed the Navigation pane by clicking the *Navigation Pane* check box in the Show group on the VIEW tab. You can also display this pane by clicking the Find button in the Editing group on the HOME tab. Use the Navigation pane to find specific text in a document. If you want to find text and then replace the text with other text, use options at the Find and Replace dialog box with the Replace tab selected. Display this dialog box by clicking the Replace button in the Editing group on the HOME tab.

Project

As you review the vacation specials document, you discover that the name of the ship is spelled incorrectly and that the ship's cabins are divided into categories rather than classes. You decide to use the Find and Replace feature to makes these changes.

Tutorial 1.7
Finding and Replacing Text

1. With **WS1-FCTVacSpecials.docx** open, press Ctrl + Home to move the insertion point to the beginning of the document. You realize that the name of the ship is the *Pacific Sky*, not the *Pacific Skye*. To change the name, click the HOME tab and then click the Replace button in the Editing group.
2. At the Find and Replace dialog box with the Replace tab selected, type **Skye** in the *Find what* text box and then press the Tab key.

   Pressing the Tab key moves the insertion point to the *Replace with* text box.

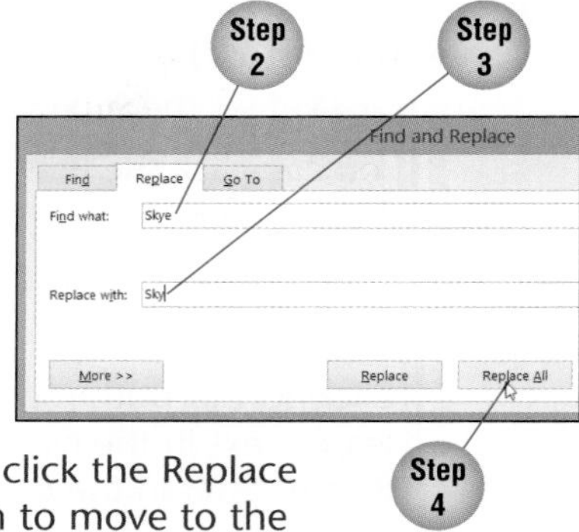

3. Type **Sky** in the *Replace with* text box.
4. Click the Replace All button located toward the bottom of the dialog box.

   Clicking the Replace All button replaces all occurrences of the text in the document. If you want control over what is replaced in a document, click the Replace button to replace text or click the Find Next button to move to the next occurrence of the text.
5. At the message telling you that four replacements were made, click the OK button.
6. Click the Close button to close the Find and Replace dialog box.
7. Looking at the document, you realize that the word "class" is used to designate cabins and the word should instead be "category." To make this change, click the Replace button in the Editing group on the HOME tab.
8. At the Find and Replace dialog box with the Replace tab selected, type **class**.

   When you open the Replace dialog box, *Skye* is automatically selected in the *Find what* text box. When you begin typing *class*, the selected text is automatically deleted.
9. Press the Tab key and then type **category** in the *Replace with* text box.

   When you type the find text and the replace text in all lowercase letters, Word will find and replace all occurrences regardless of the capitalization. For example, Word will find *Class* in the document and replace it with *Category*.

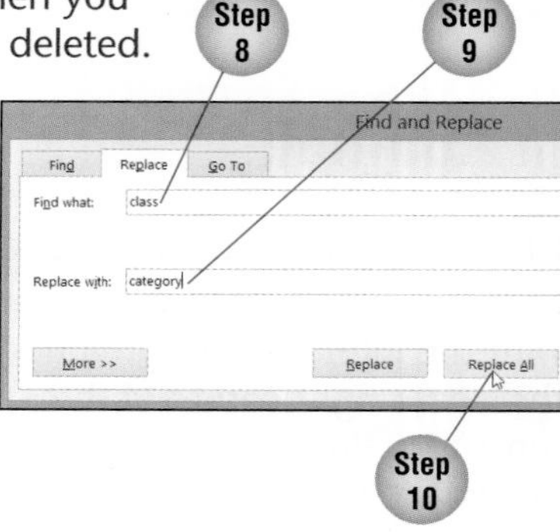

10. Click the Replace All button.

11. At the message telling you that six replacements were made, click the OK button.
12. Click the Close button to close the Find and Replace dialog box.
13. Click the Save button on the Quick Access toolbar to save the document.

In Brief

Find and Replace Text

1. Click Replace button in Editing group on the HOME tab.
2. Type find text.
3. Press Tab key.
4. Type replace text.
5. Click Replace All button.
6. Click OK.
7. Click Close button.

In Addition

Options at the Expanded Find and Replace Dialog Box

The Find and Replace dialog box contains a variety of check boxes with options you can choose for completing a find and replace. To display these options, click the More button located at the bottom of the dialog box. This causes the Find and Replace dialog box to expand as shown at the right. The options are described in the table below.

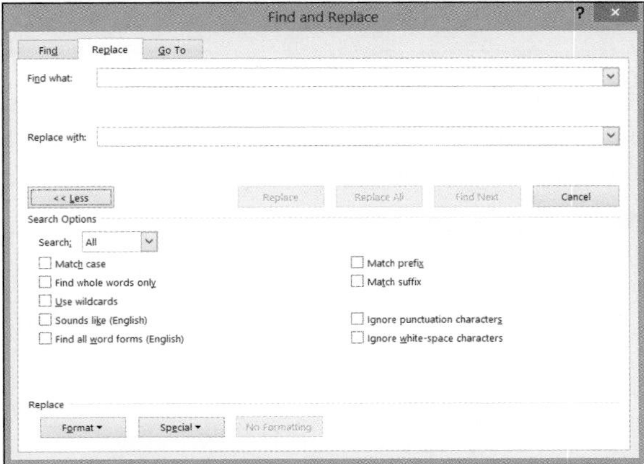

Option	Action
Match case	Exactly match the case of the search text. For example, if you search for *Book*, Word will stop at *Book* but not *book* or *BOOK*.
Find whole words only	Find a whole word, not a part of a word. For example, if you search for *her* and did not select *Find whole words only*, Word would stop at t*here*, *here*, *her*s, and so on.
Use wildcards	Search for wildcards, special characters, or special search operators.
Sounds like	Match words that sound alike but are spelled differently such as *know* and *no*.
Find all word forms	Find all forms of the word entered in the *Find what* text box. For example, if you enter *hold*, Word will stop at *held* and *holding*.
Match prefix	Find only those words that begin with the letters in the *Find what* text box. For example, if you enter *per*, Word will stop at words such as *perform* and *perfect* but will skip over words such as *super* and *hyperlink*.
Match suffix	Find only those words that end with the letters in the *Find what* text box. For example, if you enter *ly*, Word will stop at words such as *accurately* and *quietly* but skip over words such as *catalyst* and *lyre*.
Ignore punctuation characters	Ignore punctuation within characters. For example, if you enter *US* in the *Find what* text box, Word will stop at *U.S.*
Ignore white-space characters	Ignore spaces between letters. For example, if you enter *F B I* in the *Find what* text box, Word will stop at *FBI*.

Activity 1.8

Using the Help Feature; Printing a Document

Microsoft Word includes a Help feature that contains information on Word features and commands. To access Help, click the Microsoft Word Help button located in the upper right corner of the screen to display the Word Help window. You can also get help within a dialog box or at the backstage area. Display a dialog box and then click the Help button that displays in the upper right corner of the dialog box and the Word Help window displays with specific information about the dialog box.

Click the FILE tab and then click an option located at the left side of the screen and the backstage area displays with buttons and choices pertaining to the option. For example, click the *Print* option and the Print backstage area displays with buttons and choices for previewing and printing a document. At the Print backstage area, you can preview your document, specify the number of copies to print, and choose specific pages for printing. To remove the backstage area and return to your document, click the Back button located in the upper left corner of the backstage area or press the Esc key.

Project

Tutorial 1.8A
Using the Word Help Feature

Tutorial 1.8B
Previewing and Printing Documents

You are ready to print certain sections of the First Choice Travel vacation specials document, but first you want to learn more about printing a document. You decide to use the Help feature to learn about printing.

Step 1

1. With **WS1-FCTVacSpecials.docx** open, press Ctrl + Home to move the insertion point to the beginning of the document and then click the Microsoft Word Help button ? located in the upper right corner of the screen.

   You can also press the F1 function key to display the Word Help window.

2. At the Word Help window, click in the search text box, type **print**, and then press Enter.

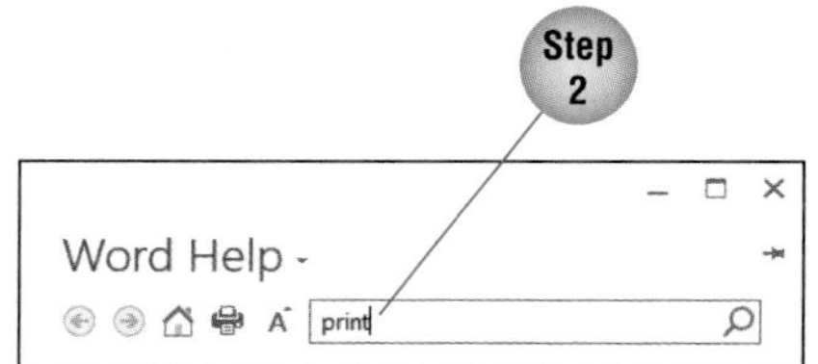

3. At the Word Help window, click a hyperlink that pertains to printing a document.
4. Read the information and then close the Word Help window by clicking the Close button located in the upper right corner of the window.
5. Click the FILE tab to display the backstage area and then click the Microsoft Word Help button located in the upper right corner of the screen.
6. Click a hyperlink in the Word Help window that interests you, read the information, and then close the window.
7. Click the *Print* option to display the Print backstage area.

   At the Print backstage area, your document displays at the right side of the screen as it will appear when printed. The left side of the Print backstage area displays three categories—*Print*, *Printer*, and *Settings*. Click the Print button in the *Print* category to send the document to the printer. Specify the number of copies you want printed with the *Copies* option in the *Print* category. Use the gallery in the *Printer* category to specify the desired printer. The *Settings* category contains a number of galleries, each with options for specifying how you want your document printed, such as whether or not you want the pages collated when printed; the orientation, page size, and margins of your document; and how many pages of your document you want to print on a page.

8. Click the Next Page button located below and to the left of the preview page to display the next page in the document.

9. Click twice on the Zoom In button (contains a plus symbol) that displays at the right side of the Zoom slider bar.

   Click the Zoom In button to increase the size of the page or click the Zoom Out button (containing a minus symbol) to decrease the size of the page.

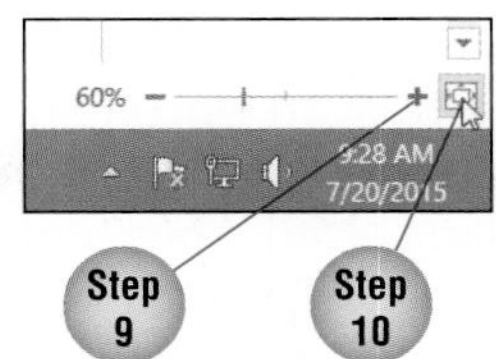

Step 9
Step 10

10. Click the Zoom to Page button located at the right side of the Zoom slider bar.

11. Print only page 2 of the document by clicking in the *Pages* text box (located in the *Settings* category), typing **2**, and then clicking the Print button.

12. Move the insertion point to any character in page 3 and then print page 3. Begin by clicking the FILE tab and then clicking the *Print* option.

13. At the Print backstage area, click the top gallery in the *Settings* category and then click *Print Current Page* at the drop-down list.

14. Click the Print button.

15. Save and then close **WS1-FCTVacSpecials.docx**.

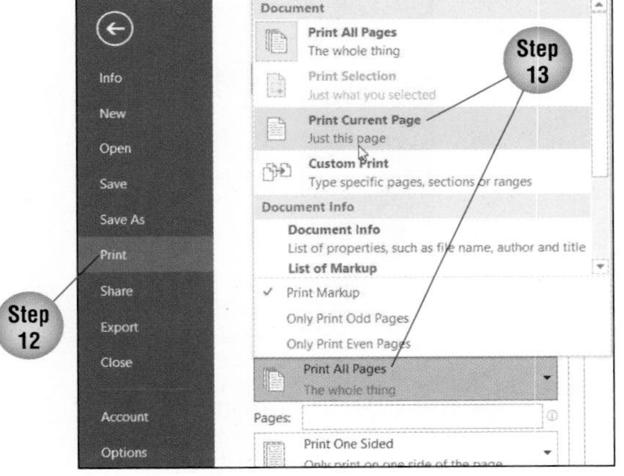

Step 12

In Brief

Use Help
1. Click Microsoft Word Help button.
2. Click desired option in Word Help window.

Print a Document
1. Click FILE tab.
2. Click *Print* option.
3. Click Print button.

Print a Specific Page
1. Click FILE tab.
2. Click *Print* option.
3. Click in *Pages* text box.
4. Type desired page number.
5. Click Print button.

Print Current Page
1. Position insertion point in desired page.
2. Click FILE tab.
3. Click *Print* option.
4. Click top gallery in *Settings* category.
5. Click *Print Current Page* at drop-down list.
6. Click Print button.

In Addition

Printing a Range of Pages

Identify a specific page, multiple pages, and/or a range of pages for printing at the Print backstage area. To print specific pages, click in the *Pages* text box and then type the page numbers of the specific pages you want to print. If you want specific multiple pages printed, use a comma to indicate *and* and use a hyphen to indicate *through*. For example, to print pages 2 and 5, you would type **2,5** in the *Pages* text box. To print pages 6 through 10, you would type **6-10**. You can also enter both commas and hyphens when specifying page numbers.

Getting Help on a Button

If you hover your mouse over some buttons, the ScreenTip that displays may include a Help icon and the text *Tell me more.* Click this hyperlinked text and the Word Help window opens with information about the button feature. You can also press F1 to display the Word Help window with information about the button feature.

Activity 1.9

Creating a Document Using a Template

Word includes a number of template documents formatted for specific uses. Each Word document is based on a template document with the *Normal* template the default. With Word templates (and Microsoft online templates), you can easily create a variety of documents, such as letters, faxes, and awards, with specialized formatting. Display available templates by clicking the FILE tab and then clicking the *New* option. Search for Microsoft online templates with the *Search for online templates* option. Type a category in the search text box and press Enter and Word displays templates matching the category. Click the desired template and then click the Create button. You must be connected to the Internet to download online templates.

Project

Tutorial 1.9
Creating Documents Using a Word Template

You are the projects coordinator for Marquee Productions, a movie production company. The company's travel agency is First Choice Travel, and you need the agency to make flight and hotel reservations for personnel involved in filming a movie in and around Toronto. You decide to use a letter template to help you format the letter.

1. Click the FILE tab and then click the *New* option.
2. At the New backstage area, click in the search text box (contains the text *Search online templates*), type **business letter**, and then press Enter.
3. Scroll down the list of templates, click the *Letter (Equity theme)* template.

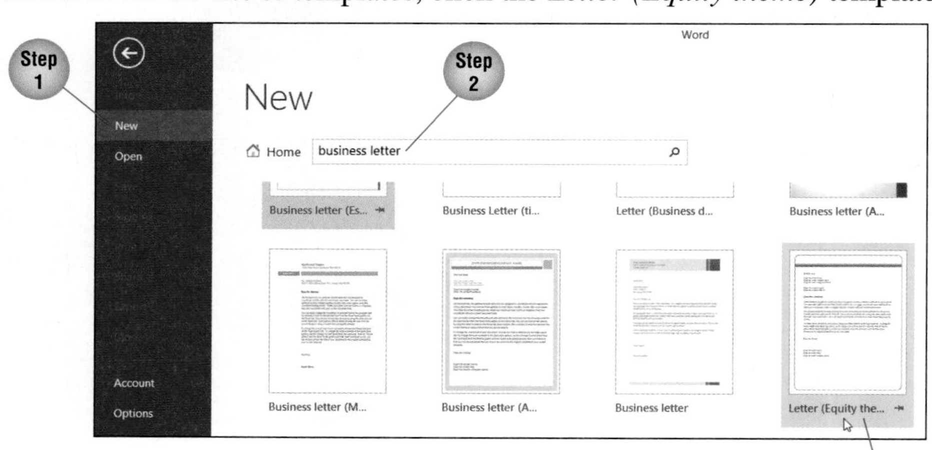

4. Click the Create button.
5. At the letter document, click the placeholder text *[Pick the date]* and then type the current date. (Your date will automatically change to numbers when you click outside the placeholder.)
6. Select the name that displays below the date and then type your first and last names.
7. Click the placeholder text *[Type the sender company name]* and then type **Marquee Productions**.
8. Click the placeholder text *[Type the sender company address]*, type **955 South Alameda Street**, press the Enter key, and then type **Los Angeles, CA 90037**.
9. Click the placeholder text *[Type the recipient name]* and then type **Ms. Melissa Gehring**.
10. Press the Enter key and then type **First Choice Travel**.
11. Click the placeholder text *[Type the recipient address]*, type **3588 Ventura Boulevard**, press the Enter key, and then type **Los Angeles, CA 90102**.

12 Click the placeholder text *[Type the salutation]* and then type **Dear Ms. Gehring:**.

13 Click on any character in the three paragraphs of text in the body of the letter and then type the text shown in Figure 1.4.

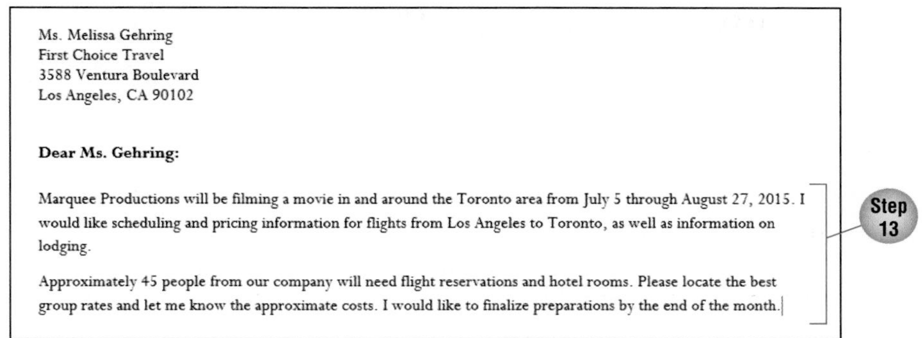

Ms. Melissa Gehring
First Choice Travel
3588 Ventura Boulevard
Los Angeles, CA 90102

Dear Ms. Gehring:

Marquee Productions will be filming a movie in and around the Toronto area from July 5 through August 27, 2015. I would like scheduling and pricing information for flights from Los Angeles to Toronto, as well as information on lodging.

Approximately 45 people from our company will need flight reservations and hotel rooms. Please locate the best group rates and let me know the approximate costs. I would like to finalize preparations by the end of the month.

14 Click the placeholder text *[Type the closing]* and then type **Sincerely,**.

15 Make sure your first and last names display below *Sincerely*. If not, select the current name below *Sincerely* and then type your first and last names.

16 Click the placeholder text *[Type the sender title]* and then type **Projects Coordinator**.

17 Click the Save button on the Quick Access toolbar.

18 At the Save As backstage area, click the *WordS1* folder that displays below the *Recent Folders* heading. (Or click your SkyDrive or the *Computer* option, click the Browse button, and then navigate to the WordS1 folder).

19 At the Save As dialog box with the WordS1 folder active (either on your SkyDrive or USB flash drive), type **WS1-MPLtrtoFCT** in the *File name* text box, and then press Enter (or click the Save button).

20 Print the letter by clicking the FILE tab, clicking the *Print* option, and then clicking the Print button.

21 Close the document by clicking the FILE tab and then clicking the *Close* option.

In Brief

Create Document Using Template
1. Click FILE tab.
2. Click *New* option.
3. Click desired template.
4. Click Create button.

FIGURE 1.4 Step 13

> Marquee Productions will be filming a movie in and around the Toronto area from July 5 through August 27, 2015. I would like scheduling and pricing information for flights from Los Angeles to Toronto, as well as information on lodging.
>
> Approximately 45 people from our company will need flight reservations and hotel rooms. Please locate the best group rates and let me know the approximate costs. I would like to finalize preparations by the end of the month.

In Addition

Specifying a Category

When you search for online templates, a Category list box displays at the right side of the screen. The list box displays the category and the number of templates that fit within the category. Click the desired category in the list box and only templates matching that category display in the New backstage area.

Activity 1.10

Creating and Renaming Folders; Saving a Document in a Different Format

As you continue working with documents, consider document management tasks such as creating a folder and copying, moving, and deleting documents. You can complete many document management tasks at the Open dialog box on one document or selected documents. By default, Word saves a file as a Word document and adds the extension *.docx* to the name. With the *Save as type* option at the Save As dialog box, you can save a document in a different format such as rich text or an earlier version of Word, or as a web page or plain text file.

Project

Since First Choice Travel will be communicating with Marquee Productions, you decide to create a folder into which you will insert Marquee Productions documents. You will also save a document in an older version of Word.

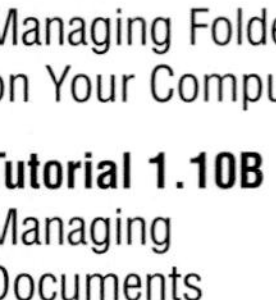

Tutorial 1.10A
Managing Folders on Your Computer

Tutorial 1.10B
Managing Documents

1. Click the FILE tab.

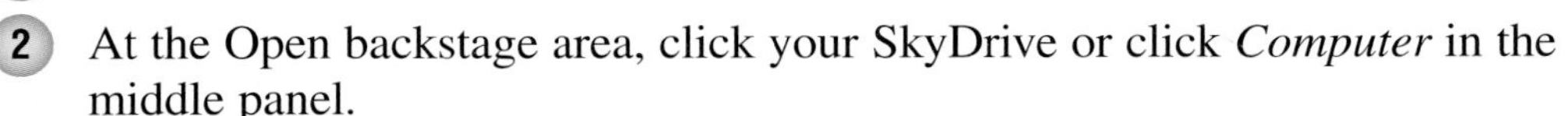

2. At the Open backstage area, click your SkyDrive or click *Computer* in the middle panel.
3. Click the *WordS1* folder that displays below the *Recent Folders* heading. (If the WordS1 folder does not display below the *Recent Folders* heading, click your location in the middle panel and then click the Browse button.)

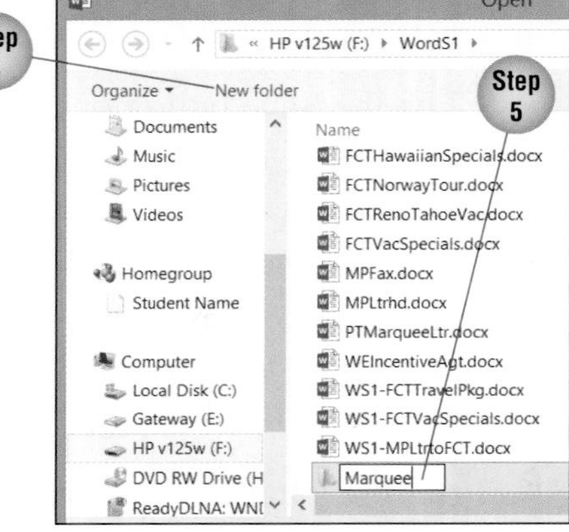

4. At the Open dialog box with WordS1 the active folder, click the New folder button.

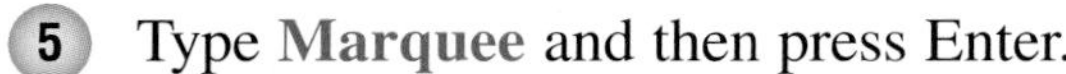

5. Type **Marquee** and then press Enter.
6. Click the document ***MPFax.docx*** in the Open dialog box list box, hold down the Ctrl key, click ***WS1-FCTVacSpecials.docx***, and then release the Ctrl key.

   Use the Ctrl key to select nonadjacent documents. Use the Shift key to select adjacent documents.

7. Right-click either of the selected documents and then click *Copy* at the shortcut menu.

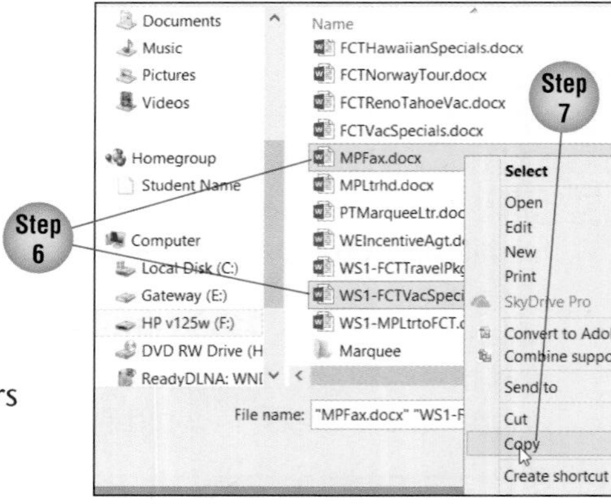

8. Double-click the *Marquee* file folder.

   File folders display in the Open dialog box list box before documents. File folders display preceded by a file folder icon and documents display preceded by a document icon.

9. Position the mouse pointer in a white portion of the Open dialog box list box, click the *right* mouse button, and then click *Paste* at the shortcut menu.

   The copied documents are inserted in the Marquee folder.

10. You need to send **WS1-FCTVacSpecials.docx** to a colleague who uses Word 2003, so you need to save the document in that format. At the Open dialog box with the Marquee folder active, double-click ***WS1-FCTVacSpecials.docx***.

11 Click the FILE tab and then click the *Save As* option.

12 At the Save As backstage area, click the *WordS1* folder that displays below the *Recent Folders* heading.

13 At the Save As dialog box, type **WS1-FCTVacSpecialsWd2003** in the *File name* text box.

14 Click the *Save as type* option box and then click *Word 97-2003 Document (*.doc)* at the drop-down list.

15 Click the Save button located in the lower right corner of the dialog box and then close the document.

If a compatibility checker message displays, click the Continue button.

16 Press Ctrl + F12 to display the Open dialog box with the WordS1 folder on your storage medium the active folder. (If it is not already the active folder, navigate to the WordS1 folder.)

17 At the Open dialog box, rename the Marquee folder. To do this, right-click the folder name and then click *Rename* at the shortcut menu. Type **MarqueeProductions** and then press Enter.

The new folder name replaces the original folder name. You can also rename a folder by clicking the Organize button, clicking *Rename*, and then typing the new folder name.

18 Delete the MarqueeProductions folder. To do this, click once on the folder to select it, click the Organize button on the toolbar, and then click *Delete* at the drop-down list. At the message asking if you are sure you want to delete the folder and all of its contents, click the Yes button.

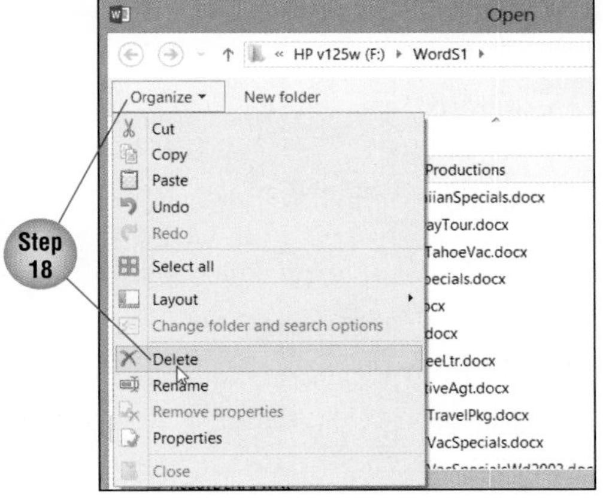

19 Close the Open dialog box.

20 Exit Word by clicking the Close button located in the upper right corner of the screen.

In Brief

Create Folder

1. Click FILE tab.
2. Click *Open* option.
3. At Open backstage area, click desired folder in *Recent Folders* section. Or, click location and then click Browse button.
4. At Open dialog box, click New folder button.
5. Type folder name.
6. Press Enter.

Save Document in Different Format

1. Open document.
2. Click FILE tab.
3. Click *Save As* option.
4. At Save As backstage area, click desired folder in the *Recent Folders* section.
5. At Save As dialog box, type document name.
6. Change *Save as type* option to desired format.
7. Click Save button.

In Addition

Editing a PDF File in Word

New to Word 2013 is the ability to open a PDF file in Word and make edits to the file. PDF stands for Portable Document Format and is a common format for sharing files. When you open a PDF file, Word converts the file to a .docx file and the data in the file may not display in the exact format as in the PDF file. Converting a PDF file to a Word document works best with text-based documents.

Features Summary

Feature	Ribbon Tab, Group	Button	Quick Access Toolbar	FILE Tab Option	Keyboard Shortcut
AutoCorrect dialog box				*Options*, Proofing, AutoCorrect Options	
close				*Close*	Ctrl + F4
Draft view	VIEW, Views				
close Word					Alt + F4
Read Mode	VIEW, Views				
Help					F1
Navigation pane	VIEW, Show				Ctrl + F
New backstage area				*New*	
Open dialog box					Ctrl + F12
Open backstage area				*Open*	Ctrl + O
Print backstage area				*Print*	Ctrl + P
Print Layout view	VIEW, Views				
redo an action					Ctrl + Y
Save As backstage area				*Save* OR *Save As*	
Save As dialog box					F12
save document					Ctrl + S
Spelling & Grammar	REVIEW, Proofing				F7
Thesaurus	REVIEW, Proofing				Shift + F7
undo an action					Ctrl + Z
Word Options dialog box				*Options*	

Knowledge Check

Completion: In the space provided at the right, indicate the correct term, command, or option.

1. This area on the screen contains tabs and commands divided into groups. ________________
2. Click this tab to display the backstage area. ________________
3. Use this keyboard command to move the insertion point to the beginning of the document. ________________
4. This toolbar contains the Undo and Redo buttons. ________________

5. To select a sentence, hold down this key and then click anywhere in the sentence. ________________
6. To begin checking the spelling and grammar in a document, click this tab and then click the Spelling & Grammar button in the Proofing group. ________________
7. This feature automatically detects and corrects some typographical errors. ________________
8. Use this feature to find synonyms for a word. ________________
9. Display a document in this view for easy viewing and reading. ________________
10. The *Navigation Pane* check box is located in this group on the VIEW tab. ________________
11. Click this button at the Find and Replace dialog box to replace all occurrences of text. ________________
12. Click this button on the Open dialog box toolbar to create a new folder. ________________
13. Select adjacent documents at the Open dialog box by holding down this key while clicking each document name. ________________
14. Select nonadjacent documents at the Open dialog box by holding down this key while clicking each document name. ________________

Skills Review

Review 1 Editing a Hawaiian Specials Document

1. Create a new folder on your storage medium (SkyDrive or USB flash drive) and name it **WordEOS**.
2. Open **FCTHawaiianSpecials.docx** from the WordS1 folder and then save it in the WordEOS folder and name it **WS1-R-FCTHawaiianSpecials**.
3. Insert the word *spectacular* between the words *the* and *Pacific* in the first sentence below the *White Sands Charters* heading.
4. Move the insertion point to the beginning of the paragraph below the *Air Adventures* heading and then type the sentence **Experience beautiful coastlines and magnificent waterfalls, and fly inside an active volcano.**
5. Select and then delete the words *Depending on weather, marine conditions, and access, your* located in the third sentence in the paragraph below the *White Sands Charters* heading.
6. Capitalize the *g* in *guides*. (This word now begins the sentence.)
7. Select and then delete the last sentence in the *Air Adventures* section (the sentence that begins *View untouched areas from*).
8. Undo the deletion and then redo the deletion.
9. Move the insertion point to the beginning of the document and then complete a spelling and grammar check on the document. (*Molokini* is spelled correctly.)
10. Use Thesaurus to change *delightful* in the paragraph in the *White Sands Charter* section to *enchanting*.
11. Save **WS1-R-FCTHawaiianSpecials.docx**.

Review 2 Creating and Using an AutoCorrect Entry

1. With **WS1-R-FCTHawaiianSpecials.docx** open, display the AutoCorrect dialog box, insert *HA* in the *Replace* text box, insert *Hawaiian* in the *With* text box, click the Add button, and then close the dialog box. Close the Word Options dialog box.
2. Move the insertion point to the end of the document and then type the text shown in Figure 1.5.
3. Save, print, and then close **WS1-R-FCTHawaiianSpecials.docx**.

FIGURE 1.5 Review 2, Step 2

> Luau Legends
>
> Enjoy a spectacular HA dinner show featuring lavish prime rib and authentic HA buffet. This uniquely HA experience includes a traditional lei greeting, exceptional food and beverages, magic music of the islands, and Hawaii's finest performers. Join us each evening beginning at 7:30 p.m. for an evening of delicious HA food and spectacular performances.

Review 3 Editing an Agreement

1. Open **WEIncentiveAgt.docx** and then save the document in the WordEOS folder and name it **WS1-R-WEIncentiveAgt**.
2. Complete a spelling and grammar check on the document. (Ignore the suggestion to revise the use of *between*.)
3. Search for all occurrences of *Employee* and replace with *Carol Shepard*.
4. Search for all occurrences of *Company* and replace with *Worldwide Enterprises*.
5. Save, print, and then close **WS1-R-WEIncentiveAgt.docx**.

Review 4 Preparing a Fax Sheet

Worldwide Enterprises

1. Click the FILE tab and then click the *New* option.
2. At the New backstage area, click in the search text box, type **equity fax**, and then press the Enter key.
3. Click the *Fax (Equity theme)* template and then click the Create button.
4. Insert the following information in the specified location:
   - To: Scott Drysdale
   - From: (Type your first and last names)
   - Fax: (213) 555-3349
   - Pages: 3
   - Phone: (213) 555-3400
   - Date: (Insert current date)
   - Re: Incentive Agreement
   - CC: (Delete this placeholder)

   Insert a capital *X* in the *Please Reply* check box. Click the *[Type comments]* placeholder and then type the following comment: **Please review the Incentive Agreement and then call me so we can schedule an appointment.**
5. Save the document in the WordEOS folder and name it **WS1-R-WEAgtFax**.
6. Print and then close the document.

Skills Assessment

Assessment 1 Editing a Letter

1. Open **PTMarqueeLtr.docx** and then save the document in the WordEOS folder with the name **WS1-A1-PTMarqueeLtr**.
2. Move the insertion point a double space below the paragraph of text in the letter and then add the following information. (Write the information as a paragraph—do not use bullets.)
   - Costume research takes approximately two to three weeks.
   - If appropriate costumes cannot be found, costumes are sewn.
   - Anticipate five working days to sew a costume.
   - Include the number of costumes and approximate sizes.
   - A price estimate will be provided before costumes are purchased or sewn.
3. Use Thesaurus to replace *regarding* in the first sentence with an appropriate synonym.
4. Save, print, and then close **WS1-A1-PTMarqueeLtr.docx**.

Assessment 2 Writing a Letter

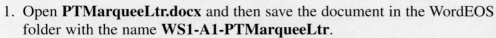

1. Display the New backstage area, search for and download the *Letter (Median theme)* template, and then use the following information to create the letter. (You determine the salutation and closing.)

   Sender's information:
   The Waterfront Bistro
   3104 Rivermist Drive
   Buffalo, NY 14280

   Recipient's information:
   Marquee Productions
   Mr. Josh Hart, Locations Director
   955 South Alameda Street
   Los Angeles, CA 90037

   Write a letter as Dana Hirsch that covers these points:

   Explain that The Waterfront Bistro is a full-service catering company with a number of menus for breakfast, lunch, dinner, and morning and afternoon snacks. Include the price ranges for breakfast, lunch, dinner, and snack menus. (You determine the ranges.) Offer a 5% discount if you cater for the duration of the filming. Tell Mr. Hart that you would like to fax a variety of menu options to him. Close the letter by telling him you are very interested in his business and say something positive about your catering service.
2. Save the completed letter document in the WordEOS folder and name it **WS1-A2-WBCateringLtr**. Print and then close the document.

Assessment 3 Preparing a Fax

1. Display the New backstage area, search for and download the *Fax (Equity theme)* template, and then insert the necessary information in the specified fields. You are Dana Hirsch and you are sending the fax to Josh Hart (see information in Assessment 2). His fax number is (612) 555-2009 and his telephone number is (612) 555-2005. Insert an *X* in the *Please Comment* check box and indicate that the fax contains 11 pages.
2. Save the fax document in the WordEOS folder and name it **WS1-A3-WBFax**.
3. Print and then close the document.

Assessment 4 Finding Information on Changing Grammar Checking Options

1. Open **FCTNorwayTour.docx** and then save the document in the WordEOS folder with the name **WS1-A4-FCTNorwayTour**.
2. Use the Help feature to learn more about spelling and grammar checking. After reading the information, display the Word Options dialog box (click the FILE tab and then click *Options*) with the *Proofing* option selected and then change the *Writing Style* option to *Grammar & Style* (this option is located in the *When correcting spelling and grammar in Word* section).
3. Complete a spelling and grammar check on the document. (*Myrdal* is spelled correctly. When the grammar checker offers corrections for *plateau, that*, choose the first option, *plateau that*.)
4. Change the *Writing style* option back to *Grammar Only*.
5. Save, print, and then close **WS1-A4-FCTNorwayTour.docx**.

Assessment 5 Individual Challenge Creating a Certificate

1. Display the New backstage area and then search for and download the *Membership certificate* template (If the *Membership certificate* template is not available, choose a similar certificate.)
2. Identify yourself as a member in good standing in the *First Choice Travel Advantage Program*.
3. Save the completed document in the WordEOS folder and name it **WS1-A5-IC-Membership**.
4. Print and then close the document.

Marquee Challenge

Challenge 1 Preparing a Business Letter

1. Open **MPLtrhd.docx** and then save the document in the WordEOS folder with the name **WS1-C1-MPLtrtoWB**.
2. Create the letter shown in Figure 1.6. (Note: When you type the email address in the last paragraph and then press the spacebar, Word automatically converts it to a hyperlink [blue underlined text].)
3. Save, print, and then close **WS1-C1-MPLtrtoWB.docx**.

Challenge 2 Editing and Formatting a Travel Document

1. Open **FCTRenoTahoeVac.docx** and then save the document in the WordEOS folder with the name **WS1-C2-FCTRenoTahoeVac**.
2. Edit and format the document so it displays as shown in Figure 1.7 on page 34. (Search for all occurrences of *Eldorado* and replace with *Sierra*. Expand the Find and Replace dialog box, insert a check mark in the *Match case* check box, and then search for all occurrences of *LT* and replace with *Lake Tahoe*. Complete a spelling and grammar check on the document.)
3. Save, print, and then close **WS1-C2-FCTRenoTahoeVac.docx**.

FIGURE 1.6 Challenge 1

V: 612 555 2005
F: 612 555 2009
info@emcp.net
www.emcp.net/marquee

(Current date) *(press Enter three times)*

Ms. Dana Hirsch *(press Shift + Enter)*
The Waterfront Bistro *(press Shift + Enter)*
3104 Rivermist Drive *(press Shift + Enter)*
Buffalo, NY 14280 *(press Enter)*

Dear Ms. Hirsch: *(press Enter)*

We will be filming a movie in and around Toronto and Buffalo from July 7 to August 30, 2015. During that time, we will require catering services for cast and crew members. The services we request include breakfast, mid-morning snack, lunch, and afternoon snack for each day of filming, including weekends. *(press Enter)*

Please send information on your breakfast and lunch catering menus and snack choices. We are interested in pricing for meals and snacks for approximately 45 people for the duration of the filming. If you have any questions about our catering needs, please contact me by telephone at (612) 555-2005 or email me at JoshH@emcp.net. *(press Enter)*

Sincerely, *(press Enter twice)*

Josh Hart *(press Shift + Enter)*
Locations Director *(press Enter)*

XX *(press Shift + Enter)*
WS1-C1-MPLtrtoWB.docx

955 South Alameda Street ■ Los Angeles, CA 90037

FIGURE 1.7 Challenge 2

VACATIONING IN RENO AND LAKE TAHOE

Reno and Lake Tahoe are home to more snow, more ski resorts, and more nightlife than any other ski destination in North America. Come visit our area and experience a vast diversity of ski terrain, scenic beauty, and entertainment options. Getting to Reno and Lake Tahoe is as easy as taking one of over 250 flights that arrive daily at the Reno/Tahoe International Airport. Getting to your accommodations can be as quick as a ten-minute shuttle ride to a hotel casino in Reno or less than a scenic hour through the Sierra foothills to a variety of Lake Tahoe properties. All of the ski slopes are between 45 and 90 minutes from the Reno Airport. Getting around is easy with a variety of transportation options.

Destinations

Convenience and great locations make Incline Village and Crystal Bay desirable destinations at Lake Tahoe. Situated between Squaw Valley and Heavenly ski resorts, the two villages, along with other great resorts such as Mt. Rose and Diamond Peak, are just minutes away. Just 30 miles from Reno/Tahoe International Airport, the villages are central to all of the Lake Tahoe ski resorts. Diamond Peak offers 2,000 acres of classic Nordic terrain, over 35 kilometers of groomed tracks, and skating lanes with incredible views of Lake Tahoe. The resort also boasts a 6.2-million-dollar complex including an eight-lane indoor swimming pool, cardiovascular and strength-training center, aerobic studio, and gym. Additional recreational offerings include sledding, sleigh rides, snowshoeing, bowling, and a movie theater.

North Lake Tahoe is a favored destination for discriminating vacationers. Visit this beautiful area for the epic powder, seven resorts, downhill and cross-country skiing, and unlimited dining choices—all for affordable prices. Consider trying ice skating at the world's highest ice rink, snowmobiling and snowshoeing in the backcountry, or touring Lake Tahoe on an authentic paddle-wheeler. Visit one of 80 restaurants boasting award-winning cuisine in lakeshore and alpine settings. Visit the historic town of Truckee, an old railroad and logging community with quaint shops and sights.

Lake Tahoe South Shore is the ideal destination for variety with an amazing selection of skiing for all skill levels. Almost endless lodging possibilities await you with over 95 luxurious hotels and casinos, all-suite resorts, motels, condominiums, cabins, and homes. Tour the Sierra backcountry on a snowmobile, take a paddle-wheeler cruise to Emerald Bay, try a peaceful sleigh ride, or see the sights from a dogsled.

Word SECTION 2

Formatting Characters and Paragraphs

Skills

- Apply fonts and font effects
- Use Format Painter
- Repeat a command
- Align text in paragraphs
- Indent text
- Change line and paragraph spacing
- Reveal formatting
- Find and replace formatting
- Insert bullets and numbering
- Insert symbols and special characters
- Set tabs and tabs with leaders
- Add borders and shading to text
- Insert a page border
- Apply styles and style sets
- Apply themes

Projects Overview

Edit and format documents on Oslo, Norway, and Petersburg, Alaska; format a document on traveling by train in Europe; and format documents on vacation packages in Oregon and Nevada and cross-country skiing vacation packages.

Prepare a letter to the chair of the Theatre Arts Division at Niagara Peninsula College requesting 20 theatre interns.

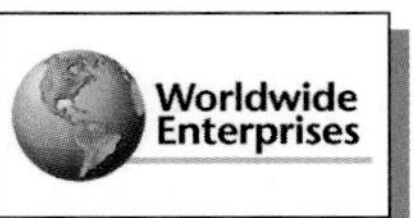

Prepare a movie distribution schedule.

Model Answers for Projects

These model answers for the projects you complete in Section 2 provide a preview of the finished projects before you begin working and also allow you to compare your own results with these models to ensure you have created the materials accurately.

WS2-FCTOslo.docx (a two-page document) is the project in Activities 2.1 to 2.5.

OSLO, NORWAY

History

The founding of Oslo took place in the turbulent period between the *Viking Age* and Norway's *Catholic Middle Ages*. Many remnants and ruins from ancient Oslo can be found in Memorial Park. The city has a fascinating, interesting, and dramatic history.

Oslo's population was substantially reduced during the time of the Black Death in 1348, which claimed over fifty percent of the inhabitants. This epidemic also had political consequences for Norway, which was reduced to a province of Denmark. During this period, Copenhagen was the actual capital of Norway. Oslo was also greatly affected by the Lutheran Protestant Reformation of 1537, with religious conflicts, political separation from the Catholic Church, and the foundation of a Protestant National Church. Many ruins of churches and monasteries bear witness to this process.

Oslo was completely destroyed by fire in 1624. Following intense renewal and advanced city planning in the spirit of the Renaissance, a completely new city was created and named Christiania. In 1814 Norway was united with Sweden, and Christiania experie
In 1905 the union with Sweden
independence. The original nam

Population

Oslo is the capital of Norway an
Approximately 900,000 people
twenty percent of the total popu

Commerce and Industry

The working population of Oslo
industry, 16%; building and con
and tourism, 69%.

Climate

Oslo's climate is temperate in the autumn and warm in spring and summer. Snow falls three to five months in the winter. Skiing conditions are good in the hills around Oslo between December and April. From May to July, the weather can be quite warm with long periods of sunshine. Drought can also occur from time to time. Statistically speaking, Oslo is Scandinavia's sunniest capital.

Holiday, Sport, and Leisure

Oslo is surrounded by forest and fjord. Preserving the fjord and the area surrounding the city for leisure and outdoor pursuits is an important part of Oslo's political tradition. Some of the major sports events in Oslo include the Grete Waitz Race, Holmenkollen Relay, Oslo Marathon, and the Holmenkollen Ski Festival. Oslo includes over 2,000 kilometers of prepared ski trails for cross-country skiing and a number of ski lifts for alpine skiing.

Sightseeing Tours

TOUR 1: MINI CRUISE
Fifty-minute cruise that departs on the hour

TOUR 2: FJORD CRUISE
Two-hour cruise that departs on the half hour

TOUR 3: FJORD CRUISE WITH DINNER
Two-hour cruise followed by dinner at Restaurant Lanternen

TOUR 4: SELECTED OSLO SIGHTSEEING
Three-hour tour of Vigeland Sculpture Park, the Holmenkollen Ski Jump, the Viking Ships, and the Kon-Tiki Raft

ALL TOURS BY BOAT AND COACH DEPART FROM PIER 3 IN FRONT OF THE OSLO CITY HALL.

Student Name
Date: 7/27/2015
Time: 12:49 PM

WS2-FCTRailTravel.docx is the project in Activities 2.6 to 2.11.

Traveling in Europe by Train

Now that you have planned your trip, bought your rail tickets, flown to Europe, and adjusted your body to jet lag, you are ready to start your rail experience. As you do so, remember the following things:

- Have your pass validated.
- Protect your pass.
- Arrive 20 minutes before train departure time.
- Be at the right train station.

Rail Ticket Bonuses

Your rail ticket offers you a variety of bonuses when traveling in Europe, including:

- Free or discount transportation on ferries, steamers, and buses
- Hotel discounts of up to 50% from participating hotels
- Special fare on the high-speed trains linking Paris to London
- Reduced rental rates with most major car rental companies

Some companies offer outstanding reductions on transportation. For example, you can travel on the ferry in Denmark between Århus and Kalundborg and between Nyborg and Korsør at a 75% discount! ScanTravel, a travel company located in Stockholm, offers the StarPass® ticket that provides you with incredible discounts on travel by train, ferry, and bus in Sweden, Norway, and Denmark.

International Airports with Train Connections

Country	City	Airport
Austria	Vienna (Wein)	Schwechat
Belgium	Brussels	Nationaal
France	Paris	Orly
Germany	Berlin	Schoenefeld
Great Britain	London	Heathrow
Italy	Rome	Fiumicino

Airport	Service
Schwechat	Train every 30 minutes
Nationaal	Train every 20 minutes
Orly	RER train every 20 minutes
Schoenefeld	S-Bahn train every 30 minutes
Heathrow	LT train every 10 minutes
Fiumicino	Train every 10 to 20 minutes

Activity 2.1

Applying Formatting with the Font Group and the Mini Toolbar

Apply character formatting to text with buttons in the Font group on the HOME tab. Formatting a document changes how the document displays and prints. The top row of the Font group contains buttons for changing the font and font size as well as changing text case and clearing formatting. The bottom row contains buttons for applying formatting such as bold, italics, underlining, strikethrough, subscript, superscript, text effects, highlighting, and font color. Microsoft Word has taken some commonly used commands and placed them on the Mini toolbar. When you select text, the Mini toolbar displays above the selected text. The Mini toolbar disappears when you move the mouse pointer away from it.

Project

You have been asked to improve the appearance of a document on Oslo, Norway, by applying a different font and various font effects to the text.

SNAP

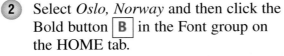

Tutorial 2.1A
Modifying the Font Using the Font Group

Tutorial 2.1B
Formatting with the Mini Toolbar

Tutorial 2.1C
Highlighting Text

1. Open **FCTOslo.docx** and then save the document and name it **WS2-FCTOslo**.
2. Select *Oslo, Norway* and then click the Bold button **B** in the Font group on the HOME tab.
3. With *OSLO, NORWAY* still selected, click the Change Case button Aa in the Font group and then click *UPPERCASE* at the drop-down list.

   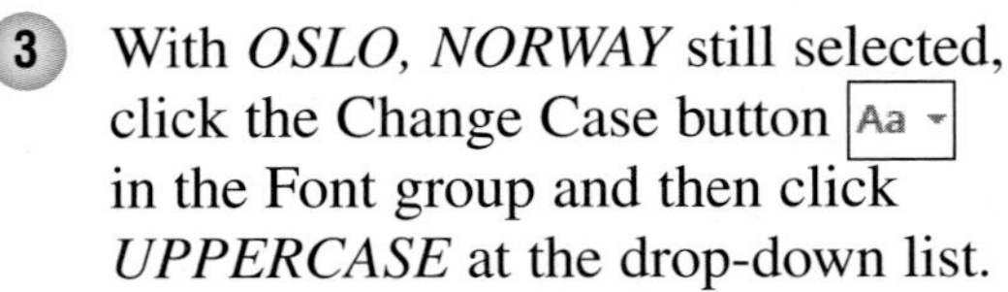

   Use options at the Change Case drop-down list to specify the case of selected text.

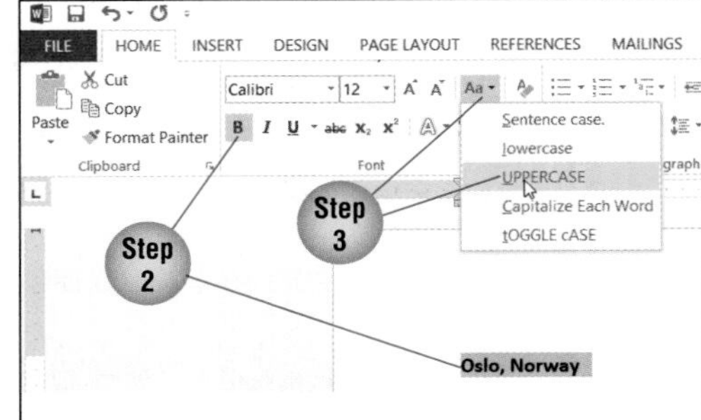

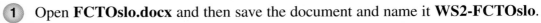

4. With *Oslo, Norway* still selected, click the Text Effects and Typography button in the Font group and then click the *Fill - White, Outline - Accent 1, Shadow* option at the drop-down gallery (fourth option in the top row).

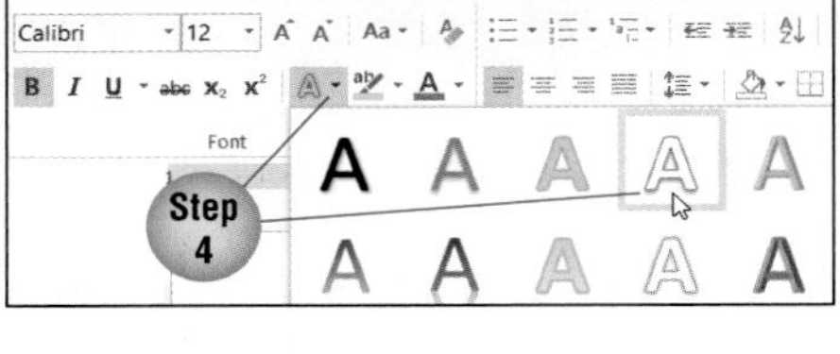

5. Select *History* and then click the Underline button U in the Font group.
6. Select and then underline the remaining headings: *Population*; *Commerce and Industry*; *Climate*; *Holiday, Sport, and Leisure*; and *Sightseeing Tours*.

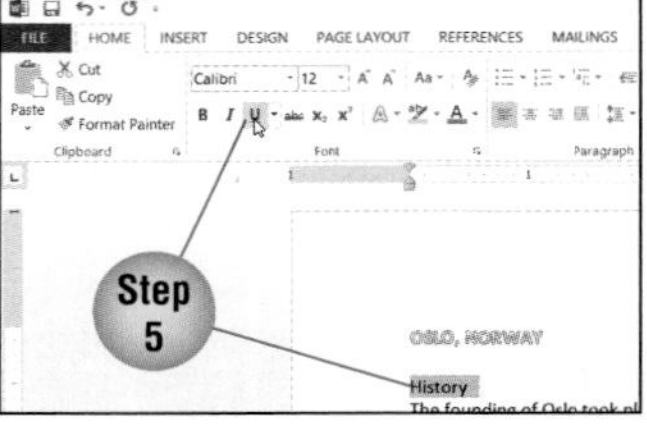

7. Select the words *Viking Age* located in the first paragraph below the *History* heading and then click the Italic button *I* on the Mini toolbar that displays above the selected text.

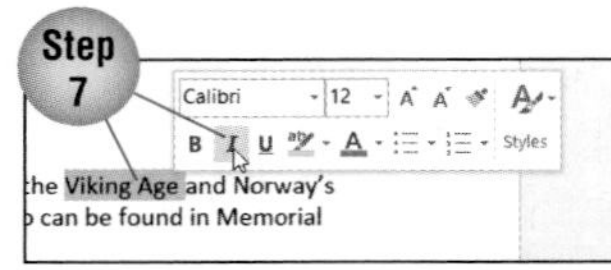

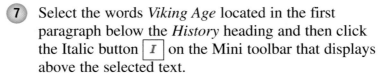

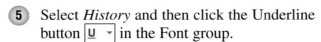

   The Mini toolbar displays above selected text. The toolbar disappears when you move the mouse pointer away from it.

8. Select the words *Catholic Middle Ages* that display in the first paragraph and then click the Italic button on the Mini toolbar.

9. Select the entire document by clicking the Select button in the Editing group on the HOME tab and then clicking *Select All* at the drop-down list.

10. Click the Font button arrow in the Font group. Hover the mouse pointer over various typefaces in the Font drop-down gallery and notice how the text in the document reflects the selected font.

    This feature is referred to as ***live preview***. It provides you with an opportunity to see how the document will appear with text formatting applied before you make a final decision.

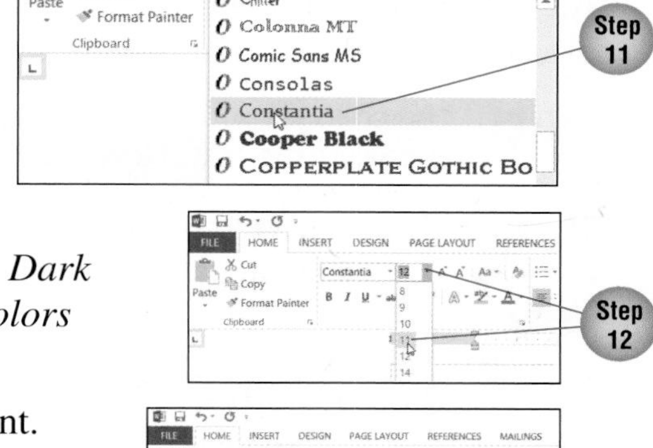

11. Scroll down the gallery and then click *Constantia.*

12. Click the Font Size button arrow and then click *11* in the drop-down gallery.

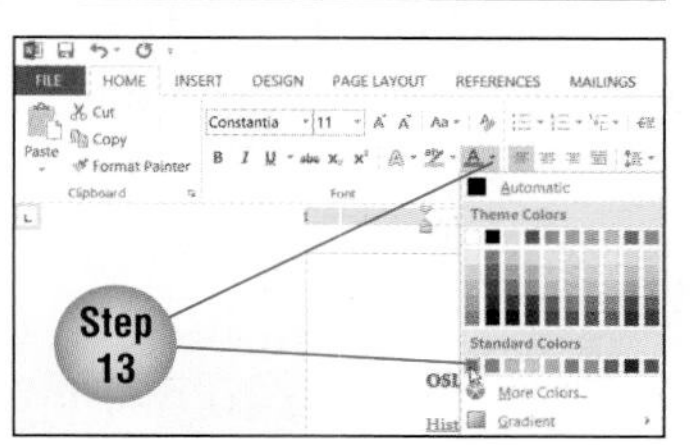

13. Click the Font Color button arrow and then click *Dark Red* in the color gallery (first color in the *Standard Colors* row).

14. Deselect the text by clicking anywhere in the document.

15. You want to identify specific text for review by colleagues so you decide to highlight the text. To do this, click the Text Highlight Color button arrow in the Font group and then click the yellow color at the drop-down list. Select the first sentence in the second paragraph (the sentence that begins *Oslo's population was substantially reduced*).

    When you click the Text Highlight Color button, the mouse pointer displays with a highlighter pen attached. Highlighting stays on until you click the Text Highlight Color button again.

16. Select the first sentence in the *Population* paragraph to highlight it and then click the Text Highlight Color button to turn it off.

17. Remove the text highlighting by pressing Ctrl + A (this selects the entire document), clicking the Text Highlight Color button arrow, and then clicking *No Color* at the drop-down list.

18. Save **WS2-FCTOslo.docx**.

In Addition

Using Typefaces

A typeface is a set of characters with a common design and shape and can be decorative or plain and either monospaced or proportional. Word refers to typeface as ***font***. A monospaced typeface allots the same amount of horizontal space for each character while a proportional typeface allots a varying amount of space for each character. Proportional typefaces are divided into two main categories: ***serif*** and ***sans serif***. A serif is a small line at the end of a character stroke. Consider using a serif typeface for text-intensive documents because the serifs help move the reader's eyes across the page. Use a sans serif typeface for headings, headlines, and advertisements.

Activity 2.2

Using the Font Dialog Box and Format Painter; Repeating a Command

In addition to buttons in the Font group, you can apply font formatting with options at the Font dialog box. With options at this dialog box, you can change the font, font size, and font style; change the font color; choose an underlining style; and apply formatting effects. Once you apply formatting to text, you can copy that formatting to different locations in the document using the Format Painter. If you apply formatting to text in a document and then want to apply the same formatting to other text, use the Repeat command. Repeat a command by pressing the F4 function key.

Project

The changes you made to the Oslo document have enhanced the readability and visual appeal of the text. Now you will turn your attention to the headings.

SNAP

Tutorial 2.2A
Applying Formatting Using the Font Dialog Box

Tutorial 2.2B
Using the Format Painter and Repeating a Command

1. With **WS2-FCTOslo.docx** open, press Ctrl + Home to move the insertion point to the beginning of the document and then select the entire document by pressing Ctrl + A.

   Ctrl + A is the keyboard shortcut to select the entire document.

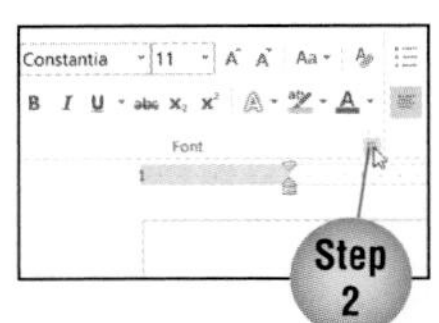

2. Click the Font group dialog box launcher.

   The dialog box launcher displays as a small button containing a diagonal arrow.

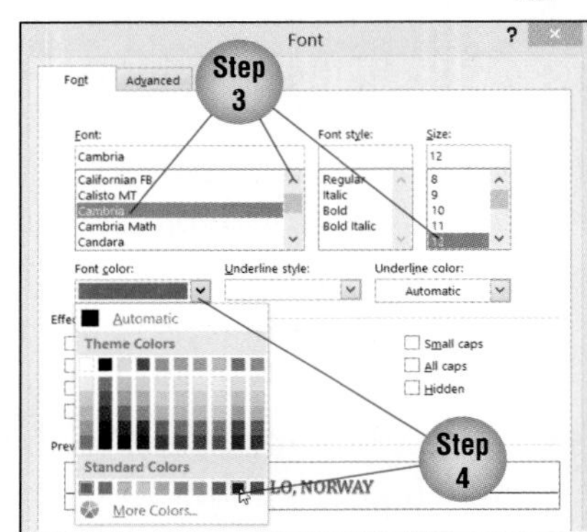

3. At the Font dialog box, click *Cambria* in the *Font* list box (you will need to scroll up the list box to display this option) and then click *12* in the *Size* list box.
4. Click the down-pointing arrow at the right side of the *Font color* option box and then click *Dark Blue* (second option from the right in the *Standard Colors* row).
5. Click OK to close the dialog box.
6. Select the heading *History* and then click the Font group dialog box launcher.

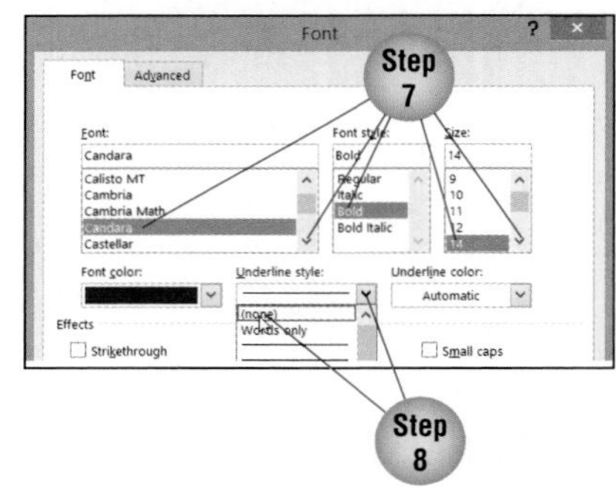

7. Click *Candara* in the *Font* list box (you will need to scroll down the list box to display this option), click *Bold* in the *Font style* list box, and then click *14* in the *Size* list box (you will need to scroll down the list box to display *14*).
8. Click the down-pointing arrow at the right side of the *Underline style* option and then click *(none)* at the drop-down list.
9. Click OK to close the dialog box and then deselect the heading.

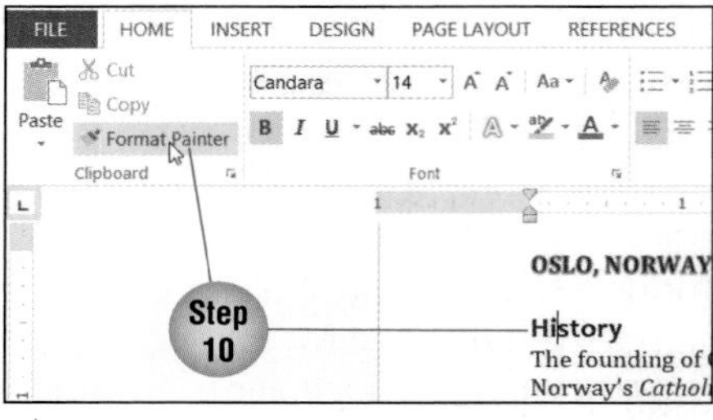

10. Click once on any character in the heading *History* and then double-click the Format Painter button in the Clipboard group on the HOME tab.

When Format Painter is active, the mouse pointer displays with a paintbrush attached. Click the Format Painter button once to apply formatting to one location only. Double-click the Format Painter button if you want to apply formatting to more than one location.

11. Select the title *OSLO, NORWAY*.

    With Format Painter active, selecting text applies formatting. Selecting the title removed the text effect and applied the same formatting that you applied to the *History* heading.

12. Scroll down the document and then click on any character in the word *Population*.

    When using Format Painter, apply formatting to a single word by clicking on any character in the word. To apply formatting to more than one word at a time, select the text.

13. Select individually each of the headings: *Commerce and Industry*; *Climate; Holiday; Sport, and Leisure*; and *Sightseeing Tours*.

14. Click once on the Format Painter button in the Clipboard group to turn off Format Painter.

15. Select the last sentence in the document (the sentence that begins *All tours by boat*) and then click the Font group dialog box launcher.

16. At the Font dialog box, click *Small caps* in the *Effects* section.

17. Click OK to close the dialog box.

18. Select the text *Tour 1: Mini Cruise* and then press F4.

    Pressing F4 repeats the previous command and applies the small caps effect to selected text.

19. Select the text *Tour 2: Fjord Cruise* and then press F4. Select the text *Tour 3: Fjord Cruise with Dinner* and then press F4. Select the text *Tour 4: Selected Oslo Sightseeing* and then press F4.

20. Press Ctrl + Home to move the insertion point to the beginning of the document, select the heading *OSLO, NORWAY,* and then change the font size to 16 points.

21. Save **WS2-FCTOslo.docx**.

In Brief

Change Font at Font Dialog Box
1. Click Font group dialog box launcher.
2. Choose desired font.
3. Click OK.

Apply Formatting with Format Painter
1. Apply formatting.
2. Double-click Format Painter button.
3. Select text.
4. Click Format Painter button to turn off.

Apply Font Effects
1. Select text.
2. Click Font group dialog box launcher.
3. Click desired effect check box.
4. Click OK.

In Addition

Using Font Keyboard Shortcuts

Along with buttons in the Font group and the Font dialog box, you can apply character formatting with the following keyboard shortcuts.

Font Group Button	Keyboard Shortcut
Font	Ctrl + Shift + F
Font Size	Ctrl + Shift + P
Increase Font Size	Ctrl + Shift + >
Decrease Font Size	Ctrl + Shift + <
Change Case	Shift + F3

Font Group Button	Keyboard Shortcut
Bold	Ctrl + B
Italic	Ctrl + I
Underline	Ctrl + U
Subscript	Ctrl + =
Superscript	Ctrl + Shift + +

Activity 2.3

Aligning and Indenting Text

Paragraphs of text in a document are aligned at the left margin by default. This default alignment can be changed to center, right, or justified. Change paragraph alignment with buttons in the Paragraph group on the HOME tab or with keyboard shortcuts. You can indent the first line of text in a paragraph, indent all lines of text in a paragraph, and indent the second and subsequent lines of a paragraph (called a hanging indent). Several methods are available for indenting text, including buttons in the Paragraph group on the HOME tab and the PAGE LAYOUT tab, markers on the horizontal ruler, options at the Paragraph dialog box with the Indents and Spacing tab selected, and keyboard shortcuts. With the keyboard shortcut Alt + Shift + D, you can insert the current date in a document. Use the keyboard shortcut Alt + Shift + T to insert the current time.

Project

You will improve the appearance of the Oslo document by changing text alignment and changing the alignment of specific paragraphs in the document.

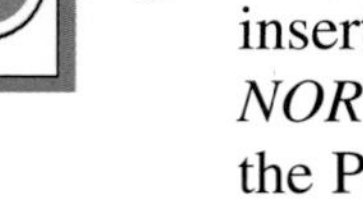

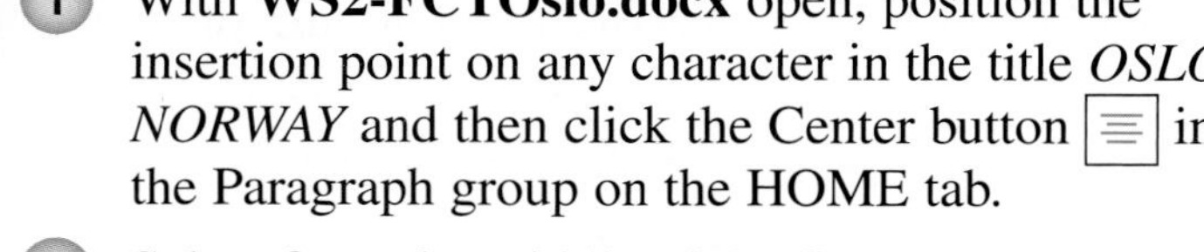

Tutorial 2.3A
Aligning Text in Paragraphs

Tutorial 2.3B
Changing Text Indentation

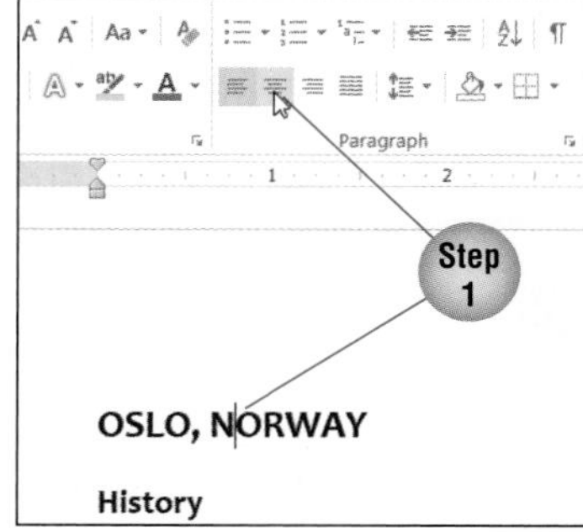

1. With **WS2-FCTOslo.docx** open, position the insertion point on any character in the title *OSLO, NORWAY* and then click the Center button in the Paragraph group on the HOME tab.

2. Select from the middle of the first paragraph of text below the *History* heading to somewhere in the middle of the third paragraph of text and then click the Justify button in the Paragraph group.

   Entire paragraphs do not have to be selected, only a portion of each paragraph.

3. Press Ctrl + End to move the insertion point to the end of the document. Click the Align Right button in the Paragraph group, type your first and last names, and then press the Enter key.

4. Type **Date:**, press the spacebar once, press Alt + Shift + D, and then press the Enter key. Type **Time:**, press the spacebar once, and then press Alt + Shift + T.

   Alt + Shift + D is the keyboard shortcut to insert the current date and Alt + Shift + T is the keyboard shortcut to insert the current time. You can also insert the date and time with options at the Date and Time dialog box. Display this dialog box by clicking the INSERT tab and then clicking the Date & Time button in the Text group.

5. Move the insertion point to the beginning of the document, select the three paragraphs below the *History* heading, and then click the Align Left button in the Paragraph group.

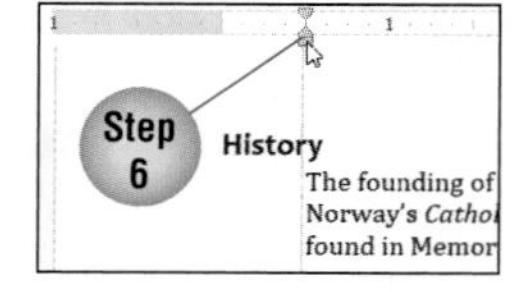

6. With the text still selected, position the mouse pointer on the Left Indent marker on the horizontal ruler, hold down the left mouse button, drag the marker to the 0.5-inch mark on the ruler, and then release the mouse button.

   If the horizontal ruler is not visible, click the VIEW tab and then click the *Ruler* check box in the Show group. The ruler indent markers are shown in Figure 2.1. To precisely position a marker on the ruler, hold down the Alt key while dragging the marker.

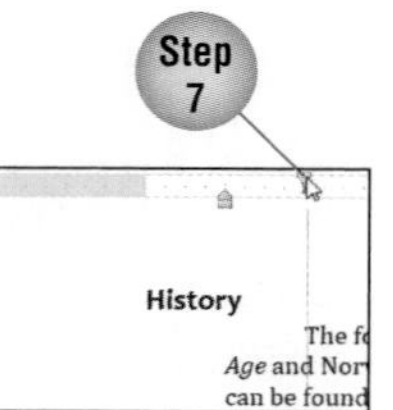

7. Position the mouse pointer on the First Line Indent marker on the horizontal ruler, hold down the left mouse button, and then drag the marker to the 1-inch mark on the ruler.

8 Position the mouse pointer on the Right Indent marker on the ruler, hold down the left mouse button, and then drag the marker to the 6-inch mark on the ruler.

9 Click anywhere in the paragraph below the *Population* heading and then click the PAGE LAYOUT tab. In the *Indent* section in the Paragraph group, click in the *Left* measurement box and then type **0.5**. Click the up-pointing arrow at the right side of the *Right* measurement box until *0.5"* displays.

10 Click anywhere in the paragraph below the *Commerce and Industry* heading and then click the Paragraph group dialog box launcher.

11 At the Paragraph dialog box, select the measurement in the *Left* measurement box in the *Indentation* section and then type **0.5**. Select the measurement in the *Right* measurement box in the *Indentation* section, type **0.5**, and then click OK.

12 Click anywhere in the paragraph below the *Climate* heading and then press F4. Click anywhere in the paragraph below the *Holiday, Sport, and Leisure* heading and then press F4.

13 Select the text below the *Sightseeing Tours* heading except the right-aligned text and then press F4.

14 Select the three paragraphs below the *History* heading and then click the Paragraph group dialog box launcher.

15 At the Paragraph dialog box, click the down-pointing arrow at the right side of the *Special* list box in the *Indentation* section and then click *Hanging* at the drop-down list.

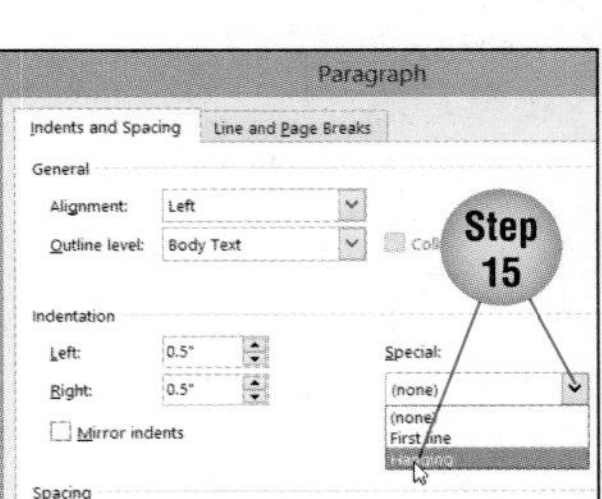

16 Click OK to close the Paragraph dialog box.

17 Save **WS2-FCTOslo.docx**.

FIGURE 2.1 Ruler Indent Markers

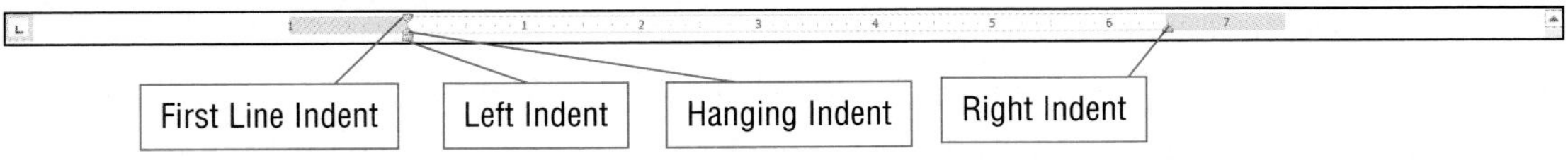

In Addition

Aligning Text

Change text alignment with the following keyboard shortcuts:

Alignment	Keyboard Shortcut
Left	Ctrl + L
Center	Ctrl + E
Right	Ctrl + R
Justified	Ctrl + J

Indenting Text

Indent text with the following keyboard shortcuts:

Indentation	Keyboard Shortcut
Indent text from left margin	Ctrl + M
Decrease indent from left margin	Ctrl + Shift + M
Create a hanging indent	Ctrl + T
Remove hanging indent	Ctrl + Shift + T

Activity 2.4

Changing Line and Paragraph Spacing

By default, line spacing is set at 1.08. This default line spacing can be changed with the Line and Paragraph Spacing button in the Paragraph group on the HOME tab, keyboard shortcuts, or with the *Line spacing* and *At* options at the Paragraph dialog box. Control spacing above and below paragraphs with options at the Line and Paragraph Spacing button drop-down list, the *Before* and *After* text boxes in the *Spacing* section in the Paragraph group on the PAGE LAYOUT tab, or with the *Before* and *After* options in the *Spacing* section of the Paragraph dialog box with the Indents and Spacing tab selected.

Project

The Oslo document project deadline is at hand. However, you have time to make a few spacing changes in the document before printing the final version.

Tutorial 2.4
Setting Line and Paragraph Spacing

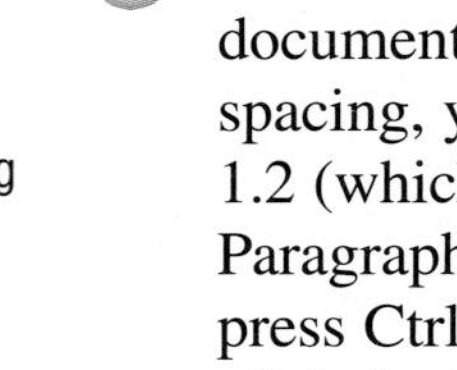

1. With **WS2-FCTOslo.docx** open, select the entire document by pressing Ctrl + A.
2. Click the HOME tab, click the Line and Paragraph Spacing button in the Paragraph group, and then click *1.5* at the drop-down list.

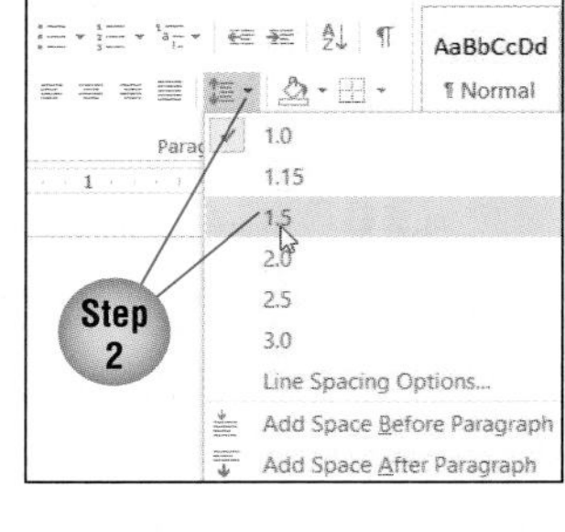

3. Deselect the text and then scroll through the document. After viewing the document in 1.5 line spacing, you decide to decrease the line spacing to 1.2 (which is not an option available at the Line and Paragraph Spacing button drop-down list). To begin, press Ctrl + A to select the entire document, click the Line and Paragraph Spacing button, and then click *Line Spacing Options* at the drop-down list.

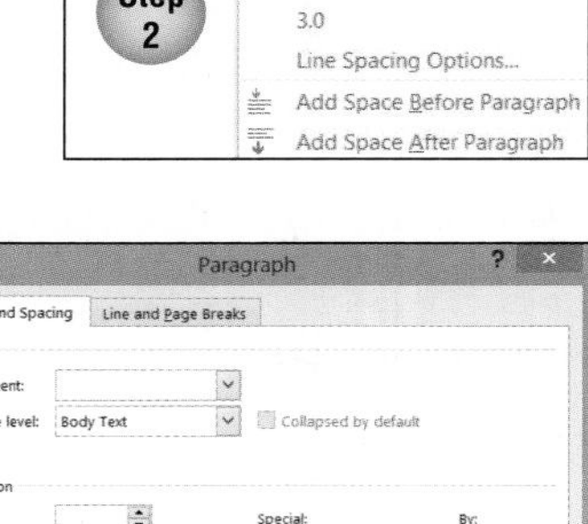

4. Type **1.2** in the *At* text box in the *Spacing* section of the Paragraph dialog box.

   The Paragraph dialog box also contains a *Line spacing* option. Click the down-pointing arrow at the right side of the option and a drop-down list displays with spacing choices.

5. Click OK to close the dialog box and then deselect the text.
6. Select the line of text beginning *Tour 1: Mini Cruise* through *Tour 4: Selected Oslo Sightseeing* and the two lines that follow.

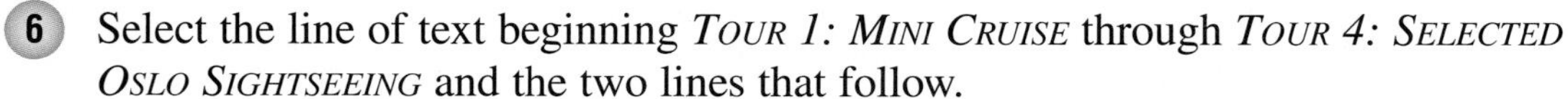

7. Click the Line and Paragraph Spacing button and then click *1.0* at the drop-down list.

   Choosing this option changes the line spacing to single for the selected paragraphs of text. You can also change line spacing with keyboard shortcuts. Press Ctrl + 1 to change to single spacing, Ctrl + 2 to change to double spacing, and Ctrl + 5 to change to 1.5 line spacing.

8. Click anywhere in the last sentence (the sentence that begins *All tours by boat*).
9. Click the Line and Paragraph Spacing button and then click *Add Space Before Paragraph.*

   This inserts 12 points of space above the sentence.

10. Press Ctrl + Home to move the insertion point to the beginning of the document,

click anywhere in the *History* heading, and then click the Paragraph group dialog box launcher.

11 At the Paragraph dialog box, click once on the up-pointing arrow at the right side of the *After* measurement box.

Clicking the up-pointing arrow at the right side of the *After* measurement box inserts *6 pt* in the text box.

12 Click OK to close the dialog box.

13 Click anywhere in the *Population* heading, click the PAGE LAYOUT tab, and then click once on the up-pointing arrow at the right side of the *After* measurement box [After: 0 pt] in the *Spacing* section of the Paragraph group.

Clicking once on the up arrow changes the point measurement to *6 pt*.

14 Click anywhere in the *Commerce and Industry* heading and then press F4.

Pressing F4 repeats the paragraph spacing command.

In Brief

Change Line Spacing

1. Click Line and Paragraph Spacing button.
2. Click desired line spacing option.

OR

1. Click Line and Paragraph Spacing button.
2. Click *Line Spacing Options*.
3. Type desired line spacing in *At* text box.
4. Click OK.

15 Click individually on any character in each of the remaining headings (*Climate*; *Holiday, Sport, and Leisure*; and *Sightseeing Tours*) and then press F4.

16 You also decide that you want to remove the hanging indent on the paragraphs in the *History* section. To do this, select the three paragraphs of text below the *History* heading and then press Ctrl + Shift + T.

Ctrl + Shift + T is the keyboard shortcut to remove hanging indent formatting.

17 Scroll down the page and notice that the heading *Climate* displays at the bottom of the first page while the paragraph that follows the heading displays at the top of the second page. You want to keep the heading with the paragraph of text. Begin by clicking on any character in the heading *Climate* and then clicking the Paragraph group dialog box launcher.

18 At the Paragraph dialog box, click the Line and Page Breaks tab, click the *Keep with next* check box to insert a check mark, and then click OK.

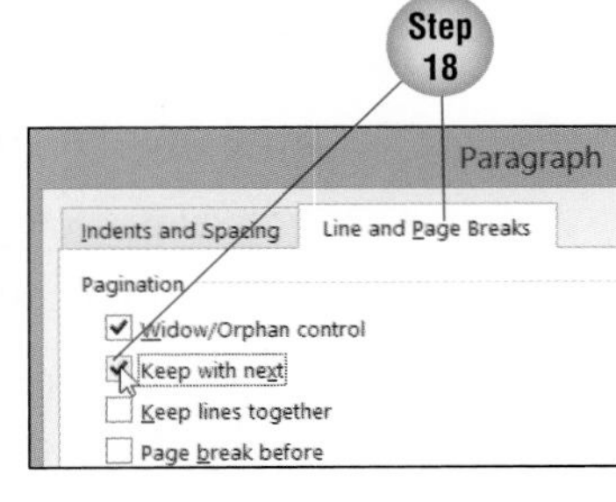

19 Save **WS2-FCTOslo.docx**.

In Addition

Spacing Above or Below Paragraphs

Spacing above or below paragraphs is added in points. A vertical inch contains approximately 72 points and a half inch contains approximately 36 points. For example, to add 9 points of spacing below selected paragraphs, click the PAGE LAYOUT tab or display the Paragraph dialog box with the Indents and Spacing tab selected. Select the current measurement in the *After* measurement box and then type *9*. You can also click the up-pointing or down-pointing arrows to increase or decrease the amount of spacing before or after paragraphs.

Activity 2.5

Revealing Formatting; Finding and Replacing Formatting

Display formatting applied to specific text in a document at the Reveal Formatting task pane. The Reveal Formatting task pane displays font, paragraph, and section formatting applied to text where the insertion point is positioned or to selected text. With options at the Find and Replace dialog box with the Replace tab selected, you can search for specific formatting or characters containing specific formatting and replace it with other formatting or characters.

Project

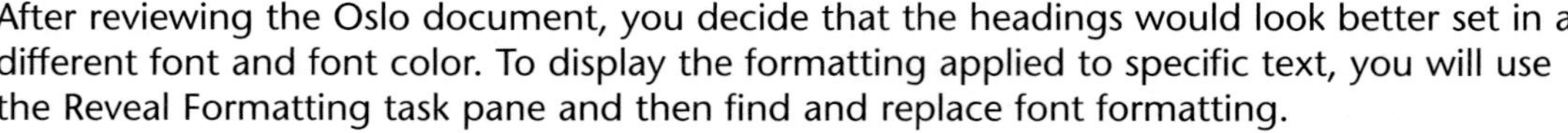

After reviewing the Oslo document, you decide that the headings would look better set in a different font and font color. To display the formatting applied to specific text, you will use the Reveal Formatting task pane and then find and replace font formatting.

First Choice TRAVEL

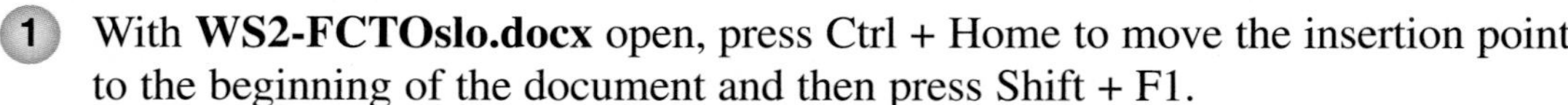

1. With **WS2-FCTOslo.docx** open, press Ctrl + Home to move the insertion point to the beginning of the document and then press Shift + F1.

   Pressing Shift + F1 displays the Reveal Formatting task pane with information on the formatting applied to the title. Generally, a black triangle precedes *Font* and *Paragraph* and a white triangle precedes *Section* in the *Formatting of selected text* section. Click the black triangle to hide any items below a heading and click the white triangle to reveal items. Some items in the Reveal Formatting task pane are hyperlinks. For example, click the FONT hyperlink and the Font dialog box displays. Use these hyperlinks to make changes to the document formatting.

Tutorial 2.5
Finding and Replacing Formatting

2. Click anywhere in the heading *History* and look at the Reveal Formatting task pane to determine the formatting.
3. Click anywhere in the paragraph of text below the heading *History* and look at the Reveal Formatting task pane to determine the formatting.
4. Close the Reveal Formatting task pane by clicking the Close button located in the upper right corner of the task pane.
5. Find text set in 14-point Candara bold and dark blue color and replace it with text set in 14-point Arial bold italic and orange color. To begin, position the insertion point at the beginning of the document and then click the Replace button in the Editing group on the HOME tab.
6. At the Find and Replace dialog box, press the Delete key. (This deletes any text that displays in the *Find what* text box.)
7. Click the More button. (If a check mark displays in the *Find all word forms* check box, click the option to remove the mark.)
8. Click the Format button located at the bottom of the dialog box and then click *Font* at the drop-down list.

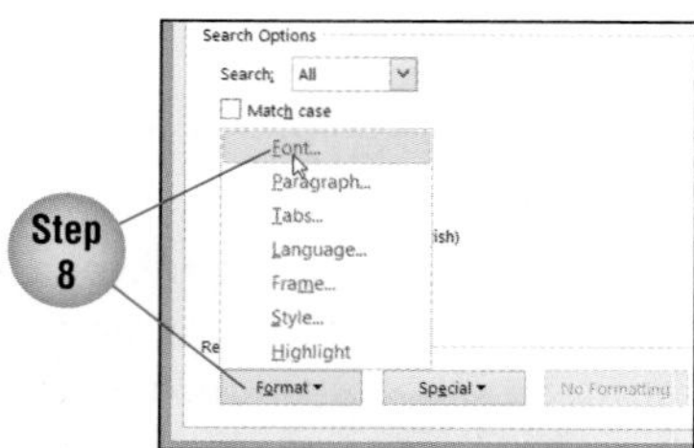

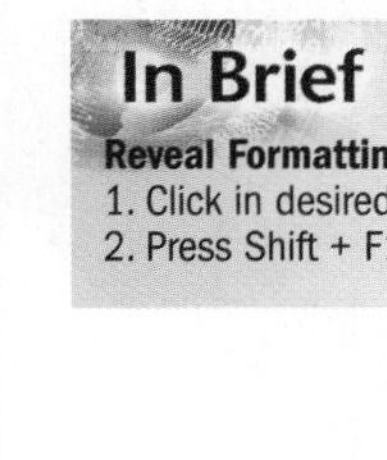

9. At the Find Font dialog box, change the font to Candara, the font style to bold, the size to 14 points, the font color to Dark Blue, and then click OK to close the dialog box.

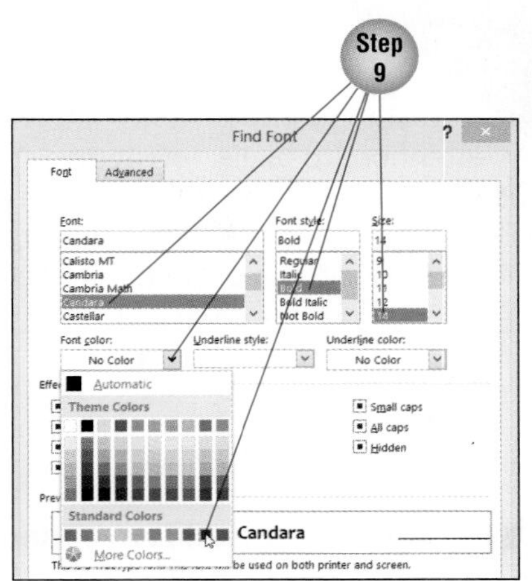

10. At the Find and Replace dialog box, select and then delete any text that displays in the *Replace with* text box.

11. With the insertion point positioned in the *Replace with* text box, click the Format button located at the bottom of the dialog box and then click *Font* at the drop-down list.

12. At the Replace Font dialog box, change the font to Arial, the font style to bold italic, the size to 14 points, and the font color to Orange, Accent 2, Darker 50% (last option in the sixth column in the *Theme Colors* section).

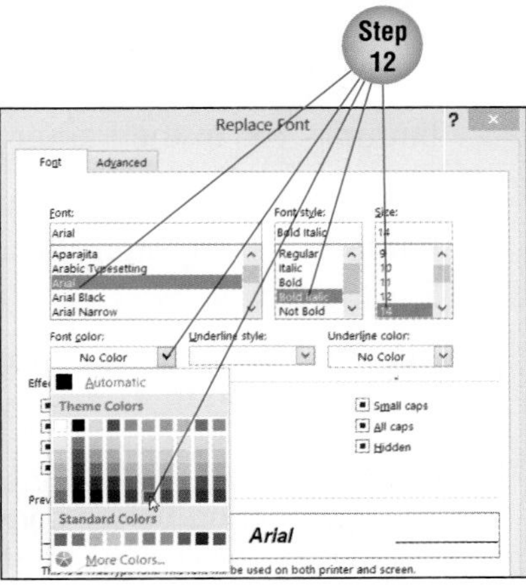

13. Click OK to close the dialog box.

14. At the Find and Replace dialog box, click the Replace All button. At the message telling you that the search of the document is complete and six replacements were made, click OK.

15. With the Find and Replace dialog box open and the insertion point positioned in the *Find what* text box, click the No Formatting button that displays at the bottom of the dialog box. Click in the *Replace with* text box and then click the No Formatting button.

16. Click the Less button to reduce the size of the Find and Replace dialog box and then close the dialog box.

17. Save, print, and then close **WS2-FCTOslo.docx**.

In Addition

Comparing Formatting

Along with displaying formatting applied to text, you can use the Reveal Formatting task pane to compare formatting of two text selections to determine what formatting is different. To compare formatting, display the Reveal Formatting task pane and then select the first instance of formatting to be compared. Click the *Compare to another selection* check box to insert a check mark and then select the second instance of formatting to compare. Any differences between the two selections will display in the *Formatting differences* list box.

Activity 2.6

Inserting Bullets and Numbering

If you want to draw the reader's attention to a list of items, consider inserting a bullet before each item. Click the Bullets button in the Paragraph group on the HOME tab to insert a bullet before items in a list. If a list of items is in a sequence, consider inserting numbers before each item with the Numbering button in the Paragraph group. Create multiple-level bulleted or numbered paragraphs with options from the Multilevel List button in the Paragraph group.

Project

First Choice Travel has a new document on traveling in Europe by train. After reviewing the document, you decide to insert numbers and bullets before selected paragraphs to make the information easier to read.

Tutorial 2.6
Creating Bulleted and Numbered Lists

1. Open **FCTRailTravel.docx** and then save the document and name it **WS2-FCTRailTravel**.
2. Select text from the paragraph *Have your pass validated.* through the paragraph *Be at the right train station.* and then click the Numbering button in the Paragraph group on the HOME tab.
3. Position the insertion point at the end of the second numbered paragraph (the paragraph that displays as *2. Protect your pass.*) and then press the Enter key.

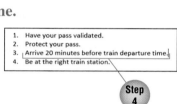

   Pressing the Enter key automatically inserts the number *3.* and renumbers the third paragraph to *4.*

4. Type **Arrive 20 minutes before train departure time.**

   Numbering before paragraphs is changed automatically when paragraphs of text are inserted and/or deleted.

5. Select text from the paragraph that begins *Free or discount transportation* through the paragraph that begins *Reduced rental rates with* and then click the Bullets button in the Paragraph group.

   Clicking the Bullets button inserts a round bullet before each paragraph. Other bullet options are available by clicking the Bullets button arrow.

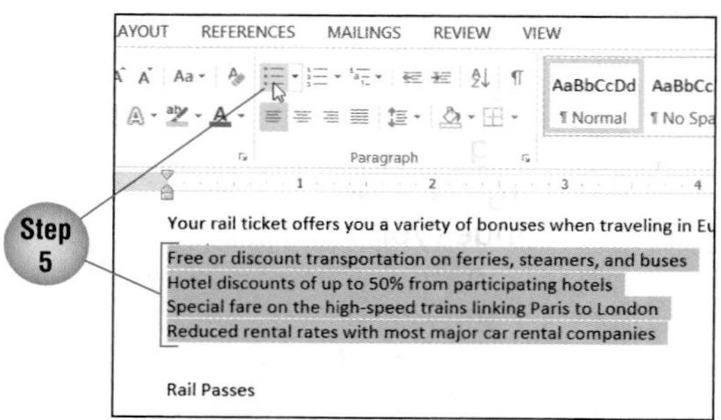

6. With the text still selected, you decide to replace the round bullet with a custom bullet. To begin, click the Bullets button arrow and then click *Define New Bullet* at the drop-down list.
7. At the Define New Bullet dialog box, click the Symbol button in the *Bullet character* section.

8. At the Symbol dialog box, click the down-pointing arrow at the right side of the *Font* list box, scroll down the drop-down list, and then click *Webdings*.

9. Scroll to the end of the symbol list, click the Earth symbol in the bottom row (as shown at the right; the location in the row may vary), and then click OK to close the Symbol dialog box.

10. Click OK to close the Define New Bullet dialog box.

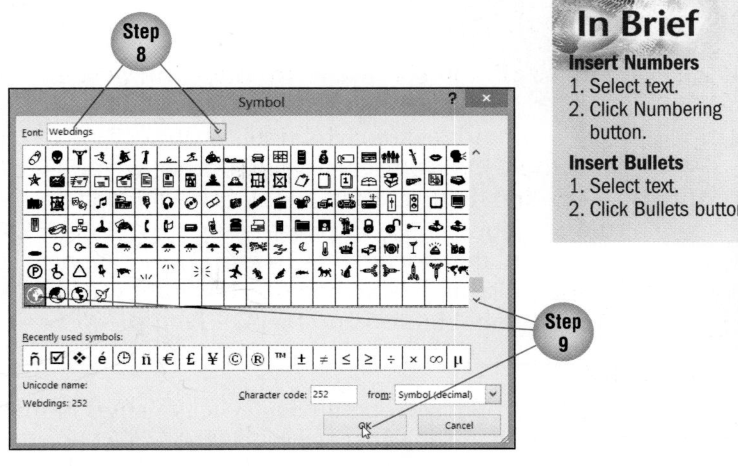

11. Select the text from *Rail Passes* through *Greece-Italy*, click the Multilevel List button in the Paragraph group, and then click the middle option in the top row in the *List Library* section.

    This applies multiple-level numbering to the selected text.

12. With the text still selected, you decide to change to bullets instead of numbers. To do this, click the Multilevel List button and then click the first option from the left in the middle row in the *List Library* section.

13. Deselect the text.

14. Save **WS2-FCTRailTravel.docx**.

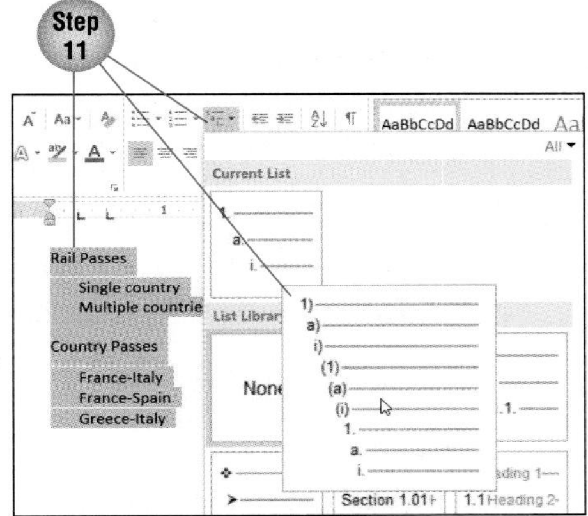

In Brief

Insert Numbers
1. Select text.
2. Click Numbering button.

Insert Bullets
1. Select text.
2. Click Bullets button.

In Addition

Creating Numbered and/or Bulleted Text

If you type *1.* and then press the spacebar, Word indents the number approximately 0.25 inch and then hang indents the text in the paragraph approximately 0.5 inch from the left margin. When you press the Enter key after typing text, *2.* is inserted 0.25 inch from the left margin at the beginning of the next paragraph. Continue typing items and Word inserts the next number in the list. Press Enter twice to turn off numbering or click the Numbering button in the Paragraph group. Bulleted lists with hanging indents are automatically created when you begin a paragraph with the symbol *, > , or -. Type one of the symbols and press the spacebar and the symbol bullet is inserted in the document. The type of bullet inserted depends on the type of character entered. For example, if you use the asterisk (*) symbol, a round bullet is inserted, and an arrow bullet is inserted if you type the greater than symbol (>).

Turning Off Automatic Numbering and/or Bulleting

If you do not want automatic numbering or bulleting in a document, turn off the features at the AutoCorrect dialog box with the AutoFormat As You Type tab selected. To display this dialog box, click the FILE tab and then click *Options*. At the Word Options dialog box, click the *Proofing* option and then click the AutoCorrect Options button. At the AutoCorrect dialog box, click the AutoFormat As You Type tab. Click the *Automatic numbered lists* check box and/or *Automatic bulleted lists* check box to remove the check mark.

Activity 2.7

Inserting Symbols and Special Characters

Insert special symbols such as é, ö, and Å with options at the Symbol palette or at the Symbol dialog box. Display the Symbol palette by clicking the INSERT tab and then clicking the Symbol button in the Symbols group. Click the desired symbol to insert it in the document. To display additional symbols, display the Symbol dialog box by clicking the Symbol button and then clicking the *More Symbols* option. Click the desired symbol at the dialog box, click the Insert button, and then click the Close button. At the Symbol dialog box with the Symbols tab selected, you can change the font and display different symbols. Click the Special Characters tab at the dialog box and a list displays containing special characters and the keyboard shortcuts to insert the characters.

Project

You have identified a few city names in the train travel document that need special letters in their spellings, as well as a special character you need to insert in the document.

Tutorial 2.7
Inserting Symbols and Special Characters

1. With **WS2-FCTRailTravel.docx** open, move the insertion point to the end of the document and then select and delete the multiple-level bulleted text.
2. With the insertion point positioned at the end of the document a double space below the bulleted text, type the text shown in Figure 2.2 up to the Å in Århus. To insert the Å symbol, click the INSERT tab, click the Symbol button Ω in the Symbols group, and then click *More Symbols* at the bottom of the palette.
3. At the Symbol dialog box with the Symbols tab selected, click the down-pointing arrow at the right side of the *Font* list box and then click *(normal text)* at the drop-down list. You may need to scroll up to see this option. Skip this step if *(normal text)* is already selected.
4. Scroll down the list box somewhere between the seventh and ninth rows and then click the Å symbol.

Need Help?

If you do not see the Å symbol, make sure *(normal text)* is selected at the *Font* list box.

5. Click the Insert button and then click the Close button.
6. Type text up to the ø symbol. To insert the ø symbol, click the Symbol button and then click *More Symbols*.

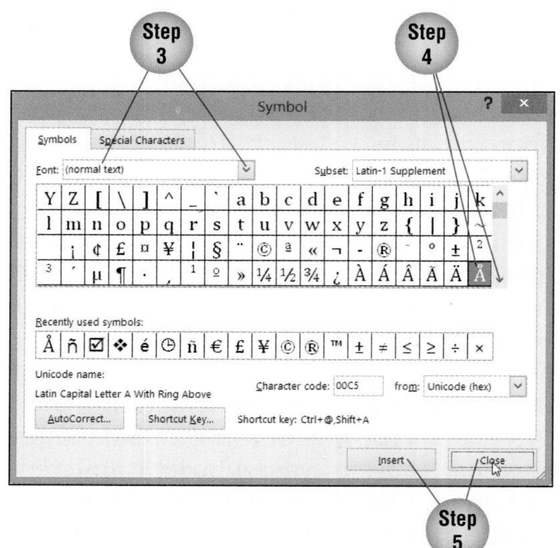

FIGURE 2.2 Steps 2–13

> Some companies offer outstanding reductions on transportation. For example, you can travel on the ferry in Denmark between Århus and Kalundborg and between Nyborg and Korsør at a 75% discount! ScanTravel, a travel company located in Stockholm, offers the StarPass® ticket that provides you with incredible discounts on travel by train, ferry, and bus in Sweden, Norway, and Denmark.

7. At the Symbol dialog box, click the ø symbol (somewhere between the tenth and twelfth rows).
8. Click the Insert button and then click the Close button.
9. Type the text up to the ® character. To insert the ® character, click the Symbol button and then click *More Symbols*.
10. At the Symbol dialog box, click the Special Characters tab.
11. Click the ® character in the dialog box list box.
12. Click the Insert button and then click the Close button.
13. Type the remaining text in Figure 2.2. Press the Enter key twice after typing the text.
14. Save **WS2-FCTRailTravel.docx**.

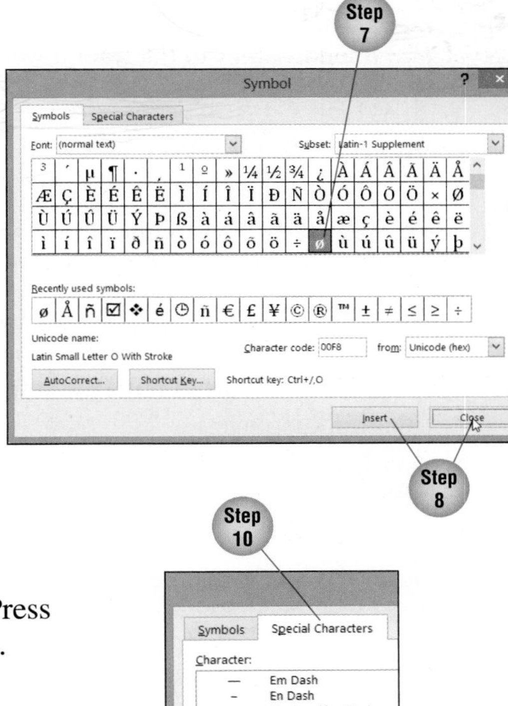

In Brief

Insert Symbol

1. Click INSERT tab.
2. Click Symbol button.
3. Click *More Symbols*.
4. Click desired symbol.
5. Click Insert button.
6. Click Close button.

Insert Special Character

1. Click INSERT tab.
2. Click Symbol button.
3. Click *More Symbols*.
4. Click Special Characters tab.
5. Click desired character.
6. Click Insert button.
7. Click Close button.

In Addition

Inserting Symbols with Keyboard Shortcuts

Another method for inserting symbols in a document is to use a keyboard shortcut. Click a symbol at the Symbol dialog box and the keyboard shortcut displays toward the bottom of the dialog box. For example, click the ø symbol and the keyboard shortcut *Ctrl + /,O* displays toward the bottom of the dialog box. To insert the ø symbol in a document using the keyboard shortcut, hold down the Ctrl key and then press the / key. Release the Ctrl key and then press the o key. Not all symbols contain a keyboard shortcut.

Inserting Symbols Using the Palette

When you click the Symbol button in the Symbols group, a drop-down palette displays with symbol choices. The palette displays the most recently used symbols. If the palette contains the desired symbol, click the symbol and it is inserted in the document.

Activity 2.8

Setting Tabs

Word offers a variety of default settings including left tabs set every 0.5 inch. You can set your own tabs using the horizontal ruler or at the Tabs dialog box. Use the horizontal ruler to set, move, and delete tabs. With a left tab, text aligns at the left edge of the tab. The other types of tabs that can be set on the horizontal ruler are center, right, decimal, and bar. The small button at the left side of the horizontal ruler is called the Alignment button. Each time you click the Alignment button, a different tab or paragraph alignment symbol displays. To set a tab, display the desired alignment symbol on the button and then click on the horizontal ruler at the desired position.

Project

You have completed some additional research on train travel in Europe with train connections. You will add airport names to the train travel document.

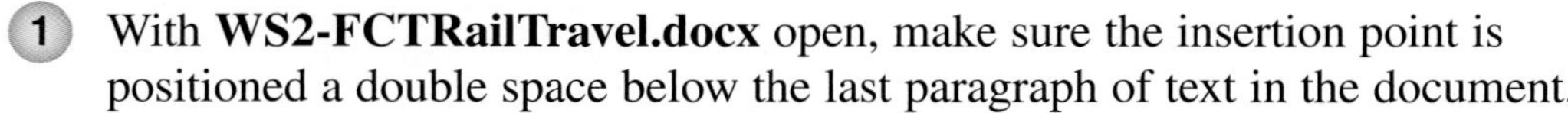

1. With **WS2-FCTRailTravel.docx** open, make sure the insertion point is positioned a double space below the last paragraph of text in the document.
2. Type **International Airports with Train Connections** and then press the Enter key twice. (If tabs display on the horizontal ruler, clear the tabs by clicking the Clear All Formatting button in the Font group on the HOME tab.)

Tutorial 2.8
Setting Tabs Using the Horizontal Ruler

3. Make sure the left tab symbol displays in the Alignment button at the left side of the horizontal ruler. (If the left tab symbol does not display in the Alignment button, click the button until the left tab symbol displays.)

   If the horizontal ruler is not visible, click the VIEW tab and then click the *Ruler* check box in the Show group.

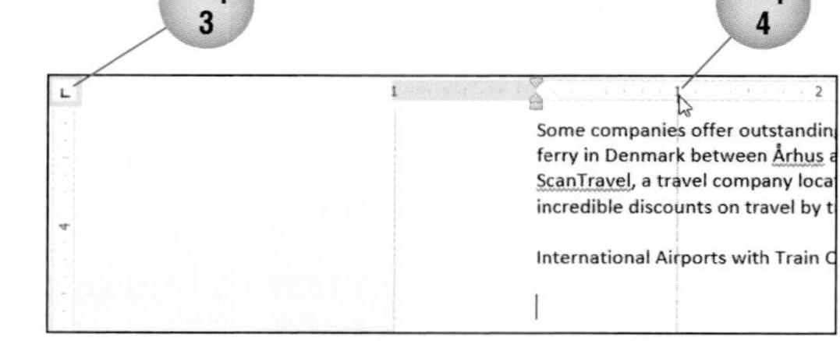

4. Position the arrow pointer below the 1-inch mark on the horizontal ruler and then click the left mouse button.
5. Click once on the Alignment button located at the left side of the horizontal ruler to display the center tab symbol.
6. Position the arrow pointer below the 3.25-inch mark on the horizontal ruler and then click the left mouse button.

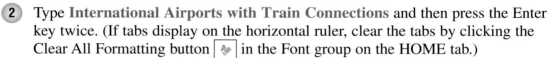

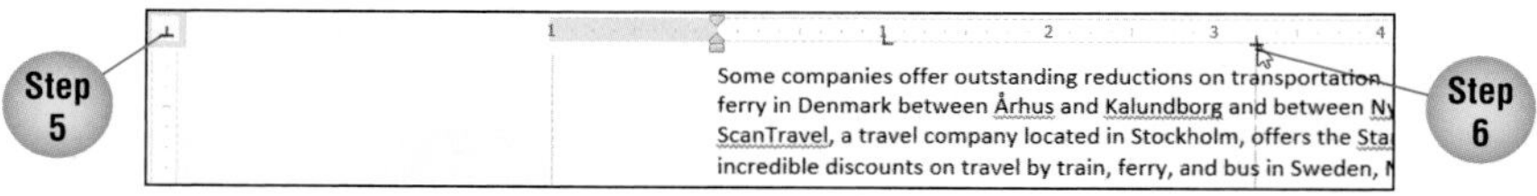

7. Click once on the Alignment button located at the left side of the horizontal ruler to display the right tab symbol.
8. Position the arrow pointer below the 5.5-inch mark on the horizontal ruler and then click the left mouse button.

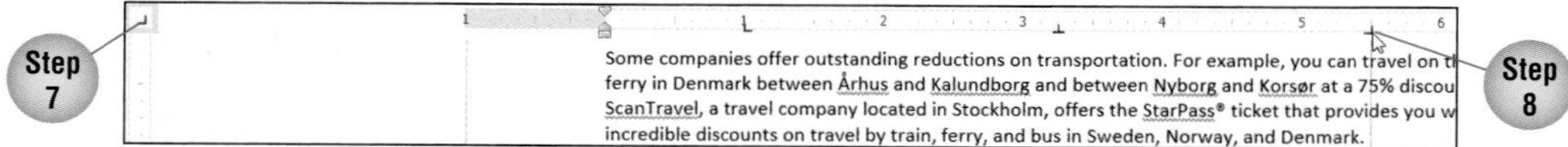

9 Type the text shown in Figure 2.3, pressing the Tab key before typing each tabbed entry. Make sure you press the Tab key before typing the entry in the first column and that you bold the text in the first row.

Need Help?

If your columns of text do not look similar to those in Figure 2.3, check to make sure you inserted the tab symbols at the correct locations on the horizontal ruler and that you pressed the Tab key before typing each entry in the first column.

10 After typing the last entry in the third column (*Fiumicino*), press the Enter key twice and then click the Clear All Formatting button in the Font group on the HOME tab.

Clicking the Clear Formatting button removes paragraph and character formatting. You can also remove paragraph formatting by pressing the keyboard shortcut Ctrl + Q and remove character formatting by pressing the keyboard shortcut Ctrl + spacebar.

11 Save **WS2-FCTRailTravel.docx**.

In Brief

Set Tab on Horizontal Ruler

1. Display desired alignment symbol on Alignment button.
2. Click on horizontal ruler at desired position.

FIGURE 2.3 Step 9

Country	**City**	**Airport**
Austria	Vienna (Wein)	Schwechat
Belgium	Brussels	Nationaal
France	Paris	Orly
Germany	Berlin	Schoenefeld
Great Britain	London	Heathrow
Italy	Rome	Fiumicino

In Addition

Moving a Tab

Move a tab on the horizontal ruler by positioning the mouse pointer on the tab symbol on the horizontal ruler, holding down the left mouse button, dragging the symbol to the new location on the ruler, and then releasing the mouse button.

Deleting a Tab

Delete a tab from the horizontal ruler by positioning the arrow pointer on the tab symbol, holding down the left mouse button, dragging the symbol down into the document screen, and then releasing the mouse button.

Setting a Decimal Tab

Set a decimal tab for column entries you want aligned at the decimal point. To set a decimal tab, click the Alignment button located at the left side of the horizontal ruler until the decimal tab symbol displays and then click on the desired position on the horizontal ruler.

Activity 2.9

Setting Tabs with Leaders

The four types of tabs can be set with leaders. Leaders are useful for material where you want to direct the reader's eyes across the page. Leaders can be periods, hyphens, or underlines. Tabs with leaders are set with options at the Tabs dialog box. To display the Tabs dialog box, click the Paragraph group dialog box launcher and then click the Tabs button at the Paragraph dialog box. At the Tabs dialog box, enter a tab position measurement, choose the type of tab, and then choose the type of leader.

Project

The information you found listing airports with train connections also includes schedule times. You will add this data to the train travel document.

Tutorial 2.9
Setting Tabs at the Tabs Dialog Box

1. With **WS2-FCTRailTravel.docx** open, move the insertion point to the end of the document.
2. Click the Alignment button at the left side of the horizontal ruler until the left tab symbol displays.
3. Position the arrow pointer below the 1-inch mark on the horizontal ruler and then click the left mouse button.
4. Click the Alignment button at the left side of the horizontal ruler until the right tab symbol displays.
5. Position the arrow pointer below the 5.5-inch mark on the horizontal ruler and then click the left mouse button.
6. Type the headings shown in Figure 2.4 by pressing the Tab key, clicking the Bold button in the Font group, and then typing **Airport**.
7. Press the Tab key and then type **Service**.
8. Press the Enter key once and then click the Clear All Formatting button to remove the bold formatting and the paragraph tab formatting.
9. Set a left tab and a right tab with leaders at the Tabs dialog box. To begin, click the Paragraph group dialog box launcher and then click the Tabs button located in the lower left corner of the Paragraph dialog box.

   You can also display the Tabs dialog box by double-clicking on any tab symbol on the horizontal ruler.

10. At the Tabs dialog box, make sure *Left* is selected in the *Alignment* section of the dialog box. (If it is not, click *Left*.) With the insertion point positioned in the *Tab stop position* text box, type **1** and then click the Set button.

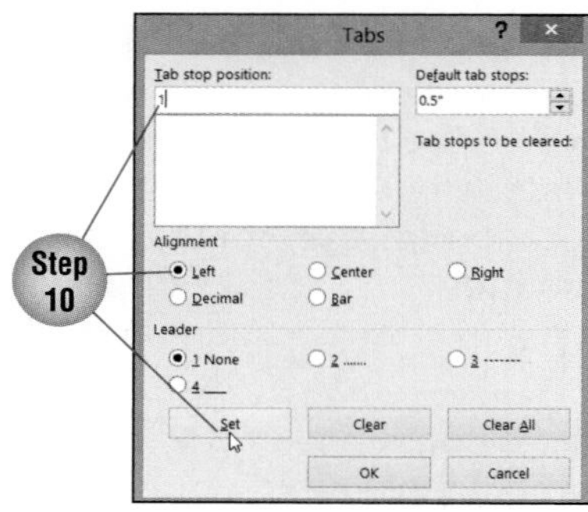

FIGURE 2.4 Step 6 and Step 13

Airport	**Service**
Schwechat	Train every 30 minutes
Nationaal	Train every 20 minutes
Orly	RER train every 20 minutes
Schoenefeld	S-Bahn train every 30 minutes
Heathrow	LT train every 10 minutes
Fiumicino	Train every 10 to 20 minutes

In Brief

Set Tab with Leaders

1. Click Paragraph group dialog box launcher.
2. Click Tabs button.
3. Type tab measurement.
4. Click desired alignment.
5. Click desired leader.
6. Click Set.
7. Click OK.

11. Type 5.5 in the *Tab stop position* text box, click *Right* in the *Alignment* section of the dialog box, and click *2.....* in the *Leader* section of the dialog box.
12. Click the Set button and then click OK to close the dialog box.

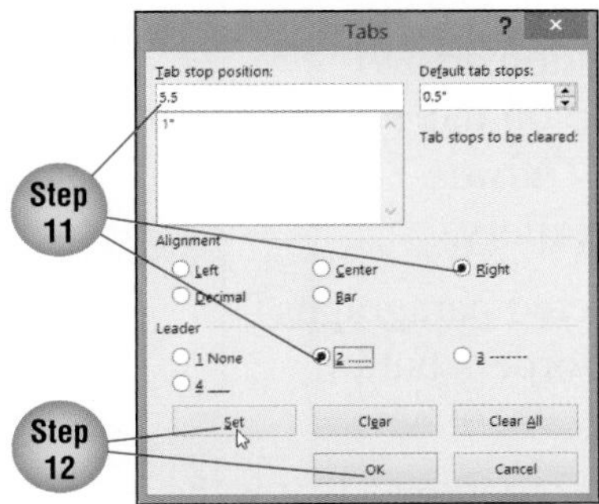

13. Type the remaining text shown in Figure 2.4, making sure you press the Tab key before typing the first text entry.

Need Help?

If your columns of text do not look similar to those in Figure 2.4, check to make sure you inserted the tab symbols at the correct measurements and that you pressed Tab before typing each entry in the first column.

14. Press Ctrl + Home to move the insertion point to the beginning of the document and then select the four numbered paragraphs.
15. With the paragraphs selected, click the Bullets button arrow and then click the Earth bullet in the *Bullet Library* section. (The Earth bullet is the bullet you selected in Activity 2.6.) If this bullet is not available at the drop-down list, complete steps similar to those in Activity 2.6, Steps 6 through 10, to select and apply the Earth bullet.
16. Save **WS2-FCTRailTravel.docx**.

In Addition

Clearing Tabs at the Tabs Dialog Box

At the Tabs dialog box, you can clear an individual tab or all tabs. To clear all tabs, click the Clear All button. To clear an individual tab, specify the tab position and then click the Clear button.

Activity 2.10

Adding Borders and Shading

Insert a border around text and/or apply shading to text in a paragraph or selected text with the Borders button and Shading button in the Paragraph group on the HOME tab or at the Borders and Shading dialog box. At the Borders and Shading dialog box with the Borders tab selected, specify the border type, style, color, and width. Click the Shading tab and the dialog box contains options for choosing a fill color and pattern style. Click the Page Border tab and the dialog box contains options for applying a page border.

Project

To highlight certain information in First Choice Travel's train travel document, you will apply a border to selected text and apply border and shading formatting to the column text. You will also apply a page border to add visual appeal.

Tutorial 2.10
Adding a Border and Shading to Selected Text

1. With **WS2-FCTRailTravel.docx** open, make sure the first four bulleted paragraphs are selected (if not, select them), click the Borders button arrow in the Paragraph group on the HOME tab, and then click *Outside Borders* at the drop-down gallery.

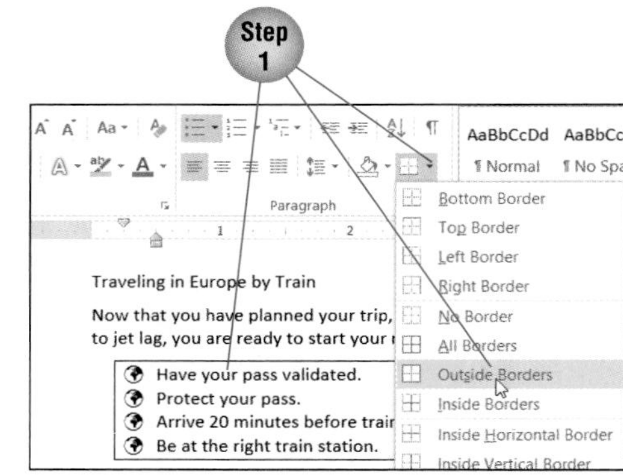

2. Select the second four bulleted paragraphs of text and then click the Borders button in the Paragraph group.

   This applies the outside border since that is the last border option you selected.

3. Select from the column headings *Country*, *City*, and *Airport* through the line of text containing the column entries *Italy*, *Rome*, and *Fiumicino*.
4. Click the Borders button arrow and then click *Borders and Shading* at the drop-down gallery.
5. At the Borders and Shading dialog box with the Borders tab selected, click the *Box* option in the *Setting* section.
6. Click the down-pointing arrow at the right side of the *Style* list box until the first double-line option displays and then click the double-line option.
7. Click the down-pointing arrow at the right side of the *Color* option box and then click *Blue, Accent 1, Darker 50%* at the color palette (bottom color in the fifth column in the *Theme Colors* section).
8. Click the down-pointing arrow at the right side of the *Width* option box and then click *¾ pt* at the drop-down list.
9. Click the Shading tab, click the down-pointing arrow at the right side of the *Fill* option, and then click *Blue, Accent 1, Lighter 80%* at the color palette (second color in the fifth column in the *Theme Colors* section).

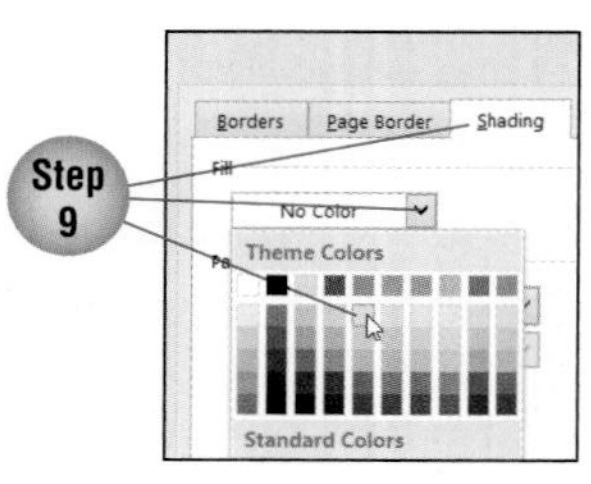

10. Click OK to close the dialog box.

11. Add the same border and shading to the other columns of text by selecting from the column headings *Airport* and *Service* through the line of text containing the column entries *Fiumicino* and *Train every 10 to 20 minutes* and then pressing F4.

12. Apply shading to the title by positioning the insertion point in the title *Traveling in Europe by Train*, clicking the Shading button arrow, and then clicking the *Blue, Accent 1, Lighter 60%* color.

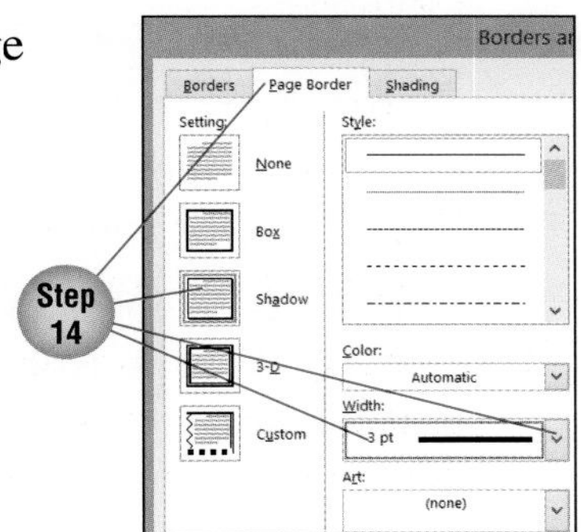

13. Apply a page border to the document. To begin, click the Borders button arrow and then click *Borders and Shading* at the drop-down list.

14. At the Borders and Shading dialog box, click the Page Border tab, click the *Shadow* option in the *Setting* section, click the down-pointing arrow at the right side of the *Width* option, and then click *3 pt* at the drop-down list.

    You can also display the Borders and Shading dialog box with the Page Border tab selected by clicking the DESIGN tab and then clicking the Page Borders button in the Page Background group.

15. Click OK to close the dialog box.

16. Change the page border to an art image. To begin, click the Borders button arrow and then click *Borders and Shading*. At the Borders and Shading dialog box, click the Page Border tab.

17. Click the *Box* option in the *Setting* section, click the down-pointing arrow at the right side of the *Art* option box, scroll down the list until the globe art images display, and then click the first set of globe images.

18. Select the measurement in the *Width* text box, type **10**, and then click OK to close the dialog box.

19. Save **WS2-FCTRailTravel.docx**.

In Brief

Insert Borders and Shading

1. Select text.
2. Click Borders button arrow.
3. Click *Borders and Shading*.
4. Choose desired border(s).
5. Click Shading tab.
6. Choose desired shading and/or pattern.
7. Click OK.

Insert Page Border

1. Click Borders button arrow.
2. Click *Borders and Shading*.
3. Click Page Border tab.
4. Choose desired options.
5. Click OK.

In Addition

Applying Borders

The Borders and Shading dialog box, with the Borders tab or the Page Border tab selected, contains a preview area you can use to insert borders at specfic locations. A diagram displays in the Preview area and you can click at the sides, top, or bottom of the diagram to insert or remove a border line. Buttons display around the diagram that you can also use to insert borders on sides of the diagram.

Activity 2.11

Applying Styles, Style Sets, and Themes

A Word document is based on a template that applies default formatting such as an 11-point Calibri font, line spacing of 1.08, and 8 points of spacing after each paragraph. You can change these default formats with buttons and options on the ribbon and also with styles. A style is a set of formatting instructions you can apply to text. To apply a predesigned style, click the desired style thumbnail in the Styles group on the HOME tab. Click the More button at the right side of the style thumbnails to display a drop-down list of additional styles. Word groups styles that apply similar formatting into style sets. Style sets are available in the Document Formatting group on the DESIGN tab. If you choose a different style set, the styles in the Styles group on the HOME tab change to reflect the currently selected style set. A style set changes the formatting applied by styles. In addition to a style set, apply formatting to a document with a theme. A theme is a set of formatting choices that includes a color theme (a set of colors), a font theme (a set of heading and body text fonts), and an effects theme (a set of lines and fill effects). Apply a theme with the Themes button in the Document Formatting group on the DESIGN tab. Customize a theme (or style set) with the Colors, Fonts, and Effects buttons.

Project

To further enhance the train travel document, you decide to apply styles, a different style set, and a theme to the document.

SNAP

Tutorial 2.11
Applying Styles, Style Sets, and Themes

1. With **WS2-FCTRailTravel.docx** open, press Ctrl + Home to move the insertion point to the beginning of the document.

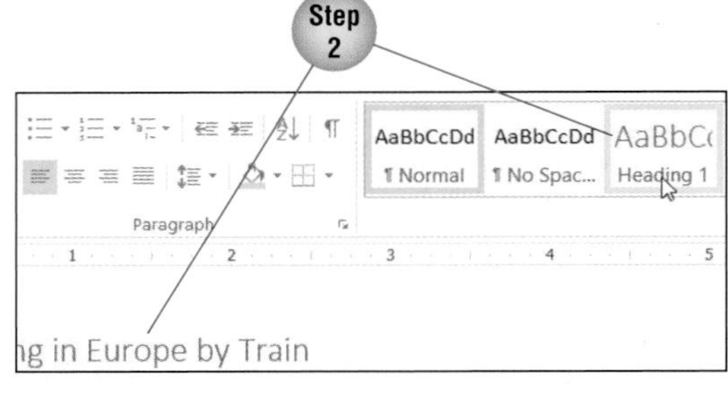

2. Click any character in the title *Traveling in Europe by Train* and then click the *Heading 1* style thumbnail in the Styles group on the HOME tab.

   The Heading 1 style in the default style set changes the font size and font color and adds 12 points of spacing above the title. Applying the heading style also removes the shading you inserted in the previous activity.

3. Click any character in the heading *Rail Ticket Bonuses* and then click the *Heading 2* style thumbnail in the Styles group.

4. Click any character in the heading *International Airports with Train Connections* and then click the *Heading 2* style.

5. Apply a different style set by clicking the DESIGN tab, clicking the More button located to the right of the style set thumbnails in the Document Formatting group, and then clicking *Lines (Stylish)*.

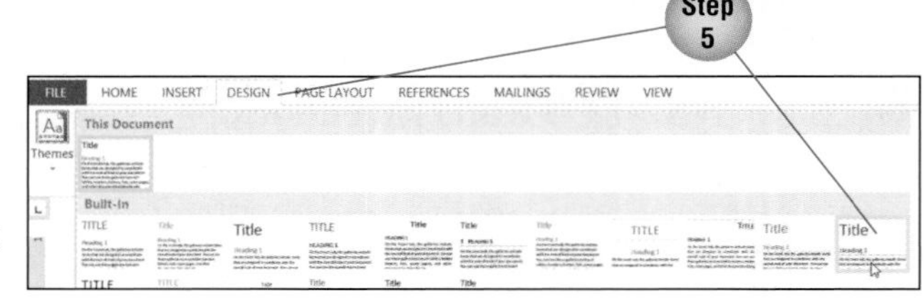

6. Apply a paragraph spacing option so the text fits on one page by clicking the Paragraph Spacing button in the Document Formatting group and then clicking *Compact* at the drop-down gallery.

   Display the paragraph and line formatting applied by a paragraph spacing option by hovering the mouse over the option at the drop-down gallery.

Step 6
Colors
Fonts
Paragraph Spacing
Style Set
Lines (Stylish)
Built-In
No Paragraph Space
Compact
Tight

7 Apply a theme by clicking the Themes button [A] in the Document Formatting group and then clicking the *Retrospect* option.

8 Change the colors applied by the theme by clicking the Colors button [ ] in the Document Formatting group and then clicking the *Green* option at the drop-down gallery.

9 Change the fonts applied by the theme by clicking the Fonts button [A] in the Document Formatting group and then clicking the *Corbel* option at the drop-down gallery.

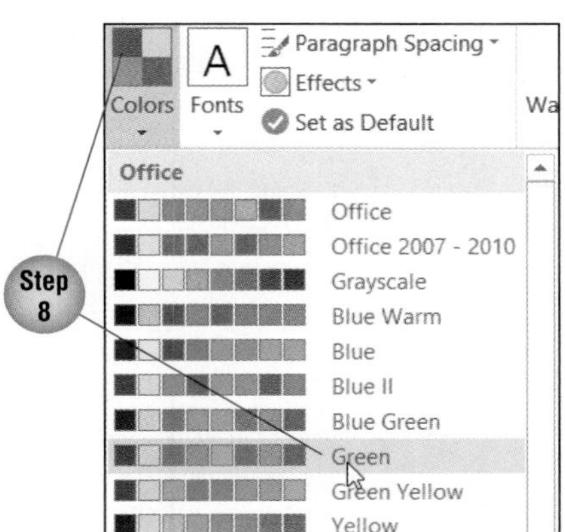

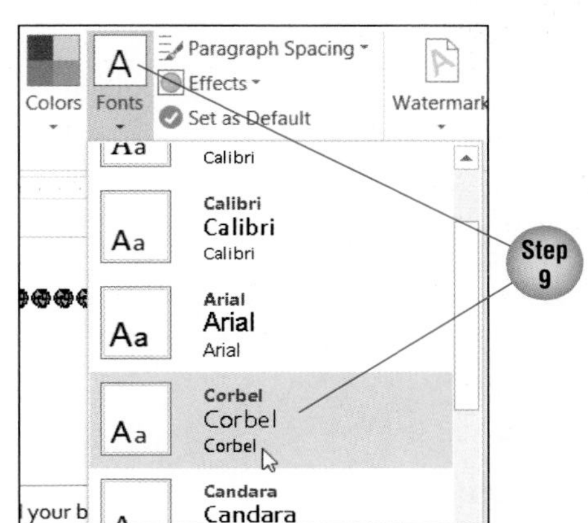

10 Select the title *Traveling in Europe by Train,* change the font size to 24 points, and change the paragraph alignment to center.

11 Save, print, and then close **WS2-FCTRailTravel.docx**.

In Brief

Apply a Style
1. Position insertion point at desired location.
2. Click style thumbnail in Styles group or click More button and then click desired style.

Change Style Set
1. Click DESIGN tab.
2. Click desired style set thumbnail in Document Formatting group.

Apply Paragraph Spacing
1. Click DESIGN tab.
2. Click Paragraph Spacing button in Document Formatting group.
3. Click desired option at drop-down gallery.

Apply a Theme
1. Click DESIGN tab.
2. Click Themes button in Document Formatting group.
3. Click desired theme at drop-down gallery.

Change Document Colors
1. Click DESIGN tab.
2. Click Colors button in Document Formatting group.
3. Click desired colors at drop-down gallery.

Change Document Fonts
1. Click DESIGN tab.
2. Click Fonts button in Document Formatting group.
3. Click desired fonts at drop-down gallery.

In Addition

Applying the No Spacing Style

By default, a blank document contains line spacing of 1.08 and 8 points of spacing after paragraphs. The increase in line spacing and spacing after paragraphs creates more space between lines and is designed to make text easier to read on a computer screen. You can change the line spacing to 1.0 and remove the spacing after paragraphs by clicking the *No Spacing* style in the Styles group on the HOME tab.

Collapsing and Expanding Headings

When you apply heading styles to text in a document, you can collapse text below the headings. By collapsing text, you can view the headings in your document and use the headings to easily navigate to specific locations. Collapse text in a document by clicking the gray triangle that displays when you hover over your text with a heading style applied. Expand a collapsed document by clicking the white triangle before a heading with a style applied.

Applying Styles at the Styles Window

The Styles window provides additional styles you can apply to text in a document. Display this window by clicking the Styles group dialog box launcher. The styles in the currently selected style set display in the window followed by a paragraph symbol (¶), indicating that the style applies paragraph formatting, or a character symbol (a), indicating that the style applies character formatting. If both characters display to the right of a style, the style applies both paragraph and character formatting. In addition to displaying styles that apply formatting, the Styles window also includes a Clear All style that clears all formatting from selected text.

Features Summary

Feature	Ribbon Tab, Group	Button	Keyboard Shortcut
1.5 line spacing	HOME, Paragraph		Ctrl + 5
align left	HOME, Paragraph		Ctrl + L
align right	HOME, Paragraph		Ctrl + R
bold	HOME, Font	B	Ctrl + B
borders	HOME, Paragraph		
bullets	HOME, Paragraph		
center	HOME, Paragraph		Ctrl + E
change case	HOME, Font	Aa	Shift + F3
clear formatting	HOME, Font		
date	INSERT, Text		Alt + Shift + D
decrease indent	HOME, Paragraph		Ctrl + Shift + M
document colors	DESIGN, Document Formatting		
document fonts	DESIGN, Document Formatting	A	
double line spacing	HOME, Paragraph		Ctrl + 2
Find and Replace dialog box with Replace tab selected	HOME, Editing		Ctrl + H
font	HOME, Font		
font color	HOME, Font	A	
Font dialog box	HOME, Font		Ctrl + D
font size	HOME, Font		Ctrl + Shift + P
Format Painter	HOME, Clipboard		Ctrl + Shift + C
hanging indent	HOME, Paragraph		Ctrl + T
highlight	HOME, Font		
increase indent	HOME, Paragraph		Ctrl + M
insert symbol	INSERT, Symbols	Ω	
italics	HOME, Font	*I*	Ctrl + I
justify	HOME, Paragraph		Ctrl + J

Feature	Ribbon Tab, Group	Button	Keyboard Shortcut
line and paragraph spacing	HOME, Paragraph		
multilevel list	HOME, Paragraph		
numbering	HOME, Paragraph		
Paragraph dialog box	HOME, Paragraph		
remove hanging indent	HOME, Paragraph		Ctrl + Shift + T
shading	HOME, Paragraph		
single line spacing	HOME, Paragraph		Ctrl + 1
spacing after	PAGE LAYOUT, Paragraph	After: 0 pt	
spacing before	PAGE LAYOUT, Paragraph	Before: 0 pt	
style sets	DESIGN, Document Formatting		
styles	HOME, Styles		
Tabs dialog box	HOME, Paragraph	, Tabs	
themes	DESIGN, Document Formatting		
time	INSERT, Text		Alt + Shift + T
underline	HOME, Font		Ctrl + U

Knowledge Check

Completion: In the space provided at the right, indicate the correct term, command, or option.

1. The Bold button is located in this group on the HOME tab. ________________
2. Click this button in the Font group and then click the *UPPERCASE* option to change selected text to uppercase letters. ________________
3. Press these keys on the keyboard to italicize selected text. ________________
4. The *Small caps* option is located in this section of the Font dialog box. ________________
5. Click this button in the Paragraph group on the HOME tab to align text at the right margin. ________________
6. Indent text from the left margin by dragging the Left Indent marker on this. ________________
7. At a new document, this is the default line spacing. ________________
8. The Line and Paragraph Spacing button displays in this group on the HOME tab. ________________
9. This is the keyboard shortcut to display the Reveal Formatting task pane. ________________
10. Click this button at the Find and Replace dialog box to display additional options. ________________

11. Click this button in the Paragraph group on the HOME tab to number selected paragraphs. ________________
12. Create multiple-level bulleted or numbered paragraphs with options from this button. ________________
13. Display the Symbol palette by clicking this tab and then clicking the Symbol button in the Symbols group. ________________
14. This is the name of the button that displays at the left side of the horizontal ruler. ________________
15. Set tabs at the Tabs dialog box or using this. ________________
16. Click this button in the Font group on the HOME tab to remove paragraph formatting from selected text. ________________
17. These can be added to a tab to help guide the reader's eyes across the page. ________________
18. Insert a page border with options at this dialog box with the Page Border tab selected. ________________
19. Style sets are available in the Document Formatting group on this tab. ________________
20. This is a set of formatting choices that includes colors, fonts, and effects. ________________

Skills Review

Review 1 Applying Character Formatting to a Travel Document

First Choice TRAVEL

1. Open **FCTPetersburg.docx** from your WordS2 folder and then save it in the WordEOS folder on your storage medium and name it **WS2-R-FCTPetersburg**.
2. Select the entire document, change the font to Cambria, the font size to 11 points, and the font color to *Blue, Accent 5, Darker 50%* (last option in the ninth column in the *Theme Colors* section).
3. Set the title *PETERSBURG, ALASKA* in 16-point Corbel.
4. Set the heading *Services* in 14-point Corbel bold and then use Format Painter to apply the same formatting to the remaining headings (*Visitor Attractions*, *Walking Tours*, *Accommodations*, and *Transportation*).
5. Use the Font dialog box to apply small caps to the last sentence in the document (the sentence that begins *If you would like more*).
6. Apply the Gradient Fill - Blue, Accent 1, Reflection text effect to the title *PETERSBURG, ALASKA* and apply bold formatting.
7. Save **WS2-R-FCTPetersburg.docx**.

Review 2 Applying Paragraph Formatting to a Travel Document

1. With **WS2-R-FCTPetersburg.docx** open, center the title PETERSBURG, ALASKA.
2. Justify the paragraph of text below the title *PETERSBURG, ALASKA*.
3. Center the last sentence in the document (the sentence that begins *IF YOU WOULD LIKE*).
4. Justify the two paragraphs of text below the *Services* heading and indent text 0.5 inch from the left. (Apply the formatting to the blank lines following the paragraphs as well as the paragraphs.) Use Format Painter to apply the same formatting to the four paragraphs below the *Visitor Attractions* heading, the one paragraph below the *Walking Tours* heading, the two paragraphs below the *Accommodations* heading, and the two paragraphs below the *Transportation* heading.
5. Move the insertion point to the end of the document, press the Enter key twice, and then change the paragraph alignment to right alignment.
6. Type **Melissa Gehring**, press Shift + Enter, and then type **First Choice Travel**.
7. Select the entire document, change the line spacing to 1.15, and then deselect the document.
8. Click anywhere in the *Services* heading and then change the paragraph spacing after to 6 points.
9. Use the Repeat command (F4) to insert 6 points of spacing after the remaining headings (*Visitor Attractions*, *Walking Tours*, *Accommodations*, and *Transportation*).
10. Save, print, and then close **WS2-R-FCTPetersburg.docx**.

Review 3 Applying Indent Formatting and Finding and Replacing Formatting in a Vacation Package Document

1. Open **FCTVacPackages.docx** from your WordS2 folder on your storage medium and then save the document in the WordEOS folder and name it **WS2-R-FCTVacPackages**.
2. Select the entire document and then change the line spacing to 1.0.
3. Select the four paragraphs of text below *Fast Facts* in the *OREGON* section, click the Decrease Indent button to remove the indent, and then insert bullets.
4. Select the four paragraphs of text below *Fast Facts* in the *NEVADA* section, click the Decrease Indent button to remove the indent, and then insert bullets.
5. Use the Find and Replace dialog box to search for all occurrences of text set in 11-point Calibri italic and replace with 12-point Corbel bold italic.
6. Move the insertion point to the end of the document and then type the text shown in Figure 2.5. ***Hint: Insert the é, è, and ñ symbols with options at the Symbol dialog box with the Symbols tab selected and the* (normal text) *font selected*.**
7. Save **WS2-R-FCTVacPackages.docx**.

FIGURE 2.5 Review 3, Step 6

Additional accommodations are available at the Ste. Thérèse Chateau and Silver Creek Resort. For information, please contact Carlos Nuñez.

Review 4 Creating Tabbed Text in a Vacation Package Document

1. With **WS2-R-FCTVacPackages.docx** open, move the insertion point to the line below the heading *Rates and Packages* in the *OREGON* section and then set a left tab at the 1-inch mark on the horizontal ruler, a center tab at the 3.5-inch mark on the horizontal ruler, and a right tab at the 5.5-inch mark on the horizontal ruler.
2. Type the three bold column headings shown in Figure 2.6 (*Accommodations*, *No. Persons*, *Daily Price*).
3. Type the tabbed text shown in Figure 2.6.
4. Move the insertion point to the line below the heading *Rates and Packages* in the *NEVADA* section and then set a left tab at the 1-inch mark on the horizontal ruler, a center tab at the 3.5-inch mark on the horizontal ruler, and a right tab at the 5.5-inch mark on the horizontal ruler.
5. Type the three bold column headings shown in Figure 2.7 (*Package*, *Length*, and *Price*) set in bold and then press the Enter key.
6. Display the Tabs dialog box, add dot leaders to the tab set at the 3.5-inch mark and the tab set at the 5.5-inch mark, and then close the dialog box.
7. Type the text in columns below the headings as shown in Figure 2.7.
8. Save **WS2-R-FCTVacPackages.docx**.

FIGURE 2.6 Review 4, Steps 2–3

Accommodations	**No. Persons**	**Daily Price**
Studio/one bedroom	2 to 4	$75 to $125
Two bedrooms	4 to 6	$95 to $225
Three bedrooms	6 to 8	$135 to $300
Four bedrooms	8 to 12	$160 to $400
Five/six bedrooms	10 to 16	$250 to $500

FIGURE 2.7 Review 4, Step 5 and Step 7

Package	**Length**	**Price**
Tuck 'n' Roll	3 days/2 nights	$269
Ski Sneak................................	4 days/3 nights	$409
Take a Break............................	6 days/5 nights	$649
Ultimate.................................	8 days/7 nights	$1,009

Review 5 Applying Borders, Shading, Styles and Themes to a Vacation Packages Document

1. With **WS2-R-FCTVacPackages.docx** open, apply the Heading 1 style to the *OREGON* title and the *NEVADA* title.
2. Apply the Heading 2 style to the headings *Fast Facts* and *Rates and Packages* in the *OREGON* section and the *NEVADA* section.
3. Insert a bottom single-line border below the title *OREGON* and below the title *NEVADA*.
4. Apply a page border with the following specifications: at the Borders and Shading dialog box with the Page Border tab selected, apply the 3-D setting, change the color to *Blue, Accent 5, Darker 25%*, and change the width to 3 points.
5. Apply the Basic (Simple) style set, the Red Orange theme colors, and the Open paragraph spacing.
6. Apply the Frame theme.
7. Select the tabbed text below the Rates and Packages heading in the *OREGON* section and apply Teal, Accent 5, Lighter 80% paragraph shading.
8. Select the tabbed text below the *Rates and Packages* heading in the *NEVADA* section and apply Teal, Accent 5, Lighter 80% paragraph shading.
9. Save, print, and then close **WS2-R-FCTVacPackages.docx.**

Skills Assessment

Assessment 1 Formatting a Cross Country Skiing Document

1. Open **FCTLakeTahoeSkiing.docx** and then save the document in the WordEOS folder and name it **WS2-A1-FCTLakeTahoeSkiing**.
2. Make the following changes to the document:
   a. Set the entire document in 12-point Constantia.
   b. Set the title in 14-point Calibri bold.
   c. Set the names of the cross-country skiing resorts in 14-point Calibri bold.
   d. Change the line spacing for the entire document to 1.3.
   e. Change the paragraph spacing after the title to 0 points.
   f. Change the paragraph spacing after each heading to 6 points.
   g. Indent one-half inch from the left margin and change the alignment to justify alignment for the paragraph of text below each cross-country skiing resort name.
   h. Center the title and apply Blue, Accent 1, Lighter 40% paragraph shading.
   i. Apply Blue, Accent 1, Lighter 80% paragraph shading and insert a single-line bottom border to each cross-country skiing resort name.
   j. Insert a shadow page border in dark blue that is 3 points in width.
   k. Apply the Integral theme.
3. Save, print, and then close **WS2-A1-FCTLakeTahoeSkiing.docx**.

Assessment 2 Preparing and Formatting a Letter

1. Open **MPLtrhd.docx** and then save the document in the WordEOS folder and name it **WS2-A2-MPLtrtoNPC**.
2. You are Neva Smith-Wilder, Educational Liaison for Marquee Productions. Write a letter using the date April 16, 2015, to Cal Rubine, Chair, Theatre Arts Division, Niagara Peninsula College, 2199 Victoria Street, Niagara-on-the-Lake, ON L0S 1J0 and include the following information (refer to page 33 for information on formatting a business letter):
   - Marquee Productions will be filming in and around the city of Toronto during the summer of 2015.
   - Marquee Productions would like to use approximately 20 interns to assist with the shoot.
   - Interns will perform a variety of tasks, including acting as extras, assisting the camera crew, working with set designers on set construction, and providing support to the production team.
   - Interns can work approximately 15 to 30 hours per week and will be compensated at minimum wage.
   - Close your letter by asking Mr. Rubine to screen interested students and then send approximately 20 names to you.
   - If Mr. Rubine has any questions, he may contact you at (612) 555-2005 or send the names to you by email at NevaSW@emcp.net. (Word will automatically convert the email address to a hyperlink.)
3. After typing the letter, apply the following formatting:
   a. Select the letter text and then change the font to Candara.
   b. Change the paragraph alignment to justify the paragraph(s) in the body of the letter.
4. Save, print, and then close **WS2-A2-MPLtrtoNPC.docx**.

Assessment 3 Setting Leader Tabs

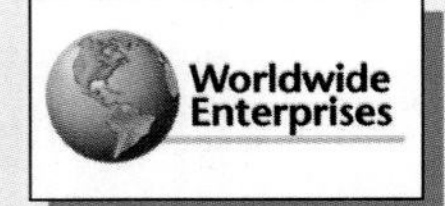

1. At a blank document, type the text shown in Figure 2.8 with the following specifications:
   a. Center, bold, and italicize the text as shown.
   b. Set the tabbed text as shown using a left tab for the first column and a right tab with leaders for the second column.
   c. After typing the text, select the entire document, change the font to Candara, and then change the spacing after paragraphs to 0 points.
2. Save the document in the Word EOS folder and name it **WS2-A3-WEDistSch**.
3. Print and then close **WS2-A3-WEDistSch.docx**.

FIGURE 2.8 Assessment 3

WORLDWIDE ENTERPRISES
Distribution Schedule
Two by Two
United States .... May 4
Canada .... June 15
Japan .... July 20
Australia/New Zealand .... August 3
Mexico .... September 21

Assessment 4 Finding Information on Controlling Page Breaks

1. Use Word's Help feature to learn how to prevent page breaks between paragraphs and how to place at least two lines of a paragraph at the top or bottom of a page to prevent a widow (last line of a paragraph by itself at the top of a page) or orphan (first line of a paragraph by itself at the bottom of a page).

2. Create a document containing the following information:
   a. Create a title for the document.
   b. Write a paragraph discussing how to prevent page breaks between paragraphs and list the steps required to complete the task.
   c. Write a paragraph discussing how to keep selected paragraphs together on a single page and list the steps required to complete the task.
   d. Write a paragraph discussing how to prevent a widow or orphan on a page in a document and list the steps required to complete the task.
3. Apply formatting to enhance the visual appeal of the document.
4. Save the completed document in the WordEOS folder and name it **WS2-A4-PageBreaks**.
5. Print and then close **WS2-A4-PageBreaks.docx**.
6. Open **FCTVacSpecials.docx**.
7. Save the document in the WordEOS folder and name it **WS2-A4-FCTVacSpecials**.
8. Select the entire document and then change the font to 12-point Cambria.
9. Search for all occurrences of *Skye* and replace with *Sky*.
10. Search for all occurrences of *Class* and replace with *Category*.
11. Complete a spelling and grammar check on the document.
12. Click anywhere in the heading *Category S* (located toward the bottom of the first page) and then insert a command to keep the heading together with the next line.
13. Save the document and then print only page 2.
14. Close **WS2-A4-FCTVacSpecials.docx**.

Assessment 5 Individual Challenge **Creating a Document with Tabbed Text**

1. Determine a city outside of your state or province that you would like to visit. Using the Internet, identify four or more airlines that will fly from the airport nearest you to the city you would like to visit and determine the round-trip airfare.
2. Using the information you find, create a document with two tabbed columns. Set the first column as a left tab and type the name of the airline in this column. Set the second column as a right tab with leaders and type the airfare price in this column.
3. Create an appropriate heading for the tabbed text. Apply a paragraph border and/or shading to enhance the visual appeal of the tabbed text.
4. Apply a page border to the document.
5. Save the completed document in the WordEOS folder and name it **WS2-A5-IC-Airfare**.
6. Print and then close **WS2-A5-IC-Airfare.docx**.

Marquee Challenge

Challenge 1 **Editing and Formatting a Document on Juneau, Alaska**

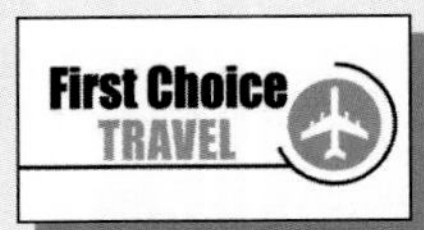

1. Open **FCTJuneau.docx** and then save the document in the WordEOS folder and name it **WS2-C1-FCTJuneau**.
2. Apply the Heading 1 style to the title and the Heading 2 style to the headings.
3. Apply the Casual style set, change the theme colors to Green, change the theme fonts to Franklin Gothic, and apply open paragraph spacing. (Make these changes with buttons on the DESIGN tab.)
4. Apply the paragraph formatting and make changes so your document appears as shown in Figure 2.9.
5. Save, print, and then close **WS2-C1-FCTJuneau.docx**.

Challenge 2 **Creating and Formatting a Flyer about a Skiing Vacation Package**

1. Create the document shown in Figure 2.10. Set the text in the Cambria font, change the line spacing to 1.5, and apply the page, border, shading, and bullet formatting as shown in the figure.
2. Save the completed document in the WordEOS folder and name it **WS2-C2-FCTSkiTahoe**.
3. Print and then close **WS2-C2-FCTSkiTahoe.docx**.

FIGURE 2.9 Challenge 1

JUNEAU, ALASKA

Juneau, Alaska's capital since 1900, sits at the base of Mt. Juneau. This capital blends its history as a mining town containing old storefronts and saloons with the modern architecture of government and Native corporations.

History

In the late 1800s, gold became the foundation of Juneau. The town contained a variety of gold mines with the Alaska-Juneau, or A-J, mine the most successful. The A-J mine buildings are still visible above town. Other gold mines include the Treadwill Mine complex at Douglas and the Alaska-Gastineau mine south of town. A massive cave-in occurred at Treadwill in 1917 and the mine closed. When gold content dropped below profitable margins in 1921, the Alaska-Gastineau mine closed. The A-J mine continued operations until World War II, when labor shortages and high costs forced its closure.

Visitor Attractions

Walking, hiking, and biking trails abound in and around the Juneau area. Scenic flights take visitors over the spectacular ice fields and the Glacier Bay National Monument. Take an exciting boat ride along Juneau's wilderness waterways. Tour buses take visitors to Mendanhall Glacier where they can climb moraines left by receding glaciers, hike nearby trails, and visit the U.S. Forest Service observatory where guides and exhibits explain glacier features. Visitors also can reach the glacier by driving or taking a charter flight.

Reminders of Juneau's past abound in the city. The Davis Log Cabin, built in 1881, was the community's first church and is now the visitor information center. Consider a visit to the St. Nicholas Russian Orthodox Church, which was built in 1894 and is considered the oldest original Orthodox Church in Southeast Alaska. Other city attractions include the Juneau Douglas City Museum, the pioneer cemetery, and the Wickersham House.

Museums

Juneau is the proud home to the Alaska State Museum, featuring permanent displays of Eskimo and Southeast Indian artifacts. The museum also offers changing displays of Alaska's political and natural history.

Visit the Juneau Douglas City Museum and learn about Juneau's history. Exhibits include features on gold mining and Juneau's historic past. A small admission fee is charged to adults. Children under the age of 18 are admitted free of charge.

The Alaska Maritime Heritage Foundation, a nonprofit group, is planning to build a tall ship for Alaska. It will be used to train sailors and people with disabilities in seamanship, environmental studies, goodwill trips, and charter work.

FIGURE 2.10 Challenge 2

Ski Lake Tahoe

Super Value Ski Package®

Our exciting new Super Value Ski Package features special rates on a full line of top-quality resort and hotel rentals for three days or more. Ask for the Super Value Ski Package and receive a blizzard of valuable savings for one low, inclusive price. Whatever resort or hotel you choose, you will receive the following items for free or at a considerable discount.

- Receive one free adult day lift ticket and ski all day.
- If you would like to travel throughout the Lake Tahoe area, rent any vehicle and receive a 25% discount coupon.
- For your comfort and convenience, we will include a coupon for a free ski rack rental.
- Book a Super Value Ski Package by October 31 and receive four $25 gift certificates you can use at any of the fine dining restaurants in the area.

Accommodations

Resort	*3 to 5 Nights*	*7+ Nights*
Ambassador Inn	$699	$959
Hanover's at Lake Tahoe	$679	$929
Moore Creek Lodge	$629	$879
Evergreen Suites	$619	$859
St. Rémi Resort	$607	$837
Cedar Ridge Lodge	$547	$757
Mountain Lodge	$539	$729
River Creek Resort	$525	$715

Word SECTION 3

Formatting and Enhancing a Document

Skills

- Cut, copy, and paste text
- Use the Clipboard task pane to copy and paste items
- Change page margins, orientation, and size
- Insert a watermark, page color, and page border
- Insert page numbering
- Insert a header and footer
- Format a document in MLA style
- Insert citations
- Create a works cited page
- Edit a source
- Use the Click and Type feature
- Vertically align text
- Insert, size, and move images
- Prepare an envelope and mailing labels

Projects Overview

Edit and format documents on Thailand and Juneau, Alaska; prepare an announcement about a workshop on traveling on a budget; format a report on the Middleton Valley in MLA style; prepare envelopes and labels for mailing fact sheets and announcements.

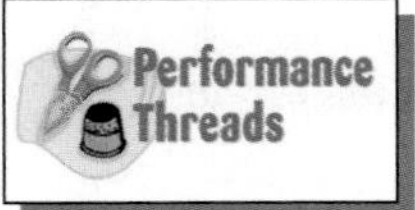

Format reports in MLA style; format a costume rental agreement.

Prepare an announcement about a workshop on employment opportunities in the movie industry; add a picture watermark.

Create an announcement for weekend work; prepare labels.

Prepare an announcement about internship positions available at Marquee Productions; prepare labels for the college.

Model Answers for Projects

These model answers for the projects you complete in Section 3 provide a preview of the finished projects before you begin working and also allow you to compare your own results with these models to ensure you have created the materials accurately.

WS3-FCTThailand.docx (a three-page document) is the project in Activities 3.1 to 3.5.

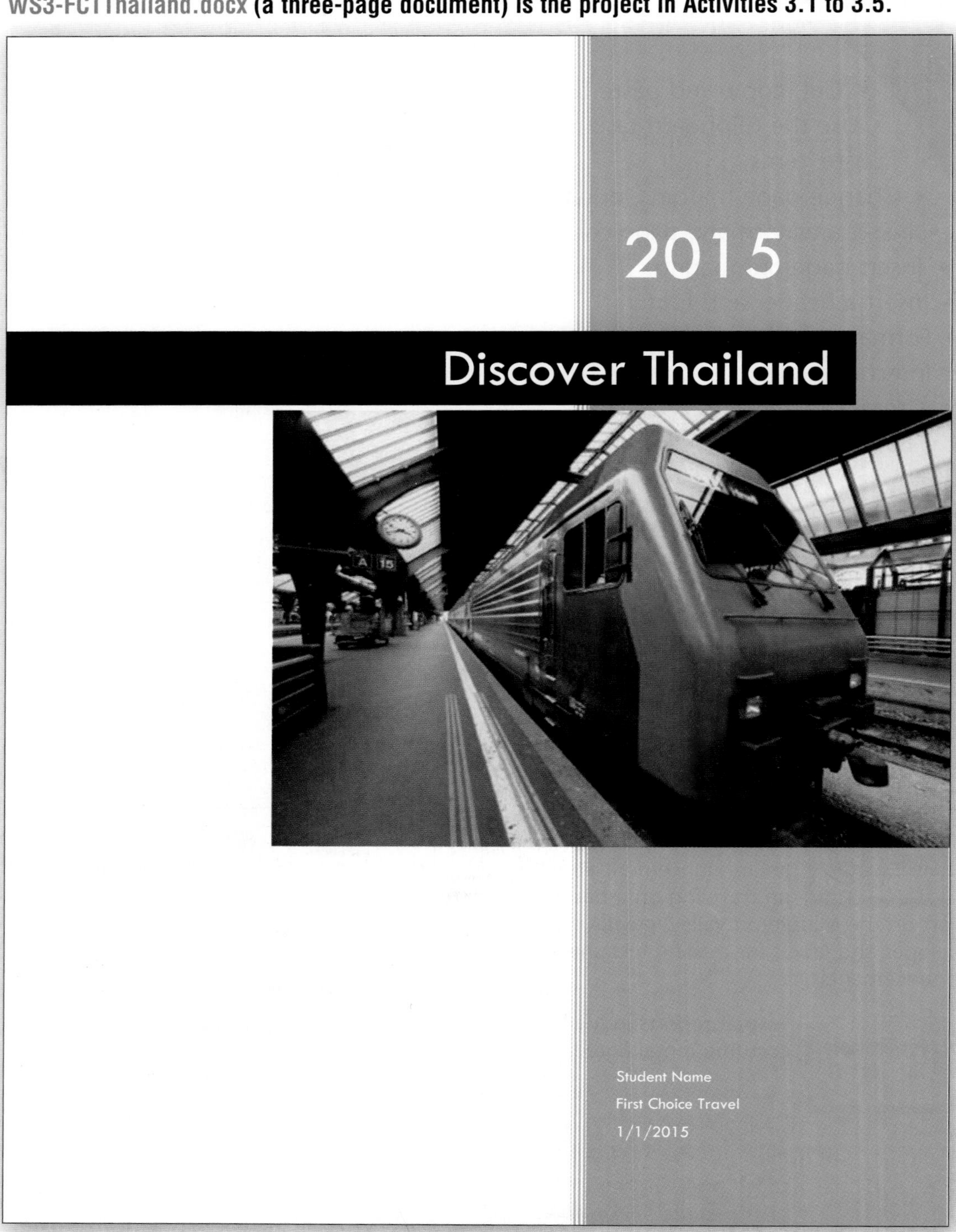

WORD SECTION 3
Project Model Answers

2

class hotels with every conceivable convenience and international standard convention facilities. Family-style hotels, bungalow complexes, guest houses, houseboats, hotels, motels, and beachside huts are available, costing from a few dollars a day to hundreds of dollars a night.

THAILAND

Thailand is a Southeast Asian country bordered to the north by Laos and Burma, to the east by Laos and Cambodia, to the south by the Gulf of Thailand and Malaysia, and to the west by the Andaman Sea. Bangkok, the capital of Thailand, is the country's largest city and the center of political, commercial, industrial, and cultural activities.

Transportation

Most visitors to Thailand enter through Bangkok's Don Muang International Airport, which is served by the world's major airlines. International flights also arrive from Malaysia and Singapore at Hat Yai and Phuket in southern Thailand, and from Hong Kong at Chiang Mai in northern Thailand.

Traveling in Thailand

Thai Airways, Thailand's domestic airline, offers tourism destinations such as Phuket and Chiang Mai with feeder routes to thriving commercial centers and provincial capitals with airfields. An efficient rail system links northern and northeastern towns with the capital and a southern route enables visitors to travel by rail into Malaysia and Singapore. Domestic express trains provide first-, second-, and third-class cars while slower trains may have only third-class seats. A modern highway system reaches into all corners of the country. If you possess a valid international driving license, you can rent an automobile. Thai automobile rental rates compare favorably with those found in other Asian countries.

Attractions

Thailand is a beautiful country with majestic mountains, national marine parks, sparkling beach resorts, ruined cities, archaeological wonders, and year-round festivals and events. Bangkok and the surrounding area boast Thailand's major attractions. While touring the capital city, visit the Emerald Buddha Temple and the Grand Palace complex. The Temple of the Dawn, the Temple of the Reclining Buddha, the Golden Mount, and the Marble Temple are popular attractions that were featured during Bangkok's Bicentennial Celebration in 1982. Take a trip to the Susan Pakkad Palace lacquer pavilion, which is decorated with seventeenth century gold leaf murals, or visit the Jim Thompson house, which contains a superb collection of Asian art and artifacts. One hour west of Bangkok is the Rose Garden, a riverside tropical park and country club that offers an 18-hole championship golf course. Just one-half hour from Bangkok is the Phra Pathom Chedi, the world's tallest Buddhist monument, which marks the spot where Buddhism was introduced to the region over 2,300 years ago.

Entertainment

Thailand offers a variety of entertainment options for visitors, such as boxing stadiums, race and golf courses, tennis and squash courts, billiard halls, nightclubs, gourmet restaurants, concert halls, teahouses, cocktail lounges, amusement parks, museums, theaters, art galleries, and cinemas. Thailand's English-language newspapers carry daily listings of current attractions.

Accommodations

Thailand offers accommodations ranging from opulent hotels to simple beachside dwellings on remote islands. Major tourism destinations such as Bangkok, Pattaya, Chiang Mai, and Phuket boast modern first-

DISCOVER THAILAND | STUDENT NAME

WS3-FCTMiddletonRpt.docx (a four-page document) is the project in Activities 3.6 and 3.7.

Last Name 4

Works Cited

Henderson, Joanne. "Natural Resources of Middleton Valley." *Planet Earth's Resources* (2014): 7-9.

Marcello, Daniel. *Middleton Valley Regional Planning Department.* 5 January 2015. 26 July 2015. <www.emcp.org/middleton>.

Last Name 3

biking, skiing, golf, and tennis. The valley boasts over 20 lodges and resorts and offers a full range of services for visitors, from those interested in camping to those preferring first-class amenities.

Last Name 2

Although the development of the Middleton Valley has come far, modern planners today use the ancient wisdom of the Native people when building in the area. Realizing the need to preserve the valley's beauty in the face of progress, the state formed the Middleton Valley Regional Planning Department in 1965 to oversee environmentally responsible development. The department's approach has enabled limitations to construction while devising a redevelopment plan that will improve the economy, tourist access, and the

y retains its
sinos, and ski
s to be the

h agriculture
ral resources
illion years
ust and
orical
e croplands

area,
r on or near
g for
some of the
rt and easily
mountain

Last Name 1

Student Name

Instructor's Name

Course Title

Current Date

Middleton Valley

The Middleton Valley is home to one of the state's largest natural freshwater lakes, the unique and beautiful Jefferson Basin, and numerous parks and recreational campgrounds. Middleton Valley has many convenient and quality visitor attractions and facilities, including a variety of lodging options to fit any budget. The Middleton Valley and surrounding area is renowned for its beautiful scenery, wildlife, and outdoor recreational opportunities.

In the 1860s, silver was discovered in the Middleton Valley area and fortune seekers flocked to the area hoping to strike it rich at the massive Milestone Lode discovered in 1860. Would-be miners rushed to the Middleton Valley over Culver Pass from the north and Myers Pass and Gulliver Pass from the south. The influx of pioneers to the valley was so great that Northridge Road was forged across the mountains. Silver was not the only valuable commodity early settlers found in the area. Middleton Valley's timber-rich forests became a necessary resource for the increasing number of people needing fuel and to support the labyrinth of mines being constructed (Henderson). The easy availability of timber soon led to the devastation of the valley forests, which were heavily logged between 1860 and 1890. The decline of the Milestone Lode probably rescued the valley's diminishing forests.

WS3-FCTTravelIntl.docx is the project in Activity 3.8.

TRAVELING INTERNATIONALLY

Traveling on a Budget

Thursday, April 16, 2015

7:00 to 8:30 p.m.

Sponsored by

WS3-FCTEnvtoMP.docx is the project in Activity 3.9.

First Choice Travel
Student Name
3588 Ventura Boulevard
Los Angeles, CA 90102

Camille Matsui
Marquee Productions
955 South Alameda Street
Los Angeles, CA 90037

WS3-FCTLALabels.docx is part of the project in Activity 3.10.

First Choice Travel
Student Name
3588 Ventura Boulevard
Los Angeles, CA 90102

First Choice Travel
Student Name
3588 Ventura Boulevard
Los Angeles, CA 90102

First Choice Travel
Student Name
3588 Ventura Boulevard
Los Angeles, CA 90102

First Choice Travel
Student Name
3588 Ventura Boulevard
Los Angeles, CA 90102

First Choice Travel
Student Name
3588 Ventura Boulevard
Los Angeles, CA 90102

First Choice Travel
Student Name
3588 Ventura Boulevard
Los Angeles, CA 90102

First Choice Travel
Student Name
3588 Ventura Boulevard
Los Angeles, CA 90102

First Choice Travel
Student Name
3588 Ventura Boulevard
Los Angeles, CA 90102

First Choice Travel
Student Name
3588 Ventura Boulevard
Los Angeles, CA 90102

First Choice Travel
Student Name
3588 Ventura Boulevard
Los Angeles, CA 90102

First Choice Travel
Student Name
3588 Ventura Boulevard
Los Angeles, CA 90102

First Choice Travel
Student Name
3588 Ventura Boulevard
Los Angeles, CA 90102

First Choice Travel
Student Name
3588 Ventura Boulevard
Los Angeles, CA 90102

First Choice Travel
Student Name
3588 Ventura Boulevard
Los Angeles, CA 90102

First Choice Travel
Student Name
3588 Ventura Boulevard
Los Angeles, CA 90102

First Choice Travel
Student Name
3588 Ventura Boulevard
Los Angeles, CA 90102

First Choice Travel
Student Name
3588 Ventura Boulevard
Los Angeles, CA 90102

First Choice Travel
Student Name
3588 Ventura Boulevard
Los Angeles, CA 90102

First Choice Travel
Student Name
3588 Ventura Boulevard
Los Angeles, CA 90102

First Choice Travel
Student Name
3588 Ventura Boulevard
Los Angeles, CA 90102

First Choice Travel
Student Name
3588 Ventura Boulevard
Los Angeles, CA 90102

First Choice Travel
Student Name
3588 Ventura Boulevard
Los Angeles, CA 90102

First Choice Travel
Student Name
3588 Ventura Boulevard
Los Angeles, CA 90102

First Choice Travel
Student Name
3588 Ventura Boulevard
Los Angeles, CA 90102

First Choice Travel
Student Name
3588 Ventura Boulevard
Los Angeles, CA 90102

First Choice Travel
Student Name
3588 Ventura Boulevard
Los Angeles, CA 90102

First Choice Travel
Student Name
3588 Ventura Boulevard
Los Angeles, CA 90102

First Choice Travel
Student Name
3588 Ventura Boulevard
Los Angeles, CA 90102

First Choice Travel
Student Name
3588 Ventura Boulevard
Los Angeles, CA 90102

First Choice Travel
Student Name
3588 Ventura Boulevard
Los Angeles, CA 90102

WS3-FCTCustLabels.docx and WS3-FCTTorontoLabels.docx are part of the project in Activity 3.10.

Moreno Products
350 Mission Boulevard
Pomona, CA 91767

Mr. Miguel Santos
12120 Barranca Parkway
Irvine, CA 92612

Mr. and Mrs. Jack Lipinski
5534 Southeast 32nd Street
Los Angeles, CA 90092

Dr. Esther Riggins
9077 Walnut Street
Los Angeles, CA 90097

Automated Services, Inc.
4394 Seventh Street
Long Beach, CA 92602

Ms. Samantha Schwartz
103-B Pacific Palms
Los Angeles, CA 90068

4277 Yonge Street
Toronto, ON M4P 2E6

4277 Yonge Street
Toronto, ON M4P 2E6

4277 Yonge Street
Toronto, ON M4P 2E6

4277 Yonge Street
Toronto, ON M4P 2E6

4277 Yonge Street
Toronto, ON M4P 2E6

4277 Yonge Street
Toronto, ON M4P 2E6

4277 Yonge Street
Toronto, ON M4P 2E6

4277 Yonge Street
Toronto, ON M4P 2E6

4277 Yonge Street
Toronto, ON M4P 2E6

4277 Yonge Street
Toronto, ON M4P 2E6

4277 Yonge Street
Toronto, ON M4P 2E6

4277 Yonge Street
Toronto, ON M4P 2E6

4277 Yonge Street
Toronto, ON M4P 2E6

4277 Yonge Street
Toronto, ON M4P 2E6

4277 Yonge Street
Toronto, ON M4P 2E6

4277 Yonge Street
Toronto, ON M4P 2E6

4277 Yonge Street
Toronto, ON M4P 2E6

4277 Yonge Street
Toronto, ON M4P 2E6

4277 Yonge Street
Toronto, ON M4P 2E6

4277 Yonge Street
Toronto, ON M4P 2E6

4277 Yonge Street
Toronto, ON M4P 2E6

4277 Yonge Street
Toronto, ON M4P 2E6

4277 Yonge Street
Toronto, ON M4P 2E6

4277 Yonge Street
Toronto, ON M4P 2E6

4277 Yonge Street
Toronto, ON M4P 2E6

4277 Yonge Street
Toronto, ON M4P 2E6

4277 Yonge Street
Toronto, ON M4P 2E6

4277 Yonge Street
Toronto, ON M4P 2E6

4277 Yonge Street
Toronto, ON M4P 2E6

4277 Yonge Street
Toronto, ON M4P 2E6

Activity 3.1

Cutting, Copying, and Pasting Text; Using Paste Special

With the Cut, Copy, and Paste buttons in the Clipboard group on the HOME tab, you can move and/or copy words, sentences, or entire sections of text to other locations in a document. You can cut and paste text or copy and paste text within the same document or between documents. Specify the formatting of pasted text with options at the Paste Special dialog box.

Project

You are working on a First Choice Travel document containing information on Thailand. You decide that some of the text in the document should be reorganized, and you also decide to add additional information to the document.

1. Open **FCTThailand.docx** and then save the document and name it **WS3-FCTThailand**.

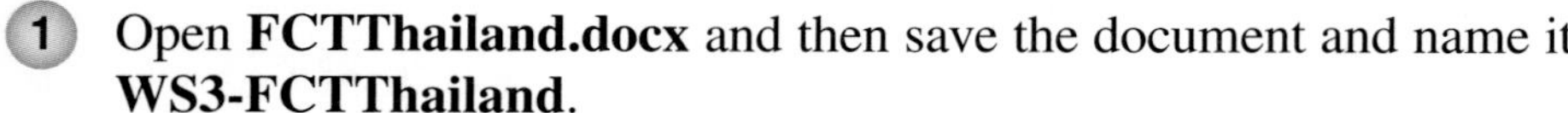

Tutorial 3.1
Cutting, Copying, and Pasting Text

2. Move the *Attractions* section below the *Traveling in Thailand* section. Begin by selecting the *Attractions* heading and the paragraph of text that follows the heading.
3. Click the Cut button in the Clipboard group on the HOME tab.

   Clicking the Cut button places the text in a special location within Word called the ***clipboard***.

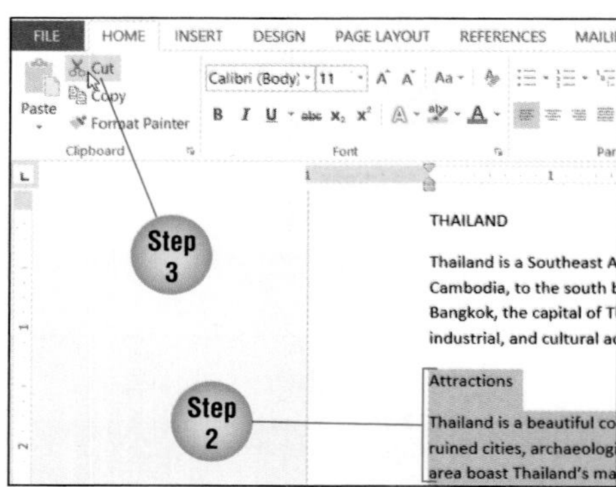

Need Help?

If you click the wrong button, immediately click the Undo button.

4. Move the insertion point to the beginning of the *Accommodations* heading and then click the Paste button in the Clipboard group on the HOME tab.

   A Paste Options button (Ctrl) displays below the pasted text. Click this button and a drop-down list of buttons displays. Use these buttons to specify the formatting of the pasted text. By default, the Keep Source Formatting button (first button from the left) is selected. With this button selected, text is pasted with the formatting from the source document. You can also click the Merge Formatting button (middle button) to merge formatting with the destination formatting or click the Keep Text Only button (third button) to keep only the text and not the formatting.

5. Open **FCTThaiStats.docx**.

   You will copy text from this document and paste it in the Thailand information document.

6. Select the *Points of Interest* heading and the four lines of text below the heading and then click the Copy button in the Clipboard group.

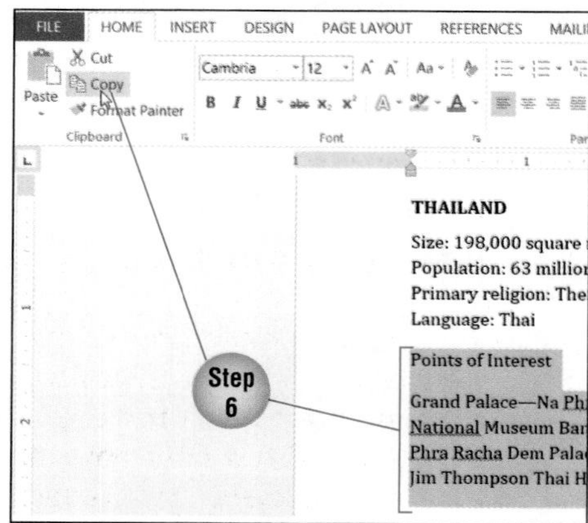

7. Click the Word button on the Taskbar and then click the **WS3-FCTThailand.docx** thumbnail.
8. Position the insertion point at the beginning of the heading *Passports/ Visas* and then click the Paste button in the Clipboard group.
9. Click the Paste Options button and then click the Merge Formatting button (middle button) at the Paste Options button drop-down list.
10. Click the Word button on the Taskbar and then click the **FCTThaiStats.docx** thumbnail.
11. Select the text *Resources:* and the three lines below it and then click the Copy button.
12. Click the Word button on the Taskbar and then click the **WS3-FCTThailand.docx** thumbnail.
13. Move the insertion point to the end of the document and then press the Enter key once. Paste the copied text into the document without the formatting by clicking the Paste button arrow and then clicking *Paste Special* at the drop-down list.

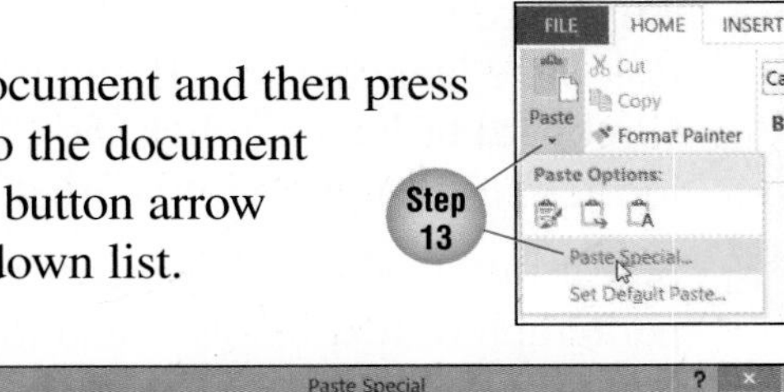

14. At the Paste Special dialog box, click *Unformatted Text* in the *As* list box and then click OK.

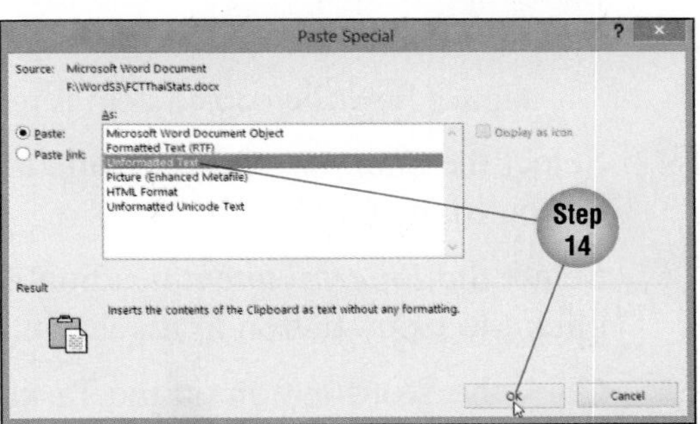

15. Select the four lines of text you just pasted in the document and then remove the spacing after the paragraphs by clicking the PAGE LAYOUT tab and then clicking twice on the down-pointing arrow at the right side of the *After* measurement box in the Paragraph group.
16. Save **WS3-FCTThailand.docx**.
17. Click the Word button on the Taskbar, click the **FCTThaiStats.docx** thumbnail, and then close the document.

Closing the **FCTThaiStats.docx** document displays the **WS3-FCTThailand.docx** document.

In Brief

Cut and Paste Text

1. Select text.
2. Click Cut button in Clipboard group.
3. Move insertion point to desired position.
4. Click Paste button in Clipboard group.

Copy and Paste Text

1. Select text.
2. Click Copy button in Clipboard group.
3. Move insertion point to desired position.
4. Click Paste button in Clipboard group.

Display Paste Special Dialog Box

1. Cut or copy text.
2. Click Paste button arrow.
3. Click *Paste Special*.
4. Click desired format in *As* list box.
5. Click OK.

In Addition

Moving and Copying Text with the Mouse

You can move selected text using the mouse. To do this, select the text with the mouse and then move the I-beam pointer inside the selected text until the I-beam pointer turns into an arrow pointer. Hold down the left mouse button, drag the arrow pointer (displays with a gray box attached) to the location where you want the selected text inserted, and then release the button. Copy and move selected text by following similar steps. The difference is that you need to hold down the Ctrl key while dragging with the mouse. With the Ctrl key down, a box containing a plus symbol displays near the gray box by the arrow pointer.

Activity 3.2

Using the Clipboard Task Pane

Using the Clipboard task pane, you can collect up to 24 different items and then paste them in various locations in a document. Display the Clipboard task pane by clicking the Clipboard group task pane launcher. Cut or copy an item and the item displays in the Clipboard task pane. If the item is text, the first 50 characters display. Paste an item by positioning the insertion point at the desired location and then clicking the item in the Clipboard task pane. When all desired items are inserted, click the Clear All button located in the upper right corner of the task pane.

Project

You will open another document with information on Thailand, copy items in the document, and then paste the items into the Thailand document.

Tutorial 3.2
Using the Clipboard Task Pane

1. Make sure **WS3-FCTThailand.docx** is open and then open **FCTThaiInfo.docx**.
2. In the **FCTThaiInfo.docx** document, display the Clipboard task pane by clicking the Clipboard group task pane launcher. If any items display in the Clipboard task pane, click the Clear All button located in the upper right corner of the task pane.

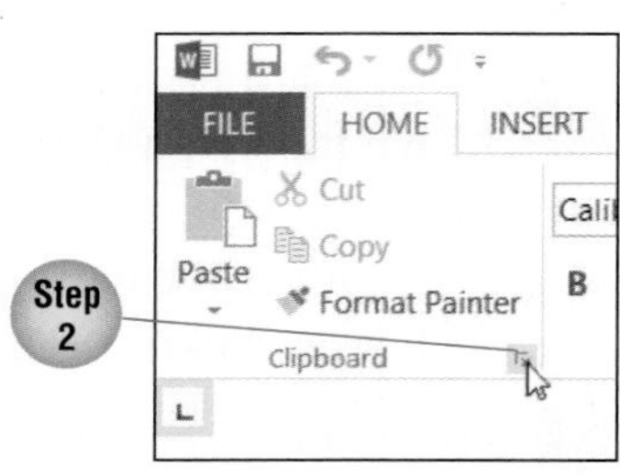

3. Select the *Food and Beverages* heading and the paragraph of text below it and then click the Copy button in the Clipboard group.

   Notice how the copied item is represented in the Clipboard task pane.
4. Select the *Shopping* heading and the paragraph below it and then click the Copy button in the Clipboard group.
5. Select the *Entertainment* heading and the paragraph of text below it and then click the Copy button in the Clipboard group.
6. Click the Word button on the Taskbar and then click the **WS3-FCTThailand.docx** thumbnail.
7. Display the Clipboard task pane by clicking the HOME tab and then clicking the Clipboard group task pane launcher.
8. Move the insertion point to the beginning of the *Accommodations* heading.
9. Click the item in the Clipboard task pane representing *Entertainment*.

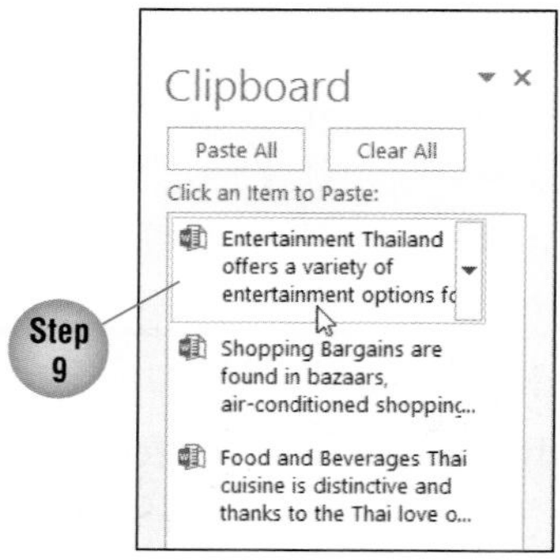

10. Move the insertion point to the beginning of the *Points of Interest* heading.

11. Click the item in the Clipboard task pane representing *Shopping*.

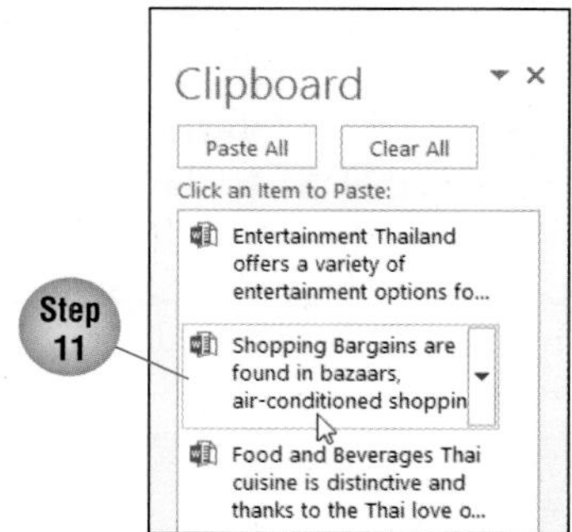

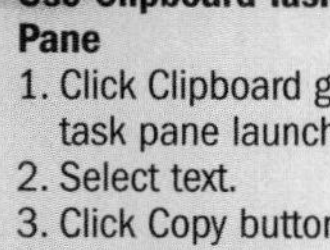

In Brief

Use Clipboard Task Pane

1. Click Clipboard group task pane launcher.
2. Select text.
3. Click Copy button.
4. Select and copy any additional items.
5. Move insertion point to desired position.
6. Click item in Clipboard task pane representing desired item.
7. Paste any other desired items from Clipboard task pane.
8. Click Clear All button.

12. Click the Clear All button located toward the upper right corner of the Clipboard task pane.
13. Close the Clipboard task pane by clicking the Close button located in the upper right corner of the task pane.
14. Click the Word button on the Taskbar, click the **FCTThaiInfo.docx** thumbnail, and then close the document.

    The **WS3-FCTThailand.docx** document displays when you close **FCTThaiInfo.docx**.

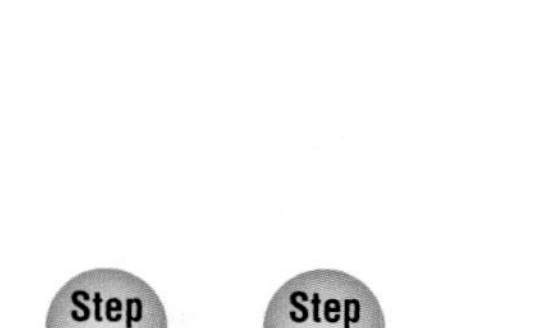

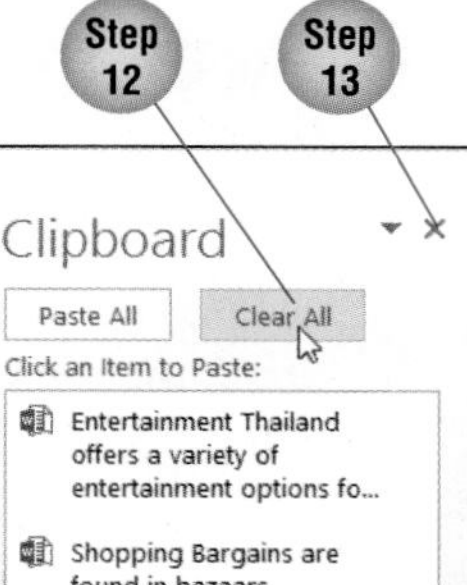

15. Press Ctrl + Home to move the insertion point to the beginning of the document, click on any character in the title *THAILAND*, and then click the *Title* style thumbnail in the Styles group on the HOME tab.
16. Apply the Heading 1 style to the headings in the document (*Transportation*, *Traveling in Thailand*, *Attractions*, *Entertainment*, *Accommodations*, *Shopping*, *Points of Interest*, and *Passports/Visas*).
17. Click the DESIGN tab and then click the *Casual* style set thumbnail in the Document Formatting group.
18. Press Ctrl + Home to move the insertion point to the beginning of the document and then center the title *THAILAND*.
19. Save **WS3-FCTThailand.docx**.

In Addition

Clipboard Task Pane Options

Click the Options button located toward the bottom of the Clipboard task pane and a pop-up menu displays with five options as shown at the right. Insert a check mark before those options you want active. For example, you can choose to display the Clipboard task pane automatically when you cut or copy text, press Ctrl + C twice to display the Clipboard task pane, cut and copy text without displaying the Clipboard task pane, display the *Office Clipboard* icon on the Taskbar when the clipboard is active, or display the item message near the Taskbar when copying items to the Clipboard.

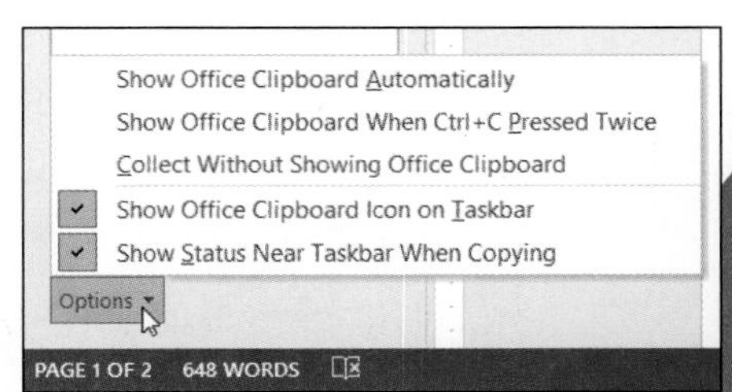

Activity 3.3

Customizing the Page Setup

In Word, a page contains a number of defaults such as a page size of 8.5 inches by 11 inches; top, bottom, left, and right margins of one inch; a portrait page orientation; and a page break after approximately 9 inches of vertical text on a page. You can change these defaults with buttons in the Page Setup group on the PAGE LAYOUT tab. Change the default margins in a document with the Margins button. With the Orientation button, you can change the orientation from the default of portrait to landscape. Use the Size button in the Page Setup group to specify a paper size.

Project

To customize the Thailand document, you will change the document margins, orientation, and page size and apply a theme.

Tutorial 3.3
Changing Margins, Page Orientation, and Paper Size

1. With **WS3-FCTThailand.docx** open, change the margins by clicking the PAGE LAYOUT tab, clicking the Margins button in the Page Setup group, and then clicking the *Wide* option at the drop-down list.

   The *Wide* option changes the left and right margins to 2 inches each.

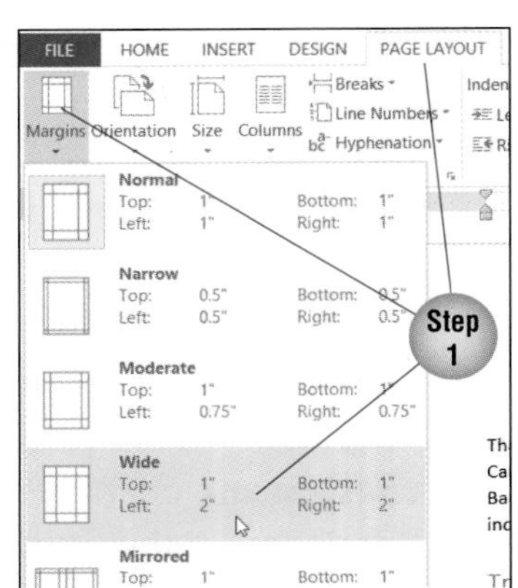

2. Change the page orientation by clicking the Orientation button in the Page Setup group on the PAGE LAYOUT tab and then clicking *Landscape* at the drop-down list.

   Word considers a page in portrait orientation to be 8.5 inches wide and 11 inches tall. Word considers a page in landscape orientation to be 11 inches wide and 8.5 inches tall. You can also change page orientation at the Page Setup dialog box with the Margins tab selected.

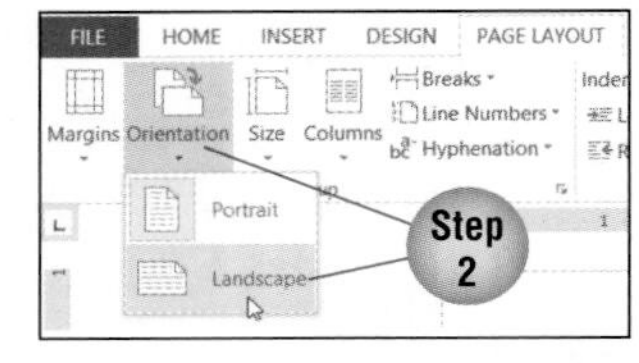

3. Change margins by clicking the Margins button in the Page Setup group on the PAGE LAYOUT tab and then clicking the *Custom Margins* option that displays at the very bottom of the drop-down list.
4. At the Page Setup dialog box with the Margins tab selected and *2"* selected in the *Top* measurement box, type **0.8**.
5. Click the down-pointing arrow at the right side of the *Bottom* measurement box until *0.8"* displays.
6. Click OK to close the Page Setup dialog box.

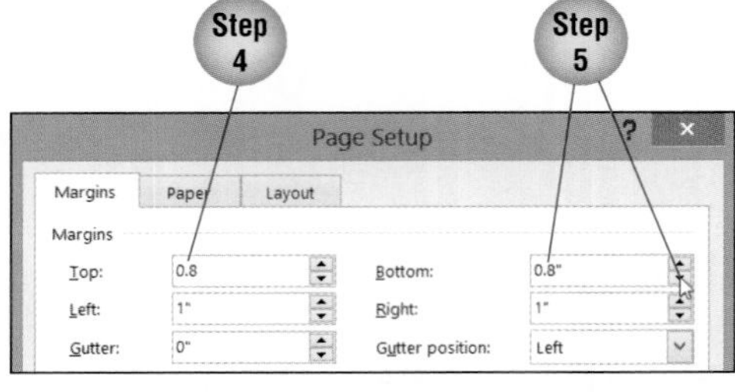

7. Change the paper size by clicking the Size button in the Page Setup group and then clicking the *Legal* option at the drop-down list.

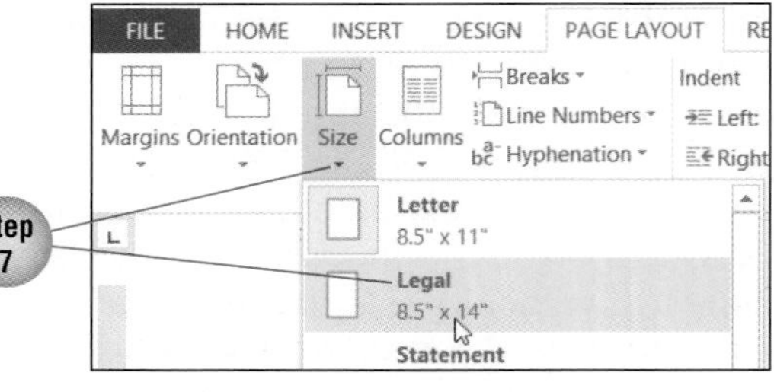

8 Scroll through the document to view the pages in legal paper size.

9 Change back to letter paper size by clicking the Size button and then clicking the *Letter* option at the drop-down list.

10 Save **WS3-FCTThailand.docx**. (Optional: Your instructor may want you to print the document at this point.)

11 Change the page orientation by clicking the Orientation button in the Page Setup group and then clicking *Portrait* at the drop-down list.

12 Change margins by clicking the Margins button in the Page Setup group and then clicking *Normal* at the drop-down list.

13 Apply a theme to the document by clicking the DESIGN tab, clicking the Themes button in the Document Formatting group, and then clicking *Integral* at the drop-down gallery.

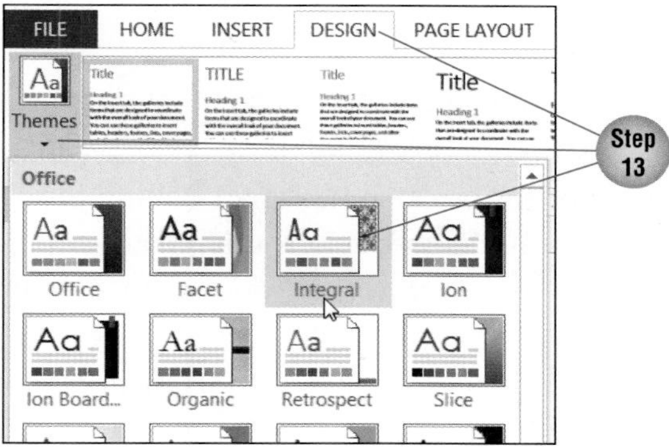

14 Change the theme colors by clicking the Colors button in the Document Formatting group and then clicking the *Red Orange* color option at the drop-down gallery.

15 Save **WS3-FCTThailand.docx**.

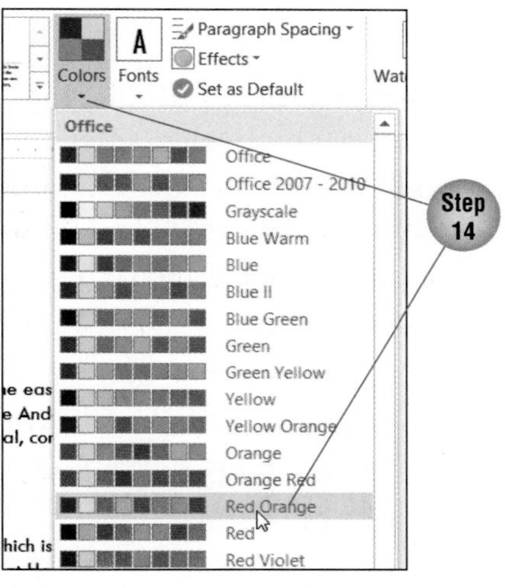

In Brief

Change Margins
1. Click PAGE LAYOUT tab.
2. Click Margins button.
3. Click desired margins option.

Change Orientation
1. Click PAGE LAYOUT tab.
2. Click Orientation button.
3. Click desired orientation option.

Change Page Size
1. Click PAGE LAYOUT tab.
2. Click Size button.
3. Click desired size option.

In Addition

Applying Landscape Orientation

Can you imagine some instances in which you might use a landscape orientation? Suppose you are preparing a company's annual report and you need to include a couple of tables that have several columns of text. If you use the default portrait orientation, the columns would need to be quite narrow, possibly so narrow that reading becomes difficult. Changing the orientation to landscape results in three more inches of usable space. Also, you are not committed to using landscape orientation for the entire document. You can use portrait and landscape in the same document. To do this, select the text, display the Page Setup dialog box, click the desired orientation, and then change the *Apply to* option to *Selected text*.

Activity 3.4

Customizing the Page and Page Background

The Page Background group on the DESIGN tab contains buttons you can use to insert a watermark, change the page color, and insert a page border. A watermark is lightened text or image that displays behind text. Word provides a number of predesigned watermark images you can insert in a document. The Pages group on the INSERT tab contains buttons for adding a cover page, a blank page, and a page break.

Project

To add visual appeal to the Thailand document, you will apply page color and a page border, and insert a cover page and blank page into the document. You will also identify the document as a draft by inserting a watermark.

Tutorial 3.4
Inserting a Watermark, Page Color, and Page Border

1. With **WS3-FCTThailand.docx** open, press Ctrl + Home. Insert a watermark by clicking the DESIGN tab, clicking the Watermark button in the Page Background group, scrolling down the drop-down list, and then clicking the *DRAFT 1* option.

   A watermark is lightened text or image that displays behind text.

2. Apply a page color to the document by clicking the Page Color button in the Page Background group and then clicking the *Gold, Accent 5, Lighter 80%* color (located in the ninth column).

   Page color is designed for viewing a document on screen and does not print.

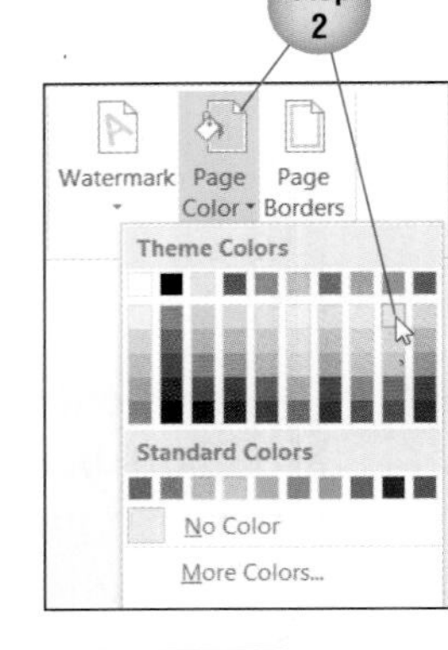

3. Click the Page Borders button in the Page Background group.

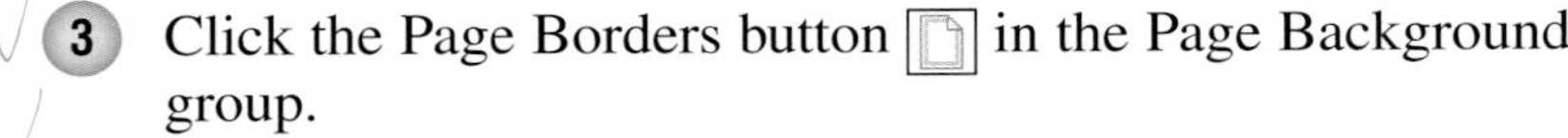

4. At the Borders and Shading dialog box with the Page Border tab selected, click the down-pointing arrow at the right side of the *Art* option box. Scroll down the list of page borders and then click the art border option shown at the right. Click OK to close the dialog box.

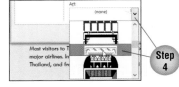

5. Press Ctrl + Home and then insert a cover page by clicking the INSERT tab, clicking the Cover Page button in the Pages group, scrolling down the drop-down list, and then clicking *Motion*.

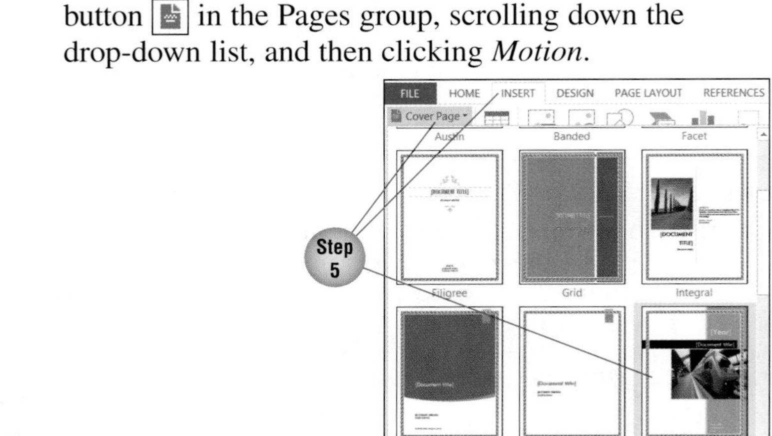

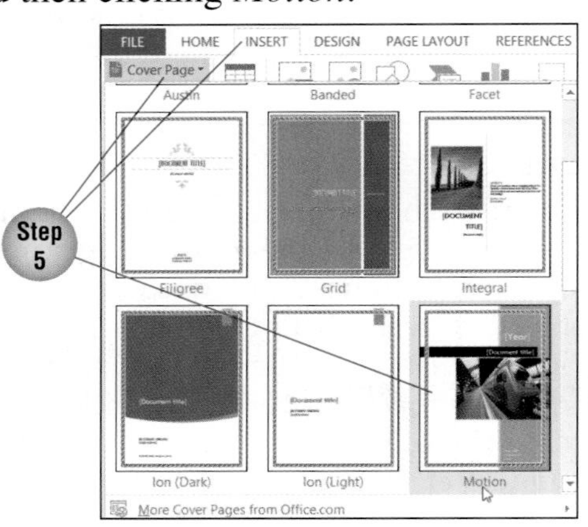

6 Click anywhere in the placeholder text *[Year]* and then type the current year.

7 Click anywhere in the placeholder text *[Document title]* and then type **Discover Thailand**.

8 Click anywhere in the placeholder text *[Company name]* and then type **First Choice Travel**. If a company name already displays above the date in the bottom right corner, click the company name, click the Company tab, and then type **First Choice Travel**.

9 Select the name that displays above *First Choice Travel* and then type your first and last names.

10 Insert the current date below *First Choice Travel* by clicking the date, clicking the down-pointing arrow at the right of the placeholder, and then clicking *Today*.

11 You need a blank page at the end of the document for information that will be added later. Press Ctrl + End to move the insertion point to the end of the document and then click the Blank Page button in the Pages group.

12 Move the insertion point to the beginning of the heading *Entertainment* and then insert a page break by clicking the Page Break button in the Pages group.

You can also insert a hard page break with the keyboard shortcut, Ctrl + Enter.

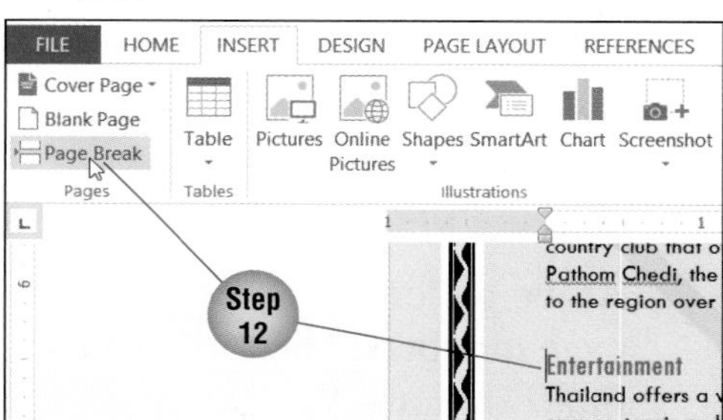

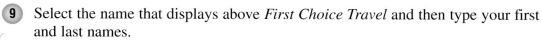

13 Save **WS3-FCTThailand.docx** and then print only pages 1 and 2.

14 Remove the page border by clicking the DESIGN tab and then clicking the Page Borders button.

15 At the Borders and Shading dialog box, click *None* in the *Setting* section and then click OK.

16 Position the insertion point on any character on page 2 and then remove page color by clicking the Page Color button in the Page Background group and then clicking *No Color* at the drop-down palette.

17 Delete the page break you inserted in Step 12 by positioning the insertion point at the end of the paragraph of text below the *Attractions* heading and then pressing the Delete key twice.

18 Remove the blank page by clicking the HOME tab and then clicking the Show/Hide ¶ button in the Paragraph group. Position the insertion point at the beginning of the page break that displays on the third page and then press the Delete key twice. Click the Show/Hide ¶ button to turn off the display of nonprinting characters.

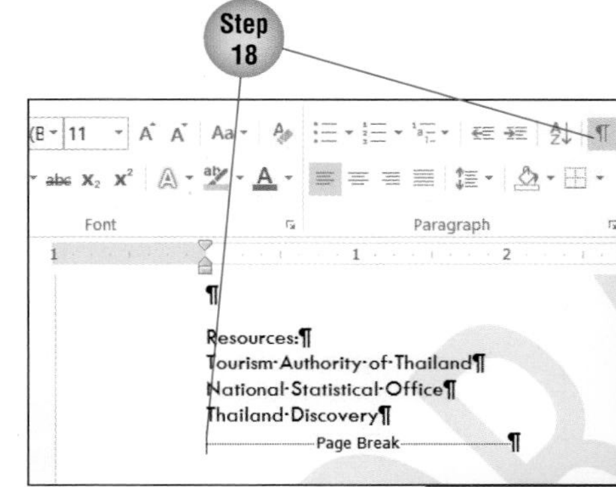

19 Save **WS3-FCTThailand.docx**.

In Brief

Apply Watermark
1. Click DESIGN tab.
2. Click Watermark button.
3. Click desired watermark option.

Apply Page Color
1. Click DESIGN tab.
2. Click Page Color button.
3. Click desired color.

Insert Page Border
1. Click DESIGN tab.
2. Click Page Borders button.
3. Click desired options at Borders and Shading dialog box.
4. Click OK.

Insert Cover Page
1. Click INSERT tab.
2. Click Cover Page button.
3. Click desired option.
4. Type text in appropriate placeholders.

Insert Blank Page
1. Click INSERT tab.
2. Click Blank Page button.

Insert Page Break
1. Click INSERT tab.
2. Click Page Break button.

OR

Press Ctrl + Enter.

Activity 3.5

Inserting Page Numbering, Headers, and Footers

Insert page numbering in a document with the Page Number button or in a header or footer. Click the Page Number button in the Header & Footer group on the INSERT tab and a drop-down list displays with options for inserting page numbers at the top or bottom of the page or in the page margins, removing page numbers, and formatting page numbers. Text that appears at the top of every page is called a ***header*** and text that appears at the bottom of every page is referred to as a ***footer***. Headers and footers are common in manuscripts, textbooks, reports, and other publications. Insert a predesigned header in a document with the Header button in the Header & Footer group on the INSERT tab. Insert a predesigned footer in the same manner as a header. Predesigned headers and footers contain formatting that you can customize.

Project

Insert identifying information in the Thailand document using a header and footer and insert page numbering.

Tutorial 3.5A
Inserting Page Numbers and Page Breaks

Tutorial 3.5B
Creating Headers and Footers

Tutorial 3.5C
Modifying Headers and Footers

1. With **WS3-FCTThailand.docx** open, move the insertion point to the beginning of the title *THAILAND* (located on the second page).
2. Number pages at the bottom of each page by clicking the INSERT tab, clicking the Page Number button in the Header & Footer group, and then pointing to *Bottom of Page*.
3. At the gallery of predesigned page numbers, click the *Accent Bar 1* option.
4. Double-click in the body of the document, and then scroll through the document and notice how the page numbers display toward the bottom of each page except the cover page.

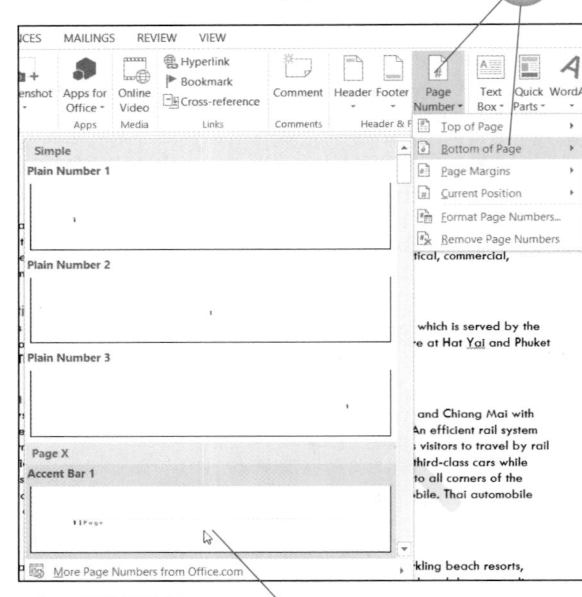

5. Remove page numbering by clicking the INSERT tab, clicking the Page Number button in the Header & Footer group, and then clicking *Remove Page Numbers* at the drop-down list.
6. Insert a header in the document by clicking the Header button in the Header & Footer group, scrolling down the header drop-down list, and then clicking the *Facet (Odd Page)* header.
7. Double-click in the body of the document.

   This makes the document active and dims the header.

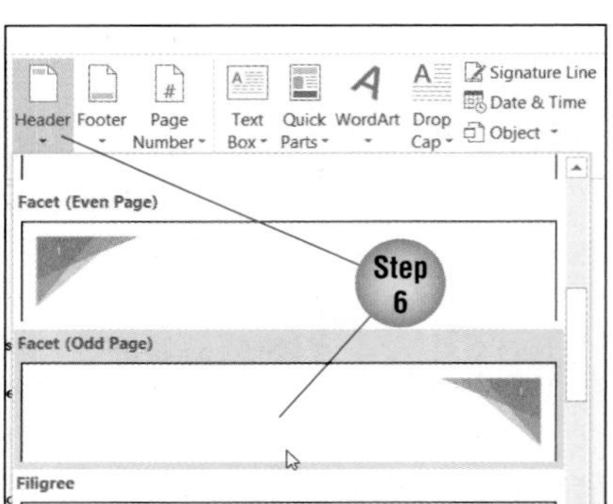

8 Insert a footer in the document by clicking the INSERT tab, clicking the Footer button in the Header & Footer group, scrolling down the footer drop-down list, and then clicking the *Ion (Dark)* footer.

Notice how the document title you entered in the cover page is inserted in the footer, as is the author's name.

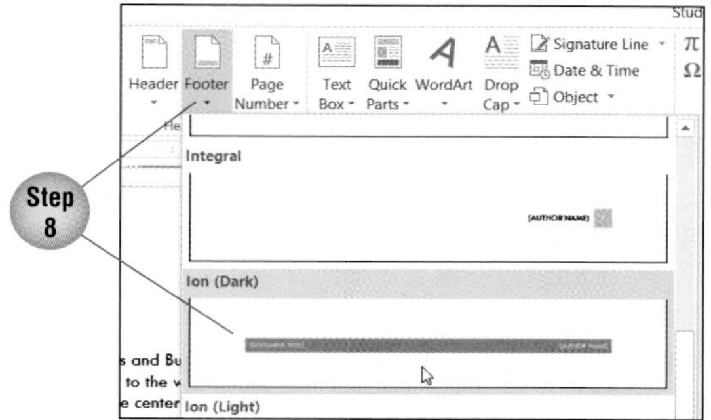

In Brief

Insert Page Numbers
1. Click INSERT tab.
2. Click Page Number button.
3. Point to desired location.
4. Click desired option at drop-down list.

Insert Header
1. Click INSERT tab.
2. Click Header button.
3. Click desired option at drop-down list.

Insert Footer
1. Click INSERT tab.
2. Click Footer button.
3. Click desired option at drop-down list.

9 Double-click in the body of the document.

10 Scroll through the document and notice how the header and footer appear on each page except the cover page.

11 Remove the header by clicking the INSERT tab, clicking the Header button in the Header & Footer group, and then clicking the *Remove Header* option at the drop-down list.

12 Insert a new header by clicking the Header button in the Header & Footer group, scrolling down the header drop-down list, and then clicking the *Ion (Dark)* header.

13 Double-click in the body of the document.

14 Edit the footer by clicking the INSERT tab, clicking the Footer button in the Header & Footer group, and then clicking *Edit Footer* at the drop-down list.

15 Select all of the text in the footer.

16 Change the font size by clicking the HOME tab, clicking the Font Size button arrow, and then clicking *10* at the drop-down list. Click the Bold button to apply bold formatting.

17 Double-click in the document.

18 Save, print, and then close **WS3-FCTThailand.docx**.

In Addition

Creating Your Own Header or Footer

Create your own header or footer using the Edit Header or Edit Footer options from the drop-down list. For example, to create a header, click the INSERT tab, click the Header button, and then click *Edit Header* at the drop-down list. This displays a Header pane in the document and also displays the HEADER & FOOTER TOOLS DESIGN tab with buttons and options for editing the header. Make the desired edits to the header with options on the tab and then close the header pane by clicking the Close Header and Footer button located in the Close group on the HEADER & FOOTER TOOLS DESIGN tab.

Activity 3.6

Formatting a Document in MLA Style; Inserting Citations

When preparing a research paper or report, consider inserting citations and a bibliography to give credit to the sources of words, ideas, and any material borrowed or summarized. Word includes some common reference styles for citing and referencing research papers and reports including the Modern Language Association (MLA) style, which is generally used in the humanities and English. To create a citation, display the Create Source dialog box by clicking the REFERENCES tab, clicking the Insert Citation button in the Citations & Bibliography group, and then clicking *Add New Source*. At the dialog box, insert bibliography information in the required fields. Once you insert source information in the Create Source dialog box, Word will automatically save the source information. To insert a citation in a document from a source that is already saved, click the Insert Citation button in the Citations & Bibliography group and then click the desired reference at the drop-down list. If you include a direct quote from another source, you will need to include the page number. To do this, click the citation in the document to select the citation placeholder, click the Citation Options arrow, and then click *Edit Citation* at the drop-down list. At the Edit Citation dialog box, type in the page or page numbers of the source from which the quote was borrowed.

Project

You are responsible for preparing and formatting a report on Middleton Valley for First Choice Travel. You have been asked to format the report in the MLA style.

Tutorial 3.6
Inserting and Modifying Sources and Citations

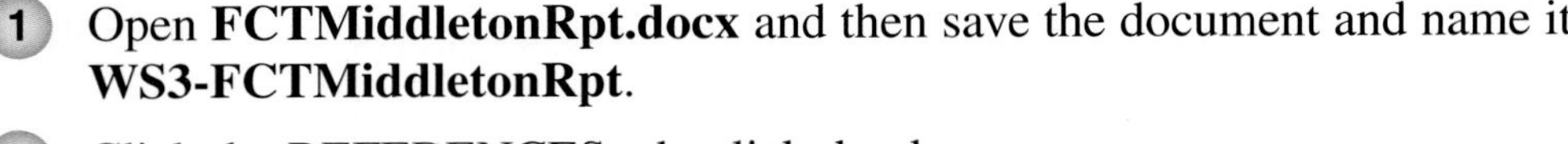

1. Open **FCTMiddletonRpt.docx** and then save the document and name it **WS3-FCTMiddletonRpt**.
2. Click the REFERENCES tab, click the down-pointing arrow at the right side of the *Style* option box in the Citations & Biblography group, and then click the *MLA* option at the drop-down list.

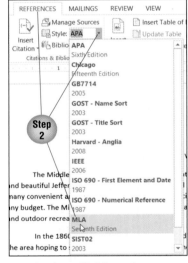

   Refer to Table 3.1 for general guidelines on formatting a research paper or report in the MLA style.
3. Press Ctrl + A to select the entire document and then change the font to 12-point Cambria.
4. With the text still selected, change the line spacing to 2.0 by clicking the Line and Paragraph Spacing button in the Paragraph group on the HOME tab and then clicking *2.0* at the drop-down list.
5. With the text still selected, remove spacing after paragraphs by clicking the PAGE LAYOUT tab, clicking in the *After* measurement box in the *Spacing* section, typing 0, and then pressing Enter.

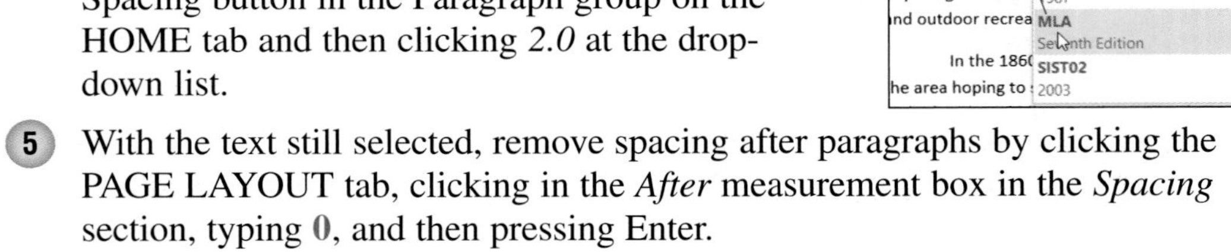

TABLE 3.1 MLA Style General Guidelines

Use standard-sized paper (8.5 × 11 inches).
Set 1-inch top, bottom, left, and right margins.
Set text in a 12-point serif typeface (such as Cambria or Times New Roman).
Double-space text.
Indent the first line of each paragraph one-half inch.
Insert page numbers in the upper right corner of pages.

6 Press Ctrl + Home to position the insertion point at the beginning of the document, type your name, and then press the Enter key.

7 Type your instructor's name and then press the Enter key.

8 Type the title of your course and then press the Enter key.

9 Type the current date.

10 Insert a header in the document by clicking the INSERT tab, clicking the Header button in the Header & Footer group, and then clicking *Edit Header* at the drop-down list.

11 Press the Tab key twice to move the insertion point to the right margin in the Header pane, type your last name, and then press the spacebar.

12 Insert page numbers by clicking the Page Number button in the Header & Footer group on the HEADER & FOOTER TOOLS DESIGN tab, pointing to *Current Position*, and then clicking the *Plain Number* option.

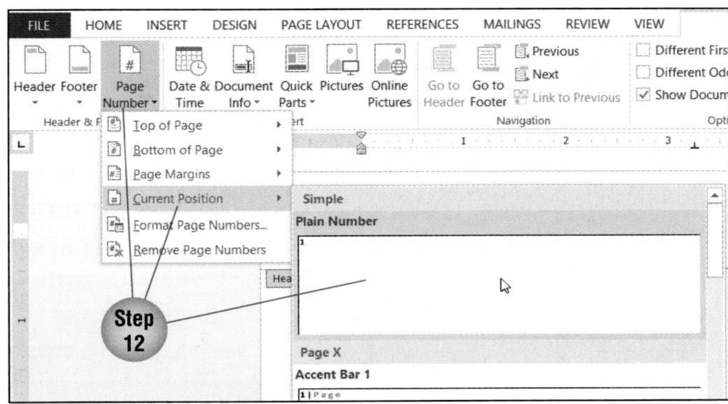

13 Press Ctrl + A to select the header text and then change the font to 12-point Cambria.

14 Double-click in the body of the document.

15 Insert a new citation in the document. Begin by positioning the insertion point immediately right of the word *constructed* (but before the period) that ends the fifth sentence in the second paragraph.

16 Click the REFERENCES tab, click the Insert Citation button in the Citations & Bibliography group, and then click *Add New Source* at the drop-down list.

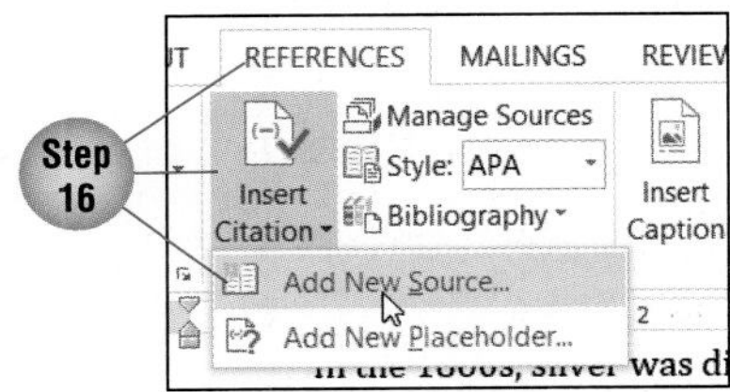

continues

17. At the Create Source dialog box, click the down-pointing arrow at the right of the *Type of Source* option and then click *Journal Article* at the drop-down list.

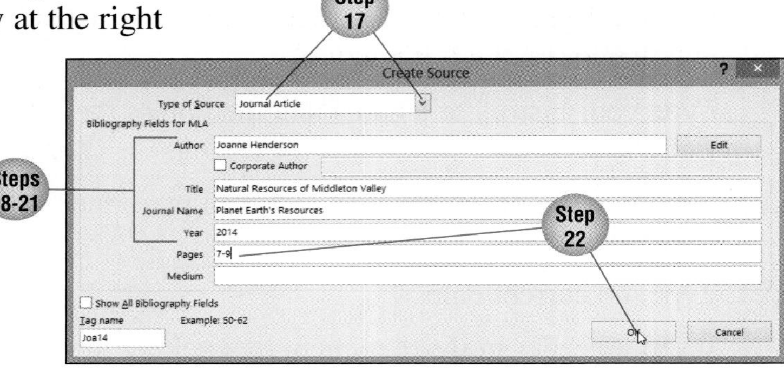

18. Click in the *Author* text box, type **Joanne Henderson**, and then press the Tab key three times.

19. Type **Natural Resources of Middleton Valley** in the *Title* text box and then press the Tab key.

20. Type **Planet Earth's Resources** in the *Journal Name* text box and then press the Tab key.

21. Type **2014** in the *Year* text box and then press the Tab key.

22. Type **7-9** in the *Pages* text box and then click OK.

23. Position the insertion point immediately right of the word *century* (but before the period) that ends the third sentence in the third paragraph, click the Insert Citation button, and then click *Add New Source* at the drop-down list.

24. At the Create Source dialog box, click the down-pointing arrow at the right of the *Type of Source* option and then click *Web site* at the drop down list. Click the *Show All Bibliography Fields* check box to insert a check mark and then type the following information in the specified fields:

    Author = **Daniel Marcello**
    Name of Web Page = **Middleton Regional Planning Department**
    Year = **2015**
    Month = **January**
    Day = **5**
    Year Accessed = (type current year)
    Month Accessed = (type current month)
    Day Accessed = (type current day)
    URL = **www.emcp.org/middleton**

25. After entering the information from a website, click OK.

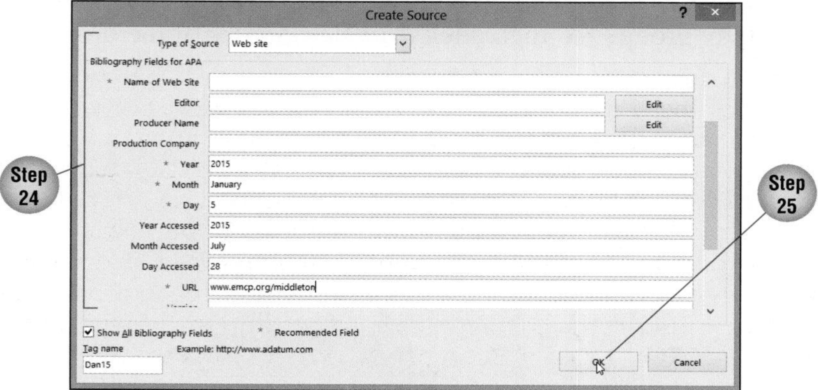

26 Insert a citation from an existing source. Begin by positioning the insertion point between the quotation mark after the word *erosion* and the period in the second sentence in the fourth paragraph.

27 Click the Insert Citation button in the Citations & Bibliography group and then click the *Henderson, Joanne* reference in the drop-down list.

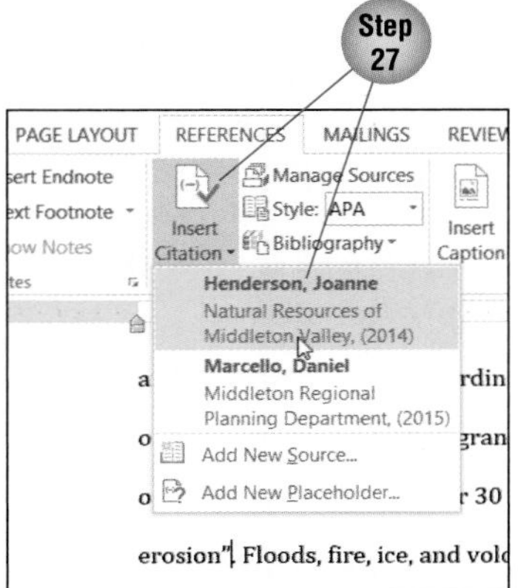

28 Because you are citing a direct quote, you need to include the page number of the journal article where you found the quote. Begin by clicking on any character in the Henderson citation you just inserted.

This displays the citation placeholder.

29 Click the Citation Options arrow that displays at the right side of the citation placeholder and then click *Edit Citation* at the drop-down list.

30 At the Edit Citation dialog box, type **8** in the *Pages* text box and then click OK.

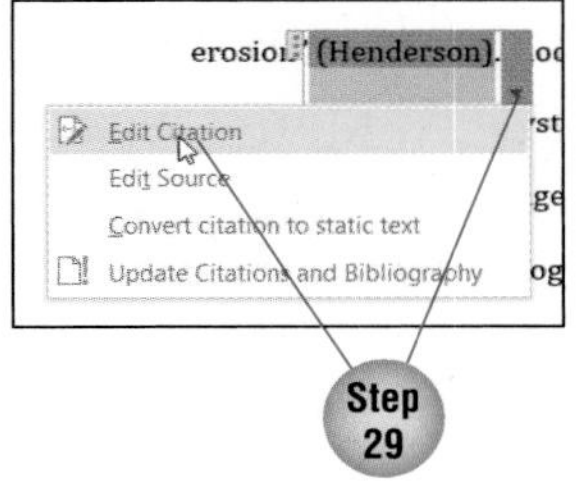

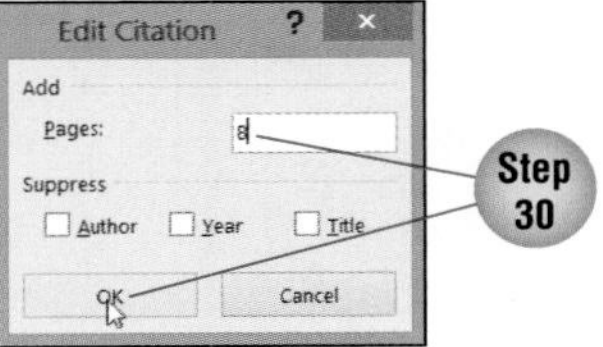

31 Save **WS3-FCTMiddletonRpt.docx**.

In Addition

Formatting the First Page of an MLA-formatted Report

Your instructor may require you to omit the header from the first page of the document. To remove the header from the first page of a document that contains a previously created header, press Ctrl + Home to move the insertion point to the beginning of the document, click the Header button in the Header & Footer group on the INSERT tab, and then click *Edit Header* at the drop-down list. Click the *Different First Page* check box in the Options group on the HEADER & FOOTER TOOLS DESIGN tab. This inserts in the document a new header pane named *First Page Header*. Since you do not want a header on the first page, leave this header blank. Click the Next button in the Navigation group on the HEADER & FOOTER TOOLS DESIGN tab and, if you previously created a header in the document, it displays in the Header pane. If the document did not include a header, type or insert the desired header text in the Header pane.

Activity 3.7

Creating a Works Cited Page; Editing Sources

Once you include citations in a report or research paper, you need to insert a works cited page on a separate page at the end of the document. A works cited page is an alphabetic list of the books, journal articles, web pages, or any other sources referenced in the document. To insert a works cited page, click the REFERENCES tab and then click the Bibliography button in the Citations & Bibliography group. At the Bibliography drop-down list, click the desired format option. If you edit a source, Word will not automatically update the works cited. To update the works cited, click anywhere in the works cited and then click the Update Citations and Bibliography tab. After inserting sources into a document, you may need to edit a citation to correct errors or change data. One method for editing a source is by clicking the desired citation in the document, clicking the Citation Options arrow, and then clicking *Edit Source* at the drop-down list. This displays the Edit Source dialog box with the information you originally typed. Make desired changes and then click OK to close the dialog box.

Project

To finish the Middleton Valley report, you need to add a works cited page, edit one of the sources, and apply MLA style formatting to the works cited page.

Tutorial 3.7
Inserting a Works Cited Page

1. With **WS3-FCTMiddletonRpt.docx** open, insert a works cited page at the end of the document. Begin by pressing Ctrl + End to move the insertion point to the end of the document and then pressing Ctrl + Enter to insert a hard page break.

2. Click the REFERENCES tab and then click the Bibliography button located in the Citations & Bibliography group.

3. Click the *Works Cited* option in the *Built-In* section of the drop-down list.

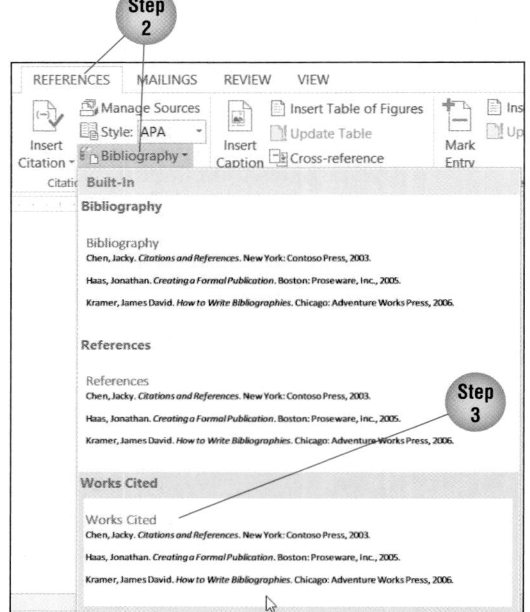

4. You realize that part of the web page title is missing and you need to edit the source. Begin by clicking on any character in the *Marcello* citation in the third paragraph located on the second page.

   This selects the citation placeholder.

5. Click the Citation Options arrow that displays at the right side of the citation placeholder and then click *Edit Source* at the drop-down list.

   This displays the Edit Source dialog box, which contains the same options as the Create Source dialog box.

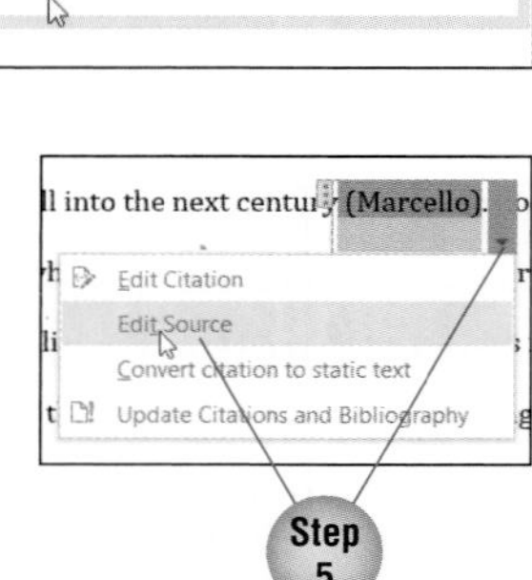

6. At the Edit Source dialog box, click in the *Name of Web Page* text box, edit the text so it displays as *Middleton Valley Regional Planning Department*, and then click OK to close the dialog box.

7. At the message telling you that the source exists in your master list and the current document and asking you if you want to update both, click the Yes button.

8 Update the works cited to include the edited source. Begin by pressing Ctrl + End to move the insertion point to the end of the document and then clicking on any character in the works cited text.

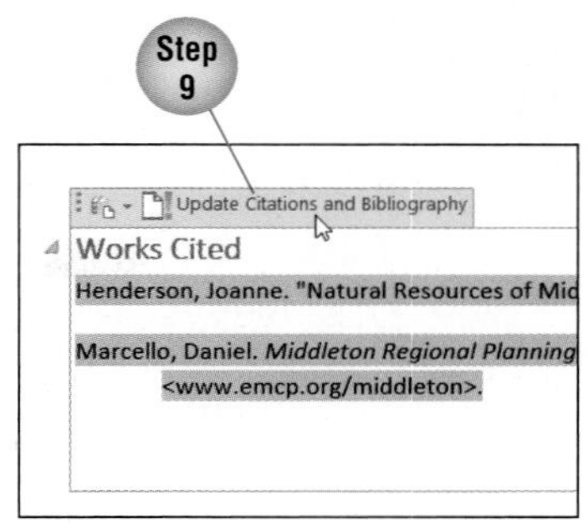

9 Click the Update Citations and Bibliography placeholder tab.

The placeholder tab displays above the *Works Cited* title. Notice that the updated works cited includes the edited web page name.

10 Format the works cited page to MLA standards, which are listed in Table 3.2. Begin by selecting the *Works Cited* heading and the entries below the heading and then clicking the *No Spacing* style in the Styles group on the HOME tab.

11 With the text still selected, change the font to Cambria, the font size to 12 points, and the line spacing to 2.0.

12 Click anywhere in the title *Works Cited* and then click the Center button in the Paragraph group.

13 Hang-indent the entries. Do this by selecting only the works cited entries and then pressing Ctrl + T.

You can also hang-indent the entries by clicking the Paragraph group dialog box launcher, clicking the down-pointing arrow at the right side of the *Special* list box in the *Indentation* section, clicking *Hanging* at the drop-down list, and then clicking OK to close the Paragraph dialog box.

14 Press Ctrl + Home to move the insertion point to the beginning of the document.

15 Save, print, and then close **WS3-FCTMiddletonRpt.docx**.

TABLE 3.2 MLA Style Works Cited Page Formatting Guidelines

Begin works cited on a separate page at the end of the document.
Include the title *Works Cited* and center the title.
Double-space between and within entries.
Begin each entry at the left margin and hang-indent second and subsequent lines in each entry.
Alphabetize the entries.

In Addition

Modifying Sources at the Manage Sources Dialog Box

Copy, delete, edit, and create new sources at the Manage Sources dialog box. Display this dialog box by clicking the REFERENCES tab and then clicking the Manage Sources button in the Citations & Bibliography group. The *Master List* section of the dialog box displays all of the citations you have created in Word, and the *Current List* section displays all of the citations included in the currently open document.

Activity 3.8

Using Click and Type; Vertically Aligning Text; Inserting, Sizing, and Moving an Image

You can change paragraph alignment with the Click and Type feature. To use the Click and Type feature, position the mouse pointer at the left margin, in the center of the page, or at the right margin until the pointer displays with the desired alignment symbol and then double-click the mouse button. By default, text is aligned at the top of the page. Change this alignment to center, justified, or bottom aligned with the *Vertical alignment* option at the Page Setup dialog box with the Layout tab selected. Microsoft Office includes a gallery of media images you can insert in a document such as clip art, photographs, and illustrations. Use the Online Pictures button on the INSERT tab to search for and insert images at Office.com. Use the Pictures button if you want to insert a picture from your computer or other computers you are connected to.

Project

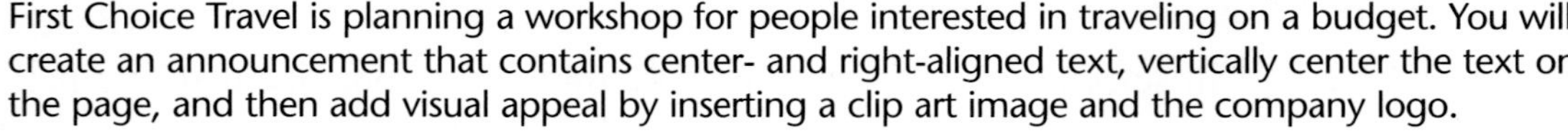

First Choice Travel is planning a workshop for people interested in traveling on a budget. You will create an announcement that contains center- and right-aligned text, vertically center the text on the page, and then add visual appeal by inserting a clip art image and the company logo.

Tutorial 3.8A
Using Click and Type

Tutorial 3.8B
Using Horizontal Alignment

Tutorial 3.8C
Inserting, Sizing, and Moving Images

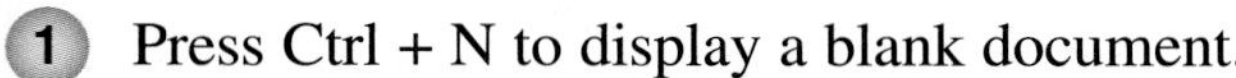

1. Press Ctrl + N to display a blank document.
2. Position the I-beam pointer in the document between the left and right margins at about the 3.25-inch mark on the horizontal ruler and approximately one inch from the top of the page. When the center alignment lines display below the I-beam pointer, double-click the left mouse button.

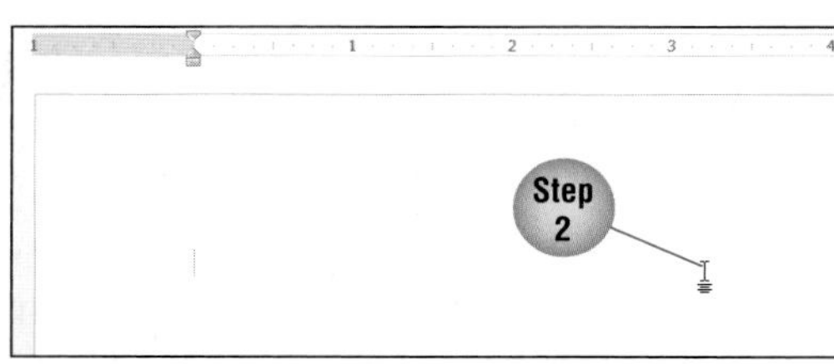

3. Type the centered text shown in Figure 3.1, pressing the Enter key once between each line of text and twice after the last line of centered text.
4. Change to right alignment by positioning the I-beam pointer near the right margin at approximately the 6.5-inch mark on the horizontal ruler until the right alignment lines display at the left side of the I-beam pointer and then double-clicking the left mouse button.

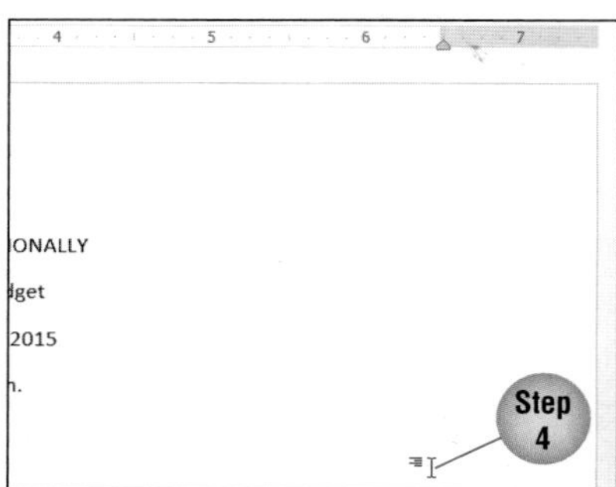

FIGURE 3.1 Step 3 and Step 5

TRAVELING INTERNATIONALLY

Traveling on a Budget

Thursday, April 16, 2015

7:00 to 8:30 p.m.

Sponsored by
First Choice Travel

5. Type the right-aligned text shown in Figure 3.1. After typing the first line of right-aligned text, press Shift + Enter to move the insertion point to the next line.

6. Select the centered text and then change the font to 14-point Candara bold. Select the right-aligned text, change the font to 10-point Candara bold, and then deselect the text.

7. Vertically center the text on the page. To do this, click the PAGE LAYOUT tab and then click the Page Setup group dialog box launcher.

8. At the Page Setup dialog box, click the Layout tab, click the down-pointing arrow at the right side of the *Vertical alignment* option, and then click *Center* at the drop-down list.

9. Click OK to close the Page Setup dialog box.

10. Save the document and name it **WS3-FCTTravelIntl**.

11. Print **WS3-FCTTravelIntl.docx**.

12. Return the vertical alignment to top alignment. To do this, click the Page Setup group dialog box launcher. At the Page Setup dialog box, click the Layout tab, click the down-pointing arrow at the right side of the *Vertical alignment* option, and then click *Top* at the drop-down list. Click OK to close the dialog box.

13. Click the INSERT tab and then click the Online Pictures button in the Illustrations group.

    This displays the Insert Pictures window with search boxes.

14. Click in the search box that displays to the right of the *Office.com Clip Art* option, type **suitcase, globe**, and then press Enter.

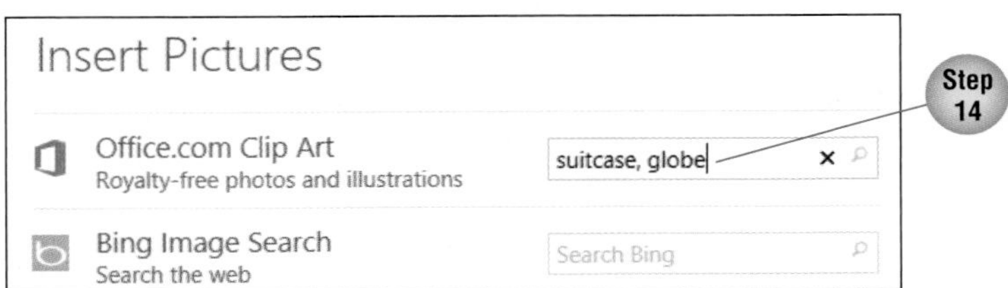

Step 14

15. Double-click the image shown at the right. If this image is not available, choose another image related to travel.

    The image is inserted in the document, it is selected (sizing handles display around the image), and the PICTURE TOOLS FORMAT tab displays as shown in Figure 3.2. A Layout Options button displays at the right side of the image. Click this button to display a list of options for positioning the image and wrapping text around the image.

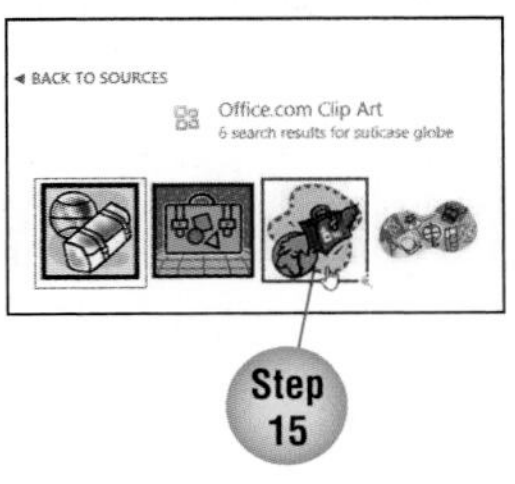

Step 15

FIGURE 3.2 PICTURE TOOLS FORMAT Tab

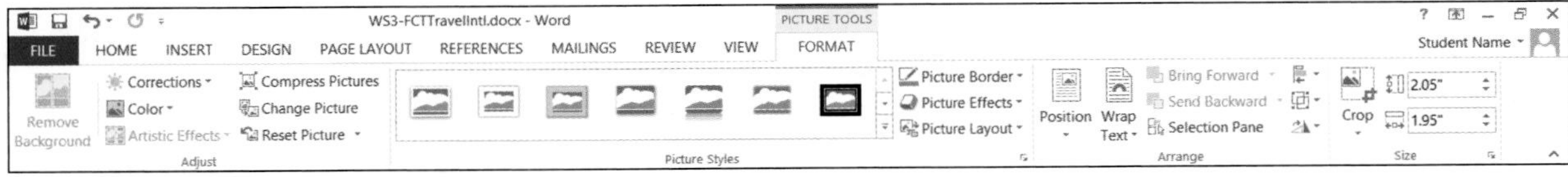

continues

16. With the image selected, click the Position button in the Arrange group and then click the *Position in Top Left with Square Text Wrapping* option in the *With Text Wrapping* section (first option in the top row).

    Apply a text wrapping style to an image to specify how you want text or other items to flow around the image. Apply text wrapping with options from the Position button or with the Wrap Text button.

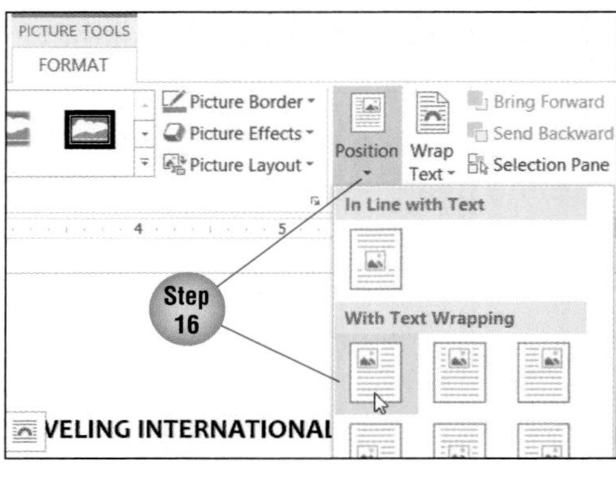

17. Add a shadow effect to the image by clicking the *Drop Shadow Rectangle* thumbnail in the Picture Styles group (fourth thumbnail).

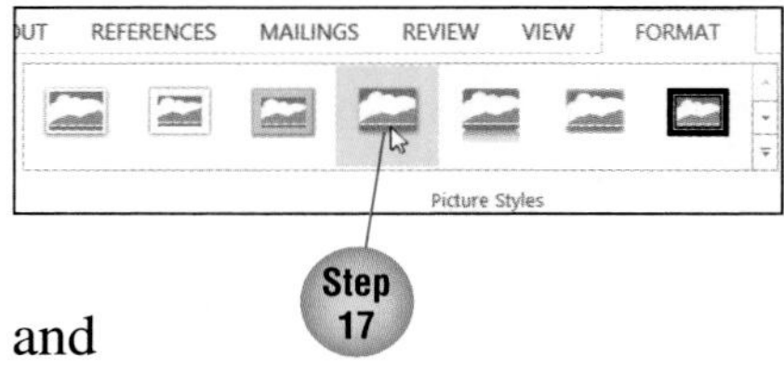

18. Click the Corrections button in the Adjust group and then click the *Brightness: -20% Contrast: +20%* option (second option in the fourth row).

19. Click the Picture Effects button in the Pictures Styles group, point to *Glow* and then click the *Blue, 5 pt glow, Accent color 1* option (first option in the top row in the *Glow Variations* section).

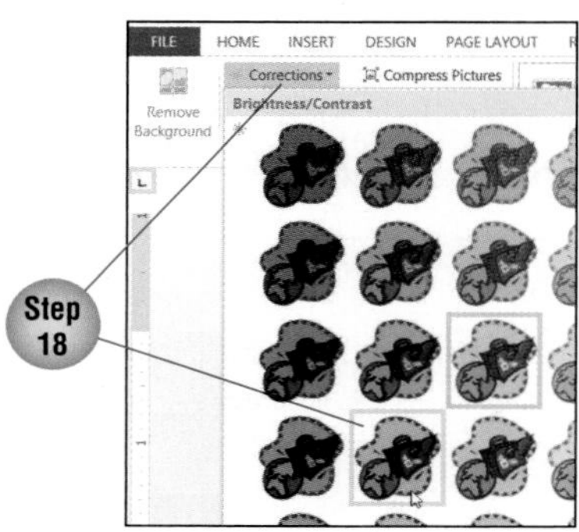

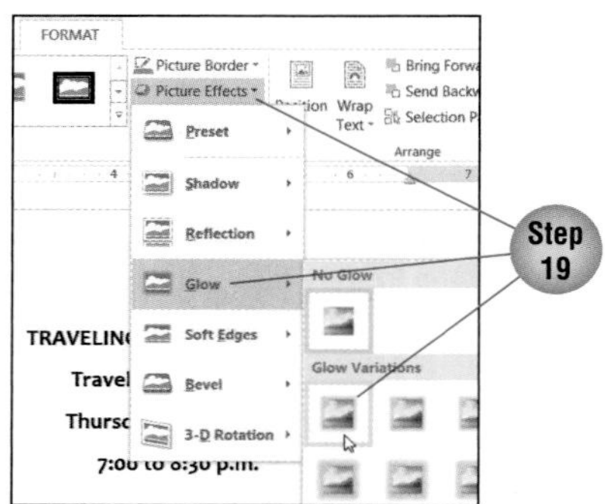

20. Click in the *Shape Height* measurement box in the Size group, type 1.7, and then press Enter.

    When you change the height measurement, the width measurement is automatically changed to maintain the proportions of the image.

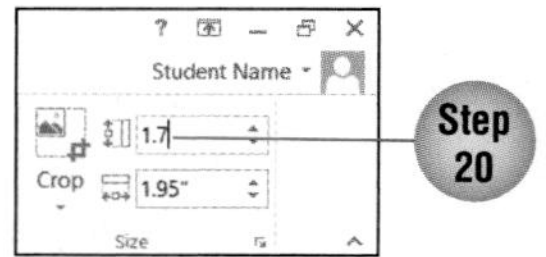

21. Select and then delete the text *First Choice Travel* that displays in small font size at the right side of the document.

22. Insert the First Choice Travel logo below *Sponsored by*. To begin, click the INSERT tab and then click the Pictures button in the Illustrations group.

23. At the Insert Picture dialog box, display the folder where your data documents are located and then double-click ***FCTLogo.jpg***.

24 With the image selected in the document, click the Layout Options button that displays outside the upper right corner of the image and then click *Tight* in the *With Text Wrapping* section of the drop-down list.

Choose a wrapping style to specify how you want text to flow around the image.

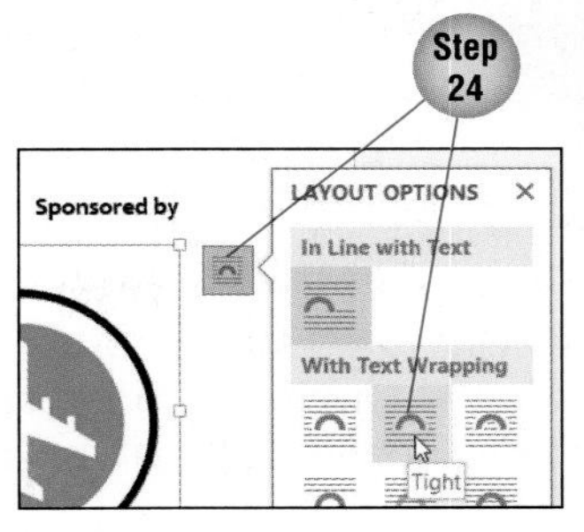

25 With the image still selected, hold down the Shift key and then drag one of the corner sizing handles (white squares) to reduce the size of the logo so it displays as shown in Figure 3.3.

Holding down the Shift key while increasing or decreasing the size of an image maintains the proportions of the image.

26 Drag the image so it is positioned as shown in Figure 3.3. To drag the image, position the insertion point inside the selected image until the arrow pointer displays with a four-headed arrow attached. Hold down the left mouse button, drag the selected image to the desired location, and then release the mouse button.

As you move an image near the top, left, right, or bottom margins of the document, green guidelines appear to help you position the image.

27 Click outside the logo to deselect it.

28 Save, print, and then close **WS3-FCTTravelIntl.docx**.

FIGURE 3.3 Activity 3.8

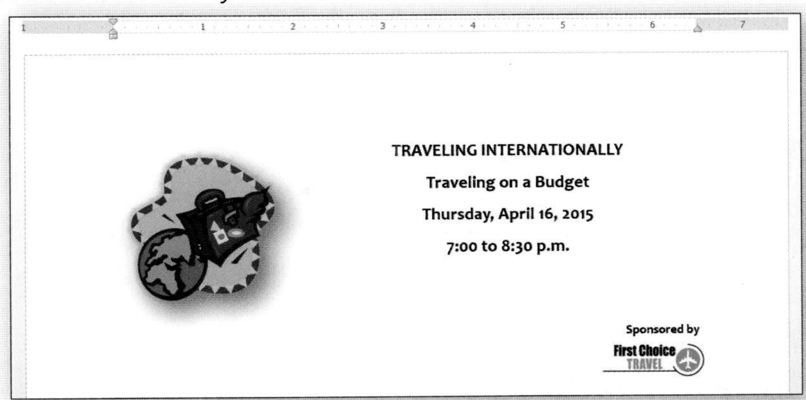

In Brief

Vertically Center Text
1. Click PAGE LAYOUT tab.
2. Click Page Setup group dialog box launcher.
3. Click Layout tab.
4. Click *Vertical alignment* option.
5. Click *Center* at drop-down list.
6. Click OK.

Insert Image
1. Click INSERT tab.
2. Click Online Pictures button.
3. Type search text in search box and then press Enter.
4. Double-click desired image.

Insert Picture
1. Click INSERT tab.
2. Click Pictures button.
3. Navigate to desired folder.
4. Double-click desired picture file.

In Addition

Formatting an Image with Buttons on the PICTURE TOOLS FORMAT Tab

Images inserted in a document can be formatted in a variety of ways, which might include adding fill color and border lines, increasing or decreasing the brightness or contrast, choosing a wrapping style, and cropping the image. Format an image with buttons on the PICTURE TOOLS FORMAT tab as shown in Figure 3.2. With buttons in the Adjust group you can correct the brightness and contrast of the image; change the image color; change to a different image; reset the image to its original size, position, and color; and compress the picture. Compress a picture to reduce resolution or discard extra information to save room on the hard drive or to reduce download time. Use buttons in the Picture Styles group to apply a predesigned style, insert a picture border, or apply a picture effect. The Arrange group contains buttons for positioning the image, wrapping text around the image, and aligning and rotating the image. Use options in the Size group to crop the image and specify the height and width of the image.

Activity 3.9

Preparing an Envelope

Word automates the creation of envelopes with options at the Envelopes and Labels dialog box with the Envelopes tab selected. At this dialog box, type a delivery address and a return address. If you open the Envelopes and Labels dialog box in a document containing a name and address, the name and address are inserted automatically as the delivery address. If you enter a return address, Word will ask you before printing if you want to save the new return address as the default return address. Answer *yes* if you want to use the return address for future envelopes or answer *no* if you will use a different return address for future envelopes.

Project

You need to create an envelope for sending the information about Thailand to Camille Matsui at Marquee Productions.

Tutorial 3.9
Creating and Printing Envelopes

1. Press Ctrl + N to display a blank document.

   You can also display a blank document by clicking the FILE tab, clicking the *New* option, and then clicking the Blank document template. Another method is to insert a New button on the Quick Access toolbar and then click the button to display a blank document. To insert the button on the Quick Access toolbar, click the Customize Quick Access Toolbar button that displays at the right side of the toolbar and then click *New* at the drop-down list.

2. Click the MAILINGS tab and then click the Envelopes button in the Create group.

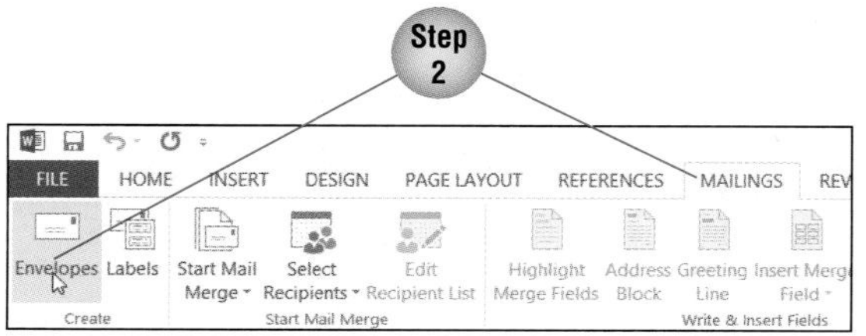

3. At the Envelopes and Labels dialog box with the Envelopes tab selected, type the following name and address in the *Delivery address* text box. (Press Enter at the end of each line, except the last line containing the city name, state, and zip code.)

   Camille Matsui
   Marquee Productions
   955 South Alameda Street
   Los Angeles, CA 90037

4. If any text displays in the *Return address* text box, delete it and then type the following name and address. Type your name where you see *Student Name*.

   First Choice Travel
   Student Name
   3588 Ventura Boulevard
   Los Angeles, CA 90102

5 Click the Add to Document button.

Clicking the Add to Document button inserts the envelope in the document. You can also send the envelope directly to the printer by clicking the Print button.

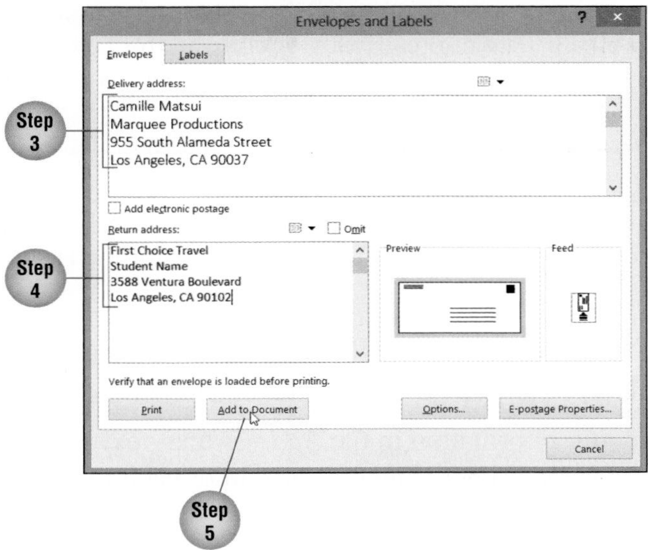

In Brief

Prepare Envelope

1. Click MAILINGS tab.
2. Click Envelopes button.
3. Type delivery address.
4. Type return address.
5. Click either Add to Document button or Print button.

6 At the message asking if you want to save the new return address as the default address, click the No button.

7 Save the document and name it **WS3-FCTEnvtoMP**.

8 Print and then close **WS3-FCTEnvtoMP.docx**. ***Note: Manual feed of the envelope may be required. Please check with your instructor before printing the envelope.***

In Addition

Customizing Envelopes

With options at the Envelope Options dialog box shown at the right, you can customize an envelope. Display this dialog box by clicking the Options button at the Envelopes and Labels dialog box. At the Envelope Options dialog box, you can change the envelope size, change the font for the delivery and return addresses, and specify the positioning of the addresses in relation to the left and top edges of the envelope.

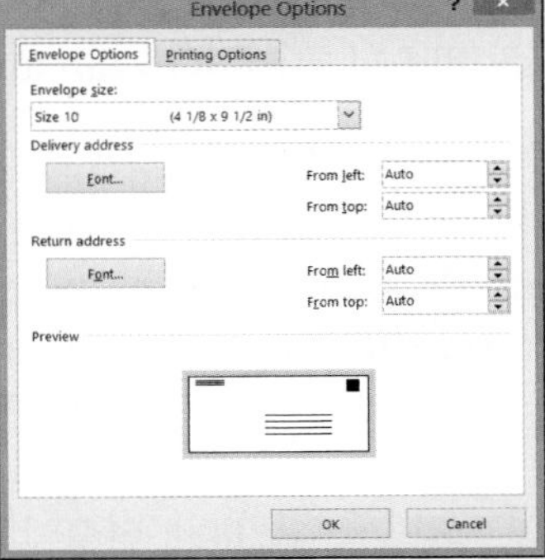

Activity 3.10

Preparing Mailing Labels

Use Word's Labels feature to print text on mailing labels, file labels, disc labels, or other types of labels. You can create labels for printing on a variety of predefined labels, which you can purchase at an office supply store. With the Labels feature, you can create a sheet of mailing labels with the same name and address or image or enter a different name and address on each label. Create a label with options at the Envelopes and Labels dialog box with the Labels tab selected.

Project

You decide to create a sheet of mailing labels containing the First Choice Travel name and address. You also need to create mailing labels for sending the Thailand document to several First Choice Travel customers. You also want to create labels for the First Choice Travel office in Toronto.

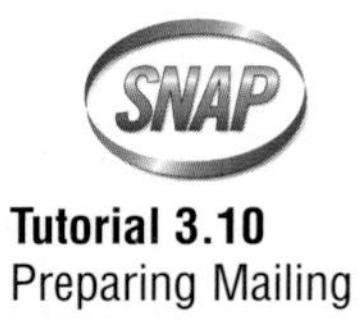

Tutorial 3.10
Preparing Mailing Labels

1. Press Ctrl + N to display a blank document.
2. Click the MAILINGS tab and then click the Labels button in the Create group.
3. Type the following information in the *Address* text box. Type your name where you see *Student Name*. (Press Enter at the end of each line except the last line.)

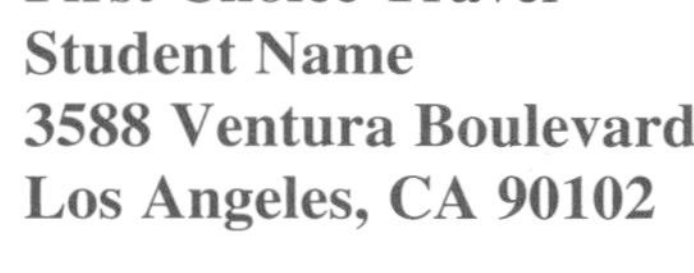

First Choice Travel
Student Name
3588 Ventura Boulevard
Los Angeles, CA 90102

4. Click the Options button.

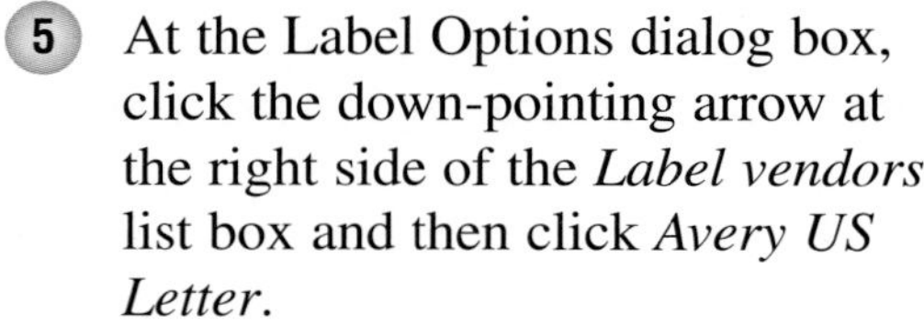

5. At the Label Options dialog box, click the down-pointing arrow at the right side of the *Label vendors* list box and then click *Avery US Letter*.

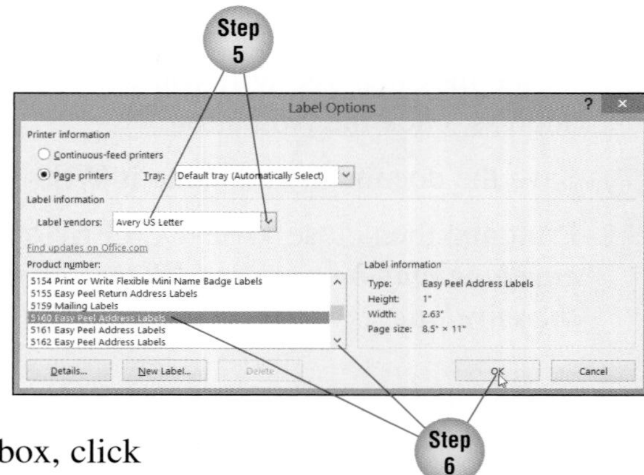

6. Scroll down the *Product number* list box, click *5160 Easy Peel Address Labels* in the list box, and then click OK to close the dialog box.
7. Click the New Document button at the Envelopes and Labels dialog box.
8. Save the document and name it **WS3-FCTLALabels**.
9. Print and then close **WS3-FCTLALabels.docx**.

   The number of labels printed on the page varies depending on the label selected at the Envelopes and Labels dialog box.

10. Click the MAILINGS tab and then click the Labels button in the Create group.
11. At the Envelopes and Labels dialog box, click the New Document button.
12. At the document, type the first name and address shown in Figure 3.4 in the first label. Press the Tab key twice to move the insertion point to the next label and then type the second name and address shown in Figure 3.4. Press the Tab key twice and then type the third name and address shown in the figure. Press the Tab key once and then type the fourth name and address. Continue in this manner until you have typed all of the names and addresses in Figure 3.4.
13. Save the document and name it **WS3-FCTCustLabels**.

14 Print and then close **WS3-FCTCustLabels.docx**.

15 At the blank document, create mailing labels for the Toronto office of First Choice Travel using an image. Begin by clicking the INSERT tab and then clicking the Pictures button in the Illustrations group.

16 At the Insert Picture dialog box, display the folder where your data files are located and then double-click ***FCTTorontoLabel.jpg***.

17 With the label image selected, click the Position button in the Arrange group and then click the *Position in Top Center with Square Text Wrapping* option (the middle option in the top row in the *With Text Wrapping* section).

18 With the image still selected, click the MAILINGS tab and then click the Labels button in the Create group.

19 At the Envelopes and Labels dialog box, make sure the Avery US Letter label number 5160 is selected and then click the New Document button.

When you click the New Document button, the label image is inserted in each label in the page and inserted in a new document.

20 Save the document and name it **WS3-FCTTorontoLabels**.

21 Print and then close **WS3-FCTTorontoLabels.docx**.

22 Close the document containing the label image without saving it.

In Brief

Prepare Mailing Labels with Same Name and Address
1. Click MAILINGS tab.
2. Click Labels button.
3. Type name and address in *Address* text box.
4. Click either New Document button or Print button.

Prepare Mailing Labels with Different Names and Addresses
1. Click MAILINGS tab.
2. Click Labels button.
3. Click New Document button.
4. At document screen, type names and addresses.

Prepare Mailing Labels with Image
1. Click INSERT tab.
2. Click Pictures button.
3. Navigate to desired folder.
4. Double-click image.
5. Click MAILINGS tab.
6. Click Labels button.
7. Click New Document button.

FIGURE 3.4 Step 12

Moreno Products 350 Mission Boulevard Pomona, CA 91767	Mr. Miguel Santos 12120 Barranca Parkway Irvine, CA 92612	Mr. and Mrs. Jack Lipinski 5534 Southeast 32nd Street Los Angeles, CA 90092
Dr. Esther Riggins 9077 Walnut Street Los Angeles, CA 90097	Automated Services, Inc. 4394 Seventh Street Long Beach, CA 92602	Ms. Samantha Schwartz 103-B Pacific Palms Los Angeles, CA 90068

In Addition

Customizing Labels

Click the Options button at the Envelopes and Labels dialog box with the Labels tab selected and the Label Options dialog box displays as shown at the right. At this dialog box, choose the type of printer, the desired label vendor, and the product number. This dialog box also displays information about the selected label, such as type, height, width, and paper size. When you select a label, Word automatically determines label margins. If, however, you want to customize these default settings, click the Details button at the Label Options dialog box.

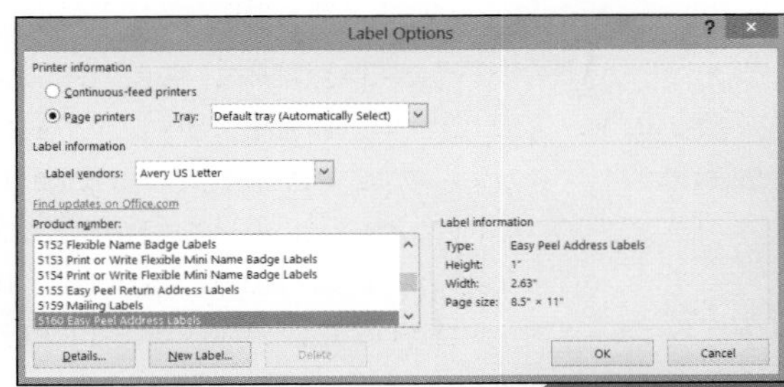

Features Summary

Feature	Ribbon Tab, Group	Button, Option	Keyboard Shortcut
blank page	INSERT, Pages		
Clipboard task pane	HOME, Clipboard		
copy selected text	HOME, Clipboard		Ctrl + C
cover page	INSERT, Pages		
Create Source dialog box	REFERENCES, Citations & Bibliography	, *Add New Source*	
cut selected text	HOME, Clipboard		Ctrl + X
Envelopes and Labels dialog box with Envelopes tab selected	MAILINGS, Create		
Envelopes and Labels dialog box with Labels tab selected	MAILINGS, Create		
footer	INSERT, Header & Footer		
header	INSERT, Header & Footer		
Insert Pictures window	INSERT, Illustrations		
Insert Picture dialog box	INSERT, Illustrations		
page borders	DESIGN, Page Background		
page break	INSERT, Pages		Ctrl + Enter
page color	DESIGN, Page Background		
page margins	PAGE LAYOUT, Page Setup		
page number	INSERT, Header & Footer		
page orientation	PAGE LAYOUT, Page Setup		
Page Setup dialog box	PAGE LAYOUT, Page Setup		
page size	PAGE LAYOUT, Page Setup		
paste selected text	HOME, Clipboard		Ctrl + V
Paste Special dialog box	HOME, Clipboard	(Ctrl), *Paste Special*	
watermark	DESIGN, Page Background		
works cited page	REFERENCES, Citations & Bibliography		

Knowledge Check SNAP

Completion: In the space provided at the right, indicate the correct term, command, or option.

1. The Cut button is located in this group on the HOME tab. ________________
2. Click this button to insert copied text in the document. ________________
3. Click this to display the Clipboard task pane. ________________
4. Click this tab to display the Margins button. ________________
5. This is the default measurement for the top, bottom, left, and right margins. ________________
6. This is the default page orientation. ________________
7. This is the default page size. ________________
8. This term refers to lightened text or image that displays behind text. ________________
9. The Cover Page button is located in the Pages group on this tab. ________________
10. Insert a page break by clicking the Page Break button in the Pages group on the INSERT tab or with this keyboard shortcut. ________________
11. Insert a footer by clicking the Footer button in this group on the INSERT tab. ________________
12. The initials MLA refer to this type of report style generally used in the humanities and English. ________________
13. General MLA style guidelines recommend this measurement for the top, bottom, left, and right margins. ________________
14. General MLA style guidelines recommend this line spacing. ________________
15. The Insert Citation button is located on this tab. ________________
16. In an MLA report, this page is an alphabetic list of the books, journal articles, web pages, or other sources referenced in the document. ________________
17. Use this feature to position the mouse pointer at the left margin, center of the page, or right margin. ________________
18. This is the default page alignment. ________________
19. Change page alignment with the *Vertical alignment* option at this dialog box. ________________
20. The Online Pictures button displays in this group on the INSERT tab. ________________
21. Click this button that displays outside the upper right corner of the image border to choose a wrapping style. ________________
22. When changing the size of an image, maintain the image proportions by holding down this key while dragging a corner sizing handle. ________________
23. To display the Envelopes and Labels dialog box, click this tab and then click the Envelopes button or the Labels button. ________________

Skills Review

Review 1 Copying and Pasting Text Between Travel Documents

1. Open **FCTJuneauAK.docx** and then save the document in the WordEOS folder and name it **WS3-R-FCTJuneauAK**.
2. Select the entire document, click the *No Spacing* style thumbnail in the Styles group, and then deselect the text.
3. Open the document named **FCTJuneauInfo.docx**.
4. Display the Clipboard task pane and then make sure the task pane is empty.
5. Select and then copy from the heading *Visitor Services* through the two paragraphs of text below the heading and the blank line below the two paragraphs.
6. Select and then copy from the heading *Transportation* through the paragraph of text below the heading and the blank line below the paragraph.
7. Select and then copy from the heading *Points of Interest* through the columns of text below the heading and the blank line below the columns of text.
8. Make **WS3-R-FCTJuneauAK.docx** the active document.
9. Display the Clipboard task pane.
10. Move the insertion point to the end of the document and then paste the text that begins with the heading *Points of Interest*.
11. Move the insertion point to the beginning of the heading *Points of Interest* and then paste the text that begins with the heading *Visitor Services*.
12. Move the insertion point to the beginning of the heading *Museums* and then paste the text that begins with the heading *Transportation*.
13. Clear the contents of the Clipboard task pane and then close the task pane.
14. Make **FCTJuneauInfo.docx** the active document and then close it.
15. Save **WS3-R-FCTJuneauAK.docx**.

Review 2 Moving and Formatting Text in a Travel Document

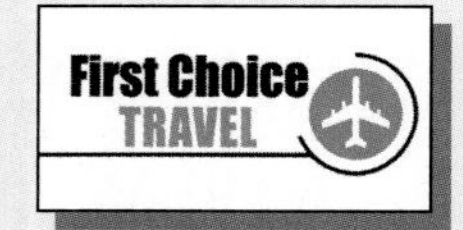

1. With **WS3-R-FCTJuneauAK.docx** open, select the heading *Visitor Centers*, the three paragraphs of text below it, and the blank line below the paragraphs, and then move the selected text before the heading *Visitor Attractions*.
2. Select the heading *Museums*, the three paragraphs of text below it, and the blank line below the three paragraphs, and then move the selected text before the heading *Visitor Attractions*.
3. Change the top and bottom margins to 1.25 inches and the left and right margins to 1 inch.
4. Apply the Heading 1 style to the title *JUNEAU, ALASKA* and apply the Heading 2 style to the other headings in the document (*History*, *Visitor Centers*, *Museums*, *Visitor Attractions*, *Transportation*, *Visitor Services*, and *Points of Interest*).
5. Apply the Lines (Stylish) style set, apply the Banded theme, and change the colors to *Blue II*.
6. Insert the Plain Number 3 page numbering style that inserts the page number in the upper right corner of each page.
7. Insert the SAMPLE 1 watermark.
8. Save, print, and then close **WS3-R-FCTJuneauAK.docx**.

Review 3 Formatting a Report in MLA Style

1. Open **PTRenaissanceRpt.docx** and then save the document in the WordEOS folder and name it **WS3-R-PTRenaissanceRpt**.
2. Select the entire document, change the font to 12-point Cambria, the line spacing to 2.0, and remove the spacing after paragraphs.
3. Move the insertion point to the beginning of the document, type your name, press Enter, type your instructor's name, press Enter, type the title of your course, press Enter, and then type the current date.
4. Insert a header that displays your last name and the page number at the right margin and changes the font to 12-point Cambria. (For help, refer to Steps 10–14 in Activity 3.6.)
5. Make sure MLA style is selected in the Citations & Bibliography group on the REFERENCES tab.
6. Position the insertion point after the word *century* (but before the period) in the last sentence in the first paragraph and then insert the source information from a journal article using the following information:
   Author = **Marcus Gerard**
   Title = **History of the Renaissance Period**
   Journal Name = **European History: Early Modern Europe**
   Year = **2015**
   Pages = **13-17**
7. Position the insertion point after the text *1494* (but before the period) in the first sentence in the third paragraph and then insert the source information from a book using the following information:
   Author = **Iris Brooke**
   Title = **A History of Renaissance Costumes**
   Year = **2014**
   City = **New York**
   Publisher = **Hudson River Publishing House**
8. Insert a works cited page as a new page at the end of the document.
9. Edit the Gerard source so the journal name displays as *European History: Western European Civilization*.
10. Update the works cited page.
11. Format the works cited page to MLA standards by making the following changes (for help, refer to Steps 10–13 in Activity 3.7):
    a. Select the *Works Cited* heading and all entries, click the *No Spacing* style, change the font to 12-point Cambria, and change the line spacing to 2.0.
    b. Center the title *Works Cited*.
    c. Hang-indent the entries.
12. Save, print, and then close **WS3-R-PTRenaissanceRpt.docx**.

Review 4 Preparing and Formatting an Announcement

1. At a blank document, use the Click and Type feature to type the text shown in Figure 3.5.
2. Select the centered text you just typed and then change the font to 14-point Candara bold.
3. Select the right-aligned text you just typed and then change the font to 10-point Candara bold.

4. Change the vertical alignment of the text on the page to center alignment.
5. Save the document in the WordEOS folder and name it **WS3-R-MPEmpOpps01**.
6. Print **WS3-R-MPEmpOpps01.docx**.
7. Save the document in the WordEOS folder with Save As and name it **WS3-R-MPEmpOpps02**.
8. Change the vertical alignment of the text on the page back to top alignment.
9. Insert a clip art image related to movies from Office.com (use the Online Pictures button). You determine the clip art image as well as the size and position of the image.
10. Delete the text *Marquee Productions* from the document and then insert the Marquee Productions logo image named **MPLogo.jpg** below the text *Sponsored by*. ***Hint: Do this at the Insert Picture dialog box.*** Adjust the size and position of the image so it displays below *Sponsored by* and is approximately 1.5 inches wide.
11. Save, print, and then close **WS3-R-MPEmpOpps02.docx**.

FIGURE 3.5 Review 4

EMPLOYMENT OPPORTUNITIES

Working in the Movie Industry

Wednesday, March 11, 2015

7:00 to 8:30 p.m.

Sponsored by

Marquee Productions

Review 5 Preparing an Envelope

1. At a blank document, prepare an envelope with the return address and delivery address shown below (type your name below *First Choice Travel* in the return address) and add the envelope to the document.

Delivery address:

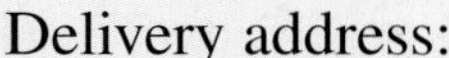

Chris Greenbaum
Marquee Productions
955 South Alameda Street
Los Angeles, CA 90037

Return address:

First Choice Travel
Student Name
3588 Ventura Boulevard
Los Angeles, CA 90102

2. Save the document in the WordEOS folder and name it **WS3-R-FCTEnv**. Print and then close **WS3-R-FCTEnv.docx**. (Manual feed of the envelope may be required.)

Review 6 Preparing Mailing Labels

1. At a blank document, prepare a sheet of mailing labels for the following name and address using the Avery US Letter 5160 Easy Peel Address Labels format (type your name below *Worldwide Enterprises*).

   Worldwide Enterprises
   Student Name
   1112-1583 Broadway
   New York, NY 10110

2. Save the mailing label document in the WordEOS folder and name it **WS3-R-WELabels**. Print and then close **WS3-R-WELabels.docx**.

Skills Assessment

Assessment 1 Formatting a Costume Rental Agreement

1. Open **PTAgreement.docx** and then save the document in the WordEOS folder and name it **WS3-A1-PTAgreement**.
2. Search for all occurrences of *Customer* and replace with *Marquee Productions*.
3. Move the *4. Alterations* section above the *3. Marquee Productions Agrees* section. Renumber the two sections.
4. Select the entire document, change the font to 12-point Constantia, and then deselect the document.
5. Change the top margin to 1.5 inches.
6. Insert the Semaphore footer.
7. Save, print, and then close **WS3-A1-PTAgreement.docx**.

Assessment 2 Creating an Announcement

1. At a blank document, create an announcement for Niagara Peninsula College by typing the text shown in Figure 3.6 on the next page.
2. Change the font for the entire document to a decorative font, size, and color of your choosing.
3. Change the line spacing to double spacing for the entire document.
4. Insert, size, and move a clip art image of your choosing from Office.com related to the subject of the announcement.
5. Save the document in the WordEOS folder and name it **WS3-A2-NPCInternship**.
6. Print and then close **WS3-A2-NPCInternship.docx**.

FIGURE 3.6 Assessment 2

NIAGARA PENINSULA COLLEGE

Internship Opportunities

June 18 through August 31, 2015

Marquee Productions, Toronto Office

Contact Cal Rubine, Theatre Arts Division

Assessment 3 Preparing Mailing Labels

1. Prepare return mailing labels with the following information (type your name below *Niagara Peninsula College*):
   Niagara Peninsula College
   Student Name
   2199 Victoria Street
   Niagara-on-the-Lake, ON L0S 1J0
2. Save the labels document in the WordEOS folder and name it **WS3-A3-NPCLabels**. Print and then close **WS3-A3-NPCLabels.docx**.

Assessment 4 Finding Information on Creating a Picture Watermark

1. Open **WS3-R-MPEmpOpps01.docx** and then save the document in the WordEOS folder and name it **WS3-A4-MPEmpOpps-Wtrmark**.
2. Use Word's Help feature to learn how to insert a picture watermark.
3. Insert the **MPLogo.jpg** file located in the WordS3 folder as a watermark.
4. Save, print, and then close **WS3-A4-MPEmpOpps-Wtrmark.docx**.

Assessment 5 Individual Challenge
Creating a Personal Letterhead

1. At a blank document, create a letterhead that includes your first and last names, address, telephone number, and insert a clip art image in the letterhead that represents you or something in which you are interested. Apply font formatting to the text in the letterhead and size and position the clip art image. (For letterhead examples, refer to **FCTLtrhd.docx** in the WordS3 folder and **MPLtrhd.docx** in the WordS2 folder. The letterheads in these two documents were created as headers. If you want to create your letterhead in a header, click the INSERT tab, click the Header button in the Header & Footer group and then click *Edit Header*.)
2. Save the document in the WordEOS folder and name it **WS3-A5-IC-Ltrhd**.
3. Print and then close **WS3-A5-IC-Ltrhd.docx**.

Marquee Challenge

Challenge 1 Formatting a Costume Document

1. Open **PTCostumes.docx** and then save the document in the WordEOS folder and name it **WS3-C1-PTCostumes**.
2. Format your document so it displays similar to the document in Figure 3.7 on the following page. To do this, apply the following formatting:
   - Change the top margin to 1.25 inches.
   - Insert, size, and position the **PTLogo.jpg** picture as shown.
   - Apply the Heading 1 style to the headings.
   - Apply the Lines (Simple) style set.
   - Apply the Green theme colors. (Use the Colors button on the DESIGN tab.)
   - Apply bold and italic formatting to the headings.
   - Apply Green, Accent 1, Lighter 80% paragraph shading to the headings.
   - Insert the page border (use the same page border you inserted in a document in Step 4 of Activity 3.4) and change the width to 15 points and the color to *Green, Accent 1, Darker 25%*.
   - Change paragraph alignment as shown.
   - Insert, size, and position the book clip art. (Use the words *three stacked books* to find the clip art image.)
   - Apply any other formatting to make your document consistent with the document in the figure.
3. Save, print, and then close **WS3-C1-PTCostumes.docx**.

Challenge 2 Preparing an Announcement

1. At a blank document, create the document shown in Figure 3.8 on page 112 with the following specifications:
   - Change the page orientation to landscape orientation.
   - When typing the text in the document, press Shift + Enter to end each line (except press Enter after typing the title).
   - Apply the page border and insert the page color as shown in the figure.
   - Use the Pictures button to insert the **WELogo.jpg** image in the upper left corner of the document. Change the background of the logo image to transparent by clicking the Color button on the PICTURE TOOLS FORMAT tab, clicking the *Set Transparent Color* option, and then clicking in a white area inside the company logo. This changes the white background of the image to a transparent background. Size and position the image as shown in the figure.
   - Use the Online Pictures button (search for *businesspeople silhouette*) to insert the image of the people in the lower right corner of the document.
   - Insert the watermark as shown.
2. Save the document in the WordEOS folder and name it **WS3-C2-WENotice**.
3. Print and then close **WS3-C2-WENotice.docx**.

FIGURE 3.7 Challenge 1

Renaissance Period

The Renaissance period was a series of cultural and literary movements that took place in the fourteenth, fifteenth, and sixteenth centuries in Europe. The word *renaissance* means "rebirth" and originated with the belief that Europeans had rediscovered the intellectual and cultural superiority of the Greek and Roman cultures. The Renaissance period was preceded by the Middle Ages, also known as the "Dark Ages," which began with the collapse of the Roman Empire in the fifth century. The term *renaissance* was coined by Jacob Burckhardt in the eighteenth century in *The Civilization of the Renaissance in Italy*.

Renaissance education was designed to produce a person well-versed in humanities, mathematics, science, sports, and art. The Renaissance person had extensive knowledge in many fields, explored beyond the boundaries of learning and geographical knowledge, and embraced free thought and skepticism. Artists, writers, explorers, architects, and scientists were motivated by a revival in classical Greek and Roman culture and a return to classical values. During the Middle Ages, interest in culture and learning was primarily confined to theologians, philosophers, and writers. During the Renaissance period, however, people from all social, political, and economic classes involved themselves in the study of classical literature and art.

Renaissance Costume

Renaissance costume developed in Italy and was introduced to Western Europe following the invasion of Italy by Charles VIII of France in 1494. Due to the warmer climate in Italy, simpler styles evolved independently from the rest of Europe. Men's clothing consisted of low-necked tunics and chemises and women's clothing consisted of simple and low-necked gowns called "Juliet" gowns. During the middle of the fifteenth century, clothing assumed a more natural appearance. Women wore dresses with attached bodices and skirts. Men's doublets became shorter and hosiery became more prominent. Interest by women in gothic headdresses declined and instead they trimmed their hair with veils, ribbons, and jewels. Lace and perfume became more prevalent during the Renaissance period.

Early in the Renaissance period, women's dress included a long, rigid, cone-shaped corset reaching below the waist to a "V" in the front. Women's gowns expanded below the waistline and by the middle sixteenth century were supported by hoops made of wire that were held together with ribbons. This hoop skirt, called a *farthingale*, reached its maximum width around the early seventeenth century and then changed to a cartwheel or drum shape. Ballooned sleeves and circular lace collars also typified the early seventeenth century costume. Men's clothing had a similar look with puffed-out hose, balloon sleeves, padded doublets, and large ruff collars.

continues

FIGURE 3.7 Challenge 1—*Continued*

Costume Vocabulary

1. Basquine: A very large skirt that was open and stretched on circles.
2. Berne: A very large, fixed, and pleated scarf that rested on the shoulder.
3. Jupon: Long-sleeved camisole generally worn by men and women in Spain.
4. Mantilla: A kind of shawl worn by women to cover the head and shoulders.

Costume Books

- Arnold, Janet, *Patterns of Fashion*
- Barton, Lucy, *Historic Costume for the Stage*
- Boucher, Francois, *20,000 Years of Fashion*
- Brooke, Iris, *A History of Costume*
- Evans, Mary, *Costume Throughout the Ages*
- LaMar, Virginia A., *English Dress in the Age of Shakespeare*

FIGURE 3.8 Challenge 2

IMPORTANT NOTICE!!

We need additional employees to work the next two weekends to complete a special distribution order. If you are interested in working any shift this weekend and/or next, please contact Rhonda Trask in Human Resources at extension 3360. We are offering overtime pay plus a bonus based on your hourly or salaried wage.

URGENT

Word SECTION 4
Formatting with Special Features

Skills

- Create and modify WordArt text
- Create a drop cap
- Insert a text box and draw a text box
- Insert and modify shapes
- Use SmartArt to create organizational charts and graphics
- Create, format, and modify tables
- Insert one file into another
- Insert a continuous section break
- Format text into columns and modify columns
- Save a document as a single file web page
- Insert a hyperlink
- Merge letters and envelopes

Projects Overview

Format a document on special vacation activities in Hawaii; prepare an organizational chart and graphic of services; create and modify a table containing information on scenic flights on Maui; format and modify a fact sheet containing information on Petersburg, Alaska; save the fact sheet as a single file web page and insert hyperlinks to an additional document and a website; create a data source and then merge a letter on cruise specials and an envelope document with the data source; format a newsletter containing information on Zenith Adventures.

Create an organizational chart and graphic for the production department.

Create and format a table with information on classes offered by the Theatre Arts Division; format and modify a newsletter.

Create a data source and then merge it with a letter asking for fabric pricing; create an organizational chart and graphic for the design department.

Create and format a table containing information on catered lunch options; create a flyer.

Create and format an announcement about an upcoming stockholders' meeting.

Model Answers for Projects

These model answers for the projects you complete in Section 4 provide a preview of the finished projects before you begin working and also allow you to compare your own results with these models to ensure you have created the materials accurately.

WS4-FCTHawaiianSpecials.docx (a two-page document) is the project in Activities 4.1 to 4.2.

HAWAIIAN SPECIALS

White Sands Charters

Sail on the Pacific Pride and visit out-of-the-way bays populated by some of Hawaii's most colorful residents. Naturalist guides help you spot humpback whales during the winter and spring seasons. Depending on weather, marine conditions, and access, your guides will also introduce you to the delightful denizens of Molokini Crater or other premier snorkeling spots. The Pacific Pride departs at 7:00 a.m. and returns at 1:00 p.m. Voyages to Molokini depart at 8:00 a.m. and return at 12:00 noon.

Air Adventures

For an adventure that will last a lifetimes, fly in Hawaii's newest and most modern jet helicopter. Each air adventure includes:

- An expert pilot
- An air-conditioned cabin
- Exclusive remote landing sites
- Video with CD sound that puts you in the picture

Sign up today for your Hawaiian adventure and enjoy spectacular beaches, Hawaii's natural undersea world, and beautiful bays.

Air Adventures puts you in a luxurious helicopter designed specifically for touring, with all seating facing forward offering 180-degree visibility. View untouched areas from the moonscapes of volcanic craters to thundering waterfalls and rugged coastlines.

Deep Sea Submarines

Journey through Hawaii's natural undersea world in a high-tech submarine to discover the island's unique marine species and explore the mysteries of the sea. Choose from the following exciting adventures:

- Island Expedition: An introduction to submarine travel and Hawaii's natural marine world
- Island Discovery: An early morning or late afternoon dive, with special savings
- Ultimate Adventure: Deep Sea Submarines' most celebrated dive, featuring a skilled team of scuba divers

All Deep Sea Submarines boats are environmentally friendly, air-conditioned vessels with state-of-the-art equipment on board.

Snorkeling Fantasies

Don't settle for an ordinary snorkeling trip—experience a Snorkeling Fantasies adventure instead! Discover sea turtles, amazing fish, and beautiful coral with a knowledgeable marine researcher as your guide. Snorkel in beautiful, out-of-the-way bays while on a sunset sail. Just bring your towel and sunscreen—we supply everything from snorkeling gear to drinks and lunch.

Bicycle Safari

Travel 38 miles downhill from the summit to the sea. View the volcano and coast through lava fields and emerald green fields. Your downhill experience includes:

- Custom-built bicycle
- Free hotel pickup
- Two volcano guides
- Vista dining
- Tour of the Orchid Flower Farm

The bicycle tour begin at the top of the volcano where you watch the sun rise over the majestic mountain. The downhill trip requires only 400 yards of pedaling, allowing you to relax and enjoy the beautiful scenery.

Sign up today for your Hawaiian adventure!

WS4-FCTStructure.docx (a two-page document) is the project in Activity 4.3.

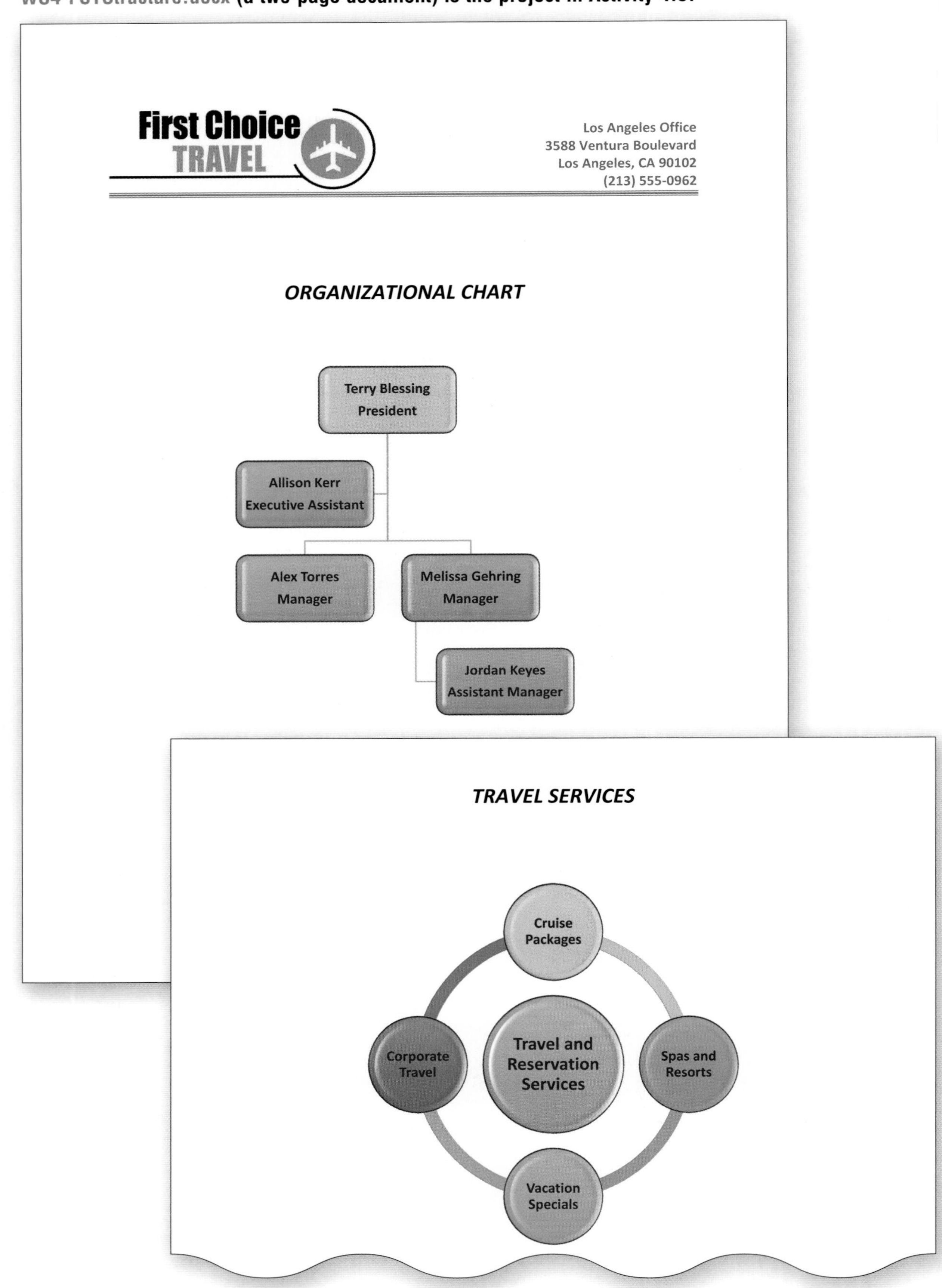

WS4-FCTIslandFlights.docx is the project in Activities 4.4 to 4.6.

ISLAND SIGHTSEEING FLIGHTS

First Choice Travel has contracted with Tropic Airlines to offer First Choice Travel customers a fantastic deal on adventurous sightseeing flights over the spectacular and breathtaking Hawaiian Islands. During your visit to any of the beautiful islands, take advantage of these Tropic Airlines flights to provide memories that will last a lifetime!

MAUI

Hawaiian Adventures	MAUI FLIGHTS			
	Adventure	Destination	Price	FCT
	Special West Maui	Waterfalls, lush tropical valleys	$49	$35
	West Maui Tropical	West Maui mountains, Hawaii's highest waterfalls	$79	$65
	Haleakala-Keane	Haleakala crater, tropical rain forest, waterfalls	$89	$75
	Molokai-West Maui	West Maui mountains, waterfalls, sea cliffs, Kalaupapa colony	$189	$175

WS4-FCTPetersburgAK.docx (a two-page document) is the project in Activities 4.7.

limits is discouraged. If you are planning to stay in a hotel, U.S. Forest Service cabin, or on the Alaska Marine Highway, you will need to make a reservation.

Transportation

Daily jet service is available from Seattle, Ketchikan, and Juneau to Petersburg. Commuter airline flights are also available from Ketchikan, Wrangell, or Juneau. The airport and seaplane base are close to town and can accommodate private aircraft. A helicopter charter service also operates at the airport.

The Alaska Marine Highway offers another option for traveling to Petersburg. Petersburg is one of the main ferry stops and service is frequent during the summer. The ferry terminal is a short walk from downtown, and taxi service is available.

If you would like more information on traveling in Alaska, check with a First Choice Travel representative.

Guided Activities

- Whale watching in Frederick Sound
- King salmon fishing
- Halibut fishing
- Wildlife cruise
- Stikine River cruise
- Leconte Glacier tour

PETERSBURG, ALASKA

Petersburg, Alaska, located on Mitkof Island, is considered Alaska's Little Norway. Petersburg grew up around a salmon cannery and sawmill built by Peter Buschmann between 1897 and 1899. Petersburg is named after Peter Buschmann and part of its charm lies in its magnificent setting and the Scandinavian design of some of its buildings and houses.

Services

Downtown merchants sell a variety of products, including gifts and souvenirs, hunting and fishing gear and licenses, camping supplies, groceries, hardware, marine supplies, automotive parts, and clothing. Unique and colorful gifts and clothes imported from Norway are available at some specialty shops. Artwork by local artists is sold at downtown shops and at an art gallery located near the ferry terminal.

The business district contains two banks, several restaurants, a laundry, a movie theater, and a bookstore. The U.S. Post Office and the U.S. Forest Service ranger district office are both located in the federal office building. Other merchants offer nearly all visitor services, including gas stations and car repair, air taxi services and charters, car rentals, RV parking, propane, and boat repairs and rentals.

Visitor Attractions

Visit the Clausen Memorial Museum at Second and Fram streets to view exhibits that explain local fishing history and Petersburg's Norwegian heritage. The museum is open daily May through September.

The recently restored Sons of Norway Hall is one of the prominent downtown landmarks. It is a favorite location for artists and photographers. The hall is on the National Register of Historic Places and is open for visitors on special occasions.

Mitkof Island offers a picnic area at Sandy Beach located north of Petersburg. Sandy Beach has a good view of Frederick Sound and offers covered picnic shelters. Camping is not allowed at the picnic grounds.

Walk through any of the boat harbors and you will usually find a friendly fisherman who will explain some of the fishing gear and fishing boats docked in the harbor. Freshly caught seafood is often available at the local markets and also is served at local restaurants.

Walking Tours

Petersburg offers several attractive walks. The city's Main Street contains brass inlays of area birds and animals, and boasts recently planted trees, custom light poles and benches, and picnic tables along Harbor Way. A boardwalk connects Mountain View Manor with the local ballpark. Other walks are the Loop Walk, Hammer Slough Walk, Harbor Walk, and the Three Lakes Loop Road Walk.

Accommodations

Accommodations in and around Petersburg include three hotels, several bed-and-breakfast establishments, a Forest Service campground, and several remote Forest Service cabins. Tent City, a municipal campground near the airport, is used primarily by the many transient cannery workers who flock to Petersburg during the summer and is not recommended for tourists.

Drivers can generally park recreational vehicles anywhere within the National Forest boundary, provided they do not interfere with logging operations. Camping or recreational vehicle parking in the city

1

WORD SECTION 4
Project Model Answers

WS4-FCTCruiseLtrMainDoc.docx is part of the project in Activity 4.9.

Los Angeles Office
3588 Ventura Boulevard
Los Angeles, CA 90102
(213) 555-0962

January 12, 2015

«AddressBlock»

«GreetingLine»

First Choice Travel has partnered with Ocean Vista Cruise Lines to offer fantastic prices on cruises along the west coast of the United States and Canada. From now until the end of September, we are offering special reduced prices for three-day and four-day cruises. With your «Membership» membership, you will receive an additional «Discount» discount.

All ground transportation is included in the special cruise price as well as a complimentary shore excursion. Consider joining one of the following cruises and enjoy the beauty of the west coast.

Three-day Cruises

Seattle, Victoria B.C., Nanaimo B.C.
$519 to $999

Vancouver B.C., San Francisco
$599 to $1399

Four-day Cruises

Seattle, Vancouver B.C., Victoria B.C., Nanaimo B.C.
$589 to $1179

Vancouver B.C., Astoria, San Francisco
$639 to $1439

Our special prices are good through September 30, 2015. Please give us a call or stop by our office and let us help you plan your dream cruise.

Sincerely,

Jordan Keyes

WS4-FCTMergedCruiseLtrs.docx **(a four-page document) is part of the project in Activity 4.9.**

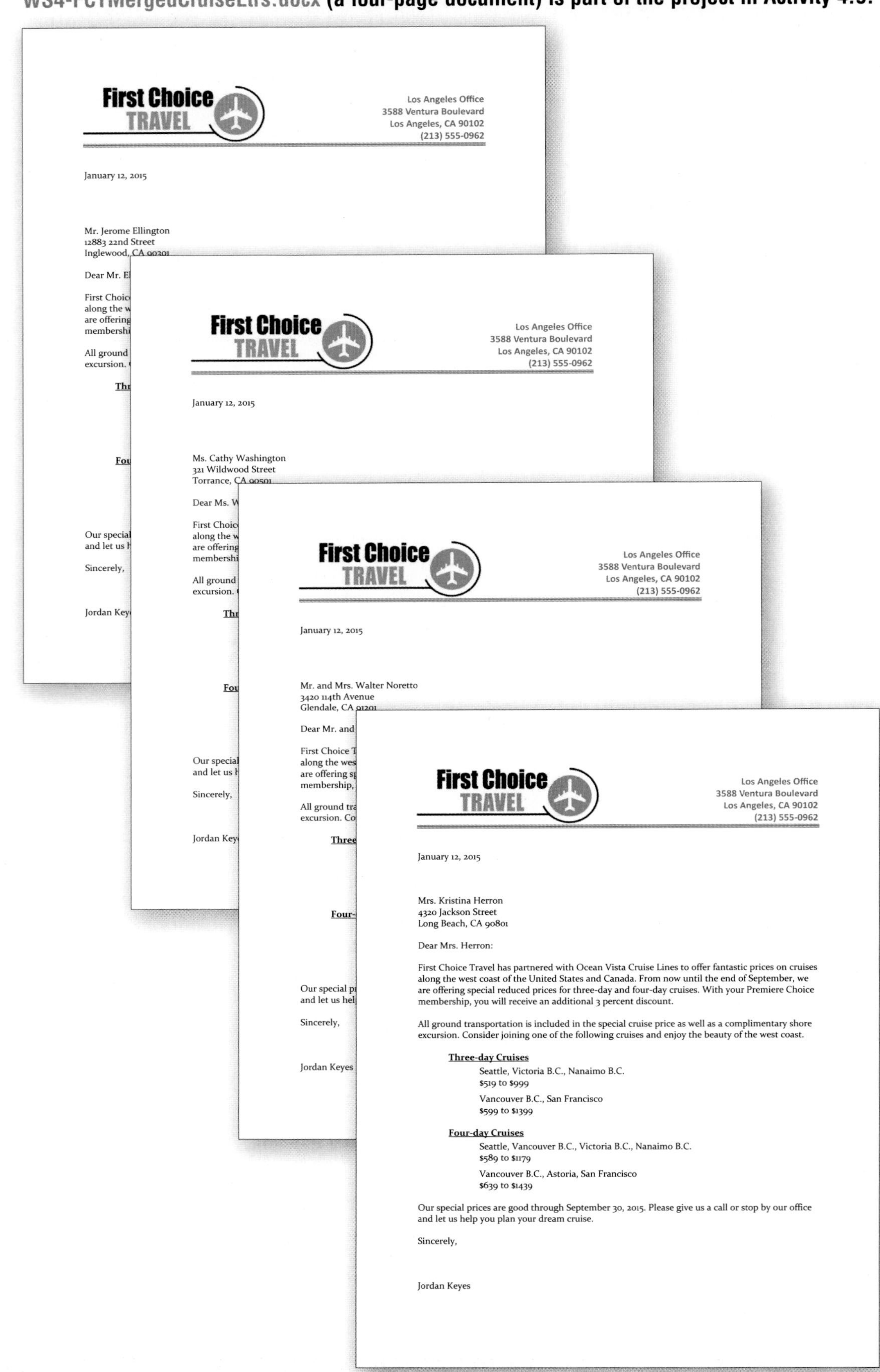

First Choice TRAVEL

Los Angeles Office
3588 Ventura Boulevard
Los Angeles, CA 90102
(213) 555-0962

January 12, 2015

Mr. Jerome Ellington
12883 22nd Street
Inglewood, CA 90301

First Choice TRAVEL

Los Angeles Office
3588 Ventura Boulevard
Los Angeles, CA 90102
(213) 555-0962

January 12, 2015

Ms. Cathy Washington
321 Wildwood Street
Torrance, CA 90501

First Choice TRAVEL

Los Angeles Office
3588 Ventura Boulevard
Los Angeles, CA 90102
(213) 555-0962

January 12, 2015

Mr. and Mrs. Walter Noretto
3420 114th Avenue
Glendale, CA 91201

First Choice TRAVEL

Los Angeles Office
3588 Ventura Boulevard
Los Angeles, CA 90102
(213) 555-0962

January 12, 2015

Mrs. Kristina Herron
4320 Jackson Street
Long Beach, CA 90801

Dear Mrs. Herron:

First Choice Travel has partnered with Ocean Vista Cruise Lines to offer fantastic prices on cruises along the west coast of the United States and Canada. From now until the end of September, we are offering special reduced prices for three-day and four-day cruises. With your Premiere Choice membership, you will receive an additional 3 percent discount.

All ground transportation is included in the special cruise price as well as a complimentary shore excursion. Consider joining one of the following cruises and enjoy the beauty of the west coast.

Three-day Cruises

Seattle, Victoria B.C., Nanaimo B.C.
$519 to $999

Vancouver B.C., San Francisco
$599 to $1399

Four-day Cruises

Seattle, Vancouver B.C., Victoria B.C., Nanaimo B.C.
$589 to $1179

Vancouver B.C., Astoria, San Francisco
$639 to $1439

Our special prices are good through September 30, 2015. Please give us a call or stop by our office and let us help you plan your dream cruise.

Sincerely,

Jordan Keyes

WS4-FCTMergedEnvs.docx (a four-envelope document) is part of the project in Activity 4.9.

Activity 4.1

Creating and Modifying WordArt Text

Use the WordArt feature to distort or modify text to conform to a variety of shapes. Consider using WordArt to create a company logo, letterhead, flier title, or heading. To insert WordArt, click the INSERT tab, click the WordArt button in the Text group, and then click the desired WordArt style at the drop-down gallery. When WordArt is selected, the DRAWING TOOLS FORMAT tab displays. Use options and buttons on this tab to modify and customize WordArt.

Project

To increase the visual appeal of a document on Hawaiian specials, you decide to insert and format WordArt.

Tutorial 4.1
Inserting and Modifying WordArt

1. Open **FCTHawaiianSpecials.docx** and then save the document and name it **WS4-FCTHawaiianSpecials**.
2. Complete a spelling and grammar check on the document. You determine what to correct and what to ignore. (The name *Molokini* is spelled correctly in the document.)
3. Click the DESIGN tab, click the Fonts button in the Document Formatting group, and then click the *Calibri Light-Constantia* option.
4. Click the Colors button and then click the *Green* option at the drop-down gallery.
5. With the insertion point positioned at the beginning of the document, click the INSERT tab.
6. Insert WordArt by clicking the WordArt button in the Text group and then clicking the *Gradient Fill - Aqua, Accent 1, Reflection* option (second option in the second row).

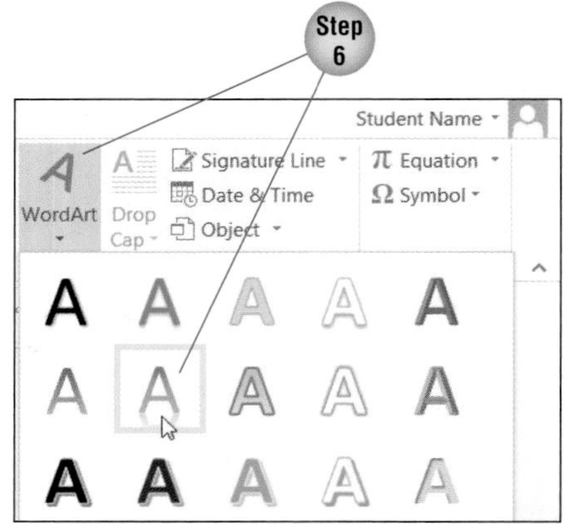

7. Type **HAWAIIAN SPECIALS**.

   This inserts the WordArt text *HAWAIIAN SPECIALS* in the document, selects the *WordArt* text box, and displays the DRAWING TOOLS FORMAT tab.
8. Select the border of the WordArt by positioning the arrow pointer on the dashed border that surrounds the WordArt and then clicking the left mouse button. (This changes the dashed border to a solid line border.)
9. Click the Text Fill button arrow in the WordArt Styles group and then click the *Blue* option (third option from the right in the *Standard Colors* row).

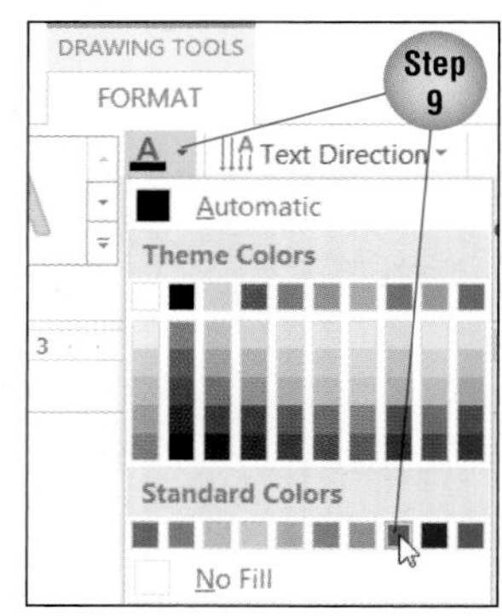

10. Click the Text Effects button in the WordArt Styles group, point to *Glow*, and then click the *Green, 5 pt glow, Accent color 1* option (first option in the first row).

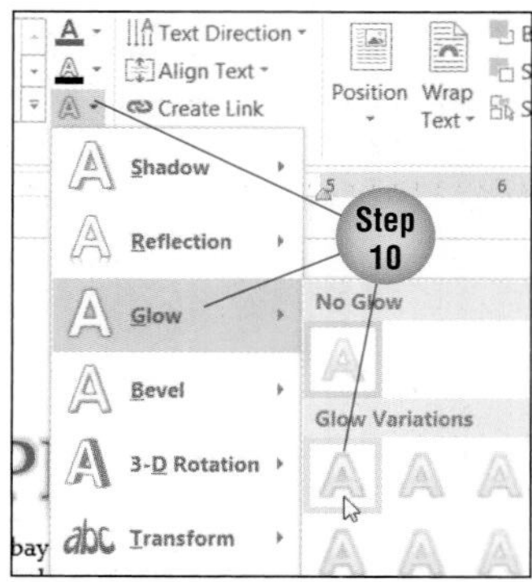

11 Increase the height of the WordArt text by clicking in the *Shape Height* measurement box in the Size group, typing **1**, and then pressing Enter.

12 Increase the width of the WordArt text by clicking in the *Shape Width* measurement box in the Size group, typing **6.5**, and then pressing Enter.

13 Click the Position button in the Arrange group and then click the *In Line with Text* option (first option in the drop-down gallery).

In Brief

Insert WordArt

1. Click INSERT tab.
2. Click WordArt button.
3. Click desired option at drop-down gallery.
4. Type desired text.
5. Format WordArt with options on DRAWING TOOLS FORMAT tab.

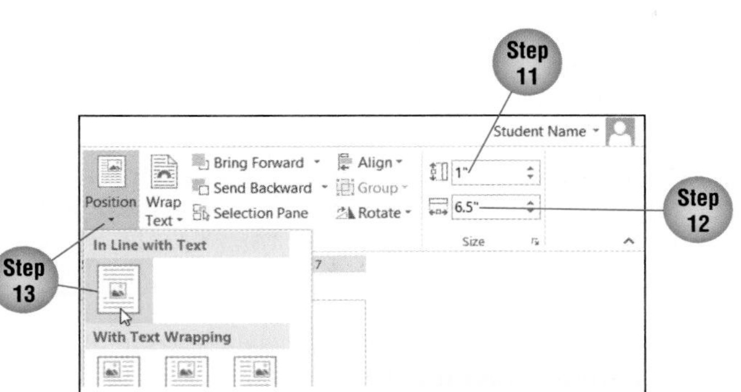

14 Click the Text Effects button in the WordArt Styles group, point to *Transform*, and then click the *Deflate* option (second option in the sixth row in the *Warp* section).

15 Apply the Heading 2 style to the following headings: *White Sands Charters*, *Air Adventures*, *Deep Sea Submarines*, *Snorkeling Fantasies*, and *Bicycle Safari*.

16 Press Ctrl + A to select the entire document and then change the font color to turquoise. To do this, click the HOME tab, click the Font Color button arrow, and then click the *Turquoise, Accent 6, Darker 50%* option (last option in the last column in the *Theme Colors* section).

17 Save **WS4-FCTHawaiianSpecials.docx**.

In Addition

Using the DRAWING TOOLS FORMAT Tab

When WordArt is selected, the DRAWING TOOLS FORMAT tab displays as shown below. Use options in the Insert Shapes group to draw a shape or text box. With options in the Shape Styles group, you can apply a predesigned style, change the shape fill color and the shape outline color, and apply shape effects. Change the style of the WordArt text with options in the WordArt Styles group, apply text formatting to WordArt with options in the Text group, specify the layering of the WordArt text with options in the Arrange group, and identify the height and width of the WordArt text box with measurement boxes in the Size group.

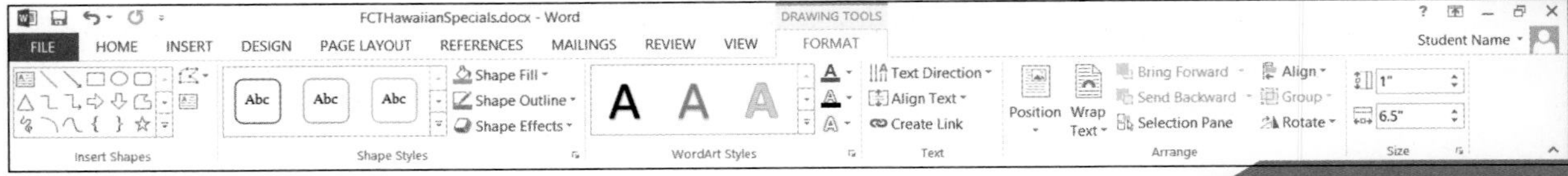

Activity 4.2

Creating Drop Caps and Text Boxes; Drawing Shapes

Use a drop cap to enhance the appearance of text. A drop cap is the first letter of the first word of a paragraph that is set into a paragraph. Drop caps identify the beginning of major sections or parts of a document. Create a drop cap with the Drop Cap button in the Text group on the INSERT tab. Use the Text Box button in the Text group to create a text box or insert a predesigned text box in a document. The Shapes button in the Illustrations group on the INSERT tab contains a number of shape options for drawing shapes in a document including lines, rectangles, basic shapes, block arrows, flow chart shapes, stars, banners, and callouts. Click a shape and the mouse pointer displays as crosshairs (plus sign). Position the crosshairs where you want the image positioned and then click the left mouse button or hold down the left mouse button, drag to create the shape, and then release the mouse button. This inserts the shape in the document and also displays the DRAWING TOOLS FORMAT tab. Use buttons on this tab to change the shape, apply a style to the shape, arrange the shape, and change the size of the shape.

Project

You continue to add visual appeal to the Hawaiian Specials document by creating a drop cap and a shape and inserting a predesigned text box.

Tutorial 4.2A
Inserting and Formatting a Shape

Tutorial 4.2B
Creating a Drop Cap and Inserting a Text Box

1. With **WS4-FCTHawaiianSpecials.docx** open, position the insertion point on any character in the heading *White Sands Charters*, click the Border button arrow in the Paragraph group on the HOME tab, and then click the *Borders and Shading* option at the drop-down list.
2. At the Borders and Shading dialog box, make sure the single line is selected in the *Style* section, click the down-pointing arrow at the right side of the *Color* option box, and then click the *Turquoise, Accent 6, Darker 50%* option (last option in the last column in the *Theme Colors* section).
3. Click the bottom of the diagram in the *Preview* section of the dialog box.

   This inserts a single turquoise line in the diagram.
4. Click OK to close the Borders and Shading dialog box.
5. Use the Repeat command, F4, to apply the same turquoise bottom border to the remaining headings in the document (*Air Adventures*, *Deep Sea Submarines*, *Snorkeling Fantasies*, and *Bicycle Safari*).

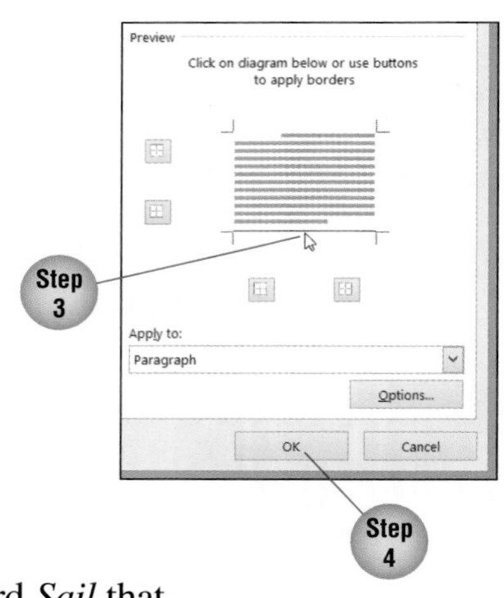

6. Move the insertion point to the beginning of the word *Sail* that displays immediately below the heading *White Sands Charters* and then click the INSERT tab.
7. Click the Drop Cap button in the Text group and then click *Dropped* at the drop-down gallery.

   If you click *Drop Cap Options*, the Drop Cap dialog box displays with options for positioning the drop cap, changing the font, identifying the number of lines for the drop cap, and setting the distance from the drop cap to the text.

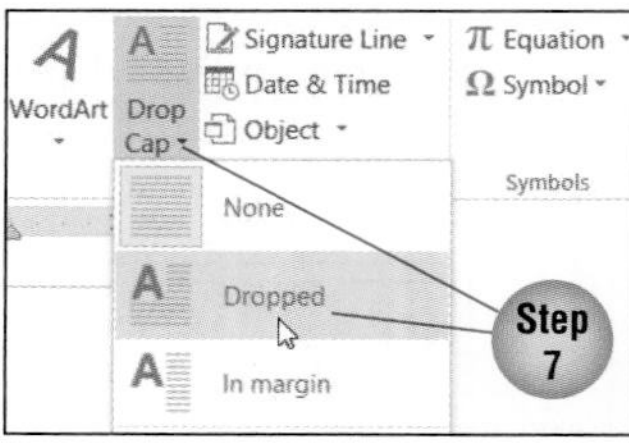

8 Click anywhere in the text on the first page to deselect the *S*.

9 Insert a text box on the first page by clicking the Text Box button [button] in the Text group on the INSERT tab and then clicking the *Austin Quote* option.

Predesigned text boxes are listed in alphabetical order.

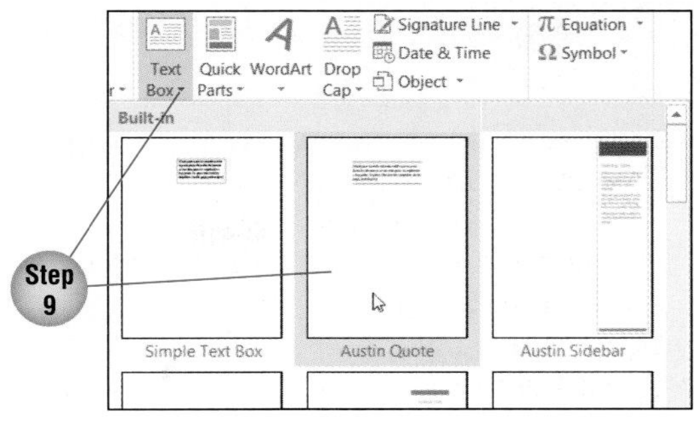

10 Type the following text in the text box: **Sign up today for your Hawaiian adventure and enjoy spectacular beaches, Hawaii's natural undersea world, and beautiful bays.**

11 With the DRAWING TOOLS FORMAT tab active, click the More button [button] at the right side of the shape style thumbnails in the Shape Styles group, and then click the *Subtle Effect - Aqua, Accent 5* option (sixth option in the fourth row).

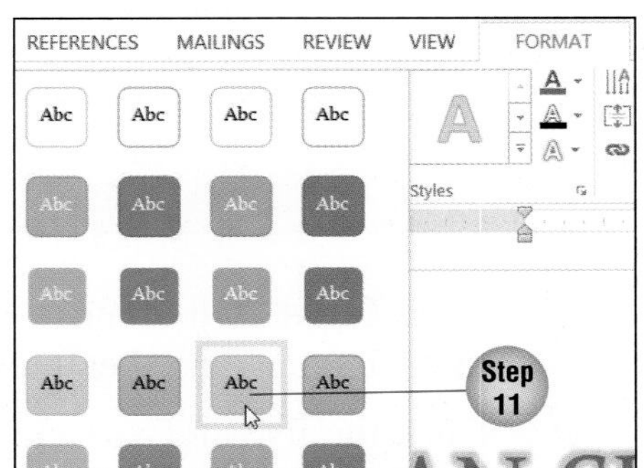

12 Press Ctrl + A to select the text in the text box, click the Text Fill button arrow, and then click the *Turquoise, Accent 6, Darker 50%* option (last option in the last column in the *Theme Colors* section).

13 With the text still selected, press Ctrl + B to apply bold formatting and then press Ctrl + Shift + < to decrease the font size. Press the Right Arrow key to deselect the text but keep the text box selected.

14 Click the Shape Effects button [button], point to *Glow*, and then click the *Turquoise, 5 pt glow, Accent color 6* option (last option in the first row in the *Glow Variations* section).

15 Click the Shape Effects button, point to *Bevel*, and then click the *Circle* option (first option in the top row in the *Bevel* section).

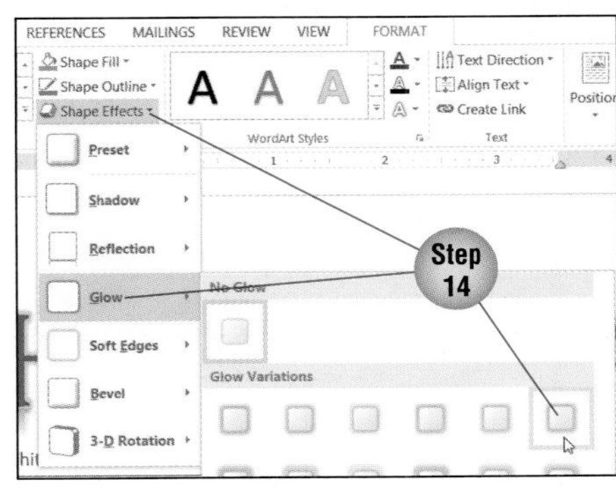

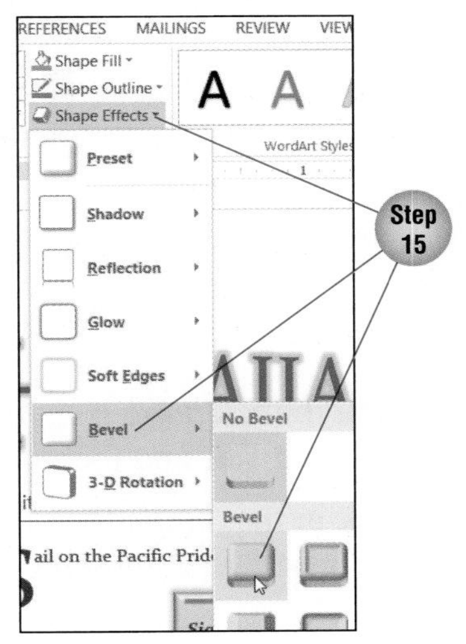

continues

16 Click in the *Shape Width* measurement box in the Size group, type **2.9**, and then press Enter.

17 Click the Wrap Text button in the Arrange group and then click *Tight* at the drop-down gallery.

18 Drag the text box so it is positioned similarly to what is shown below.

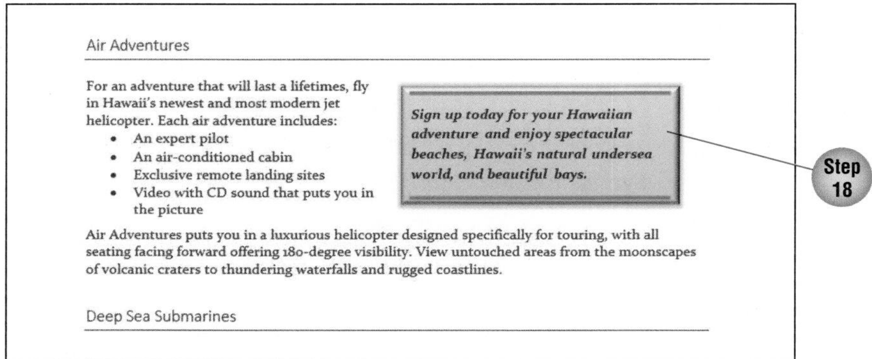

Air Adventures
For an adventure that will last a lifetimes, fly in Hawaii's newest and most modern jet helicopter. Each air adventure includes:
• An expert pilot
• An air-conditioned cabin
• Exclusive remote landing sites
• Video with CD sound that puts you in the picture
Sign up today for your Hawaiian adventure and enjoy spectacular beaches, Hawaii's natural undersea world, and beautiful bays.
Air Adventures puts you in a luxurious helicopter designed specifically for touring, with all seating facing forward offering 180-degree visibility. View untouched areas from the moonscapes of volcanic craters to thundering waterfalls and rugged coastlines.
Deep Sea Submarines
Step 18

19 Press Ctrl + End to move the insertion point to the end of the document and then press the Enter key twice.

20 Click the INSERT tab and then click the Shapes button in the Illustrations group.

21 Click the *Bevel* shape in the *Basic Shapes* section.

22 Click in the document at the location of the insertion point.

This inserts a bevel shape in the document that is 1.14 inches in width and height.

23 Apply a shape style by clicking the More button at the right side of the shape style thumbnails in the Shape Styles group and then clicking the *Subtle Effect - Aqua, Accent 5* option (sixth option in the fourth row).

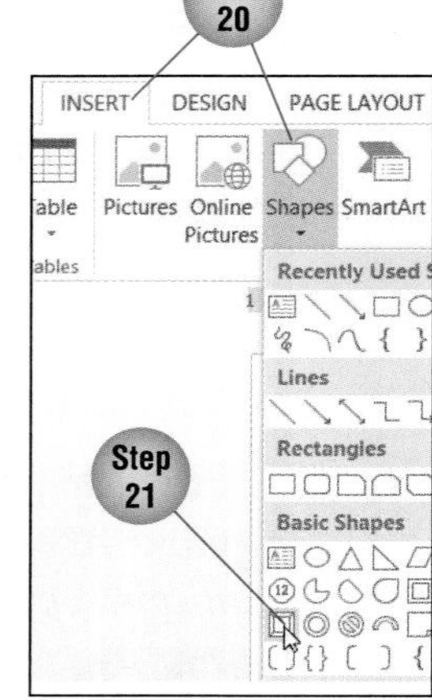

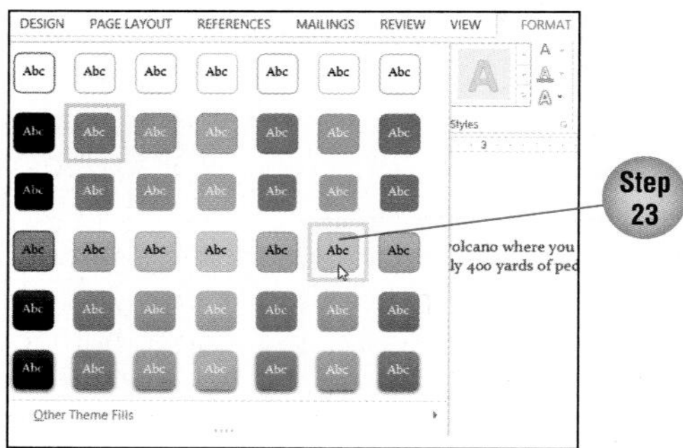

24 Click in the *Shape Height* measurement box, type **1.5**, and then press Enter.

25 Click in the *Shape Width* measurement box, type **5.5**, and then press Enter.

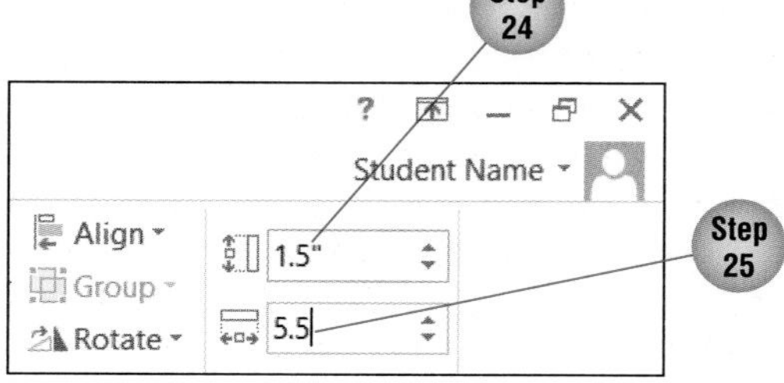

26 Click the Align button in the Arrange group and then click *Distribute Horizontally* at the drop-down list.

27 With the shape selected, type **Sign up today for your Hawaiian adventure!**

28 Select the text you just typed, click the HOME tab, change the font size to 14 points, change the font color to dark blue, and then click the Bold button and the Italic button.

Your text box should appear similar to what is shown below.

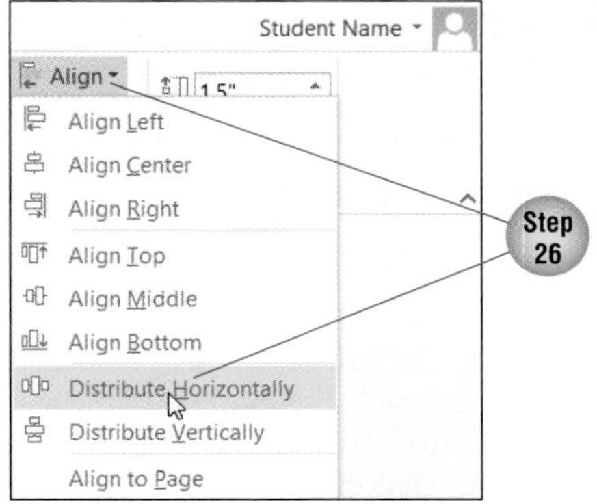

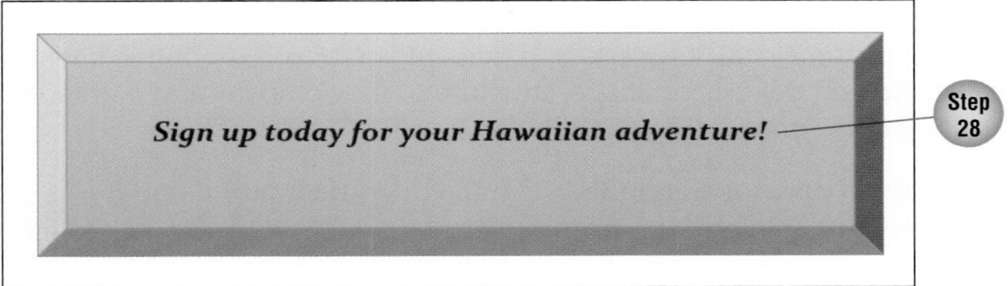

29 Press Ctrl + Home to move the insertion point to the beginning of the document.

30 Save, print, and then close **WS4-FCTHawaiianSpecials.docx**.

In Brief

Create Drop Cap
1. Click INSERT tab.
2. Click Drop Cap button.

Insert Text Box
1. Click INSERT tab.
2. Click Text Box button.
3. Click desired predesigned text box option.

Insert Shape
1. Click INSERT tab.
2. Click Shapes button.
3. Click desired shape at drop-down list.
4. Click in document or drag with mouse to draw shape.

In Addition

Drawing Lines

The Shapes button drop-down list contains a number of options for drawing lines in a document. Click the *Curve* option in the *Lines* section to draw curved lines by clicking at the beginning position, dragging to the location where you want the curve to appear, and then clicking the mouse button again. Continue in this manner until you have drawn all the desired curved lines. Click the *Freeform* option in the *Lines* section to draw free-form in a document. After clicking the *Freeform* option, drag in the document screen. When you want to stop drawing, double-click the left mouse button. You can also use the *Scribble* option to draw free-form in a document. The difference between the Freeform tool and the Scribble tool is that you have to double-click to stop drawing with Freeform but you only need to release the mouse button to stop drawing with the Scribble tool.

Drawing and Formatting Text Boxes

Draw your own text box in a document by clicking the INSERT tab, clicking the Text Box button in the Text group, and then clicking *Draw Text Box* at the drop-down list. The mouse pointer displays as a crosshairs. Position the crosshairs in the document and then drag to create the text box. When you insert a text box in a document, the DRAWING TOOLS FORMAT tab becomes active. Use options on this tab to customize and format the text box.

Activity 4.3

Creating SmartArt Graphics

Use SmartArt to create a variety of graphics to visually illustrate and present data. SmartArt includes graphics for presenting hierarchical data; lists of data; showing data processes, cycles, and relationships; and presenting data in a matrix or pyramid. To display SmartArt graphics, click the INSERT tab and then click the SmartArt button in the Illustrations group. This displays the Choose a SmartArt Graphic dialog box with *All* selected in the left panel and all available predesigned graphics displayed in the middle panel. Click the desired graphic type in the left panel and then click a graphic in the middle panel and the name of the graphic displays in the right panel along with a description of the graphic type. Double-click a graphic in the middle panel and the graphic is inserted in the document. Use buttons on the SMARTART TOOLS DESIGN tab and the SMARTART TOOLS FORMAT tab to customize a graphic. Some graphics are designed to include text. Type text in a graphic by selecting the shape and then typing text in the shape or type text in the *Type your text here* window that displays at the left side of the graphic.

Project

Terry Blessing, president of First Choice Travel, has asked you to prepare a document containing information on the organizational structure of the company and a graphic that illustrates the services provided by First Choice Travel.

Tutorial 4.3
Creating SmartArt

1. Open **FCTStructure.docx** and then save the document and name it **WS4-FCTStructure**.

2. Move the insertion point a double space below the heading *ORGANIZATIONAL CHART* and then create the organizational chart shown in Figure 4.1. To begin, click the INSERT tab and then click the SmartArt button in the Illustrations group.

Step 3

3. At the Choose a SmartArt Graphic dialog box, click *Hierarchy* in the left panel of the dialog box and then double-click the first option in the middle panel, *Organization Chart*.

   This displays the organizational chart in the document with the SMARTART TOOLS DESIGN tab selected. Use buttons on this tab to add additional boxes, change the order of the boxes, choose a different layout, apply formatting with a SmartArt Style, and reset the formatting of the organizational chart.

4. If a *Type your text here* window displays at the left side of the organizational chart, close it by clicking the Text Pane button in the Create Graphic group.

   You can also close the window by clicking the Close button that displays in the upper right corner of the window.

5. Delete the bottom right box in the organizational chart by clicking the border of the box in the lower right corner to select it and then pressing the Delete key.

   Make sure that the selection border that surrounds the box is a solid line and not a dashed line. If a dashed line displays, click the box border again. This should change it to a solid line.

6. With the bottom right box selected, click the Add Shape button arrow in the Create Graphic group and then click the *Add Shape Below* option.

   Your organizational chart should contain the same boxes as shown in Figure 4.1.

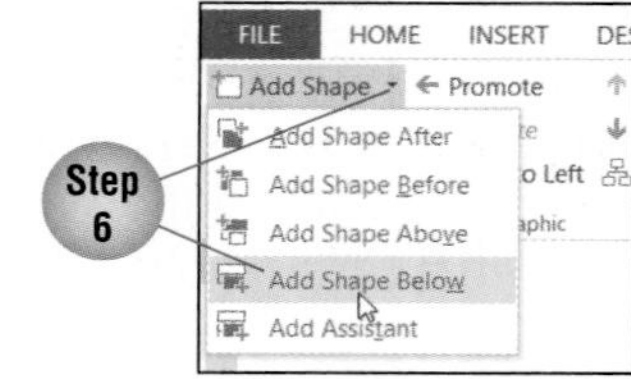

7 Click *[Text]* in the top box, type **Terry Blessing**, press the Enter key, and then type **President**. Click in each of the remaining boxes and type the text as shown in Figure 4.1.

FIGURE 4.1 Organizational Chart

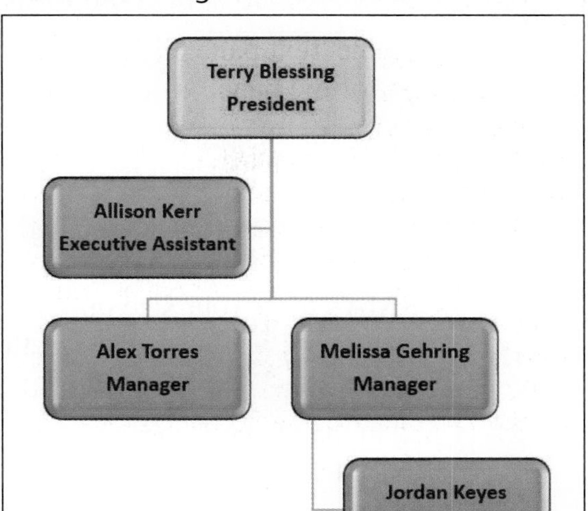

8 Click inside the organizational chart border but outside any shapes in the chart.

This deselects the shape in the chart but keeps the chart selected.

9 Click the More button located at the right side of the thumbnails in the SmartArt Styles group and then click the *Inset* option located in the *3-D* section.

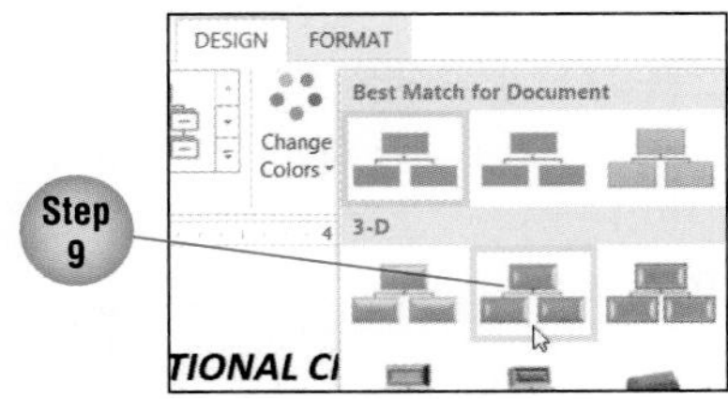

10 Click the Change Colors button in the SmartArt Styles group and then click the *Colorful Range - Accent Colors 5 to 6* option (last option in the *Colorful* section).

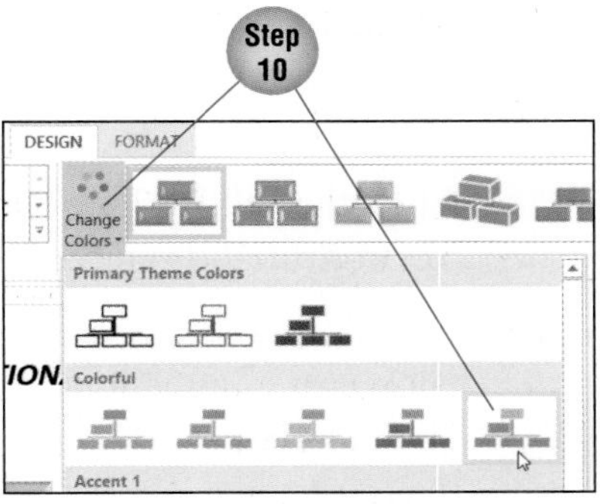

11 Click the SMARTART TOOLS FORMAT tab.

The SMARTART TOOLS FORMAT tab contains buttons for changing the box shape; applying shape styles; applying WordArt styles to text; applying text fill, outline, and effects; and arranging and sizing the organizational chart.

12 Click the tab (displays with a left-pointing triangle) that displays at the left side of the diagram border.

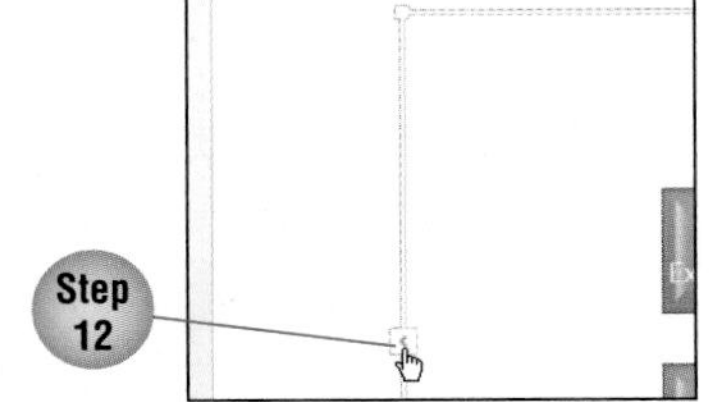

13 Click any character in the *Type your text here* window and then press Ctrl + A.

This selects all of the text and shapes in the organizational chart.

14 Click the Change Shape button in the Shapes group and then click the Rounded Rectangle option (second shape in the top row) in the *Rectangles* section.

15 Click the Shape Outline button arrow in the Shape Styles group and then click the *Dark Blue* color in the *Standard Colors* section (second color option from the right).

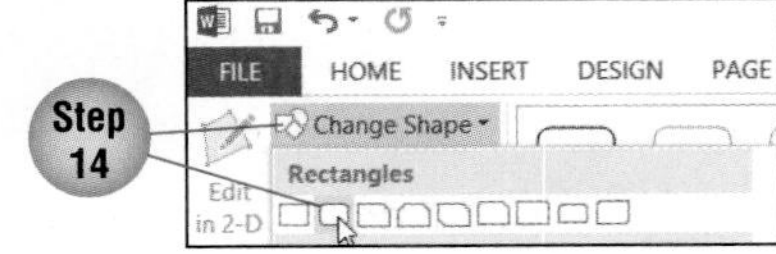

16 Click the Text Fill button arrow in the WordArt Styles group and then click the *Dark Blue* color in the *Standard Colors* section.

continues

17 Press Ctrl + B to apply bold formatting to the text.

18 Close the Text pane by clicking the Close button that displays in the upper right corner of the pane.

19 Deselect the shapes (but not the chart) by clicking inside the organizational chart border but outside any shapes in the chart.

20 Click the Size button located at the right side of the SMARTART TOOLS FORMAT tab. (Your size options may display in the Size group rather than the Size button.)

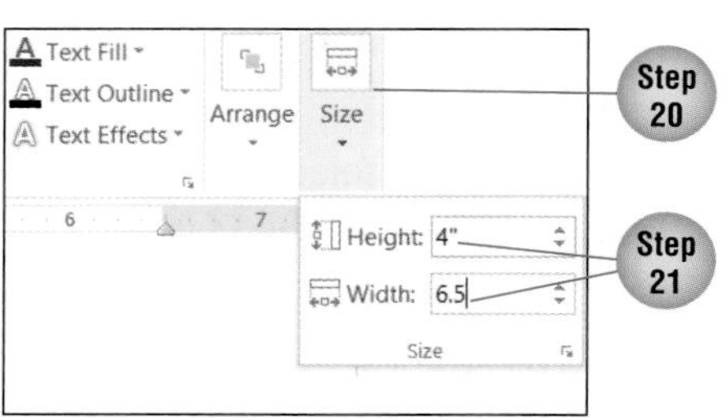

21 Click in the *Shape Height* measurement box, type **4**, click in the *Shape Width* measurement box, type **6.5**, and then press Enter.

In addition to the *Shape Height* and *Shape Width* measurement boxes, you can increase or decrease the size of a SmartArt graphic by dragging a corner of the graphic border. To maintain the proportions of the graphic, hold down the Shift key while dragging the border.

22 Press Ctrl + End to move the insertion point below the title *TRAVEL SERVICES* located on the second page.

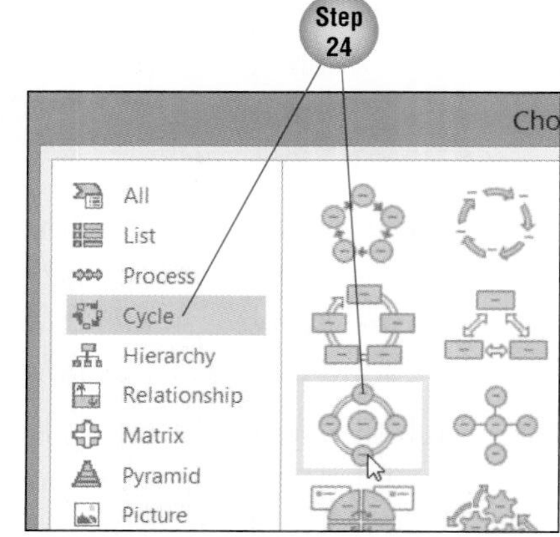

23 Click the INSERT tab and then click the SmartArt button in the Illustrations group.

24 At the Choose a SmartArt Graphic dialog box, click *Cycle* in the left panel and then double-click the *Radial Cycle* graphic (first graphic in the third row).

25 Click in each of the shapes in the graphic and type the text as shown in Figure 4.2.

FIGURE 4.2 Services Diagram

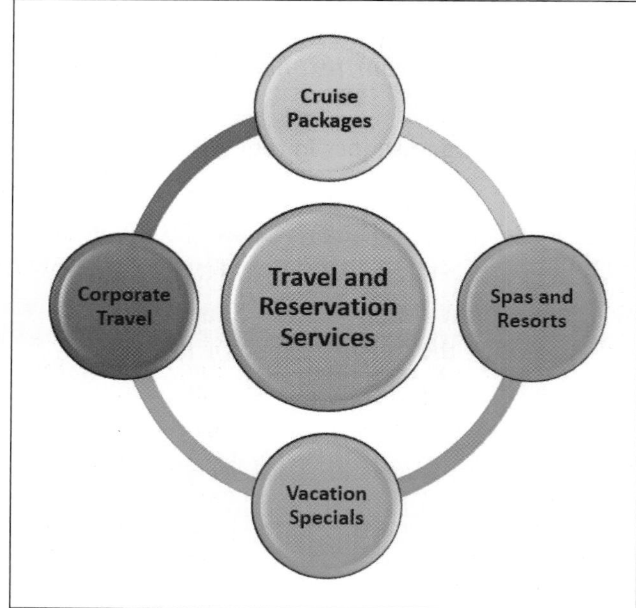

26 Click inside the graphic but outside any shapes.

27 Click the More button located at the right side of the SmartArt Styles group and then click the *Inset* option (second column, first row in the *3-D* section).

28 Click the Change Colors button in the SmartArt Styles group and then click the *Colorful Range - Accent Colors 4 to 5* option (fourth option in the *Colorful* section).

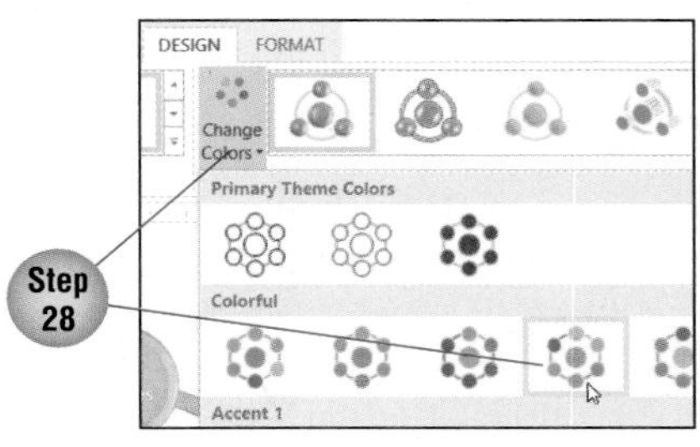

29 Click the SMARTART TOOLS FORMAT tab.

30 Hold down the Shift key, click each of the circles in the graphic, and then release the Shift key.

This selects all of the circle shapes in the graphic.

31 Click once on the Larger button in the Shapes group to slightly increase the size of the circles.

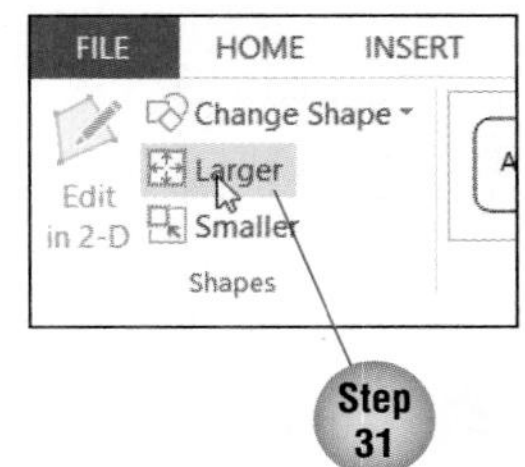

32 Click the Shape Outline button arrow in the Shape Styles group and then click the *Dark Blue* color (ninth option in the *Standard Colors* section).

33 Click the Text Fill button arrow in the WordArt Styles group and then click the *Dark Blue* color in the *Standard Colors* section.

34 Press Ctrl + B to apply bold formatting to the text.

35 Deselect the shapes by clicking inside the graphic but outside any shapes.

36 Click the Size button, click in the *Shape Height* measurement box, type 4, click in the *Shape Width* measurement box, type 6.5, and then press Enter. (Your size options may display in the Size group rather than the Size button.)

37 Click outside the graphic to deselect it.

38 Save, print, and then close **WS4-FCTStructure.docx**.

In Brief

Create a SmartArt Organizational Chart
1. Click INSERT tab.
2. Click SmartArt button.
3. Click *Hierarchy* at Choose a SmartArt Graphic dialog box.
4. Double-click desired organizational chart.

Create SmartArt Graphic
1. Click INSERT tab.
2. Click SmartArt button.
3. Click desired category in left panel of Choose a SmartArt Graphic dialog box.
4. Double-click desired graphic.

In Addition

Wrapping Text

Apply a text wrapping style to a SmartArt graphic to specify how you want text or other items to flow around the graphic. To apply text wrapping, click the Layout Options button that displays to the right of the SmartArt border and then click an option at the drop-down list. You can also click the Arrange button on the SMARTART TOOLS FORMAT tab, click the Position button or the Wrap Text button, and then click the desired wrapping style at the drop-down list.

Moving a SmartArt Graphic

Move a SmartArt graphic by positioning the arrow pointer on the graphic border until the pointer displays with a four-headed arrow attached, holding down the left mouse button, and then dragging the graphic to the desired location. As you move a graphic near the top, left, right, or bottom margins of the document, green guidelines appear to help you position the image.

Activity 4.4

Creating and Modifying a Table

Word's Table feature is useful for displaying data in columns and rows. This data may be text, values, and/or formulas. Create a table using the Table button on the INSERT tab or with options at the Insert Table dialog box. Once you specify the desired number of rows and columns, Word displays the table and you are ready to enter information into the cells. A ***cell*** is the "box" created by the intersection of a column and a row. Modify the structure of the table by inserting or deleting columns and/or rows and merging cells.

Project

You are developing a new First Choice Travel information document about sightseeing flights around the island of Maui. You decide to create a table to display the data and then modify the table.

Tutorial 4.4
Creating a Table

1. Open **FCTIslandFlights.docx** and then save the document and name it **WS4-FCTIslandFlights**.
2. Press Ctrl + End to move the insertion point to the end of the document.
3. Click the INSERT tab and then click the Table button in the Tables group.
4. Drag the mouse pointer down and to the right until the number above the grid displays as *3x6* and then click the mouse button.
5. Type the text in the cells as shown in Figure 4.3. Press the Tab key to move the insertion point to the next cell or press Shift + Tab to move the insertion point to the previous cell.

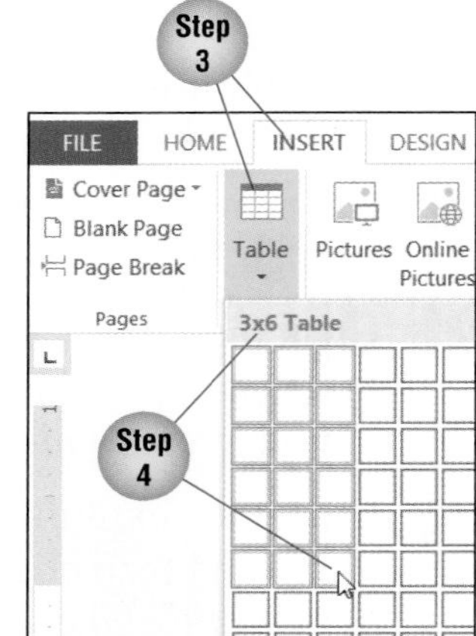

When typing text in the cells in the second column, do not press the Enter key to end a line. Type the text and let the word wrap feature wrap the text within the cell. After typing text in the last cell, do not press the Tab key. This will insert another row. If you press the Tab key accidentally, immediately click the Undo button. To move the insertion point to different cells within the table using the mouse, click in the desired cell.

FIGURE 4.3 Step 5

Adventure	Destination	Price
Special West Maui	Waterfalls, lush tropical valleys	$49
West Maui Tropical	West Maui mountains, Hawaii's highest waterfalls	$79
Haleakala-Keane	Haleakala crater, tropical rain forest, waterfalls	$89
Special Circle Island	Hana, Haleakala, West Maui mountains, tropical rain forest, waterfalls	$169
Molokai-West Maui	West Maui mountains, waterfalls, sea cliffs, Kalaupapa colony	$189

6 You decide to add First Choice Travel discount prices to the table. To do this, position the insertion point in the *Price* cell, click the TABLE TOOLS LAYOUT tab, and then click the Insert Right button in the Rows & Columns group.

Figure 4.4 displays the TABLE TOOLS LAYOUT tab.

7 Click in the top cell of the new column, type **FCT**, and then press the Down Arrow key. Type the money amounts in the remaining cells as shown at the right. (Press the Down Arrow key to move to the next cell down.)

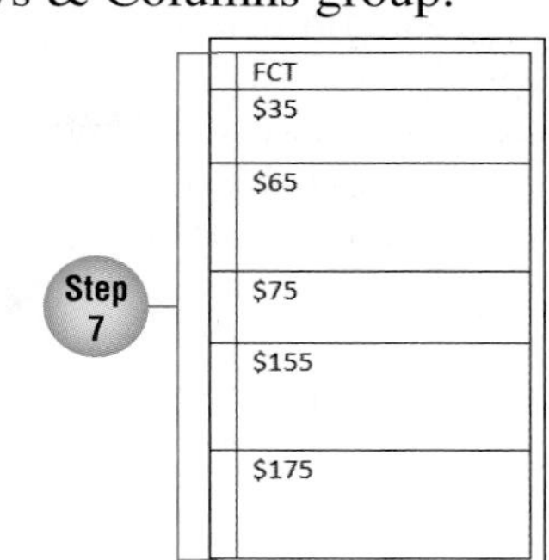

8 Delete the *Special Circle Island* row. To do this, click anywhere in the text *Special Circle Island*, make sure the TABLE TOOLS LAYOUT tab is active, click the Delete button in the Rows & Columns group, and then click *Delete Rows* at the drop-down list.

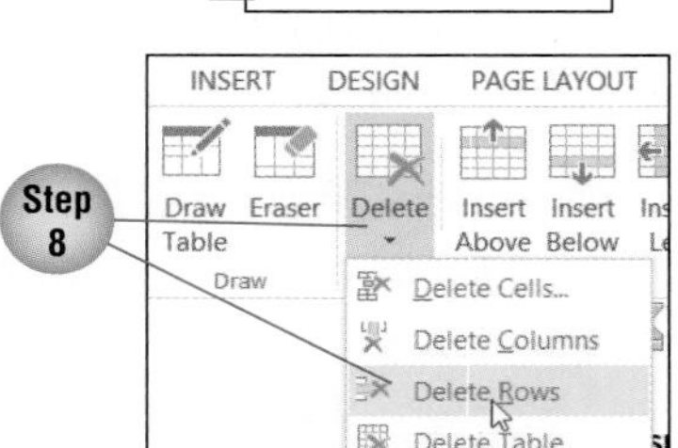

9 Insert a row above *Adventure*. To do this, click anywhere in the text *Adventure* and then click the Insert Above button in the Rows & Columns group.

10 With the new top row selected, merge the cells by clicking the Merge Cells button in the Merge group.

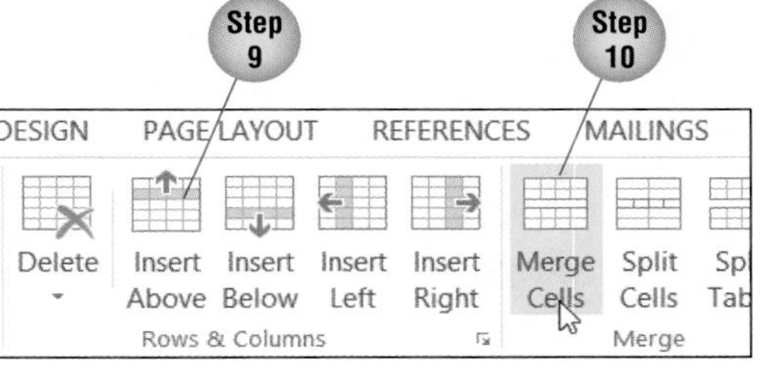

11 Type **MAUI FLIGHTS** in the top row.

12 Select all cells in the table by clicking the table move handle that displays in the upper left corner of the table (a square with a four-headed arrow inside).

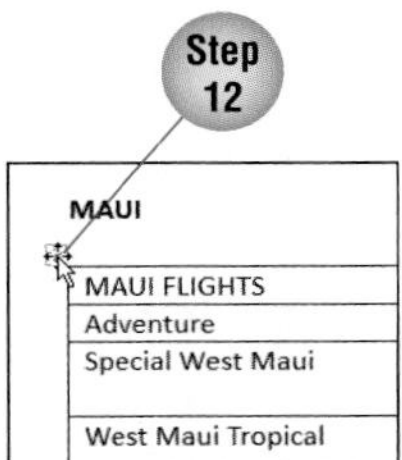

13 Click the HOME tab, change the font to Constantia and the font size to 12 points, and then click outside the table to deselect it.

14 Save **WS4-FCTIslandFlights.docx**.

> **In Brief**
>
> **Create Table**
> 1. Click INSERT tab.
> 2. Click Table button.
> 3. Drag in grid to select desired number of columns and rows.

FIGURE 4.4 TABLE TOOLS LAYOUT Tab

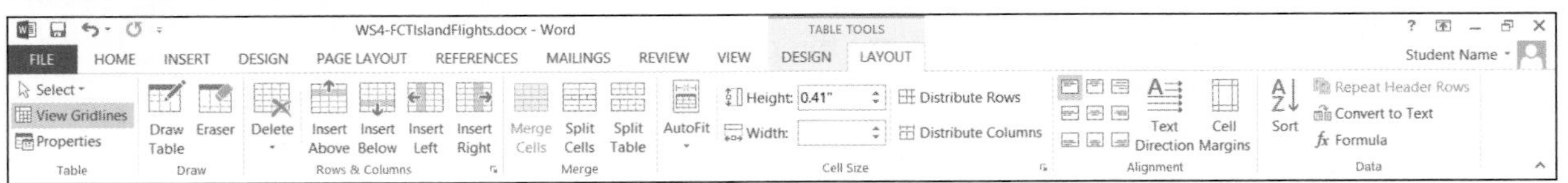

In Addition

Other Methods for Creating a Table

Other methods for creating a table include using options from the Insert Table dialog box or drawing a table. Display the Insert Table dialog box by clicking the INSERT tab, clicking the Table button, and then clicking *Insert Table* at the drop-down list. Specify the desired number of columns and rows and then click OK to close the dialog box. Another method for creating a table is to draw a table by clicking the Table button and then clicking *Draw Table* at the drop-down list. The mouse pointer changes to a pencil. Drag in the document screen to create the desired columns and rows.

Activity 4.5

Changing the Table Layout

In the previous activity, you added a column and a row and deleted a row using buttons on the TABLE TOOLS LAYOUT tab. This tab contains additional buttons for customizing the table layout such as changing cell size, alignment, direction, and margins; sorting data; and converting a table to text. You can also vertically and horizontally center a table on the page with options at the Table Properties dialog box. When you create a table, columns are the same width and rows are the same height. The width of columns depends on the number of columns as well as the document margins. Change column widths and row heights using a variety of methods including dragging the gridlines. Apply formatting to text in cells by selecting text or selecting multiple cells and then applying formatting.

Project

The Maui Flights table needs adjustments to improve its appearance. You will increase and decrease column widths, increase the height of a row, apply formatting to the entire table and to specific cells in the table, and vertically center the table on the page.

Tutorial 4.5
Changing the Table Layout

1. With **WS4-FCTIslandFlights.docx** open, click in the top cell containing the text *MAUI FLIGHTS*, click the TABLE TOOLS LAYOUT tab, click in the *Table Row Height* measurement box in the Cell Size group, type **0.4**, and then press Enter.

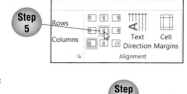

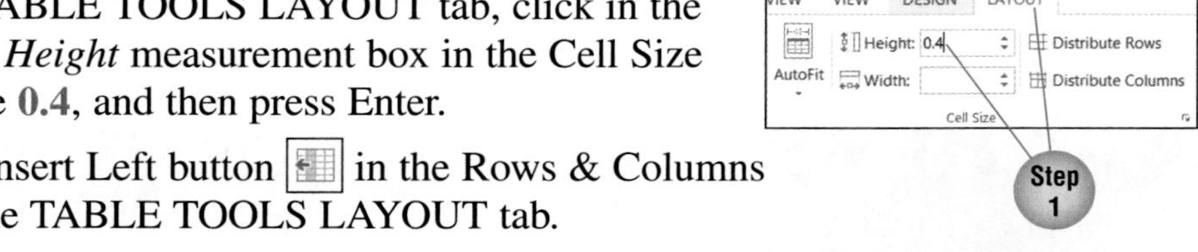

2. Click the Insert Left button in the Rows & Columns group in the TABLE TOOLS LAYOUT tab.
3. With the cells in the new column selected, click the Merge Cells button in the Merge group.
4. Type **Hawaiian Adventures** in the new cell and then click twice on the Text Direction button in the Alignment group.

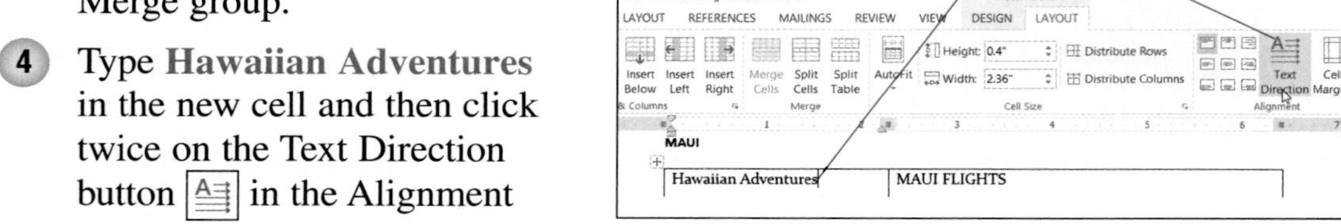

5. Click the Align Center button in the Alignment group to change the horizontal and vertical alignment of text in the cell.

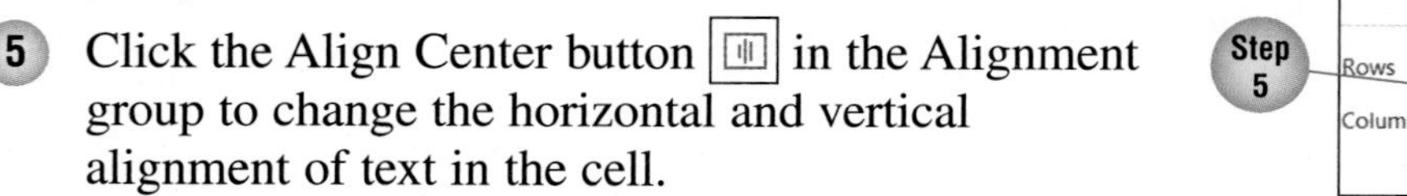

6. Position the mouse pointer on the gridline between the first and second columns until the pointer turns into a double-headed arrow pointing left and right with a short double line between. Hold down the left mouse button, drag to the left until the table column marker displays at approximately the 0.5-inch mark on the horizontal ruler, and then release the mouse button.

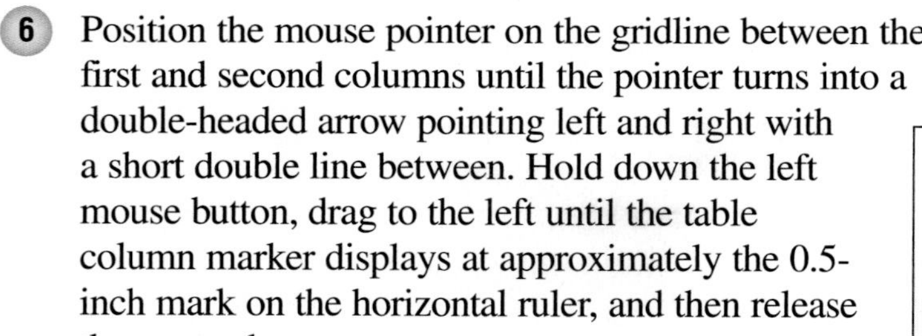

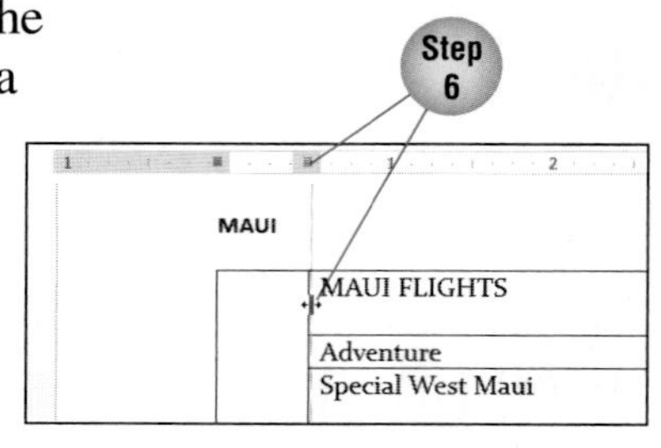

7. Position the mouse pointer on the gridline between the second and third columns until the pointer turns into a double-headed arrow pointing left and right, and then drag to the left until the table column marker displays at the 2.25-inch mark on the horizontal ruler.

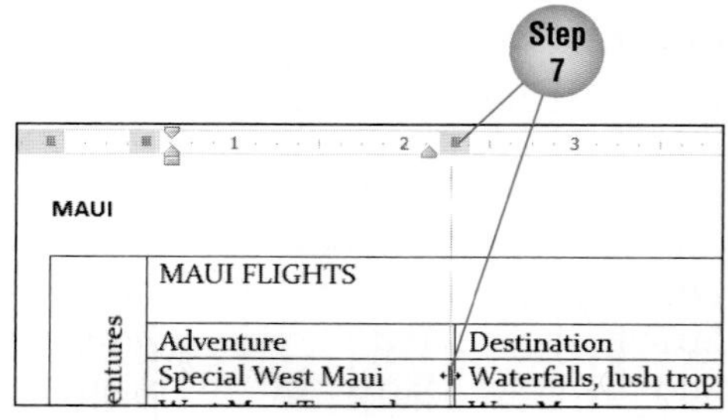

8 Following the same procedure, drag the gridline between the third and fourth columns to the left until the table column marker displays at the 4.25-inch mark on the horizontal ruler.

9 If you hold down the Alt key while dragging a gridline, column measurements display on the horizontal ruler. Use these measurements to change the width of the fourth column. To do this, position the mouse pointer on the gridline between the fourth and fifth columns, hold down the Alt key, drag the gridline to the left until the measurement for the fourth column on the horizontal ruler displays as *0.68"*, release the Alt key, and then release the mouse button.

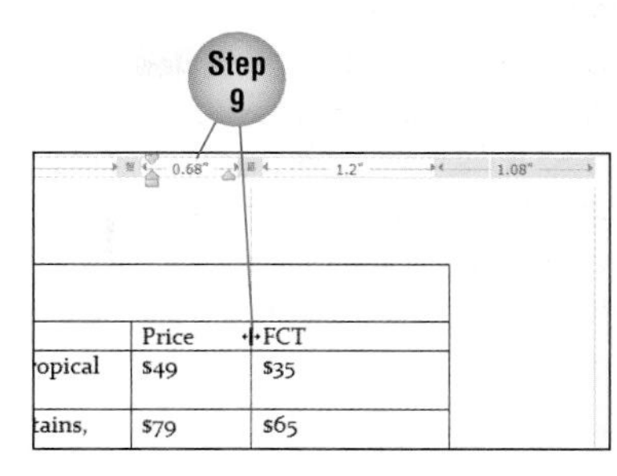

10 Position the mouse pointer on the gridline at the right side of the table, hold down the Alt key, drag the gridline to the left until the measurement for the fifth column on the horizontal ruler displays as *0.68"*, release the Alt key, and then release the mouse button.

11 Click anywhere in the *MAUI FLIGHTS* text and then click the Align Center button in the Alignment group on the TABLE TOOLS LAYOUT tab.

This changes the horizontal and vertical alignment to center for text in the cell.

12 Select the four cells containing the headings *Adventure*, *Destination*, *Price*, and *FCT*. To do this, position the mouse pointer in the *Adventure* cell, hold down the left mouse button, drag to the *FCT* cell and then release the mouse button.

13 With the cells selected, click the Align Center button in the Alignment group and then press Ctrl + B to apply bold formatting.

14 Select all of the cells containing prices and then click the Align Top Center button in the Alignment group.

15 Horizontally center the table on the page. Begin by clicking the Properties button in the Table group on the TABLE TOOLS LAYOUT tab.

16 At the Table Properties dialog box with the Table tab selected, click the *Center* option in the *Alignment* section and then click OK.

17 Click anywhere outside the table to deselect the cells.

18 Save **WS4-FCTIslandFlights.docx**.

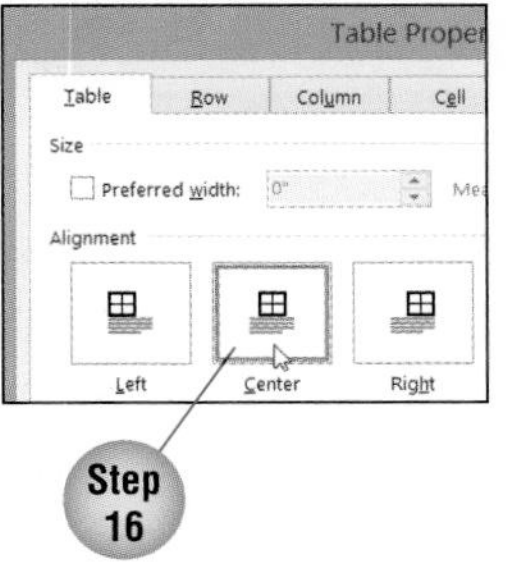

In Brief

Increase/Decrease Column/Row

1. Position mouse pointer on gridline until it turns into a double-headed arrow.
2. Hold down left mouse button, drag to desired position, then release mouse button.

In Addition

Selecting Cells with the Keyboard

Besides using the mouse, you can also select cells using the following keyboard shortcuts:

To select	Press
the next cell's contents	Tab
the preceding cell's contents	Shift + Tab
the entire table	Alt + 5 (on the numeric keypad with Num Lock off)
adjacent cells	Hold Shift key and then press an arrow key repeatedly.
a column	Position insertion point in top cell of column, hold down the Shift key, and then press Down Arrow key until column is selected.

Activity 4.6

Changing the Table Design

The TABLE TOOLS DESIGN tab contains a number of options for enhancing the appearance of the table. With options in the Table Styles group, apply a predesigned style that applies color and border lines to a table. Maintain further control over the predesigned style formatting applied to columns and rows with options in the Table Style Options group. For example, if your table contains a row for totals, you would insert a check mark in the *Total Row* option. Apply additional formatting to cells in a table with the Shading and Borders buttons in the Table Styles group. With options in the Borders group, you can customize the borders of cells in a table. Display a list of predesigned border lines; change the line style, width, and color; add or remove borders; and apply the same border style formatting to other cells with the Border Painter button.

Project

You will add final design formatting to the Maui Flights table by applying a table style and then customizing the formatting with additional options.

Tutorial 4.6
Changing the Table Design

1. With **WS4-FCTIslandFlights.docx** open, select *MAUI FLIGHTS*, change the font size to 16 points, and then turn on bold.

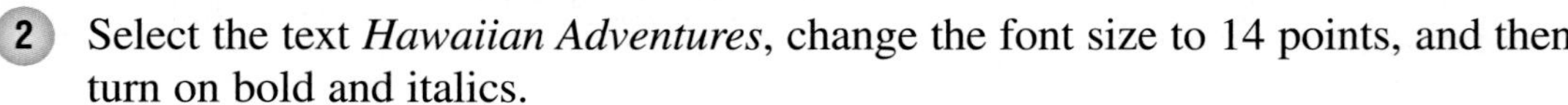

2. Select the text *Hawaiian Adventures*, change the font size to 14 points, and then turn on bold and italics.

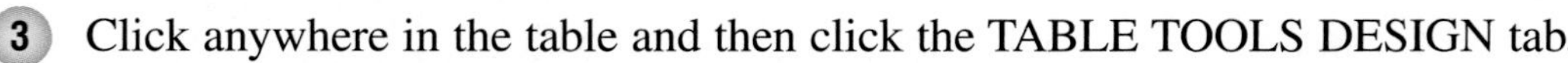

3. Click anywhere in the table and then click the TABLE TOOLS DESIGN tab.
4. Click the More button that displays at the right side of the thumbnails in the Table Styles group.

   This displays a drop-down gallery of style choices.

5. Click the *Grid Table 4 - Accent 2* option (third option in the fourth row in the *Grid Tables* section).

   Notice the color and border style formatting applied and also notice how the style changed the cell alignment for *MAUI FLIGHTS* and *Hawaiian Adventures* from Align Center to Align Top Center.

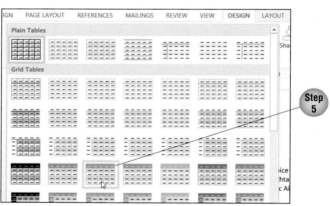

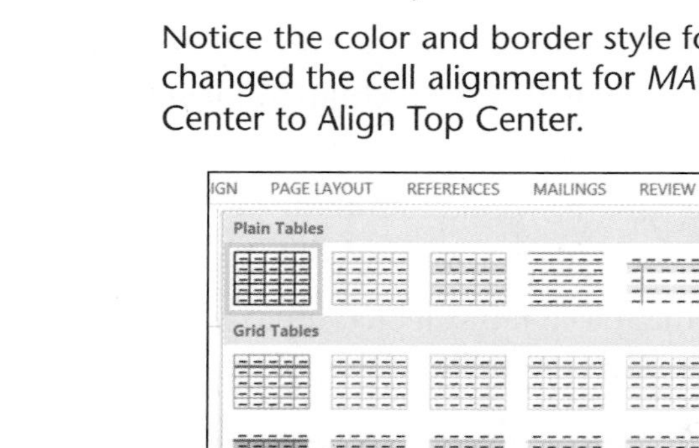

6. Experiment with an additional style by clicking the More button at the right side of the thumbnails in the Table Styles group and then clicking the *Grid Table 4 - Accent 1* option (second option in the fourth row in the *Grid Tables* section).

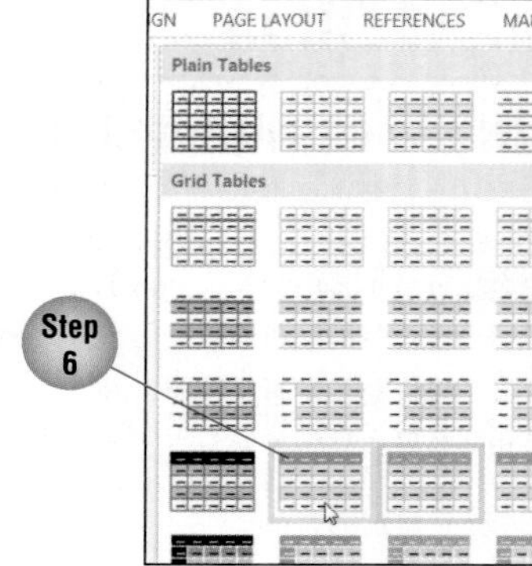

7 Change the formatting by clicking the *Banded Rows* option in the Table Style Options group to remove the check mark. Click the *Banded Columns* option to insert a check mark. Click the *Header Row* option to remove the check mark and click the *First Column* option to remove the check mark.

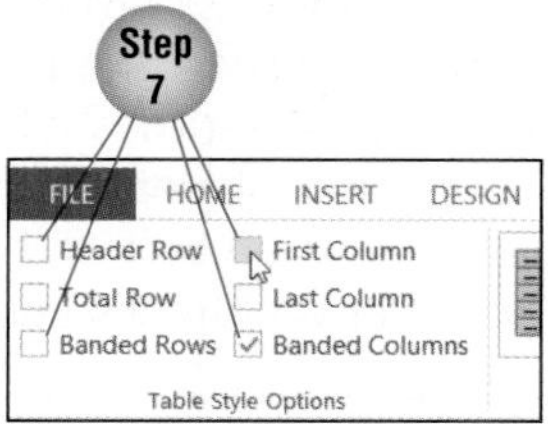

8 Save and then print **WS4-FCTIslandFlights.docx**.

9 With the insertion point positioned in a cell in the table and the TABLE TOOLS DESIGN tab selected, click the *Header Row* option in the Table Style Options group to insert a check mark, and click the *First Column* option to insert a check mark. Click the *Banded Columns* option to remove the check mark, and click the *Banded Rows* option to insert a check mark.

10 Applying the table styles removed the horizontal alignment of the table. Horizontally align the table by clicking the TABLE TOOLS LAYOUT tab, clicking the Properties button in the Table group, clicking the *Center* option in the *Alignment* section of the Table Properties dialog box, and then clicking OK to close the dialog box.

11 Apply the Heading 1 style to the heading *ISLAND SIGHTSEEING FLIGHTS* and the heading *MAUI*.

12 Click the DESIGN tab and then apply the Lines (Simple) style set, change the style colors to Blue Green, and change the fonts to Calibri Light-Constantia.

13 Save, print, and then close **WS4-FCTIslandFlights.docx**.

In Addition

Sorting in a Table

Sort text in a table alphabetically, numerically, or by date with options at the Sort dialog box. Display this dialog box by positioning the insertion point in a cell in the table and then clicking the Sort button in the Data group on the TABLE TOOLS LAYOUT tab. Make sure the column you want to sort is selected in the *Sort by* option and then click OK. If the first row in the table contains data such as headings that you do not want to include in the sort, click the *Header row* option in the *My list has* section of the Sort dialog box. If you want to sort specific cells in a table, select the cells first and then click the Sort button.

Inserting a Row Using the Mouse

You can use the mouse to insert a row by moving the mouse pointer immediately left of the row where you want the new row inserted. As you move the mouse pointer to the left side of a row, a plus symbol inside a circle displays along with thin, blue, double lines that display across the top or bottom of the row. Move the image and lines to the bottom of the row, click the plus symbol and a new row is inserted below the current row. Move the symbol and lines to the top of the row and click the plus symbol and a row is inserted above the current row.

Activity 4.7

Inserting a File and Section Break; Creating and Modifying Newspaper Columns

Use the Object button in the Text group on the INSERT tab to insert one document into another. To increase the ease with which a person can read and understand groups of words (referred to as the ***readability*** of a document), consider setting text in the document in newspaper columns. Newspaper columns contain text that flows up and down on the page. Create newspaper columns with the Columns button in the Page Setup group on the PAGE LAYOUT tab or with options at the Columns dialog box. If you want to apply column formatting to only a portion of a document, insert a section break in the document with options at the Breaks button drop-down list.

Project

You are working on an informational document on Petersburg, Alaska, and realize that you need to insert additional information from another file. You also decide to improve the readability of the document by setting the text in newspaper columns.

Tutorial 4.7A
Inserting Section Breaks

Tutorial 4.7B
Creating Newspaper Columns

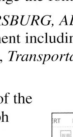

1. Open **FCTPetersburgAK.docx** and then save the document and name it **WS4-FCTPetersburgAK**.
2. Press Ctrl + End to move the insertion point to the end of the document and then click the INSERT tab.
3. Insert a document into **WS4-FCTPetersburgAK.docx** by clicking the Object button arrow in the Text group and then clicking the *Text from File* option at the drop-down list.
4. At the Insert File dialog box, navigate to the WordS4 folder on your storage medium and then double-click ***FCTPetersburgActivities.docx***.
5. Select the text you just inserted and then change the font to Constantia.
6. Apply the Heading 1 style to the title *PETERSBURG, ALASKA* and apply the Heading 2 style to the headings in the document including *Services*, *Visitor Attractions*, *Walking Tours*, *Accommodations*, *Transportation*, and *Guided Activities*.
7. Position the insertion point at the beginning of the first paragraph in the document (the paragraph that begins *Petersburg, Alaska, located on*), click the PAGE LAYOUT tab, and then click the Breaks button in the Page Setup group.
8. At the Breaks drop-down list, click *Continuous* in the *Section Breaks* section.

   The section break is not visible in Print Layout view. A continuous section break separates the document into sections but does not insert a page break. Click one of the other three options in the *Section Breaks* section of the Breaks drop-down list if you want to insert a section break that begins a new page.

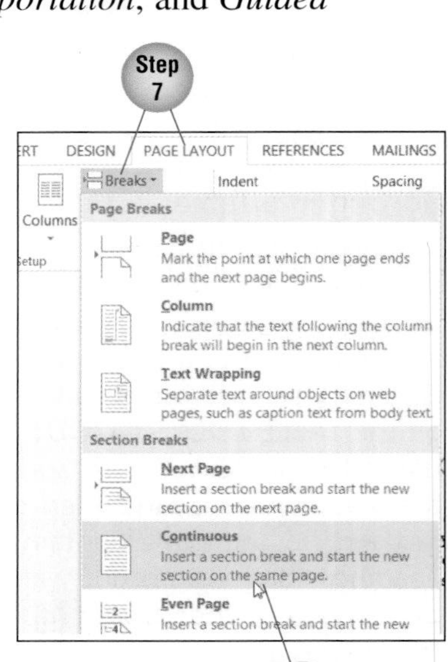

9 Click the VIEW tab and then click the Draft button in the Views group.

In Draft view, the section break displays in the document as a double row of dots with the words *Section Break (Continuous)* in the middle.

10 With the insertion point positioned below the section break, format the text below the section break into three newspaper columns by clicking the PAGE LAYOUT tab, clicking the Columns button in the Page Setup group, and then clicking *Three* at the drop-down list.

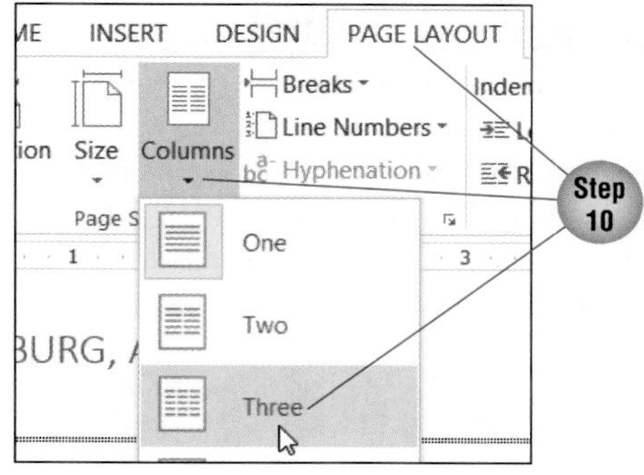

Formatting text into columns automatically changes the view to Print Layout.

11 As you view the document, you decide that the three columns are too narrow. To change the columns, click the Columns button in the Page Setup group and then click *More Columns* at the drop-down list.

12 At the Columns dialog box, click *Two* in the *Presets* section.

13 Increase the spacing between the two columns by clicking the up-pointing arrow at the right side of the *Spacing* option in the *Width and spacing* section until *0.7"* displays in the measurement box and make sure a check mark displays in the *Equal column width* check box. (If not, click the option to insert the check mark.)

14 Click the *Line between* option to insert a check mark and then click OK to close the dialog box.

Choosing the *Line between* option inserts a line between the two columns. The *Preview* section of the dialog box provides a visual representation of the columns.

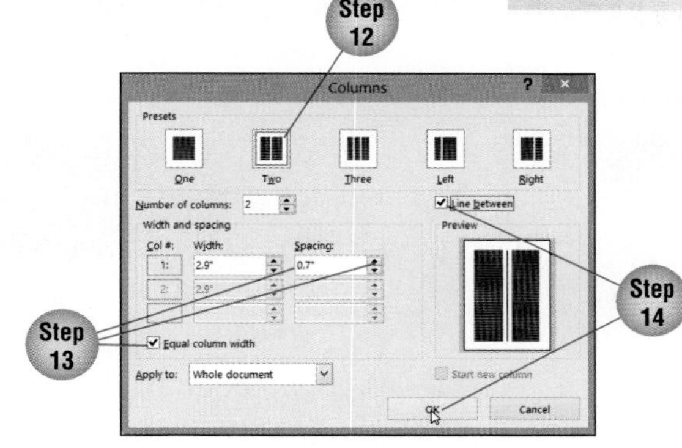
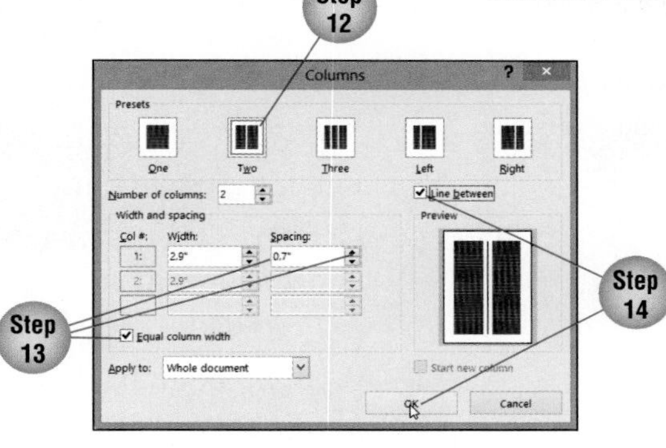

15 Insert page numbering by clicking the INSERT tab, clicking the Page Number button in the Header & Footer group, pointing to *Bottom of Page*, and then clicking the *Plain Number 2* option. Double-click in the document.

16 Press Ctrl + End to move the insertion point to the end of the document. Looking at the columns on the last (second) page, you decide to balance the two columns. To do this, click the PAGE LAYOUT tab, click the Breaks button in the Page Setup group, and then click *Continuous* in the *Section Breaks* section.

17 Save and then print **WS4-FCTPetersburgAK.docx**.

In Brief

Insert One File into Another
1. Click INSERT tab.
2. Click Object button arrow.
3. Click *Text from File* option.
4. At Insert File dialog box, double-click desired document.

Insert Continuous Section Break
1. Click PAGE LAYOUT tab.
2. Click Breaks button in Page Setup group.
3. Click *Continuous*.

Format Text into Columns
1. Click PAGE LAYOUT tab.
2. Click Columns button in Page Setup group.
3. Click desired number of columns.

Display Columns Dialog Box
1. Click PAGE LAYOUT tab.
2. Click Columns button in Page Setup group.
3. Click *More Columns* option.

In Addition

Changing Column Width

One method for changing column width in a document is to drag the column marker on the horizontal ruler. To change the width (and also the spacing) of columns of text, position the arrow pointer on the left or right edge of a column marker on the horizontal ruler until the pointer turns into a double-headed arrow pointing left and right. Hold down the left mouse button, drag the column marker to the left or right to make the column wider or narrower, and then release the mouse button. Hold down the Alt key while dragging the column marker and measurements display on the horizontal ruler.

Activity 4.8

Saving a Document as a Web Page; Creating a Hyperlink

You can save a Word document as a web page and apply formatting to the web page. When you save a document as a web page, Word automatically changes to the Web Layout view. In this view, the page displays as it will appear when published to the Web or an intranet. In an organization, a Word document can be saved as a web page and posted on the company intranet as a timely method of distributing the document to the company employees. You can save a Word document as a single web page or as a conventional web page. If you choose the *Single File Web Page* option, all data in the document such as graphics and other supplemental data is saved in a single web file. If you choose the *Web Page* option, Word creates additional files for supplemental data and saves the files in a subfolder. A third option *Web Page, Filtered*, is similar to the *Web Page* option except only the essential data is saved. You can create a hyperlink in a document or web page that connects to a site on the Internet or to another document.

Project

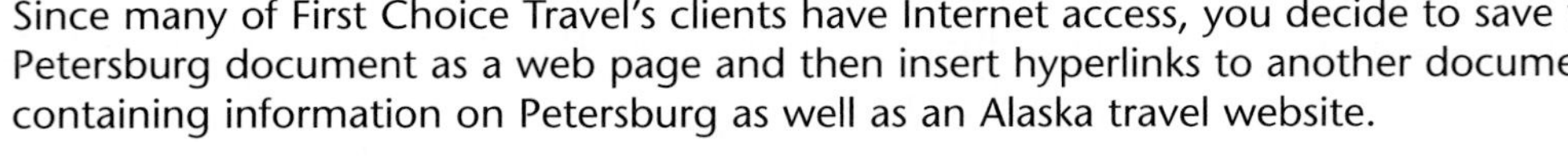

Since many of First Choice Travel's clients have Internet access, you decide to save the Petersburg document as a web page and then insert hyperlinks to another document containing information on Petersburg as well as an Alaska travel website.

Tutorial 4.8A
Saving a Document as a Web Page

Tutorial 4.8B
Creating and Editing Hyperlinks

1. With **WS4-FCTPetersburgAK.docx** open, save the document as a single web page by clicking the FILE tab and then clicking the *Save As* option.
2. At the Save As backstage area, navigate to the WordS4 folder on your storage medium.
3. At the Save As dialog box, click the *Save as type* option box and then click the *Single File Web Page (*.mht; *.mhtml)* option.
4. Click the Save button.

   This saves the document with the name **WS4-FCTPetersburgAK.mht** and displays the document in a format for viewing on the Internet. Notice how some of the formatting has been removed.
5. Apply a page background color by clicking the DESIGN tab, clicking the Page Color button in the Page Background group, and then clicking the *Gold, Accent 4, Lighter 80%* option (located in the eighth column).
6. Press Ctrl + End to move the insertion point to the end of the document and then type **Additional Information**.
7. Select the text *Additional Information.*
8. Insert a hyperlink by clicking the INSERT tab and then clicking the Hyperlink button in the Links group.

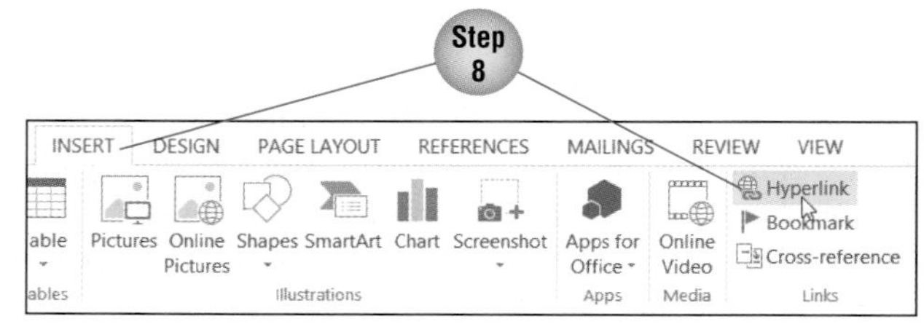

9. At the Insert Hyperlink dialog box, click the down-pointing arrow at the right side of the *Look in* option, navigate to the WordS4 folder on your storage medium, and then double-click ***FCTPetersburgStats.docx***.

   The Insert Hyperlink dialog box closes and *Additional Information* displays as hyperlink text.

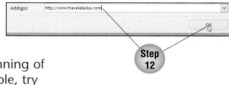

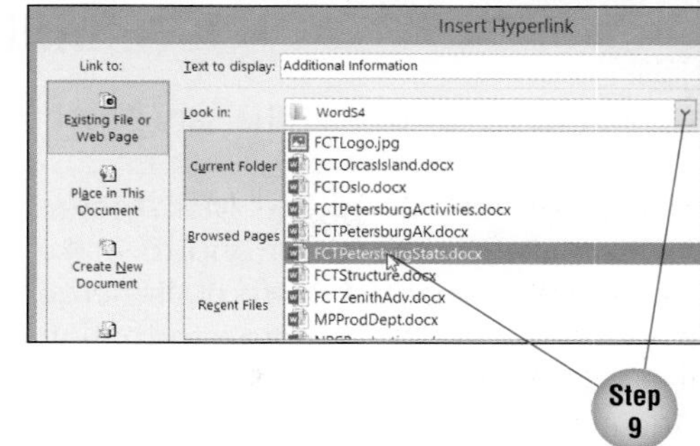

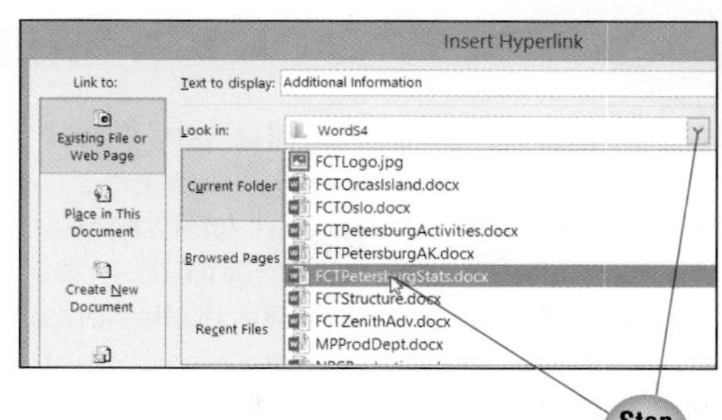

10. Press Ctrl + End, press the Enter key once, and then type **Alaska Tourism**.
11. Create a hyperlink to the tourism site by selecting *Alaska Tourism* and then clicking the Hyperlink button in the Links group.
12. At the Insert Hyperlink dialog box, type **www.travelalaska.com** in the *Address* text box and then click OK.

    Word automatically adds *http://* to the beginning of the web address. If this website is not available, try www.state.ak.us.

13. Display the document containing additional information on Petersburg by holding down the Ctrl key and then clicking the Additional Information hyperlink.
14. After reading the information in the document, close the document.
15. Make sure you are connected to the Internet and then connect to the Alaska tourism site by holding down the Ctrl key and then clicking the Alaska Tourism hyperlink.

    If you are not able to connect to the Alaska Tourism website, check with your instructor.

16. At the Alaska Tourism web page, click on any hyperlinks that interest you. When you are finished, click the Close button in the upper right corner of the browser window.
17. Print only page 2 of the document.

    The page prints with the original formatting applied.

18. Save and then close **WS4-FCTPetersburgAK.mht**.

In Brief

Save Document as Single File Web Page
1. Click FILE tab.
2. Click *Save As* option.
3. At Save As backstage area, navigate to desired folder.
4. At Save As dialog box, click *Save as type* option box.
5. Click *Single File Web Page (*.mht; *.mhtml)*.
6. Click Save.

Insert Hyperlink
1. Select text.
2. Click INSERT tab.
3. Click Hyperlink button in Links group.
4. Type file name or web address.
5. Click OK.

In Addition

Downloading and Saving Web Pages and Images

You can save the image(s) and/or text that displays when you open a web page as well as the web page itself. Copyright laws protect much of the information on the Internet, so check the site for restrictions before copying or downloading. If you do use information, make sure you properly cite the source. To save a web page as a file, display the desired page, click File on the Internet Explorer Menu bar, and then click *Save as*. At the Save Webpage dialog box, specify the folder where you want to save the web page. Select the text in the *File name* text box, type a name for the page, and then click the Save button. Save a specific web image by right-clicking the image and then clicking *Save picture as*. At the Save Picture dialog box, type a name for the image in the *File name* text box and then press Enter.

Activity 4.9

Merging Documents and Envelopes

If you need to mail the same basic letter to a number of clients or customers, consider using the Mail Merge feature to make the job easier and to make the letter more personalized. With mail merge you can use a data source containing information on your clients to merge with a main document containing the letter. You can also create an envelope document you can merge with a data source. Click the MAILINGS tab to display a number of buttons for preparing a mail merge document. Generally, a merge takes two documents — the ***data source*** and the ***main document***. The data source document contains the variable information that will be inserted in the main document. Use buttons on the MAILINGS tab to create main documents and data source documents for merging.

Project

First Choice Travel is offering a special cruise package, and Melissa Gehring has asked you to prepare a data source document with client information and merge it with a letter describing the cruise special and then print envelopes for the letters.

Tutorial 4.9
Merging Documents

1. At a blank document, click the MAILINGS tab, click the Select Recipients button in the Start Mail Merge group, and then click *Type a New List* at the drop-down list.

   This displays the New Address List dialog box with predesigned fields. You can use these predesigned fields as well as create your own custom fields.

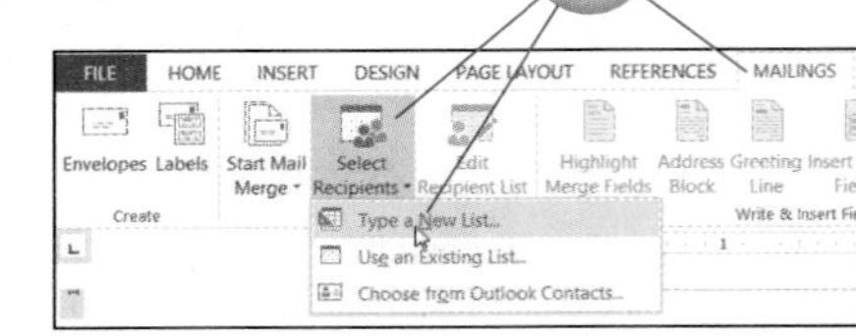

2. Click the Customize Columns button located toward the bottom of the dialog box.

   The predesigned fields offer most of the fields you need for your data source document, but you decide to delete six of the predesigned fields and insert two of your own fields.

3. At the Customize Address List dialog box, click *Company Name* to select it and then click the Delete button.

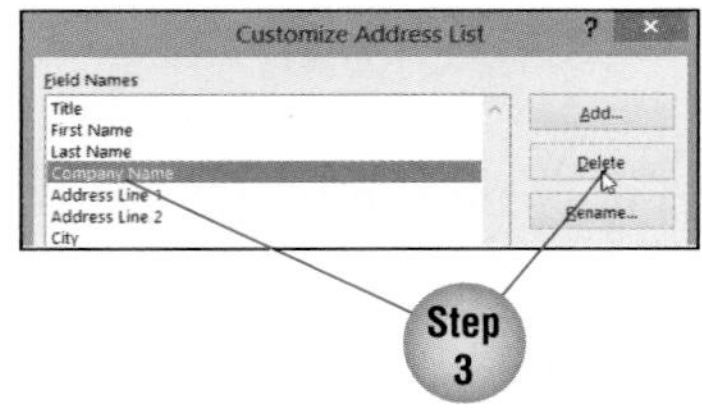

4. At the message that displays, click the Yes button.
5. Complete steps similar to those in Steps 3 and 4 to delete the following fields: *Address Line 2*, *Country or Region*, *Home Phone*, *Work Phone*, and *E-mail Address*.
6. Click the Add button.

   If the New Address List dialog box does not provide for all variable information, create your own custom field.

7. At the Add Field dialog box, type **Membership** and then click OK.
8. Click the Add button, type **Discount**, and then click OK.
9. Click OK to close the Customize Address List dialog box.

10 At the New Address List dialog box with the insertion point positioned in the *Title* field, type **Mrs.** and then press the Tab key.

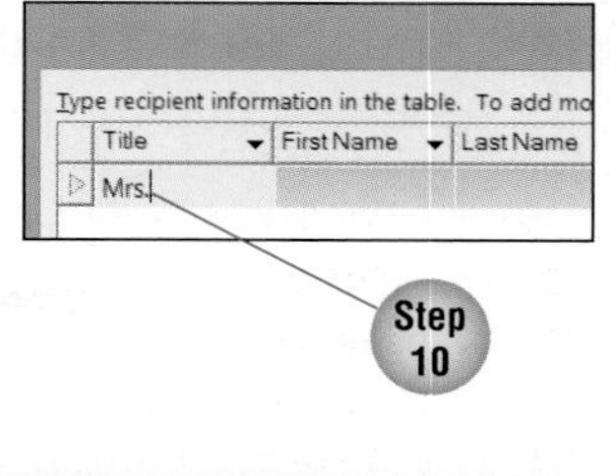

Pressing the Tab key moves the insertion point to the *First Name* field. Press the Tab key to move the insertion point to the next field and press Shift + Enter to move the insertion point to the previous field.

11 Continue typing text in the specified fields as indicated in Figure 4.5. After entering all of the information for the last client in Figure 4.5, click the OK button.

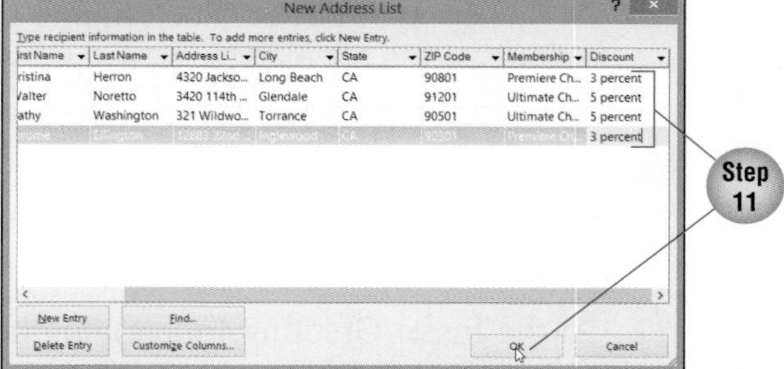

After typing **3 percent** for Jerome Ellington, do not press the Tab key. If you do, a new blank client record will be created.

12 At the Save Address List dialog box, navigate to your WordS4 folder. Click in the *File name* text box, type **WS4-FCTDataSource**, and then press Enter.

Word automatically saves the data source as an Access database.

13 Open **FCTCruiseLtr.docx** and then save the document and name it **WS4-FCTCruiseLtrMainDoc**.

14 Click the MAILINGS tab, click the Select Recipients button in the Start Mail Merge group, and then click *Use an Existing List* at the drop-down list.

FIGURE 4.5 Step 11

Title	**Mrs.**	*Title*	**Mr. and Mrs.**
First Name	**Kristina**	*First Name*	**Walter**
Last Name	**Herron**	*Last Name*	**Noretto**
Address Line 1	**4320 Jackson Street**	*Address Line 1*	**3420 114th Avenue**
City	**Long Beach**	*City*	**Glendale**
State	**CA**	*State*	**CA**
ZIP Code	**90801**	*ZIP Code*	**91201**
Membership	**Premiere Choice**	*Membership*	**Ultimate Choice**
Discount	**3 percent**	*Discount*	**5 percent**
Title	**Ms.**	*Title*	**Mr.**
First Name	**Cathy**	*First Name*	**Jerome**
Last Name	**Washington**	*Last Name*	**Ellington**
Address Line 1	**321 Wildwood Street**	*Address Line 1*	**12883 22nd Street**
City	**Torrance**	*City*	**Inglewood**
State	**CA**	*State*	**CA**
ZIP Code	**90501**	*ZIP Code*	**90301**
Membership	**Ultimate Choice**	*Membership*	**Premiere Choice**
Discount	**5 percent**	*Discount*	**3 percent**

continues

15 At the Select Data Source dialog box, navigate to your WordS4 folder and then double-click the document named ***WS4-FCTDataSource.mdb***.

16 Move the insertion point a double space above the first paragraph of text in the letter and then click the Address Block button in the Write & Insert Fields group.

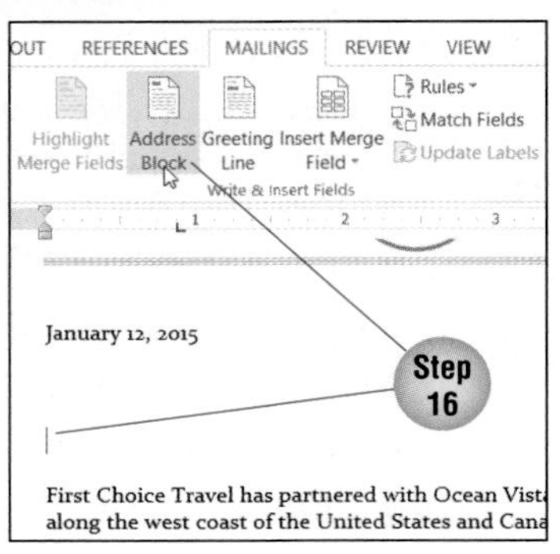

17 At the Insert Address Block dialog box, click OK.

This inserts the necessary field code to insert the client name and address in the letter.

18 Press the Enter key twice and then click the Greeting Line button in the Write & Insert Fields group.

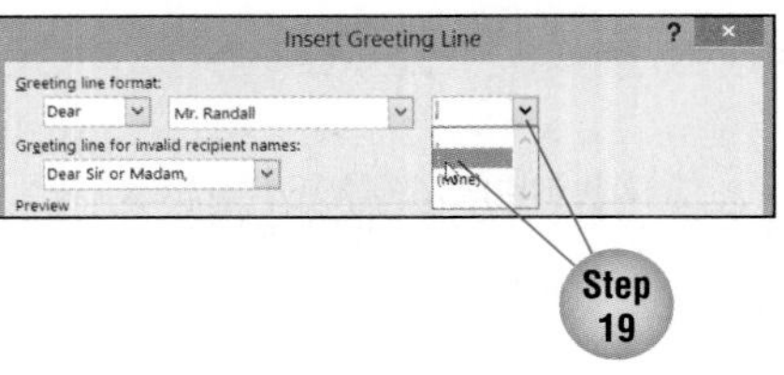

19 At the Insert Greeting Line dialog box, click the down-pointing arrow at the right side of the option box containing the comma (the box to the right of *Mr. Randall*) and then click the colon at the drop-down list.

20 Click OK to close the dialog box.

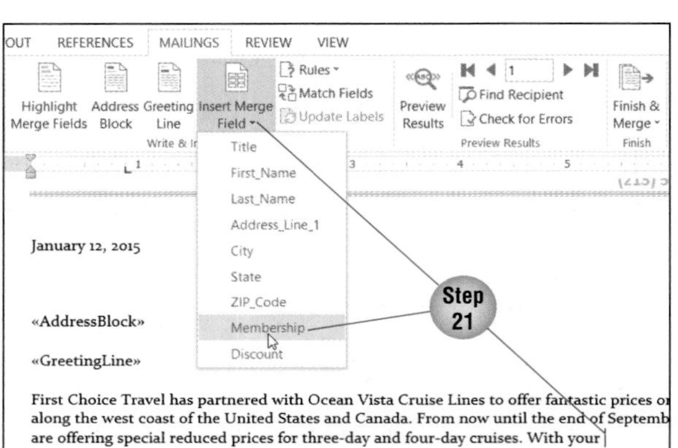

21 Move the insertion point to the end of the first paragraph, type **With your**, press the spacebar, and then insert the *Membership* field by clicking the Insert Merge Field button arrow and then clicking *Membership* at the drop-down list.

22 Press the spacebar and then type **membership, you will receive an additional**.

23 Press the spacebar and then insert the *Discount* field by clicking the Insert Merge Field button arrow and then clicking *Discount* at the drop-down list.

24 Press the spacebar, type **discount**, and then type a period.

The sentence you just typed should look like this: *With your «Membership» membership, you will receive an additional «Discount» discount.*

25 Click the Save button on the Quick Access toolbar.

26 Merge the letter with the records in the data source. Begin by clicking the Finish & Merge button in the Finish group on the MAILINGS tab and then clicking *Edit Individual Documents* at the drop-down list.

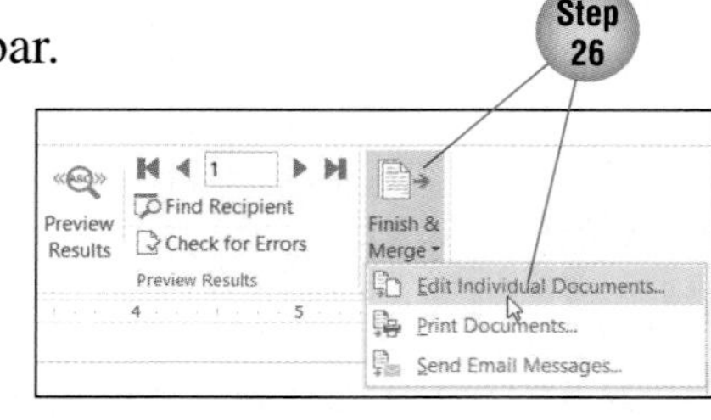

27 At the Merge to New Document dialog box, click the OK button.

The letters are merged with the records and displayed in a new document.

28. Save the merged letters in the normal manner and name the document **WS4-FCTMergedCruiseLtrs**.
29. Print and then close **WS4-FCTMergedCruiseLtrs.docx**.

    Four letters will print.
30. Save and then close **WS4-FCTCruiseLtrMainDoc.docx**.
31. At a blank document, prepare envelopes for the four letters. Begin by clicking the MAILINGS tab, clicking the Start Mail Merge button, and then clicking *Envelopes* at the drop-down list.

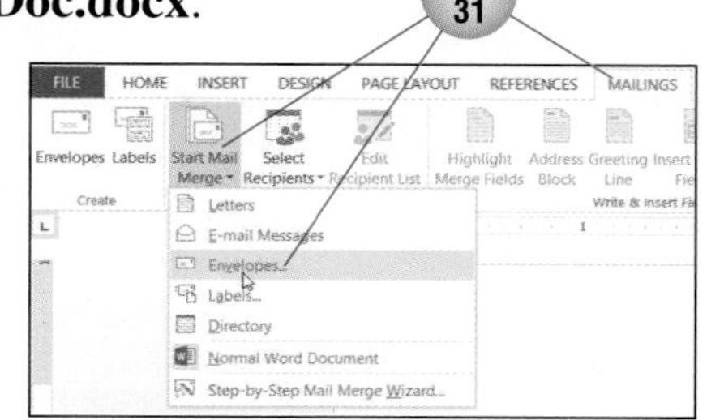

32. At the Envelope Options dialog box, click OK.
33. Click the Select Recipients button in the Start Mail Merge group and then click *Use an Existing List* at the drop-down list.
34. At the Select Data Source dialog box, navigate to the WordS4 folder and then double-click ***WS4-FCTDataSource.mdb***.
35. Click in the approximate location in the envelope in the document where the client's name and address will appear.

    This causes a box with a dashed gray border to display. If you do not see this box, try clicking in a different location on the envelope.
36. Click the Address Block button in the Write & Insert Fields group.
37. At the Insert Address Block dialog box, click OK.
38. Click the Finish & Merge button in the Finish group and then click *Edit Individual Documents* at the drop-down list.
39. At the Merge to New Document dialog box, click OK.
40. Save the merged envelopes document and name it **WS4-FCTMergedEnvs**.
41. Print **WS4-FCTMergedEnvs.docx**.

    This document will print four envelopes. Check with your instructor about specific steps for printing envelopes. You may need to hand feed envelopes into your printer.
42. Close **WS4-FCTMergedEnvs.docx**.
43. Close the envelope main document without saving it.

In Brief

Mail Merge

1. Click MAILINGS tab.
2. Click Select Recipients button.
3. Click *Type a New List*.
4. Click Customize Columns button.
5. At Customize Address List dialog box, delete and/or insert fields.
6. Click OK to close dialog box.
7. At New Address List dialog box, type text in fields.
8. Click OK.
9. At Save Address List dialog box, navigate to desired folder.
10. Click in *File name* text box, type name, press Enter.
11. Open main document.
12. Click MAILINGS tab.
13. Click Select Recipients button.
14. Click *Use an Existing List*.
15. At Select Data Source dialog box, navigate to desired folder, then double-click desired data source document.
16. Insert desired fields in document.
17. Click Finish & Merge button.
18. At Merge to New Document dialog box, click OK.

In Addition

Using the Mail Merge Wizard

The Mail Merge feature includes a Mail Merge wizard that guides you through the merge process. To access the Wizard, click the MAILINGS tab, click the Start Mail Merge button, and then click the *Step-by-Step Mail Merge Wizard* option at the drop-down list. The first of six Mail Merge task panes displays at the right side of the screen. Completing the tasks at one task pane displays the next task pane. The options in each task pane may vary depending on the type of merge you are performing.

Features Summary

Feature	Ribbon Tab, Group	Button	Option
columns	PAGE LAYOUT, Page Setup		
Columns dialog box	PAGE LAYOUT, Page Setup		*More Columns*
drop cap	INSERT, Text		
Drop Cap dialog box	INSERT, Text		*Drop Cap Options*
Insert Address Block dialog box	MAILINGS, Write & Insert Fields		
insert file	INSERT, Text		*Text from File*
Insert Greeting Line dialog box	MAILINGS, Write & Insert Fields		
Insert Hyperlink dialog box	INSERT, Links		
insert merge field	MAILINGS, Write & Insert Fields		
Insert Table dialog box	INSERT, Tables		*Insert Table*
merge documents	MAILINGS, Finish		
section break (continuous)	PAGE LAYOUT, Page Setup		*Continuous*
select recipients	MAILINGS, Start Mail Merge		
shapes	INSERT, Illustrations		
SmartArt	INSERT, Illustrations		
start mail merge	MAILINGS, Start Mail Merge		
table	INSERT, Tables		
text box	INSERT, Text		
WordArt	INSERT, Text		

Knowledge Check SNAP

Completion: In the space provided at the right, indicate the correct term, command, or option.

1. Use this feature to distort or modify text to conform to a variety of shapes. ________________
2. This is the first letter of the first word of a paragraph that is set into a paragraph. ________________
3. When you draw a shape in a document, this tab becomes active. ________________
4. To display a menu of SmartArt choices, click the INSERT tab and then click the SmartArt button in this group. ________________

5. In a SmartArt graphic, click this button in the Create Graphic group to close the *Type your text here* window. ____________
6. Create a table using the Table button on the INSERT tab or with options at this dialog box. ____________
7. Press this key to move the insertion point to the next cell in a table. ____________
8. Press these keys to move the insertion point to the previous cell in a table. ____________
9. To insert a row in a table above the current row, click this button in the Rows & Columns group on the TABLE TOOLS LAYOUT tab. ____________
10. Merge selected cells in a table by clicking the Merge Cells button in this group. ____________
11. Rotate text in a cell by clicking this button in the Alignment group on the TABLE TOOLS LAYOUT tab. ____________
12. Use this button in the Text group on the INSERT tab to insert one file into another. ____________
13. Insert a section break with options at this button drop-down list. ____________
14. To display the Columns dialog box, click the PAGE LAYOUT tab, click the Columns button, and then click this option at the drop-down list. ____________
15. If you want to save a Word document as a single file web page, choose this option at the *Save as type* option box drop-down list at the Save As dialog box. ____________
16. To navigate to a hyperlinked document or website, hold down this key while clicking the hyperlink. ____________
17. A merge generally takes two documents—the main document and this. ____________
18. Use buttons on this tab to merge documents. ____________

Skills Review

Review 1 Formatting a Travel Document

First Choice TRAVEL

1. Open **FCTZenithAdv.docx** and then save the document in the WordEOS folder and name it **WS4-R-FCTZenithAdv**.
2. Move the insertion point to the beginning of the heading *Upcoming Adventures* and then insert the file named **FCTBicyclingAdv.docx**. ***Hint: Do this with the Object button on the INSERT tab.***
3. Position the insertion point in the top cell in the first column in the table in the *Bicycling Adventures* section and then change the width to 1.7 inches. ***Hint: Do this with the* Table Column Width *measurement box in the Cell Size group on the TABLE TOOLS LAYOUT tab.*** Position the insertion point in the top cell in the middle column and then change the width to 0.7 inch. Position the insertion point in the top cell in the last column and then change the width to 0.7 inch.
4. With the insertion point positioned in any cell in the table in the *Bicycling Adventures* section, apply the Grid Table 4 - Accent 1 table style (second style in the fourth row in the *Grid Tables* section of the Table Styles drop-down gallery), and then click the *First Column* check box in the Table Style Options group on the TABLE TOOLS DESIGN tab to remove the check mark.
5. Apply the same table style (remove the check mark from the *First Column* check box) to the other two tables in the document.

6. Select the heading *Antarctic Zenith Adventures* and then apply the Intense Reference style. ***Hint: Click the More button at the right side of the style thumbnails in the Styles group on the HOME tab to display this style.***
7. Apply the Intense Reference style to the remaining three headings in the document.
8. Use the Colors button on the DESIGN tab to apply the Red color theme.
9. Use the Fonts button on the DESIGN tab to apply the Arial-Times New Roman font theme.
10. Save **WS4-R-FCTZenithAdv.docx**.

Review 2 Inserting Objects and Applying Column Formatting in a Travel Document

1. With **WS4-R-FCTZenithAdv.docx** open, move the insertion point to the beginning of the document and then insert WordArt with the following specifications:
   a. Click the *Fill - Dark Red, Accent 1, Shadow* option at the WordArt button drop-down list (second option in the top row).
   b. Type **Zenith Adventures** as the WordArt text.
   c. Change the WordArt text height to 1 inch and the width to 6.5 inches.
   d. Change the position of the WordArt to *In Line with Text*. (Do this with the Layout Options button that displays to the right of the WordArt border.)
   e. Click the Text Effects button, point to *Transform*, and then click the *Can Up* option (third option in the fourth row in the *Warp* section).
2. Move the insertion point to the beginning of the first paragraph in the document and then insert a continuous section break.
3. Create two newspaper columns with 0.4 inch of spacing between columns.
4. Insert a text box with the following specifications:
   a. Insert the Simple Text Box text box in the document and then type the following in the text box: **First Choice Travel is teaming with Zenith Adventures to provide our clients with thrilling and extreme outdoor adventures.**
   b. Change the text box shape style to *Colored Outline - Orange, Accent 2* (third option in the top row).
   c. Select the text in the text box and then change the font size to 10 points and apply bold and italic formatting.
   d. Change the height of the text box to 0.8 inch and the width to 2.1 inches.
   e. Change the position of the text box to *Position in Middle Center with Square Text Wrapping*.
5. Create a drop cap with the first letter of the first paragraph in the document (the letter *W* in *We*) and then change the font color for the letter to *Dark Red, Accent 1, Darker 25%* (located in the fifth column in the *Theme Colors* section of the drop-down color palette).
6. Move the insertion point to the end of the document and then insert a continuous section break (this balances the columns on the second page).
7. Press Ctrl + End to move the insertion point to the end of the document after the continuous section break and then press the Enter key.
8. Click the PAGE LAYOUT tab, click the Columns button, and then click *One* at the drop-down list.
9. Draw and format the shape and insert text as shown in Figure 4.6 using the following specifications:
   a. Insert the Up Ribbon shape in the *Stars and Banners* section at the location of the insertion point.

b. Change the height of the drawn shape to 1.5 inches and the width to 4.2 inches.
c. Use the Align button on the DRAWING TOOLS FORMAT tab to horizontally distribute the shape.
d. Change the shape style to *Subtle Effect - Orange, Accent 2* (third option in the fourth row).
e. Type the text in the shape as shown in Figure 4.6. Apply italic and bold formatting and change the font size to 22 points.

10. Save, print, and then close **WS4-R-FCTZenithAdv.docx**.

FIGURE 4.6 Review 2, Step 9

Review 3 Creating and Formatting SmartArt

1. Open **MPProdDept.docx** and then save the document in the WordEOS folder and name it **WS4-R-MPProdDept**.
2. Press Ctrl + End and then create the organizational chart shown in Figure 4.7 with the following specifications:

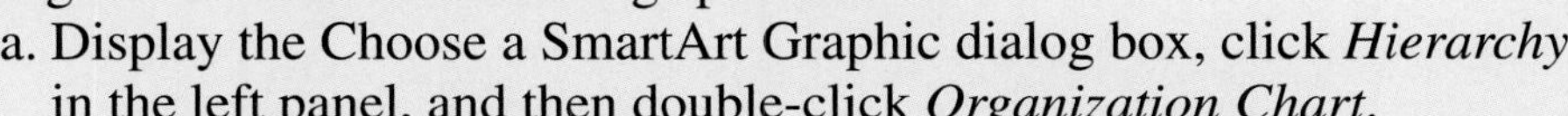

a. Display the Choose a SmartArt Graphic dialog box, click *Hierarchy* in the left panel, and then double-click *Organization Chart*.
b. Select the organizational chart graphic (not a specific shape in the graphic) and then apply the Cartoon SmartArt style and change the colors to *Colorful Range - Accent Colors 5 to 6*.
c. Change the height of the SmartArt graphic to 2.5 inches and the width to 5 inches. (Do this with the Size button on the SMARTART TOOLS FORMAT tab.)
d. Type the text in the boxes as shown in Figure 4.7. (Press Shift + Enter after typing the names.)
e. Select the SmartArt graphic (not an individual shape in the graphic) and then change the text fill color to *Black, Text 1* using the Text Fill button arrow.

FIGURE 4.7 Review 3 SmartArt Organizational Chart

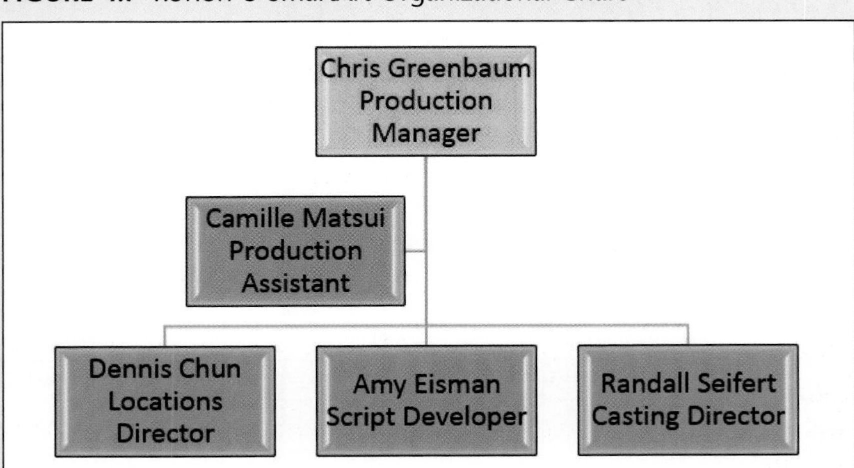

3. Create the graphic shown in Figure 4.8 with the following specifications:
   a. Press Ctrl + End to move the insertion point to the end of the document and then press the Enter key three times.
   b. Display the Choose a SmartArt Graphic dialog box, click *Process* in the left panel, and then double-click *Continuous Block Process*.
   c. Select the SmartArt process graphic (not a specific shape in the graphic) and then change the SmartArt style to *Polished*.
   d. Change the colors to *Colorful Range - Accent Colors 5 to 6*.
   e. Click the SMARTART TOOLS FORMAT tab and then change the height to 2.5 inches and the width to 5 inches.
   f. Type the text in the boxes as shown in Figure 4.8.
4. Make sure the organizational chart and graphic fit on the page.
5. Save, print, and then close **WS4-R-MPProdDept.docx**.

FIGURE 4.8 Review 3 SmartArt Graphic

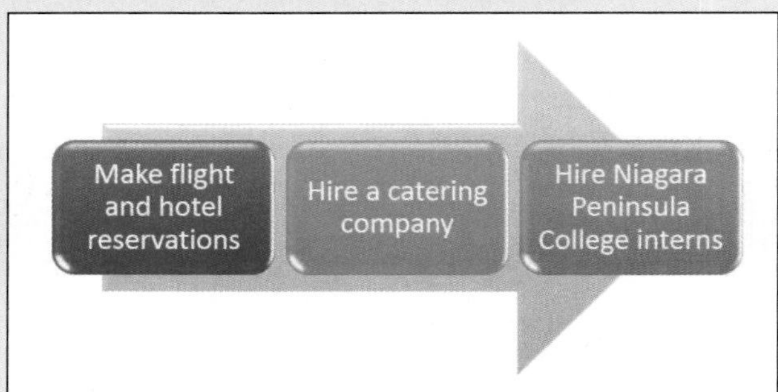

Review 4 Preparing, Modifying, and Formatting a Table

1. At a blank document, create a table with four columns and five rows.
2. Type the text in the cells as shown in Figure 4.9.
3. Insert a new column at the right side of the table and then type the following text in the new cells:

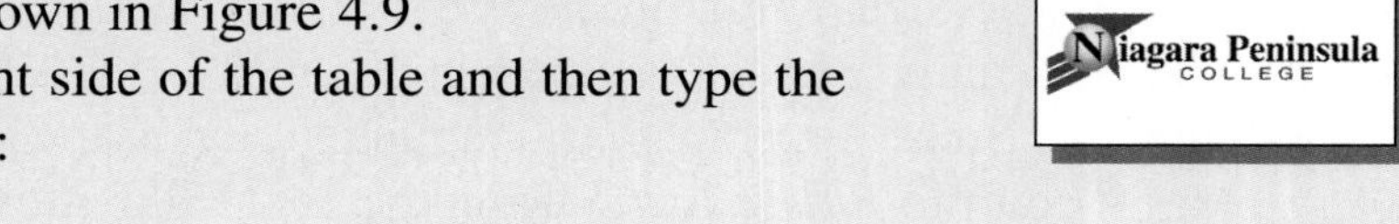

   Instructor
   Crowe
   Rubine
   McAllister
   Auve

FIGURE 4.9 Review 4

Course	Name	Days	Time
TR 101	Intro to Theatre	MTWRF	8:00-8:50 a.m.
TR 125	Beginning Acting	MTWR	9:00-9:50 a.m.
TR 211	Set Design	MTW	10:00-10:50 a.m.
TR 251	Costume Design	MW	3:00-4:20 p.m.

4. Change the width of each column to the following measurements:
   First column = 0.6 inch
   Second column = 1.3 inches
   Third column = 0.7 inch
   Fourth column = 1.25 inches
   Fifth column = 1 inch
5. Insert a new row above the first row and then with the new row selected, merge the cells.
6. Type **THEATRE ARTS DIVISION FALL SCHEDULE** in the cell and then bold and center the text.
7. Select the second row (contains the text *Course*, *Name*, *Days*, and so on) and then bold and center the text.
8. Display the TABLE TOOLS DESIGN tab, remove all check marks from the options in the Table Style Options group *except* the *Header Row* and *Banded Rows* options.
9. Change the table style to *Grid Table 5 Dark - Accent 2* (third option in the fifth row in the *Grid Tables* section).
10. Select the text in the first row (*THEATRE ARTS DIVISION FALL SCHEDULE*), change the font size to 14 points, and turn on bold formatting.
11. Horizontally center the table on the page. ***Hint: Do this at the Table Properties dialog box with the Table tab selected.***
12. Save the document in the WordEOS folder and name it **WS4-R-NPCFallSch**.
13. Print and then close **WS4-R-NPCFallSch.docx**.

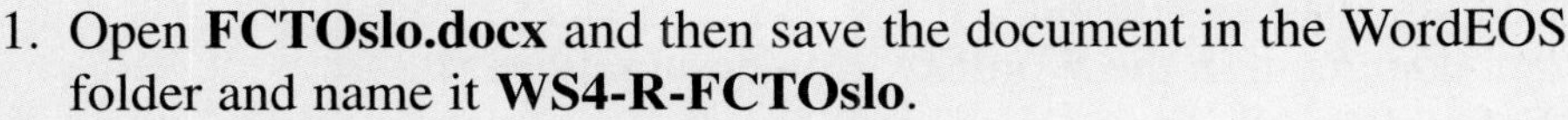

Review 5 Saving a Document as a Web Page; Inserting a Hyperlink

1. Open **FCTOslo.docx** and then save the document in the WordEOS folder and name it **WS4-R-FCTOslo**.
2. Change the bottom margin to 0.8 inch.
3. Apply the Title style to the text *Oslo*, *Norway* and apply the Heading 2 style to the headings in the document (*History*; *Population*; *Commerce and Industry*; *Climate*; *Holiday, Sport, and Leisure*; and *Sightseeing Tours*).
4. Apply the Word 2010 style set.
5. Move the insertion point to the beginning of the heading *History*, insert a continuous section break, and then create two newspaper columns with a line between.
6. Save and then print **WS4-R-FCTOslo.docx**.
7. Save the document as a single file web page with the name **WS4-R-FCTOslo.mht**.
8. Move the insertion point to the end of the document, press the Enter key twice, and then type **Additional Information on Norway**.
9. Select the text *Additional Information on Norway* and then insert a hyperlink to the official site of Norway for the United States at www.norway.org.
10. Make sure you are connected to the Internet, hold down the Ctrl key, and then click the Additional Information on Norway hyperlink.
11. At the Norway site, click on any hyperlink that interests you. When you are finished, close the web browser.
12. Save and then close **WS4-R-FCTOslo.mht**.

Review 6 Merging Letters and Envelopes

1. Create a data source document with the following names and addresses. (You determine the fields to delete; use the *State* field for the ON [Ontario] province; use the ZIP Code field for the postal codes.)

   Mr. Frank Tolentino
   Royal Fabrics and Supplies
   3220 Wilson Avenue
   Toronto, ON M4C 3S3

   Mrs. Andrea Jones-Leigh
   JL Fabrics and Crafts
   1230 Sheppard Avenue
   Toronto, ON M6H 4J2

   Mrs. Anna Strassburg
   Millwood Fabrics
   550 Jane Street
   Toronto, ON M4B 2C7

   Mr. Donald Enslow
   Wright Fabrics and Design
   8744 Huron Street
   London, ON N5V 2K8

2. Save the data source document in the WordEOS folder and name it **WS4-R-PTDataSource**.
3. Open **PTFabricLtr.docx**, save the document in the WordEOS folder, and then name it **WS4-R-PTFabricLtrMD**.
4. Specify **WS4-R-PTDataSource.mdb** as the data source.
5. Insert the *Address Block* field and the *Greeting Line* field in the appropriate locations in the letter.
6. Move the insertion point immediately right of the word *company* located in the last sentence of the third paragraph, type a comma, and then press the spacebar. Insert the *Title* field, press the spacebar, insert the *Last Name* field, and then type a comma.
7. Merge all of the records to a new document.
8. Save the merged letters document in the WordEOS folder and name it **WS4-R-PTMergedFabricLtrs**. Print and then close the document.
9. Save and then close **WS4-R-PTFabricLtrMD.docx**.
10. Create an envelope document, specify **WS4-R-PTDataSource.mdb** as the data source, and then merge the envelopes.
11. Save the merged envelopes document in the WordEOS folder and name it **WS4-R-PTMergedEnvs**. Print and then close the document.
12. Close the envelope main document without saving it.

Skills Assessment

Assessment 1 Formatting a Theatre Arts Division Newsletter

1. Open **NPCTheatreNewsltr.docx** and then save the document in the WordEOS folder and name it **WS4-A1-NPCTheatreNewsltr**.
2. Move the insertion point to the end of the document and then insert the document named **NPCProductions.docx**.
3. Use the Fonts button on the DESIGN tab to change the fonts to Calibri Light-Constantia and then apply the Heading 2 style to the three headings in the document.
4. Insert a continuous section break at the beginning of the *Division Description* heading and then format the text into two columns.

5. Move the insertion point to the beginning of the document and then insert the text *Theatre Arts Division* as WordArt. You determine the layout and format of the WordArt. Increase the height of the WordArt to 1 inch and the width to 6.5 inches. Apply a transform effect and change the position of the WordArt to *In Line with Text*.
6. Move the insertion point to any character in the heading *Division Description* and then insert the Simple Text Box text box and then type the text **The Niagara Peninsula College theatre experience can be the beginning of a lifelong interest in the art of theatre**. Select the text in the text box, change the font size to 9 points, and apply bold and italic formatting. Change the shape style to *Subtle Effect - Blue, Accent 1* and then change the position of the text box to *Position in Middle Center with Square Text Wrapping*.
7. Move the insertion point to the end of the document and insert a continuous section break.
8. Save, print, and then close **WS4-A1-NPCTheatreNewsltr.docx**.

Assessment 2 Creating SmartArt Graphics

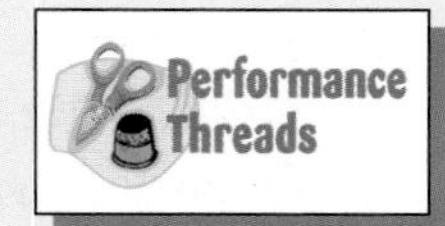

1. Open **PTDesignDept.docx** and then save the document in the WordEOS folder and name it **WS4-A2-PTDesignDept**.
2. Move the insertion point to the end of the document and then create a SmartArt organizational chart with the following information:

Camilla Yong
Design Manager

Scott Bercini
Designer

Terri Cantrell
Designer/Sewer

Paul Gottlieb
Designer/Sewer

3. Apply formatting and/or design to enhance the visual display of the organizational chart.
4. Move the insertion point below the organizational chart and then create a SmartArt graphic with the following text (use the Converging Radial graphic in the *Relationship* group in the Choose a SmartArt Graphic dialog box):

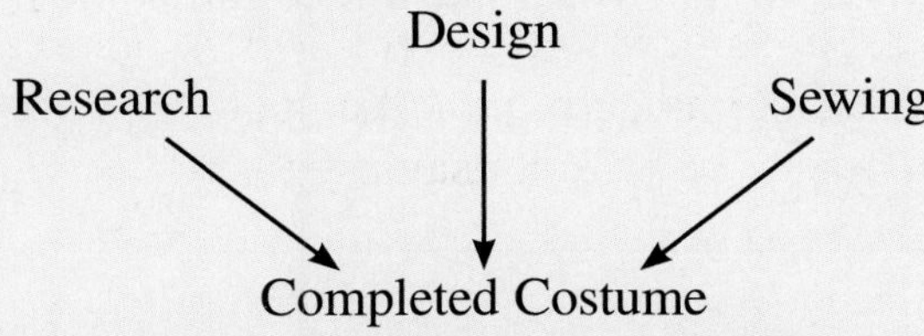

5. Apply formatting and/or design to enhance the visual display of the graphic. Change the text wrapping to *Tight* and then move the graphic below the organizational chart.
6. Make any necessary adjustments to spacing and/or size to ensure that the organizational chart and graphic fit on one page.
7. Save, print, and then close **WS4-A2-PTDesignDept.docx**.

Assessment 3 Creating a Table for the Waterfront Bistro

1. At a blank document, create a table with the text shown in Figure 4.10.
2. Apply design and layout features to enhance the visual appeal of the table.
3. Center the table horizontally on the page.
4. Save the document in the WordEOS folder and name it **WS4-A3-WBLunchOptions**.
5. Print and then close **WS4-A3-WBLunchOptions.docx**.

FIGURE 4.10 Assessment 3

CATERED LUNCH OPTIONS			
Option	Contents	Cost per Person	Discount Price
Option A: Hot	Vegetarian quiche, Caesar salad, vegetables, dressing, dessert, and beverages	$11.75	$10.95
Option B: Deli	Turkey or ham sandwiches, chips, vegetables, dressing, brownies, and beverages	$9.75	$9.30
Option C: Continental	Bagels, rolls, cream cheese, vegetables, dressing, cookies, and beverages	$8.95	$8.50

Assessment 4 Finding Information on Flipping and Copying Objects

1. Use Word's Help feature to learn how to flip objects and copy objects, or draw a shape and then experiment with the Rotate button on the DRAWING TOOLS FORMAT tab.
2. At a blank document, create the document shown in Figure 4.11. Use the Pictures button in the Illustrations group on the INSERT tab to insert the logo **WELogo.jpg** located in the WordS4 folder on your storage medium. Create the arrow at the left with the Striped Right Arrow shape in the *Block Arrows* section. Apply the Intense Effect - Gold, Accent 4 arrow shape style, the Angle shape effect (in the *Bevel* section), and the Offset Diagonal Top Left shadow shape effect. Copy and flip the arrow to create the arrow at the right side.
3. Save the completed document in the WordEOS folder and name it **WS4-A4-WEStockholderMtg**.
4. Print and then close **WS4-A4-WEStockholderMtg.docx**.

FIGURE 4.11 Assessment 4

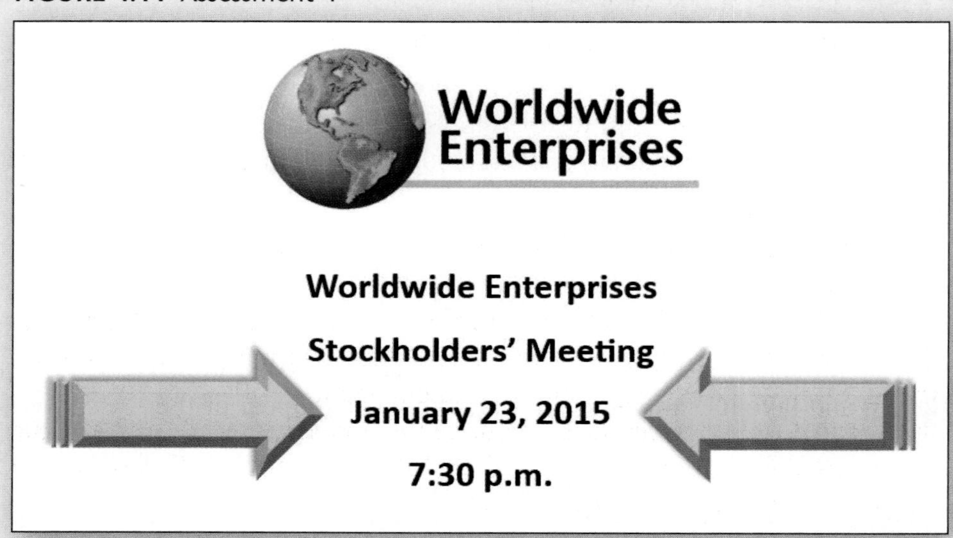

Assessment 5 Individual Challenge **Locating Information and Creating a Table**

1. Using the Internet, search for information on car rentals in your area. Locate pricing information on economy and midsize cars and also minivans. Find out the daily rental fees for each, as well as the weekly rental fee.
2. At a blank document, create a table that contains the information you found on car rentals. Modify and format the table so the information in the table is attractive and easy to read.
3. Save the document in the WordEOS folder and name it **WS4-A5-IC-CarRentalInfo**.
4. Print and then close **WS4-A5-IC-CarRentalInfo.docx**.

Marquee Challenge

Challenge 1 **Formatting a Document on Orcas Island**

1. Open **FCTOrcasIsland.docx** and then save the document in the WordEOS folder and name it **WS4-C1-FCTOrcasIsland**.
2. Format the document so it displays as shown in Figure 4.12 on the next page, with the following specifications:
   - Change the colors to Blue Green and the fonts to Century Gothic-Palatino. (Use the Colors button and the Fonts button on the DESIGN tab.)
   - Apply the Heading 2 style to the headings.
   - Format the text in two columns as shown in the figure.
   - Create the drop cap as shown. Change the font color for the drop cap to *Aqua, Accent 1, Lighter 40%*.
   - Create the WordArt with the Fill - Aqua, Accent 1, Shadow WordArt style (second option in the first row), change the height to 1 inch and the width to 6.5 inches, change the position to *In Line with Text*, and apply the Can Down transform text effect and the Offset Top shadow text effect.
   - Insert the image of the lighthouse (search for *Bodie Island Lighthouse*), make sure the height displays as 2 inches and the width displays as 1.91 inches and change the position to *Position in Middle Center with Square Text Wrapping*.
   - Balance the columns on the second page.
3. Save, print, and then close **WS4-C1-FCTOrcasIsland.docx**.

Challenge 2 **Preparing a Flier for The Waterfront Bistro**

The Waterfront
B·I·S·T·R·O

1. At a blank document, create the document shown in Figure 4.13 on page 158 with the following specifications:
   - Insert the Waterfront Bistro logo (**TWBLogo.jpg**) as a picture and change the text wrapping to *Behind Text*.
   - Set the text in the Candara font (you determine the sizes) and in the Dark Blue color.
   - Insert the art page border (down approximately one-third in the *Art* drop-down list).
   - Insert the line below the logo as a border and change the color to Dark Blue.
   - Apply any other formatting required to create the document as shown in Figure 4.13.
2. Save the completed document in the WordEOS folder and name it **WS4-C2-WBFlier**.
3. Print and then close **WS4-C2-WBFlier.docx**.

FIGURE 4.12 Challenge 1

Orcas Island

The San Juan Islands in Washington State include a number of islands including Orcas Island, which has long been a favorite destination for generations of vacationers. Located approximately 60 miles north of Seattle, it lies in the Strait of Georgia between Anacortes and Vancouver Island. To the north, on the mainland, is Vancouver, B.C. With its fjord-like bays and sounds, deep harbors, lakes, streams, and waterfalls, Orcas is considered the most spectacular of the islands. The island is over 56 square miles in size and has more than 125 miles of saltwater shoreline. Winding roads fan out from the business and social center of Eastsound village to the nearby communities of Deer Harbor, Orcas, and Olga. One of the greatest assets of the island is Mt. Constitution in Moran State Park, which offers panoramic views of the entire archipelago and is surrounded by miles of trails and sparkling lakes.

Activities on Orcas

Orcas Island offers an unhurried setting to enjoy the spectacular scenery and wildlife, with a wide variety of recreation. Activities include hiking, biking, golfing, sailing, kayaking, shopping, flying, and fishing. During the summer and on weekends and holidays, several resorts and lounges offer live music. Throughout the year, Orcas Theatre and Community Center offers concerts, plays, art exhibits, dances, workshops, movies, and many special events.

Bicycling Safety

Orcas Island is the most challenging of the islands for bicyclists. This is due to the narrow, winding roads and hilly terrain. When bicycling on the island, ride single file and keep to the right side of the road. Make stops on a straight-of-way rather than at the top of a hill or on a curve. Motorists cannot negotiate blind approaches safely with a bicyclist on the road. When stopping to rest or regroup, enjoy the scenery, but please move completely off the road. As you enjoy the scenery, be alert for potential traffic and the condition of the roadway. When leaving the ferry, pull over to the side of the road and let the automobiles pass.

continues

FIGURE 4.12 Challenge 1—*Continued*

Marine Parks

These marine parks are accessible only by boat:

- Sucia Island: Cluster of 11 islands; trails, bays, and bluffs; 2.5 miles from Orcas Island
- Patos: Two buoys, four campsites, trails (no water)
- Matis: One hundred and fifty acres, two buoys, and ten campsites

Directions to Orcas Island

You can reach Orcas Island either by ferry or by airplane. The primary departure point for the Washington State Ferry is Anacortes. To reach Anacortes, take Interstate 5 to State Highway 20 (exit 230) and travel west about 20 miles to the ferry terminal. The ferry ride lasts approximately one hour and fifteen minutes. Consider arriving at least one hour ahead of your desired departure time. Kenmore Air and West Isle Air each offer scheduled flights from Anacortes and Bellingham to Orcas Island. Flights arrive at Eastsound Airport, Rosario, or Westsound. Landings in Rosario and Westsound require float planes.

FIGURE 4.13 Challenge 2

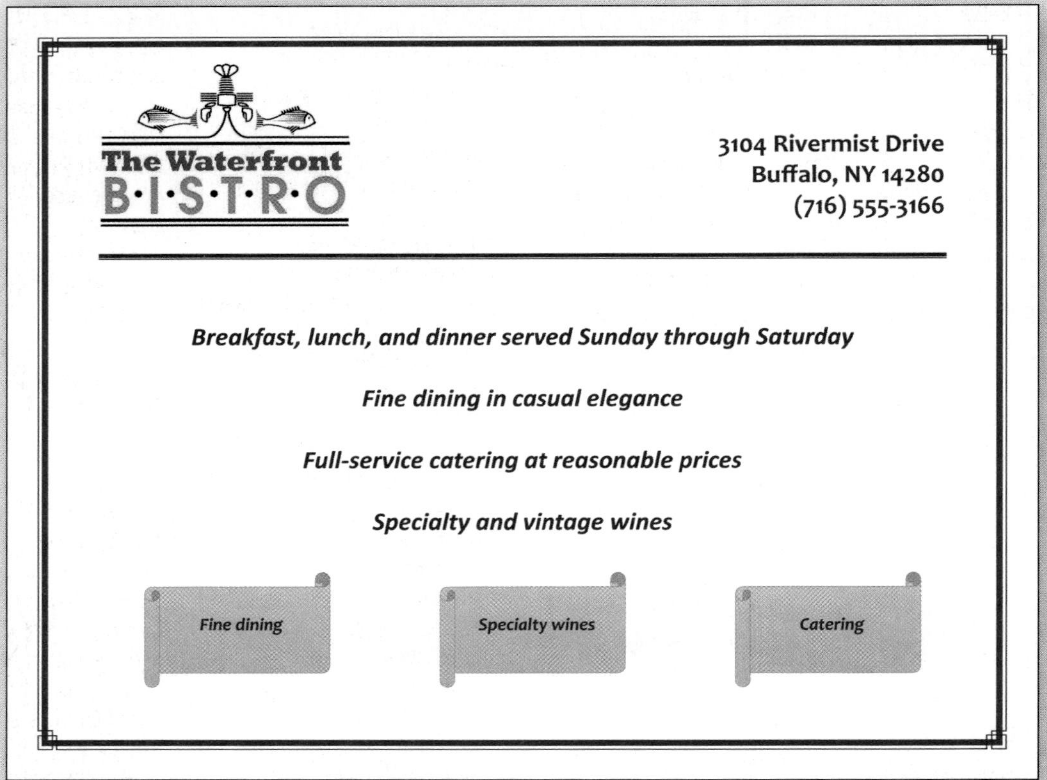

INDEX

A

B

C

D